MAKING MEN IN GHANA

MAKING MEN
IN GHANA

Stephan F. Miescher

INDIANA UNIVERSITY PRESS
BLOOMINGTON AND INDIANAPOLIS

The author and publisher acknowledge permission to use scattered excerpts from the following material:

Stephan F. Miescher, "The Life Histories of Boakye Yiadom (Akasease Kofi of Abetifi, Kwawu): Exploring the Subjectivity and 'Voices' of a Teacher-Catechist in Colonial Ghana," in *African Words, African Voices: Critical Practices in Oral History*, ed. L. White, S. F. Miescher, and D. W. Cohen (Bloomington: Indiana University Press, 2001), 162–93.

Stephan F. Miescher, "The Making of Presbyterian Teachers: Masculinities and Programs of Education in Colonial Ghana," in *Men and Masculinities in Modern Africa*, ed. L. A. Lindsay and S. F. Miescher (Portsmouth, N.H.: Heinemann, 2003), 89–108.

This book is a publication of

Indiana University Press
601 North Morton Street
Bloomington, IN 47404-3797 USA

http://iupress.indiana.edu

Telephone orders   800-842-6796
Fax orders   812-855-7931
Orders by e-mail   iuporder@indiana.edu

© 2005 by Stephan F. Miescher

No part of this book may be reproduced or utilized in any form or by any means, electronic or mechanical, including photocopying and recording, or by any information storage and retrieval system, without permission in writing from the publisher. The Association of American University Presses' Resolution on Permissions constitutes the only exception to this prohibition.

The paper used in this publication meets the minimum requirements of American National Standard for Information Sciences—Permanence of Paper for Printed Library Materials, ANSI Z39.48-1984.

Manufactured in the United States of America

Library of Congress Cataloging-in-Publication Data
Miescher, Stephan.
   Making men in Ghana / Stephan F. Miescher.
      p. cm.
   Includes bibliographical references and index.
   ISBN 0-253-34636-3 (cloth : alk. paper)—ISBN 0-253-21786-5 (pbk. : alk. paper) 1. Men—Ghana. 2. Men—Ghana—History—20th century,   I. Title.
      HQ1090.7G4M54 2005
      305.31'096—dc22
                                                    2005016231

1 2 3 4 5   10 9 8 7 6 5

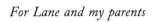

For Lane and my parents

CONTENTS

Acknowledgments

The initial ideas for this book were first tossed around in a coffee shop on Chicago's north side during the fall of 1990. As a brand-new graduate student I talked with my adviser, David William Cohen, who was immediately enthusiastic about a dissertation project exploring understandings of masculinity in twentieth-century Ghana. I am deeply grateful to David for his unwavering encouragement and intellectual prodding. He is one of those rare people who have the ability to listen and then ask provocative questions that push one's preconceived notions. In the subsequent writing of this book I have received enormous intellectual, emotional, and financial support from individuals and institutions on three continents. It is a great pleasure to acknowledge them here.

At Northwestern University I was privileged to study with a group of inspiring teachers who challenged me intellectually and introduced me to a wide range of issues in and beyond African Studies: David William Cohen, James Campbell, Jonathan Glassman, Karen Tranberg Hansen, James Oakes, Ivor Wilks, and, as extramural mentor, Tom McCaskie. In the early 1990s David William Cohen gathered at Northwestern's Program of African Studies a cohort of lively and talented students including Leslie Ashbaugh, Keith Breckenridge, Catherine Burns, Catherine Cole, Michele Mitchell, Keith Shear, Ben Soares, and Lynn Thomas. When Northwestern launched the Institute of Advanced Study and Research in the African Humanities, its preceptors took an interest in my work: Ivan Karp, Karin Barber, and Kofi Anyidoho. Visiting scholars including Kofi E. Agovi, Emmanuel Akyeampong, Corinne Kratz, Luise White, and Kwesi Yankah commented on my project as it took shape, as did the next group of students, among them Sylvester Ogbechie and Gregory Mann. I learned much from all of them.

In Ghana I am most grateful to the men and women who agreed to speak with me about their lives. Their names are listed in the notes and the bibliography. Still, a profound thank-you belongs to the cohort at the center of this study: E. K. Addo, Rev. E.K.O. Asante, Ɔkyeame Kwabena Asante, Kofi Ankoma, Ɔpanyin Kwaku Marfo, E. F. Opusuo, J. A. Wahyee, and A. K. Boakye Yiadom. At the University of Ghana, Professor Kwame Arhin (Nana Brempong Arhin) granted me research affiliation with the Institute of African Studies. Others were helpful, too: Professors Kofi E. Agovi, Kofi Baku, John Collins, Takyiwaa Manuh, Akosua Perbi, and Kwesi Yankah. In Kwawu I am indebted to Dasebre Akuamoa Boateng, Ɔmanhene of Kwawu; and Nana Asiedu Agyeman III, Adɔntenhene of Kwawu, for permitting me to conduct research. I owe much gratitude to my Twi teachers and research assistants for their interest in my research and for their friendship: Joseph Kwakye, Kwame Fosu, and Yaw Douglas Ansomani. They were later joined by Pearl A. Ofosu, Yaw Tweneboa, and Joe Acquah. Others shared their wealth of knowledge and became informal advisers: in Abetifi, Nana Annor Boama III; Rev. Felix Maafo, former warden of the Ramseyer Training Center; and Mark Schramm, SVD, former director of the Divine Word Language Center; in Pepease, Akɔmfoɔhene Yaa Animwaa, Ɔkɔmfo Ama Yeboah of Pepease, and G.G.Y. Dovi; in Abene, S. O. Boateng; in Akropong, Kwame Asare Ofori and Ofori Boahene, former principal of the Presbyterian Training College; and in Accra, Kwabena Ofori Atta Addo. I am grateful to Mrs. Felicia Akyepommaa, Mrs. Agovi, and Mrs. Emily Asiedu, as well as Mr. and Mrs. E. A. Saka, for opening their hearts and homes in Abetifi and Accra.

In Switzerland I am indebted to Martin Schaffner, my former mentor at the University of Basel, and to colleagues who provided inspiration and guidance at various junctures: Sibylle Brändli, Peter Haenger, Jakob Tanner, Kuno Trüeb, and Helmut Puff (now in the United States). During visits to the United Kingdom I was welcomed by a stimulating community of Africanists, among them Karin Barber, Lynne Brydon, Paulo de Moraes Farias, Tom McCaskie, Stephanie Newell, Richard Rathbone, Keith Shear, and Megan Vaughan. When hired for my first job at Bryn Mawr College, colleagues offered advice about juggling the demands of teaching and finishing a dissertation: among them Sharon Ullman, Mary Osirim, Madhavi Kale, Harvey Glickman, Mimi Doi, and Tim Burke. At the University of California, Santa Barbara (UCSB), I have found a permanent academic home in a collegial history department. I have enjoyed discussions about shared intellectual concerns with Erika Rappaport, Alice O'Connor, Cecilia Méndez, Carol Lansing, Joan Judge, Mary Furner, Sabine Frühstück, Sharon

Farmer, Adrienne Edgar, and Eileen Boris. Africanists at UCSB urged me to think about broader contexts and larger epistemological issues, among them Peter Bloom, Catherine Cole, Tim Mechlinski, Bianca Murillo, Sylvester Ogbechie, and Oyèrónké Oyĕwùmí.

A project like this depends on numerous individuals and institutions facilitating archival work. In Ghana former registrar E. A. Apeadu granted me ideal working conditions at the Kwawu Traditional Council in Mpraeso. I received generous assistance from the staff at the National Archives of Ghana in Accra and Koforidua, particularly Frank Ablorh and Desmond Duah Abrokwa. Moderator Rt. Rev. Dr. Sam Prempeh allowed me to conduct research in the Presbyterian Church Archive, facilitated by Rev. H. A. Opong and E. Obeng Ntow. Rev. T.K.A. Addy enabled me to consult Presbyterian session records in Abetifi. In Switzerland Paul Jenkins, Guy Thomas, and Barbara Frey Näf provided assistance at the Basel Mission Archive. In the United Kingdom Megan Vaughan offered hospitality and a formal introduction to the Rhodes House Library at Oxford University. Thanks also to the staff at the University of Michigan library, the Melville J. Herskovits Memorial Library at Northwestern University, and the Davidson Library at UCSB, particularly Sylvia Curtis and Sherri Barnes. Sjaak van der Geest, Rebecca Afua Van-Dyck, Victoria Tashjian, Lynn Thomas, Dennis Laumann, Natasha Gray, and Jean Allman generously shared research material and unpublished work.

Several institutions provided financial support for research and writing. The University of Basel, La Roche Stiftung, and Northwestern University helped during graduate studies. The Wenner-Gren Foundation, the Janggen-Pöhn Stiftung, the John D. and Catherine T. MacArthur Foundation, Northwestern University's Center for Humanities, and the International Institute at the University of Michigan supported dissertation research and writing. I am also grateful for travel and research grants from Bryn Mawr College, the University of California, Santa Barbara, and the American Historical Association (Bernadotte E. Schmitt Grant).

Revising the dissertation, I benefited from colleagues who read chapter drafts and freely shared their insights: Luise White, Lynn Thomas, Leila Rupp, Erika Rappaport, Takyiwaa Manuh, Nancy Rose Hunt, Nancy Gallagher, Catherine Cole, and Leslie Ashbaugh. Lisa Lindsay, Carol Lansing, and Emmanuel Akyeampong read the entire manuscript and offered extensive comments. Late in the process Jay Jennings provided crucial editorial advice. Dee Mortensen of Indiana University Press believed in this project from early on, and had patience and sympathy; without her, this would have been a very different book. Rita Bernhard, Marvin Keenan, and Jane Lyle saw it through the production process. Thanks to all of them.

Friends and family have given me various forms of assistance and affection in the long process of writing this book. Without their presence in my life I would not have been able to complete this project. Catherine Cole and Kwame Braun were fellow Twi students at Northwestern, shared research stays in Ghana, and eventually led the way to California. Stephen Liu came to Ghana for what was to be a brief visit, yet remained for the next year as an apprentice to an Abetifi tailor, and kept me connected with Kwawu. In Switzerland my parents, Felix and Elisabeth Miescher; my brothers, Andreas and Giorgio Miescher; as well as their partners, Doris Gräve and Lorena Rizzo have taken a genuine interest in this project, and offered hospitality and warmth. When my grandmother, Clara Löw-Suter, learned about my work in the Basel Mission Archive, she stopped by and helped me read nineteenth-century German script. Now a centenarian, she belongs to the same generation as the oldest men in this book. She often asked whether she would live long enough to see it in print. I am happy to report that she has. For the past six years I have been blessed to live in the mountains above Santa Barbara. There a group of friends have provided a nurturing community: Elizabeth and Gianni Vallino, Thorsten von Eicken, Angela Moll, Adwoa A. Gyata, Ruthie and Alex Drogomiretsky, and Lane Clark. They not only offered practical support like computer upgrades and photo selections but also cooked delicious meals, turned up the music, and reminded me of the joys in life beyond my desk.

My parents have encouraged me to pursue my intellectual passions and have supported my unconventional life choices. Lane Clark has not only been a companion on three continents but also an emotional and intellectual partner, whose commitment cannot be surpassed. This book is for them.

Abbreviations

AHR	*American Historical Review*
ASR	*African Studies Review*
APC	Abetifi Presbyterian Church (Abetifi, Ghana)
AP	E. K. Addo's Papers (Abetifi and Accra, Ghana)
ASP	Rev. E.K.O. Asante's Papers (Abetifi, Ghana)
BMA	Basel Mission Archive (Basel, Switzerland)
BYP	A. K. Boakye Yiadom's Papers (Abetifi, Ghana)
CEP	Commissioner, Eastern Province
CJAS	*Canadian Journal of African Studies*
CPP	Convention People's Party
CS	Colonial Secretary
DC	District Commissioner
GA	Government Agent
GCR	Gold Coast Regiment
GCTJ	*Gold Coast Teachers' Journal*
HA	*History in Africa*
HB	*Evangelischer Heidenbote*
IJAHS	*International Journal of African Historical Studies*
JAH	*Journal of African History*
JAS	*Journal of African Studies*
JB	*Jahresbericht der Evangelischen Missions-Gesellschaft zu Basel*
JSAS	*Journal of Southern African Studies*
KTC	Kwawu Traditional Council (Mpraeso, Ghana)
NAG	National Archives of Ghana (Accra, Ghana)
NAG-K	National Archives of Ghana (Koforidua, Ghana)
OP	E. F. Opusuo's Papers (Pepease, Ghana)
PCA	Presbyterian Church Archive (Accra, Ghana)
PNDC	Provisional National Defense Council

Abbreviations

RH	Rhodes House (Oxford University, United Kingdom)
SNA	Secretary of Native Affairs
TWA	*Times of West Africa*
UAC	United Africa Company
UGCC	United Gold Coast Convention
UTC	Union Trading Company

Prologue and Personae

I first visited Ghana at the end of a trans-Sahara journey in 1989. During this trip I not only became painfully aware of my ignorance and Eurocentric education but was taken with West Africa, particularly with its warm, hospitable people. In contrast to my ignorance of Africa, the Africans I met were extremely knowledgeable about my European world. I decided to learn more by pursuing graduate studies in African history. In 1991 I returned to Ghana looking for a research site where I could use archival material from the Basel Mission, an abiding interest of mine through family history. In November 1992, the day after J. J. Rawlings's election as the first president of Ghana's Fourth Republic, I landed in Accra with my partner Lane Clark for an extended stay of thirteen months.

We based ourselves in Abetifi, Kwawu. While Lane worked on a video documentary about Akan proverbs, I conducted historical research about what it meant to be a man in a West African society since the nineteenth century. I wanted to explore how ideas of masculinity had changed under colonialism, how men had dealt with conflicting cultural ideals. I hoped such questions would provide a fuller understanding of the working of gender.

I faced a crucial problem: (how can we learn about changing constructions of masculinity in an African society?) Although I consulted documentary sources in archives in Ghana, Britain, and Switzerland, asking men directly about their personal experiences and gathering their life histories became the heart of my research. Reading government and missionary reports, court records, Presbyterian Church diaries, chronicles, and minutes, ethnographic writings, and newspapers enabled me to situate men's life histories in larger historical contexts.[1] I took my time conducting interviews. To improve my Twi I enrolled at the Abetifi Divine Word Language Center, whose highly qualified teachers, Yaw Douglas Asomani, Kwame Fosu, and Joseph Kwakye, later became my research assistants. Learning Twi opened many doors. Exploring Abetifi, greeting elders, and engaging in small talk became my daily routine. I requested an interview only after several visits. I looked for men and women, born early in the twentieth century, with fine memories and a willingness to share their recollections. Some of them had attended (mainly) Presbyterian schools and had become clerks and teachers; others had no school experience but worked as farmers, petty traders, and artisans. I also conduced a few interviews with retired teachers in Akuapem. It is difficult to pose questions about an abstract concept like masculinity. Instead, I asked about childhood, gendered games, sexuality, marriage, child rearing, work, and migration, as well as involvement in hometown communities while becoming elders. I inquired about expectations from parents and uncles. I requested my interview partners to identify role models whom they emulated. I asked about their hopes for their children, nieces, and nephews. Finally, I solicited advice for young people. Such open questions produced elaborations that allowed me to distill their gender ideals. Over 110 interviews were recorded on tape, transcribed, and, those in Twi, translated; about half of them were in English. When not working with a tape recorder, I took notes during or after conversations.

By 1994 I had identified the cohort of eight men at the center of this study. I selected them based on the richness of our initial conversations and the quality of our personal rapport. I was also concerned about a range of life experiences and differences in socioeconomic status. As elders, some lived in poverty with small or no pensions. Others had secure resources owing to personal or inherited wealth, or to reliable pensions or well-positioned children or both. Within Kwawu, these men belong to two clusters. E. K. Addo, Rev. E.K.O. Asante, E. F. Opusuo, J. A. Wahyee, and A. K. Boakye Yiadom were members of the Presbyterian Church and lived in the Christian Quarters of Abetifi and Pepease; Ɔkyeame Kwabena Asante, Kofi Ankoma, and Kwaku Marfo were involved with the Pepease Tegare shrine. Increasingly our conversations on specific stages of their life cycle drew my attention to forms of self-presentation. My interview partners switched oral genres, depending on whether we met informally, just the two of us, or whether I conducted a taped interview with the help of a research assistant. The latter often attracted an audience: the narration became a performance. There are indeed "complex connections between genre and the construction of self."[2]

I was involved in different communities in Abetifi and Pepease. Close to our house, I attended Presbyterian Church services. With an invitation from our adopted wɔfa (maternal uncle), Yao Edward Opoku Annor, now Nana Annor Boama III, I participated in gatherings of our abusua (matrilineage), including funerals, "outdoorings" of children (naming ritual performed eight days after birth), *Adae* celebrations, and ritual offerings to the Tano ɔbosom (lesser god), administered by Ɔkɔmfo Anɔbea. At *Akwasidae* celebrations, I paid respect to Dasebrɛ Akuamoa Boateng, Ɔmanhene (paramount chief) of Kwawu, and his elders in Abene, and to other chiefs in Abetifi and Pepease. Frequently I not only witnessed Tegare *agorɔ* (ritual performance) in Pepease but followed its main actors to their farms and other gatherings in Nkwantanan, Afram Plains. Accompanying Kwawu elders, shaking many hands upon arrival, and then sitting hours on hard benches, I listened to their proceedings, watched the slaughtering of sheep, and partook in ritual drinking. These experiences provided me with a lived contrast to stories I heard in interviews and read about in archives. They gave me a better understanding of how men of different age and status groups engaged with one another, and with women. I witnessed the performance of masculinity, particularly senior masculinity, at the *ahenfie* (chief's palace) and other settings of elders, during the presentation of a drink, and in formal speech. Since ideas about masculinity are expressed and negotiated through language, I learned about Akan proverbs and about the gendered meaning of Twi terms like *ɔbarima* (man), *aberanteɛ* (young man), *ɔpanyin* (elder), and *suban* (character)—terms whose semantics have changed in the course of the twentieth century.[3]

Long-term research became part of my methodology. In 1994 I returned for a four-month stay, followed by briefer visits in 1997, 2000, and 2001. Returning changed my status and increased my familiarity with interview partners. In 1994 I asked for photographs; looking at them triggered additional stories. Some of the literate men shared letters, diaries, and other autobiographical writings. These documents enriched oral accounts, especially since I found only a few references to the eight men in the archives. I also began sharing drafts with literate interview partners. Their comments not only expressed concerns about correct names but sharpened my interpretations. In Switzerland I interviewed former Basel missionaries who had worked in Ghana between the 1940s and 1970s. Still, the research for such a project is never completed. Because my focus is on self-presentation and subjectivity, the eight men's recollections take center stage.

Most scholars who publish life histories position themselves, commenting on the intersubjectivity between themselves and their interview partners.[4] This is not merely self-serving, fitting current feminist practice and postmodern fashion, but is crucial to the life-history methodology. Oral accounts are produced in interaction with interviewers, research assistants, and others present, narrated for an intended audience and imagined readership. My Swiss heritage and bourgeois family background mattered. The once dominant Basel Mission, now a donor of the Presbyterian Church, has its headquarters in my hometown. Some Kwawu Christian Quarters are still called *baselmu* (in Basel); its inhabitants refer to themselves as *baselfoɔ* (Basel people). Although I have family connections to the Basel Mission (my maternal grandfather served on its board for thirty-five years), I grew up outside its *Heimatgemeinde* (home congregation). Some interview partners connected me with their European teachers.

And as I listened to Reverend Asante, for example, he reminded me of an old relative. His habitus and body language seemed familiar. I wondered whether this was the shared exposure to remnants of Pietist values brought to Ghana by the Basel Mission. Had he received norms and ideas from the same source as my grandparents, first through the filter of his teachers trained in Basel Mission schools, and then during his career in direct contact with the early missionaries' successors? For me, his style recalled the mood prevalent around my mother's family, most noticeable at my grandparents' home. And, indeed, he was their contemporary.

In the course of this project my relationships evolved. In the beginning I was the young Swiss student doing research on behalf of a U.S. university. Later, having completed my Ph.D. and secured an academic job, I was attributed more status, although oddly; because I was still unmarried, in local perception I was not quite an adult. That I am labeled gay in my own culture and have forged a fitting identity was of little relevance in Ghana. Since there was no similar social category, at least for my older interview partners, I was seen as the *aberantee* who needed guidance, particularly regarding questions of adult masculinity and marriage. Many stories came with well-intended pieces of advice. Moreover, since I was the one asking my interview partners to produce knowledge about their lives, they were the experts and I the learner. My limited, childlike Twi served as a reminder of my position, well captured in these proverbs: "*Ɔhoho ani akɛse-akɛse, nanso enhu ne hwe*" (The stranger has big eyes but does not see) and "*Ɔhoho te sɛ abofra*" (The stranger is like a child).

Still, as a student with a fellowship large enough that I could afford a car, there was a pronounced imbalance in economic resources. During visits I offered food or toiletries. As a "social lubricant," I presented beverages like beer or schnapps to non-Christian seniors, since "the transfer of schnapps in exchange for knowledge from elders is key to the success" of scholarly research in Akan societies.[5] After learning that prosperous men were expected to help elders financially, I made gifts of money that were much appreciated.

In a research relationship there exist "multiple kinds of power" and "many ways in which researchers are dependent upon those with whom they seek such a relationship."[6] As a genre, "the life history is a hybrid form that inscribes the doubled voices of the native speaker and the translator."[7] Yet, ultimately, the power of translation, arrangement, and interpretation rests with the researcher. This is a responsibility. In writing this book I have sought to do justice to these lives. The book is not a rendering of unmediated voices devoid of interpretation. Instead, while my analysis is not uncritical, I offer it with respect for my interview partners' dignity as elders, particularly since most are no longer alive to correct this record.

I have included extended quotes from interview transcripts, either in the original English or in translation from Twi. I have not used pseudonyms. Everyone I cite or mention in the notes asked to be represented by his or her name. In fact, one reason my interview partners talked with me was their desire to occupy a place within this book. They hoped that their names and lives might receive some permanence. Many Kwawu elders are concerned about their personal legacy. In Akan culture, the memory of important ancestors is evoked by calling their names during libation. Since not all my interview partners will be included in future libations, this book should, at least partially, fulfill their wishes. I look forward to sharing copies with them or their descendants.[8]

In order to help the reader distinguish the cohort of eight men at the center of this book, I offer brief vignettes. Four lived in the town of Abetifi and three in nearby Pepease, both of which are divided into Christian Quarters and an old town; in addition, Pepease is home of the Tegare religious shrine. The final interview partner came from Obo.

In Abetifi

Rev. E.K.O. Asante (1911–1997)

Rev. E.K.O. Asante's house is at the edge of the Christian Quarters close to the old town. The blue shutters, in lieu of glass windows, can be seen from far away. Opposite the house, across the washed-out road, lies his garden, fenced in like a sanctuary, with citrus and avocado trees giving shade to tender vegetable plants. Although there is a wide, blue double door facing the street, everybody uses the side entrance leading into the cement yard (see Fig. 0.1). In his sitting room a mechanical clock strikes every half hour, a bookcase shows his literate status, and a poster bears the inscription,

> Christ is the Head of this house.
> The unseen Guest at every meal.
> The silent listener to every conversation.

Asante, an elder of his *abusua*, was always available for consultation. During our interviews visitors frequently came by to greet the *osafo* (pastor). There was something warm and intimate about our conversations, which often ran for hours. Usually we shared the same couch with just enough room between us for my notebook. Only if other people joined us did Asante reclaim his position as *ɔpanyin* (elder), taking a seat in the center of the room. I recall rainstorms that caused power outages and kept me there until deep into the night. Since Asante's English was superb, there was never any language barrier. Nevertheless, as a former teacher, he made a point to open and close the conversation in Twi. Later in my stay, if I just stopped by for a chat, we spoke Twi.

Asante had a prominent pastoral career. In the Presbyterian Church, as well as in Basel Mission circles, he was well known for his pioneer service in Ghana's Northern Territories. Reverend Asante died only days prior to my return in 1997. Entering the courtyard, seeing his wife, daughter, and other women in mourning cloth, I wept unabashedly. His wife, Felicia, comforted me and assured me that he was now in a better place. Over the years I have known most of his ten children and corresponded with some of them.

E. K. Addo (1904–1998)

When I wished to speak with a Kwawu trader, Reverend Asante sent me to his paternal relative, E. K. Addo. There are two large older buildings at the end of the central road through Abetifi's Christian Quarters, Sober House No. 1 and No. 2. The latter was built by Addo, a well-to-do businessman living in Accra and Abetifi. In 1994 Addo was full of energy, frequently making the strenuous journey from Accra by public transport. Entering his living quarters, I had a sense of taking a journey into the past. Never had I seen in Abetifi such a well-preserved example of a colonial sitting room, equipped with skillfully crafted furniture and the ubiquitous wall clock. I was fascinated by the photographs, among them a hand-colored reproduction of King George V. Usually Addo offered me a chair upholstered in burgundy, while he took his seat next to a small coffee table, covered with

Fig. 0.1. Rev. E.K.O. Asante in front of his house, Abetifi, 1993.
Photo, S. F. Miescher.

papers. Often in a forceful move revealing his determination, he pushed the papers aside to make room for a welcome drink. Addo had a commanding appearance, and it was a challenge not to be intimidated by his authority. Wearing cloth, the outfit of an Akan elder, his searching eyes scrutinized the visitor through a pair of thick glasses (see Fig. 0.2). Toward me he was welcoming and eager to share his thoughts about Ghana's history. He could be quite opinionated and did not hesitate to critique younger generations whom he considered not hard-working. I spent intensive times with him in Abetifi and Accra during my visit in 1997. Preoccupied with his own death, he was making detailed funeral arrangements.

J. A. Wahyee (1900–1999)

When I met J. A. Wahyee in 1993, this former cocoa farmer and elder of the Presbyterian Church rarely left his house in Abetifi's Christian Quarters. Usually his wife of over sixty years led me to his sitting room. Waiting there, I admired the woodwork, particularly the delicate carpentry of doors, windows, shutters, and ceilings that show the craftsmanship of the 1930s. The sitting room is spacious with four windows and a double door opening into the courtyard of the compound house; four doors lead into adjacent rooms. In one corner, there was a pile of carved Akan stools; on the wall ticked a clock. Wahyee took his seat opposite me in a large yellow plastic chair padded with pillows. He seemed to disappear into his chair, looking tired and very old. Whenever he spoke, a vividness reentered his body (see Fig. 0.3). Though frail, his mind was sharp and blessed with a detailed memory. Visitors addressed Wahyee as *wɔfa*, *agya*, or *papa* (father), thereby showing respect to this widely recognized elder.

A. K. Boakye Yiadom (1910–)

I met A. K. Boakye Yiadom, a retired teacher-catechist of Abetifi's Christian Quarters, through his younger brother. In 1993 we had a few conversations and one longer interview. Boakye Yiadom pursued me, even writing to the United States. Transcribing our first interview, I noticed the richness of his narrative. Upon my return in 1994, we began working more intensively. He lives in a modest compound house that belongs to relatives of his late wife, Susana Ansomaah. As caretakers, they occupied one room with a narrow veranda, where they entertained visitors (see Fig. 0.4). In spite of his advanced age, Boakye Yiadom is remarkably fit. He receives only a

Fig. 0.2. Mr. E. K. Addo in his sitting room, Sober House No. 2,
Abetifi, 1994. Photo, R. Lane Clark.

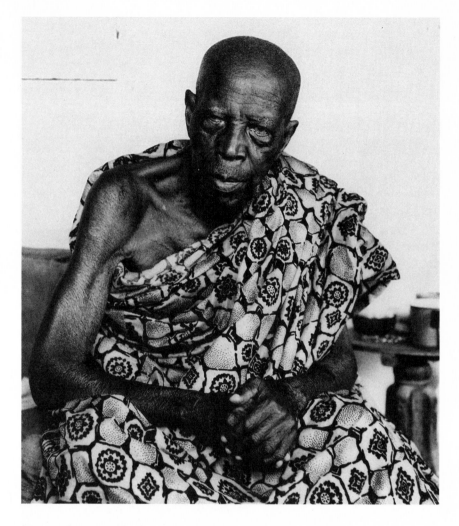

Fig. 0.3. Ɔpanyin J. A. Wahyee in his sitting room, Abetifi, 1994.
Photo, S. F. Miescher.

small pension and depends on a cocoa farm that he still works. Over the years we have spent much time in each other's company, once traveling to his second hometown of Kurofa, Asante-Akyem. Boakye Yiadom often visited me at the house where I was living in Abetifi. I have met many of his seventeen children, his nephews, his former wives, and other relatives. In 2000 I was among the guests of honor at his ninetieth birthday party. Boakye

Fig. 0.4. Mr. A. K. Boakye Yiadom in his old scouting uniform, Abetifi, 1994. Photo, S. F. Miescher.

a Yiadom is a passionate collector and writer, and has granted me access to his personal archive.

In Pepease

E. F. Opusuo (ca. 1923–)

The former teacher and education officer E. F. Opusuo lives in the small Christian Quarters of Pepease, his house hidden behind a grove of plantain trees. I first visited Opusuo on the recommendation of E. K. Opoku, principal of the Training College and known as "Blackman," who provided me with names of elderly graduates of the Presbyterian Training College, Akropong. Since retirement Opusuo has been engaged in community work, serving in the Kwawu District Assembly, and as an elder for his *abusua*. He also attended to his farm (see Fig. 0.5). Opusuo is an unassuming, soft-spoken man who expresses himself very deliberately. He was accommodating, open to talk about any aspect of his life. Most of our conversations took place in the comfortable sitting room at his house, which he then shared with his wife and their three small children. In 1992 I accompanied him to a district assembly meeting about HIV/AIDS prevention, then a little-known disease in Kwawu. Since I often went to Pepease to participate in the activities of a Tegare shrine, I stopped at Opusuo's house, sometimes accompanied by an entourage of friends. Opusuo introduced me to Nana Okyere Ampadu II, the long-serving Pepease chief and *Kyidomhene* of Kwawu, and arranged interviews. Opusuo visited me in Abetifi, and we ran into each other at funerals.

Kwaku Marfo (ca. 1905–2000)

Kwaku Marfo was the Kwawu *Nsumankwaahene*, the caretaker of royal charms, amulets, and talismans of the *Ɔmanhene*. As a palace elder, he wore only cloth and had a shaven head (see Fig. 0.6). Marfo shared a house in Pepease with Ɔkɔmfo Yaa Animwaa, the *Akɔmfoɔhene* (chief diviner) of Pepease. Marfo's father, Kwasi Nyame, had been Ɔkɔmfo Yaa's predecessor, divining the two *abosom* (gods) at their house. I had become friends with Ɔkɔmfo Yaa whom I encountered at the Pepease Tegare shrine in 1992, where Lane began playing with the drummers and later videotaped the *agorɔ*. Visiting Ɔkɔmfo Yaa, I greeted the old man but never engaged in a longer

Fig. 0.5. Mr. E. F. Opusuo attending a funeral, Pepease, 1993.
Photo, S. F. Miescher.

Fig. 0.6. Ɔpanyin Kwaku Marfo in front of the shrine at his house, Pepease, 1993. Photo, R. Lane Clark.

conversation. Then I learned that Marfo was sick. He had an open infection on his leg, and herbal remedies did not seem to help. After a few days I could no longer watch him suffer and offered to take him to the health center. Following several injections of antibiotics and regular dressings, the infection healed. Marfo regained his strength and managed to walk again. With a new lease on life, he volunteered to share some of his recollections.

Ɔkyeame Kwabena Asante (1911–1999)

Kwabena Asante was the *ɔkyeame* (spokesperson) and principal attendant of the Pepease Tegare (Gare) shrine. I remember first noticing him during a dramatic *agorɔ* when Gare, embodied by Ɔbosomfo Kwadwo Amoa, swirled across the large cemented yard of the *ɔbosomfie* (shrine house). In ritually critical moments Ɔkyeame Asante poured water on the ground and fired an old shotgun into the air. I began to greet him at his house in the center of Pepease. Usually he was sitting on the porch puffing his beloved pipe. Ɔkyeame Asante was of slight build, with gray hair and a moustache. He had sparkling, inquisitive eyes and was eloquent (see Fig. 0.7). After our first conversation about his life as a Catholic-raised *odunsini* (herbalist), ex-serviceman, and Tegare *ɔkyeame*, I left impressed with his compassion and sense of humor.

In Obo

Kofi Ankoma (1914–1996)

The former policeman and lorry driver Kofi Ankoma belonged to the *mpanyinfoɔ* (elders) at the Gare shrine in Pepease. For *Anwona*, Gare's principal festival and coinciding with *Fieda Fofie* (ritually important Friday, ten days before *Akwasidae* on the Akan calendar), Ankoma traveled from his hometown of Obo to Pepease to attend the performance. Sitting among the elders on the elevated platform watching the *agorɔ*, I started a conversation in my halting Twi. Laughingly, he went along but then switched into English. He invited me to visit him in Obo to improve my Twi (see Fig. 0.8). He was eager to know what I felt seeing the "fetish priests" dance; I hoped to learn about his life. Ankoma abhorred churches and thought pastors talked too much. Still, once on a funeral Sunday we went to the Obo Anglican Church. Halfway through the service he left, bored by the long prayers. A

Fig. 0.7. Ɔkyeame Kwabena Asante, Pepease, 1994.
Photo, R. Lane Clark.

Fig. 0.8. Ɔpanyin Kofi Ankoma during Kwasi Mawu's funeral, Pepease, 1993. Photo, S. F. Miescher.

tall, slender man, he had an abundant dry wit and was always ready for a drink. Since one hip had become stiff from an accident, he could only walk with the aid of a cane. I spent one intense week with Ankoma in Obo, sharing his daily routine. Drinking alcohol in various places structured our days. In the morning we stayed for hours at the palm-wine bar in a shady street, engaged in lively talk with other men curious about Ankoma's new friend. I loved to play *ɔware* (a board game), although I was too slow for the men gathered there. Following an afternoon nap, we retreated to Ankoma's sitting room—a small hallway in front of his bedroom—for beer and conversation with the tape recorder running. In the evening we walked to his favorite *akpeteshie* (local gin) bar. Later I combined trips to the archive at the Kwawu Traditional Council in Mpraeso with visits in Obo and gave him rides to Pepease. He complimented me on my habit of shifting gears to slow the car; I learned about the lorry driver's practice of honking his horn whenever crossing a stream to greet the *ɔbosom* (lesser god). Unfortunately Ankoma passed away before I could show him the first drafts of my book.

MAKING MEN IN GHANA

"TO BE A MAN IS HARD": MASCULINITIES AND LIFE HISTORIES

1

In Ghana many of the road transport lorries and buses bear painted slogans. Some are in English, some in Twi or another West African language. They might say, "No Hurry in Life" or "All Shall Pass" or "Trust in God" or "Good Father." I became curious and asked drivers about the meanings of these slogans. I was told that they reflect a driver's philosophy, referring to significant experiences in his life. Once, while riding up from the coastal capital city of Accra to inland Kwawu (the primary site of this study), I noticed a truck with the inscription "To Be a Man Is Hard." I was in no position to ask questions of the driver of that truck, but the ideas and anxieties that seemed to underlie the slogan traveled with me up to Kwawu. What does it mean to be a man in Ghana? Why did this driver decide to inform the public about his hardship? The slogan seemed to me a way to explore changing expectations for men in Ghana and, in particular, whether colonialism challenged older understandings of masculinity.

Since the 1970s gender studies have provided compelling analysis of the economic and social position of African women, cultural questions about customary law, motherhood and reproduction, sexuality and the body, as well as about the formation of identities. Most of this work conflates women with gender.[1] Scholars have only begun to explore how shifting meanings of gender have affected African men, and how constructions of masculinity have been challenged and transformed within African history. As gendered social actors, men were not a unified category. Instead, they worried about ideals and expectations surrounding masculinities. Reading Mau Mau fighters' autobiographies, Luise White has noted that men wrote "about being men." They wrote about courtship and domestic arrangements, "about being husbands, lovers, fathers, gender roles that were an integral part of their political struggle."[2] White's insights are important. We need to look closely at men's recollections about their private lives, since this is where gender relations are not only intimately practiced but are contested and transformed. At the same time understandings of masculinity are linked to histories of institutions and economic structures. Scholars have studied how "industrial man" came to colonial Africa, how urban men's organized leisure activities like football "became entangled in definitions of masculinity," how masculinity remains contested among lawyers in postcolonial Africa.[3] Yet historians have posed fewer questions about intersections between changing notions of masculinities, men's self-presentation, and men's subjective experience.

A fast-growing literature on masculinity in the humanities and social sciences draws mostly on examples from North America, Europe, and Australia. R. W. Connell's formulation has been influential: masculinity "as a configuration of practice *within* a system of gender relations."[4] In Western societies different patterns of masculinity are structured by hierarchy and power. Among them *one* form of masculinity is dominant, that is, hegemonic, because it is based on patriarchal claims. Subordinate forms of masculinity carry less privilege. African societies can be complicated because of colonialism and the imposition of outside gender norms. It is not always obvious which forms of masculinity were dominant, since understandings of gender depended on specific contexts, power relations, and actors' subject positions. Connell's model fails to acknowledge situations in which different hegemonic forms might coexist.[5] While his approach offers a helpful way to think about a multitude of masculinities, this book ultimately disagrees with his conclusion, particularly in a colonial context. In contrast, the ideas presented in the collection *Men and Masculinities in Modern Africa* provide a useful framework to build on.[6] *Making Men in Ghana* establishes and explores the complex processes of how a group of men negotiated with different and at times competing notions of masculinities. Elders and kinship groups in Akan societies promoted forms like adult masculinity, senior masculinity, and big-man status, and a mission church advocated what I call Presbyterian masculinity. As school graduates, some men became "middle figures," crucial players in colonial encounters but at odds with older ideas of seniority.[7]

Because expectations about responsibilities and obligations were contested, members of this group had to redefine themselves as men, struggling with complicated ideas about gender, authority, seniority, and Christian education. They varied in social status and in religious affiliations. They were born between 1900 and 1923, and include a cocoa farmer, a policeman and driver, a trader and businessman, two teachers, one pastor, and two shrine attendants. In the course of their lives they traveled extensively, maintaining relationships with hometowns while sojourning outside Kwawu. These men lived through the changes of the twentieth century: the establishment of colonial rule, the presence of mission churches, social mobility through Western education, economic opportunities in trading and cocoa farming, wage labor, a new material culture, resistance and nationalism, challenges to established forms of authority and social relations, as well as the hopes and crises of postcolonial Ghana.

Kwawu and Akan Societies

These days, traveling from Accra to Kwawu, a visitor leaves the motor road to Kumase in the entrepôt of Nkawkaw and turns right toward an imposing mountain ridge. A small road with dangerous curves climbs the steep escarpment. A spectacular view opens up over Nkawkaw: fertile agricultural land and remnants of the tropical forest (see Fig. 1.1). The Kwawu ridge, one hundred miles north of the coast, is densely populated with a dozen towns and many more villages, where most people continue to practice

Fig. 1.1. View from the Kwawu ridge toward Nkawkaw, 1993.
Photo, R. Lane Clark.

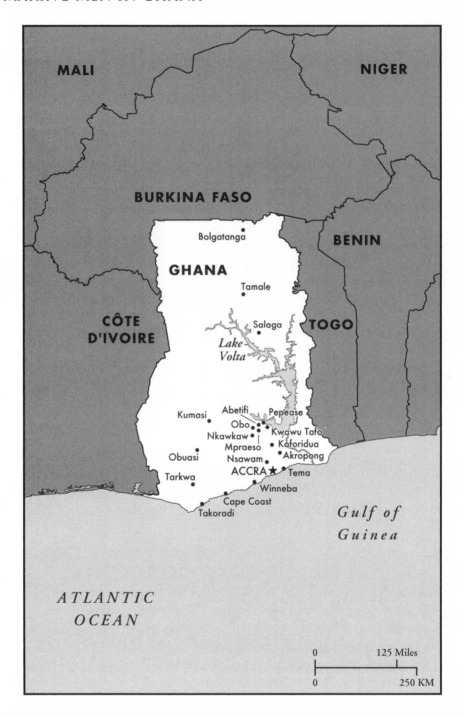

Ghana in 2004. Map by Greg Hajic, Map & Imagery Laboratory, UCSB.

matrilineal descent and speak Akan-Twi. Kwawu also encompasses lands in the forest south of the ridge and portions of the northern savannah in the Afram Plains. The ridge towns enjoy a cool climate. At the highest elevation of two thousand feet lies Abetifi, with about eight thousand inhabitants, and the hometown of four men in the cohort: E. K. Addo, Rev. E.K.O. Asante, J. A. Wahyee, and A. K. Boakye Yiadom. Three men, Ɔkyeame Kwabena Asante, Kwaku Marfo, and E. F. Opusuo, hail from neighboring Pepease, half the size of Abetifi and situated at the lorry road's terminus above the Afram Plains. One man, Kofi Ankoma, comes from Obo, a town southwest of Abetifi, renowned for its large buildings and close to the administrative center of Mpraeso.[8]

Abetifi, like other southern Ghanaian communities with an old missionary presence, is divided into two sections: the old town with the *ahenfie* (chief's palace), the market, a bank, stores, and shrine houses, and, across a valley on a hill, the Christian Quarters or *Salem*, with large houses and a stone church whose steeple can be seen from far away. This dichotomy physically and geographically represents two important competing areas of masculinity that prevailed throughout the lives of these men. The Christian Quarters owes its existence to the arrival of the Basel Mission in 1876, welcomed by Kwawu chiefs after breaking with their Asante overlord (see Fig. 1.2). The Basel missionaries were instrumental in negotiating the Protectorate Treaty of 1888 with the British, gradually incorporating Kwawu into the Gold Coast Colony. The Basel Mission—a pietistic organization from Switzerland with strong ties to southern Germany—made a deliberate effort to separate its followers from local people. In Abetifi the missionaries acquired land for twenty-six pounds and offered plots to converts. Within the *Salem*, converts were expected to live according to the *Gemeindeordnung*, a set of rules that intervened in every aspect of daily life and reconstructed gender relations. The missionaries repeated this settlement scheme as they founded congregations in other Kwawu towns. Like mission societies elsewhere, the Basel Mission made a conscious effort to reshape personhood, promoting specific notions of masculinity and femininity. According to these guidelines—and contrary to Akan practice—husband and wife were expected to live with their children, and to share meals and worship. For sons, schooling was compulsory; for daughters, it was optional but recommended.[9]

The Basel Mission encountered difficulties in Kwawu. Strikes hindered construction of buildings. First, laborers demanded a raise in their daily salaries from one six pence to one shilling; then, skilled coastal workers demanded even higher wages. Although four young men were baptized dur-

Fig. 1.2. "Mission house in Abetifi," ca. 1890. Photo, F. Ramseyer. (Copyright Basel Mission Archive, D-30.14.008.)

ing the chapel dedication in 1878, converts hesitated before moving to the *Salem*. Only in 1891 could Friedrich Ramseyer report that all Abetifi Christians, with one exception, had relocated. By 1910 the Kwawu congregation had more than twenty-seven hundred members. These mission settlements became "centres of diffusion of architectural models," engaging in "agricultural experiments" with new cash crops, introducing "new skills and tools," and promoting "changes in life style."[10] During World War I the Basel Mission was expelled from the Gold Coast and replaced by the Scottish Mission. Although the latter granted congregations more independence, reorganizing them as the Presbyterian Church in 1926, Basel Mission gender ideals did not lose their importance. Separate Christian Quarters expanded during the interwar period; Abetifi had become a "twin town."[11]

Although Kwawu is now known as an educational center, the expansion of Western education was a slow process. After the Basel Mission created the first primary school in the 1870s, it took almost fifty years to open a middle school. By 1944 the Presbyterian Church still managed the vast majority of schools. Following the implementation of self-rule in 1951 the government, then ruled by the Convention People's Party (CPP), incorporated denominational schools into the state system. In 1956 a Presbyterian secondary school opened in Abetifi, and four years later a Catholic one in Nkwatia. In 1960 the Presbyterian Church established the Abetifi Training College. According to a 1950 study, about 80 percent of male children attended school. Yet most of them stopped attending after primary school to assist their uncles in stores. Among the few girls enrolled, most quit earlier, with pregnancy listed as the "chief source of interference to girls' education."[12]

Mission churches were not the only cultural innovators in twentieth-century Kwawu. Three men in this study were involved with the Tegare shrine, brought first to Nkwantanan, Kwawu, from Ypala in the Northern Territories ca. 1938. They were followers of Ɔbosomfo Kwasi Mawu, one of Kwawu's most prominent Tegare priests. Tegare *aduru* (medicine) belongs to so-called witch-finding cults, which offer protection from evil forces, promise prosperity, and help with impotence and sterility. Since the 1870s these cults appeared in waves across southern Ghana with changing names: Domankama, Aberewa, Hwe-me-so, Kune, Tongo, Tegare, and Mframa.[13] The colonial government tried to suppress them as a threat to its authority. Although the Native Administration Ordinance gave chiefs the right to judge witchcraft cases, a 1930 government order prohibited the practice of witch finding. Two years later this ban was revised, permitting voluntary participation in witch-finding oracles. The law contributed to the transformation of witch cleansing from a coercive, court-ordered process to "a voluntary, therapeutic practice centered on confession."[14] This applied to Tegare. In the 1940s and 1950s social scientists interpreted these shrines as reactions to the socioeconomic transformations, particularly cocoa, sweeping across southern Ghana. Since people's lives were deeply altered, the argument went, they experienced a high degree of anxiety that led to a "search for security."[15] Nevertheless Tegare was controversial. Mission churches perceived its popularity as a direct threat. Colonial administrators dismissed it as merely a money maker. From my perspective, it is more important to recognize that a Tegare shrine provided a sense of community. Its priest could acquire big-man status, representing a specific type of masculinity.[16]

Crucially setting a foundation for these twentieth-century developments was the long history of Akan societies, which dominate southern Ghana. Among them are Asante, Akuapem, Akyem, Bron, Denkyera, Fante, and

Kwawu. Akans share a culture, speak the same language, and belong to several matrilineages (*mmusua*) that are localized segments of territorially dispersed matriclans (*mmusua kɛseɛ*). Today Akans form Ghana's largest ethnic group. Originally from the Ofin-Pra basin, Akans spread across the forest and to the coast, matriclans providing mechanism for absorbing outsiders. An Akan state (*oman*) consisted of a town (*kuro*) with male and female leaders (*ɔhene* and *ɔhemaa*) who were custodians of ceremonial stools representing ancestors, and dependent villages (*nkuraa*). In Akan cosmology, people distinguished between a supreme god (*Ɔnyame*), an earth goddess (*Asase Yaa*), lesser gods (*abosom*), and a cult of ancestors (*nsamanfoɔ*). Diviners (*akɔmfoɔ*) mediated between the powers of a spiritual world and the world of the living. Asante, the most prominent Akan state, emerged in the late seventeenth century and dominated what is now Ghana over the next two hundred years.[17]

Kwawu lies at Asante's eastern border and was settled by Akans beginning in the seventeenth century. According to oral traditions, Osei Twum and Kwaw Baadu from Denkyera founded the town of Bokuruwa; then Ampon Agyei from Adanse established the towns of Abene, Pepease, Aduamoa, and Abetifi. Other migrants followed, founding Obo, Obomeng, and Mpraeso. By the 1740s Ampon Agyei's successor, Nana Odiawuo, had installed the Tena matriclan as the ruling lineage. Kwawu was a province of Greater Asante until its rebellion in 1875, following the Anglo-Asante war of 1873–74 (see Fig. 1.3).[18]

In the nineteenth century Asante and its Akan provinces were hierarchical societies. Patriarchy and gerontocracy dominated. These societies consisted of commoners, slaves, as well as more privileged groups like the *nhenkwaa* (palace attendants) and *adehyeɛ* (royals of a stool or office). The state mediated sexuality and gender relations, recognizing male sexual needs but not those of women. As a sign of wealth, elite men sought to accumulate women through various forms of marriage, as well as to acquire subjects and land. Men and women who were commoners jointly produced foodstuff for subsistence, and increasingly commodities like kola nuts or gold for internal and external markets.[19]

Akan societies have a long history of contested masculinity and femininity, although this is best documented for Asante. Since the eighteenth century an emphasis on war as a male occupation altered relations between men and women, seniors and juniors. In the absence of a standing army, free male subjects furnished their own weapons (see Fig. 1.4). Individual gun possession became an "indicator of adult male status."[20] In the Asante state

Fig. 1.3. "Chief in compound," *nhenkwaa* (attendants) at the *ahenfie* (chief's palace) of Abetifi; in the foreground, the *Ɔnyame dua* (basin on a tree trunk), a place to pour libation; ca. 1890. Photo, F. Ramseyer. (Copyright Basel Mission Archive, QD-32.024.0082.)

"militaristic values were held up among the highest collective values."[21] A man excelling on the battlefield was called *ɔbarima* (valiant man) or *ɔkatakyie* (hero). Praise poetry portrayed the *Asantehene* (Asante ruler) as the model warrior. Yet women were not completely absent from warfare. They supplied fighting men with provisions and performed the *mmobomme* ritual: spiritual warfare, involving prayer, partial nudity, inversion of gender roles, and abuse of male cowards. Each *oman* had a female stool (symbolizing political office), occupied by the *ɔhemaa* (queenmother), and each linage an *ɔbaapanyin* (female elder). Senior women maintained political and spiritual powers, symbolized in their menstrual blood. In exceptional cases, women beyond menopause could occupy male stools and serve as military leaders; they had become ritual men.[22]

By the late nineteenth century, in addition to the warrior ideal, there were at least three other important notions of masculinity in Akan societies:

Fig. 1.4. "Asante warrior," ca. 1888. Photo, F. Ramseyer. (Copyright Basel Mission Archive, QD-30.043.0026.)

adult masculinity signified by marriage, senior masculinity reflected in the figure of an *ɔpanyin* (elder), and the status of an *ɔbirɛmpɔn* (big man). Adult masculinity, mediated by male and female elders, signified a free man's independence and permission to marry. Prior to colonial conquest, gun ownership reflected this status. In Kwawu a married man was expected to provide for his wife and help her farm. As a father, he should look after his children but could demand their labor, even after divorcing their mother. An adult man also had obligations toward his *abusua* (matrilineage). Senior masculinity, the position of an *ɔpanyin*, did not depend on a person's specific age and wealth but rather on comportment, reputation, and the ability to mediate conflicts and provide advice. The *ɔbirɛmpɔn* ideal "has an enduring and alluring appeal in the history of southern Ghana" going back to the founders of Akan settlements in the forest.[23] Originally a chiefly title, by the late nineteenth century the big-man status related to men who had amassed fortunes trading items like kola and rubber. Big men were expected to share their wealth and act like the precolonial *ɔbirɛmpɔn*, famous for their generosity and conspicuous display of wealth.[24]

From the mid-nineteenth century a series of changes complicated these understandings of masculinity. Colonial conquest and Pax Britannica ended warfare as an activity of Akan men, even to the point that most members of the Gold Coast Constabulary were recruited not among Akans but among "Hausas" with alleged martial qualities from Lagos, the Niger Valley, and then northern Ghana.[25] In Kwawu colonial observers portrayed the people as industrious farmers who cultivated land around their towns and in farming villages south of the ridge, growing crops like "mountain rice, yams, plantains, bananas, maize, white and red beans, tomatoes, garden eggs [eggplant] and okra."[26] Men hunted in the plains and fished in the Afram River. Kwawu people are well known for trading. In the nineteenth century, traders focused on northern markets exchanging kola nuts, imported fabric, and glass beads for hides, metal craft, and slaves. Early in the twentieth century they reoriented toward the southern commercial centers. Traders invested profits in cash crops, launching a Kwawu cocoa industry, and erected large cement buildings in their hometowns to demonstrate their wealth. As big men, they began surpassing chiefs.[27]

Further, mission societies contested established ideas of masculinity. Since the 1840s Basel and Wesleyan missionaries founded schools to shape young boys into a new kind of men: monogamous husbands who showed primary allegiance to wife and children and secondarily to their *abusua*. School graduates, *akrakyefoɔ*, occupied the new social positions of clerks,

11

teachers, and church leaders. In work environments they had to redefine their masculine and professional identities.[28]

Slave emancipation, in the Gold Coast Colony in 1874 and in Asante in 1902, led not only to an increased availability of male wage labor but to conflicts about social dependencies, involving issues of authority and masculinity.[29] Prior to World War I migration and urbanization accelerated across southern Ghana. Young men hoped through wage labor in cities and mines to accumulate wealth and ultimately return to their hometowns as big men. For women, urban migration was "an end in itself": some became "big women."[30] Migration caused generational struggles as well, as male elders lost their position as gatekeepers over youths reaching adult and senior masculinity. From the 1890s the cocoa industry altered gender relations. Owing to an absence of slave labor, men made increasing demands on their wives to help with cocoa farming. This caused a feminization of pawning. Because men moved into more lucrative endeavors like cocoa, women took over the markets. Further, new colonial institutions like the Boy Scouts and the civil service created male arenas with distinct behavioral codes.[31]

Colonial Ghana thus had a complex plurality of masculinities (and femininities). The cocoa-growing areas saw "gender chaos" during the interwar years. Chiefs and colonial officials expressed concerns about independent women accusing them of spreading venereal disease.[32] In Kwawu commoners forced chiefs to accept a set of Asafo Laws that curbed their influence by regulating court fines, adultery fees, and marriage payments. The colonial government, in response, strengthened chiefs' positions by formalizing indirect rule, with the Colony's Native Administration Ordinance of 1927, followed by the reconstituted Asante Confederacy in 1935. Empowered to reassert their authority, male elders used their control over native tribunals and other sites of dispute settlement to promote their ideas about gender— often in direct opposition to those of mission churches and other cultural innovators. By the 1950s new mass parties like the CPP and the National Liberation Movement (NLM) in Asante also articulated their gendered agenda.[33] Many of these big events, however, seemed to touch the interviewed men only marginally, at least in retrospect in their self-presentations. The focus here is more on the personal and individual and less on the institutional or governmental.

Moreover, in the twentieth century none of these institutions or movements fabricated a single hegemonic understanding of masculinity. Rather, expectations for masculine behavior differed by social context. Mining companies and the colonial state could issue guidelines about the personal comportment of their workers, or of male civil servants, policemen, and rail-waymen. These norms did not hold in all situations. When a clerk employed in Accra returned to his hometown, the elders expected him to act according to local norms as a member of the matrilineage. Similarly the Basel Mission, and later the Presbyterian Church sought to exercise close control over their members. Frequent conflicts about proper male behavior between church officials and local big men show that these norms remained contested. The Presbyterian concept of fatherhood, which privileges patrilineal relations, conflicted with matrilineal practices of Akan societies. Outside the congregation, church leaders not only failed to achieve the adoption of their ideas about masculinity but found themselves in competition with the expectations of other actors, such as lineage elders, wives and girlfriends, and employers.[34]

For more than one hundred years colonial and Western norms, which changed through the century, collided with local systems of longer standing, which were themselves being constantly adapted and revised. This many-fronted conflict manifested itself in the private lives of the men who shared with me their narratives over a decade of discussion and interaction. It was a battle being joined in countless areas on other continents affected by colonialism as well, and it is hoped that the deep investigation provided here will illuminate and define its complexities.

Life Histories and Subjectivity

In order to explore understandings of masculinities and sense of self among eight Kwawu men, I have focused on the life cycle. While there is a wealth of anthropological studies addressing how Africans think about personhood and the life cycle, this approach also allows for the examination of change in masculinity. A focus on individual life histories not only provides rich evidence of personal experience and subjectivity but also reveals "impersonal and collective processes."[35] Since the late 1980s Africanists have published life histories to give "voice" to people subjected to the colonial project. Most archival documents remain silent about the experiences of women, rural dwellers, migrant laborers, and other disadvantaged groups, and rarely provide African perspectives. As a result, oral research has been a way to supplement the shortcomings of colonial archives. Historians have asked African men and women to talk about their personal lives, to share their tales about repression and resistance. Listening to these accounts, feminist researchers created a new genre presenting African history through collections of women's life histories. Some scholars have foregrounded "unmediated voices" which means edited first-person accounts, kept separate from interpretation and historical contextualization. Other scholars have taken a different approach by extensively citing interview transcripts combined with their interpretations, while also drawing on archival evidence.[36]

I am interested in subjectivities, reading and presenting my interview transcripts as evidence of self-presentations, moments of subjective reflections about the past. The outcome can be interpreted as collective biographies, but this is reached through the presentation of individual selves. In my approach, intersubjectivity, the transforming relationship between elicitor and narrator, is crucial for the presentation of the account. The narrative can be "envisioned as a product of the interaction and desire of understanding between teller and listener." Still, the importance of the researcher in the production of the narration should not be overemphasized. Narrators of life histories have their own agenda and are involved in a "myriad of processes involving numerous relationships," in addition to the one with the researcher.[37] Oral history is the product of a dialogue, "the result of a relationship, of a shared project, in which both the interviewer and the interviewee are involved together."[38]

Unlike an earlier generation that developed rigid methodologies for using oral sources in the reconstruction of Africa's precolonial past, Africa's more recent social historians have been less concerned with evaluating oral accounts. Europeanists, however, have raised sophisticated methodological questions about oral testimonies as historical evidence.[39] I do not treat oral accounts about the interviewed men's lives as written documents, as if they were texts of the past. Instead, I read them as transcripts of our conversations about the past, as ways to explore their self-presentations. As these men narrated episodes about their lives, they reconstituted their selves, their lived experiences. Life histories are about subjectivities. Constituted out of collective experience, subjectivity is not static "but a dynamic process during which individuals take up and change positions in discourse."[40] As a product of history, subjectivity is multiple, gendered, and located in bodies. While the body has attracted much attention among scholars of the cultural turn, historians have been reluctant to investigate self and subjectivity. I seek to explore historical constructions of masculinity in connection with formations of subjectivity. I do not view a self as purely relational, culturally and socially determined. Instead, I focus on a "narrative self" that links culture and mind, social and reflexive qualities.[41]

In examining narrated selves of twentieth-century Africans one needs to avoid the projection of Western histories of the self. Some argue that in the West the transition to modernity meant that the self moved from communalism to subjective individualism. Even if this were true of the Western self, it does not mean that people in other societies followed a similar trajectory. Rather, ideas about selfhood and personhood must be examined in specific cultural contexts.[42] Although historians have been slow to historicize self and subjectivity in emerging modern African societies, there is an extensive anthropological and philosophical literature. There are two aspects of personhood, the "objective side," which means "distinct qualities, capacities and roles with which society endows a person," and the "subjective side," how "the individual, as actor, knows himself to be—or not to be—the person he is expected to be in a given situation and status."[43] Personhood has a temporal dimension and intersects with other social qualifications like descent, gender, and status. In the course of a life an individual may go through different stages of personhood. Ghanaian philosopher Kwame Gyekye has noted that, for Akan societies, personhood "is not innate but is earned in the ethical arena; it is an individual's moral achievement that earns him the status of a person."[44] Here the focus is on the individual process, on "how life is experienced and lived from within the mind of the person."[45] I am interested in "the *experience* of the subject in its various modalities and in a variety of settings."[46] A self is not unified. Rather, a self, reflected by its subjectivity, may include different identities, explored in this study as a multitude of masculine identities. Attaining personhood was linked to notions of masculinity, like adult and senior masculinity, in twentieth-century Akan societies.

African philosophers have suggested that communitarian values supersede any notion of self in African societies. More nuanced, Gyekye, in a plea for a "moderate communitarianism," sees the self "both as a communal being *and* as an autonomous, self-assertive being with a capacity for evaluation and choice."[47] The shift to modernity did not lead to a self separated from the social or collective. By subjectivity, I refer to a person's ability to experience the material reality of the world, to what the person does with that experience, and to the person's distinct agency as a subject. This understanding refutes the notion of "one familiar mode of subjectivity, modern subjectivism," as "irresistibly on the march."[48] I do not argue for a fragmented or fractured self as suggested by postcolonial thinkers. Instead, in narrating their selves, the men at the center of this study created selves and acted as subjects that in their view were not problematic, fragmented, or in need of liberation.[49] Although the twentieth century was a time of struggle and contestations, these men, speaking near the end of their lives, came to see themselves as integrated individuals, no longer steeped in conflict.

Despite ideas of masculinity changing in the course of the twentieth century, no single notion became dominant in these men's lives. Rather, the men created their own synthesis of different cultural practices, shaped by specific social contexts, while navigating this non-hegemonic landscape. Since they took the role of elders and teachers in our conversations, they deemphasized the hurdles and challenges of their lives. Instead, they offered a more balanced view of themselves. Only by enriching their narratives through archival research, by comparing them with other accounts, and especially by closely reading their autobiographical writings does it become possible to historicize these men's subjectivities and reconstruct the tensions they experienced. The interpretative work laid out here shows how they, as gendered actors, engaged creatively with historical opportunities embedded in structural constraints that reflected West Africa's transformations over the last hundred years.

CHILDREN AND CHILDHOOD:
WORK AND PLAY, 1900–1930

2

In early-twentieth-century Kwawu work was the dominant experience of *mmofraase* (childhood).[1] At a young age children's lives were gendered as they learned about norms and expectations for men and women. Talking about childhood, the eight men provided vivid descriptions of tasks they performed and games they played. They were exposed to notions of masculinity, particularly ideas about senior masculinity, the social position of an *ɔpanyin* (elder). Embedded in their upbringing were the historical conditions that transformed the social fabric of colonial Ghana. Yet recollections went beyond reconstructing the bygone world of their youth. Rather, the act of remembering offered insights about current subjectivities. Speaking to me as *mpanyinfoɔ* (elders), advising the *aberanteɛ* (young man), they formulated ideas about cross-generational relationships. Telling childhood stories, they reconnected with older role models.

There is an extensive literature on childhood and youth in African studies.[2] For Ghana, social scientists have written about children's diet, relations to parents, and sexual development.[3] For Akan societies, there is a rich and influential ethnography of Asante, dominated by R. S. Rattray's work in the 1920s. Deploring the changes wrought by colonialism, and deeply suspicious of Asante people who had received a school education, Rattray proposed an idealized reconstruction of precolonial Asante.[4] A child was positioned between *ena* (mother), *agya* (father), and *wɔfa* (maternal uncle). Connected by *mogya* (blood) to their mother, children belonged to her *abusua* (matrilineage) and were under the *wɔfa's* authority. Although structurally less significant, father-child relationships tended to be more intimate. A child inherited from the father a *ntɔrɔ* or *ntɔn*, a totemic spirit that implied taboos and responsibilities. I found that by the mid-twentieth century the *ntɔrɔ* was no longer relevant; none of my interview partners could fully explain its significance.[5] Listing norms and proverbs about children's "training," Rattray argued that young children were daily "undergoing unconscious instruction, mostly perhaps by a process of imitation of their elders." Attentive to gender differences, he noted that while mothers took care of girls, "the bringing up of a boy seem[ed] naturally to have fallen on the father." A boy learned from his father about social etiquette, the dangers of oaths, and sexual matters like the masturbation taboo and adultery sanctions. A boy was admonished to recognize people's property and to respect elders.[6]

In the 1940s Meyer Fortes conducted a large-scale investigation of the effects of colonialism on Asante social organization. Fortes found that "in spite of rapid social and cultural change during the past forty years," Rattray's principles still prevailed. He concluded that "kinship is not only the source of the critical norms governing the jural and personal relations of individuals in many fields of social life, but it also determines the structure of the corporate groups on which the political organization is based." Fortes updated Rattray's childhood findings and noted a father's new responsibilities concerning formal education. Aware that realities were often more complex than his normative, system-oriented approach, Fortes made *time* an analytical factor.[7] Historians Jean Allman and Victoria Tashjian argue that both Rattray and Fortes presented a system of child rearing "governed by notions of reciprocity," duty, and obligations in exchange for "rights of use." This brought a husband/father and his wife's children and *abusua* "in an ongoing process of exchange." While this system appears to have been intact in the early twentieth century, fatherly care became increasingly monetized over the following decades, and rights of use in children were replaced by "inalienable rights, detached from reciprocal obligations."[8] While Allman and Tashjian explore childhood through parenting, the perspective here is reversed. I have foregrounded individual experiences of childhood to reveal the aspirations boys entertained in the first decades of the last century, and how these aspirations were shaped not only by the changing political economy but also by their role models.

Social Contexts and Elders

As children, the eight men lived in the towns of Abetifi, Pepease, Nteso, and Obo, and in farming villages. This was a period of major socioeconomic transformations. In 1906 Traveling District Commissioner Francis Crowther reported that "the cocoa industry has not developed yet to an extraordinary extent in Okwawo."[9] Yet ten years later these men's memories testify that the "cocoa revolution" had reached Kwawu. Farmers planted cocoa trees around Nkawkaw and on the ridge behind Kwawu-Tafo and began profiting from this new cash crop. Since the 1910s Kwawu had become more closely integrated into the infrastructure of the Gold Coast. Footpaths were turned into roads to accommodate "motor lorries," like the one from Kwawu-Tafo down the north side of the ridge and along the Afram River to Makrong. From there cocoa was shipped down the Volta. Easier access to the coast introduced imported commodities, too. When the railway reached Kwawu in 1922, the hamlet Nkawkaw, south of the escarpment, became the new commercial center. Politically Kwawu had several upheavals during the first three decades of the twentieth century, because commoners, so-called young-men, challenged Kwawu chiefs who enjoyed the support of the colonial government. These changes formed the background of the eight men's child-hoods.[10]

The eight men emphasized memories about fathers, mothers, and *wɔfanom* (maternal uncles) who were formative. They identified individuals who had the characteristics of senior masculinity: widely respected in their communities with polished speech and comportment, and recognized accomplishments. These elders exercised power based on their access to spiritual knowledge, their economic resources, or their political office as lineage head or subchief. Emmanuel Akyeampong distinguishes *tumi* (power), the ability to produce change through knowledge about the spiritual world, from authority, "the enforceable right to command others" by controlling social institutions. For Akan people, as in most precolonial African societies, spiritual power was "rooted in the cosmos" and access to it was theoretically "unlimited."[11] Yet mechanisms of control included secrecy by those who knew about the spiritual world, as well as attempts by political rulers to neutralize forms of power harmful to those with authority. In the men's recollections, important elders were men and a few older women representing a form of female masculinity. Although most of the eight did not follow these elders' occupations, the latter's status and expression of senior masculinity never lost significance. Especially after the men had advanced in years, when they shared their childhood recollections with me, they reconnected with the role models of their youth. Their presentations of senior masculinity provide a way to historicize their subjectivity.

Colonial writers used much ink to deplore the "indolent" and "lazy" people of the Gold Coast, illiterate boys and young men only interested in play. This perspective is echoed in Sophy Osafo's study of child rearing in Kwawu. She noted that "most of the boys when they are of school age and do not go to school, roam about idly in the villages, both day and night and are a potential source of delinquency."[12] Yet the narratives of the interviewed men sketch a different picture of their lives as children. Days were filled with work and with obligations toward fathers, mothers, uncles, or other relatives. *Adwuma* (work) is presented as the *central* experience of childhood. Already as young children, both boys and girls were expected to help around the house and run errands. After the age of six their work became more gendered, as they began learning the skills needed for adulthood. Girls assisted their mothers in domestic work, trading, and cultivating farms; boys joined their fathers, or other relatives, in tilling, weeding, and harvesting or other activities like hunting and fishing. Growing up required that they learn the patterns of appropriate activities and behavior that would be expected of them as boys and girls, and later as men and women.[13]

Working for Fathers

As small children, most of the interviewed men stayed with their mothers. Later, as five of them highlighted, they started spending time with their fathers and acquired gendered skills. J. A. Wahyee, born in 1900, lived with his mother, Afua Yeboah, who was an offspring of the *ɔdehyeɛ* (royal) Tena *abusua* of Abetifi. More dominant in his memories was learning from his father, Kwaku Frempong. Wahyee belonged to the last generation that was introduced to the art of big-game hunting—elephant (*ɛsono*), bongo antelope (*ɔtrommo*), and the yellow-backed duiker (*ɔkwadu*). At the beginning of the twentieth century Kwawu hunters found plenty of game in Aframso (Afram Plains). By the third decade large animals had "virtually disappeared."[14] In Wahyee's childhood hunters regularly left Abetifi for an extended period. He followed his father to Kwawu's northern boundaries toward "Kete-Krachi and Atebubu." Members of an *ekuo* (hunters' association) camped in temporary villages from which experienced hunters departed on their own. It was the task of *ayawfoɔ* (hunter's attendants) to carry the smoked meat back to Abetifi, presenting a share to the *ɔhene* (chief); if hunters had killed an *ɛsono,* one of the tusks belonged to the chief. Hunting, like other crafts, was passed down in the patrilineal line; Wahyee's father, Kwaku Frempong, had learned from his father, Kofi Nkonko. In Wahyee's words:

> What I remember is the way to kill the animals; how you tiptoe quietly towards the animal and kill it; how to prepare the gun. As for the "long gun" [Danish gun, muzzle loader], if you don't clean it and prepare it well, it won't shoot.

When you see the animal, you have to aim carefully and then shoot; it will fire right away. Again, we had to learn how to watch the animals, their eyes and ears; otherwise you will miss the target.

Referring to "the way" of killing these animals, Wahyee implied the elaborate steps a hunter had to observe in order to overcome these spiritually dangerous animals, so-called *sasammoa*. When hunters returned to their hometowns, *sasammoa* were awarded a funeral performance. But, as a Presbyterian elder, Wahyee did not provide much detail about these "heathen" practices.[15]

British officials expressed concerns about the dwindling numbers of big game, especially elephants. After inspecting the Afram Plains in 1908, H. N. Thompson, conservator of forests, argued that local people should be restricted in their hunting. His report provides a description of the hunting economy Wahyee experienced with his father:

> Judging from the game tracks met with, elephants and buffalo [bongo antelopes] must be very plentiful. Large numbers of them are slaughtered every year and the flesh taken up to Abetifi for sale. We met numbers of people almost everyday who were employed in carrying the smoked flesh to that town. The slaughter of elephants must be great as one of our guides told me that he had shot ten in one month. Several had been killed just before we arrived at Abetifi. Elephant meat can be purchased almost any day at Abetifi. . . . Abetifi is the great center to which the bulk of the smoked flesh is brought. . . . Some of the more well-to-do inhabitants own small hunters' villages down on the plain and a portion of everything shot in the vicinity has to be sent up to them for disposal.[16]

At the beginning of the twentieth century Abetifi was a well-known market for ivory, attracting European traders. According to Decima Moore, who stayed there in 1906, it was a common sight to see elephant skulls "used as seats outside the houses." Wahyee also recalled "Germans" purchasing ivory (see Fig. 2.1).[17]

In a discussion with his nephew, Yaw Apea, Wahyee reflected on the disappearance of the hunting profession. This *adwuma* ceased to exist because the old hunters had died and young men "were no longer interested." Although both Wahyee and Apea mentioned the extinction of big game, in their perception men's changing preferences and government interference were more important. Yaw Apea noted:

> The animals are not finished, but the government has taken over the land on which the animals live. The government has "quarantined" the land . . . and made it into a "forest reserve." Nobody is allowed to go and kill any animals

Fig. 2.1. "Elephant jaws under a fetish tree in Abetifi," ca. 1902. Photo, M. O. Schulz. (Copyright Basel Mission Archive, D-30.14.062.)

there. At the moment, if you want to go to hunt there, you have to get a special permit. Because of that, the hunting profession has almost disappeared. . . . The young men growing up [these days] also don't like hunting. They kill little animals such as the *opuro* [squirrel], the *akrantɛɛ* [hedgehog], and the *nkokɔ hwedeɛ* [bush fowl].

Yaw Apea then reminded his audience about the important achievements for hunters:

Before you get a big name as a real hunter, you have to kill an ɛsono [elephant]. If you only kill *awansan* [antelopes] and *opuro*, you will not make a name for yourself, except if you kill big animals. But these days there are no large animals anymore.[18]

In Wahyee's youth, hunters were categorized in grades; a man who succeeded in killing one elephant became an *ɔbɔmmɔfo* (pl. *abɔmmɔfoɔ*), a junior hunter. An *ɔbɔmmɔfo* distinguished himself from apprentices assisting hunters. He was widely respected among Kwawu men. One song praises "the *ɔbɔmmɔfo* as a valiant man—*ɔbɔmmɔfo yɛ ɔbarima.*" Senior hunters, those who had killed three elephants, were elevated to the top rank of *abɔfoɔ* (master hunters) and formed an *ekuo*, or professional hunters association, which acted as a link between hunters and the chief. Wahyee never killed an elephant, although his father, Kwaku Frempong, had achieved this special trophy.[19]

In his remarkable childhood memoir, T. E. Kyei of Agogo included a chapter on the "honoured profession that is no more." Kyei's maternal grandmother was a daughter of a big-game hunter who hunted in Aframso to the west of Kwawu. In her stories the grandmother emphasized the high status of hunters, ranked next to the Agogo chief and *akɔmfoɔ* (diviners). A hunter not only had connections to the spiritual world but his "income earning capability" made "him an influential member of the community till his profession was superseded by the cocoa industry."[20] This economic potential was declining for Wahyee's father. Moreover, it is striking that Wahyee did not dwell on his father's spiritual knowledge as a hunter. Instead, he emphasized Kwaku Frempong's role in introducing him to the Basel Mission congregation. Kwaku Frempong told his son Bible stories. After learning "more about the scriptures," Wahyee joined a baptismal class. In 1920 he was confirmed and accepted as a full church member. Although Wahyee never enrolled in school, the Bible introduced him to the written word. Later he taught himself basic literacy skills in Twi.[21] In Wahyee's account of his father as a role model, he sketched aspects of senior masculinity, particularly the father's bravery and experience as a hunter. Yet when linking these memories with his own life as a respected elder and former presbyter of the Presbyterian Church, the father was no longer a hunter with powerful connections to a dangerous spiritual world but, instead, was the one who opened doors to the Christian faith.

Kwaku Marfo also had an intense spiritual connection with his father, Kwasi Nyame, a renowned big man with fifty-eight children. Marfo, *Nsumankwaahene* of Kwawu (leader of those responsible for royal charms), was born ca. 1905 in Pepease. Since Marfo was without a maternal family in Pepease, he was adopted into his father's Agona *abusua*. As a child, Marfo and his Fante mother stayed with the father. Marfo recalled:

> My father married many women. So, when the children grew up, they went back to their family or returned to their hometowns; those who did return to their families learned from their uncles and mothers. As for myself and my brother, however, our mother was a Fante from Mankesim-Dominase [Central Region]. Therefore, when my other brothers and sisters went back to their

families, my mother remained with my father. I was born *and* bred here, while those, who had to go, left. As we had nowhere to go, we stayed with our father. . . . When my mother died, she was . . . buried here.

While growing up in Pepease, Marfo accompanied his mother to her hometown. After she died, the journeys to Fanteland stopped. Because his maternal uncles and other relatives from her *abusua* never played an important role, the bonds to his father grew stronger. Marfo and his brother learned the father's trade. The father, well-versed in herbal and spiritual medicines, was closely connected to chiefs in Kwawu and Asante.

My father Kwasi Nyame first lived in Aduamoa [Kwawu town]. There he was born. He was the grandchild of the Aduamoahene. When they gave birth to him, he stayed there until he came of age. From there, he traveled to Kumase to become a *nsumankwaa* of the Asantehene.[22]

In Kumase, Kwasi Nyame was responsible for a royal *suman* Domfe Kyerefi. *Asuman* were handmade objects like charms and amulets worn around the neck or limbs. When the father moved back to Pepease, he was possessed by two local *abosom* (lesser gods) of his *abusua*, Fofie Anim and Yentumi. Subsequently he became a powerful ɔkɔmfo (diviner), still remembered by the older generation.[23]

Because of his spiritual responsibilities and chiefly patronage, Kwasi Nyame never had to grow foodstuff, nor did he expect Marfo and his elder brother, Kwadwo Frempong, to engage in farmwork. With a smile on his face, Marfo stated that he "did not know how to weed." Instead, Marfo recounted his father's wish that his sons should "learn his *adwuma*," particularly his knowledge about herbs, "so that in the future we would remember him." As long as the father lived, Marfo worked closely with him. Proudly, but with a sad face, he recalled that Kwasi Nyame "died in [his] arms." Marfo took his father as a guiding example of senior masculinity and sought to emulate him. When asked about the advice he received from his father, Marfo emphasized respect for seniority:

He warned his children not to insult elders. "You are always with the chiefs, therefore learn from my behavior towards chiefs. Learn from how I walk with these chiefs, and from this you will be able to move with them. Learn from me, so that you become one with your neighbors. Do not be too talkative. It is not necessary to offend any other person, be it an adult or a child. Do not develop hatred for elders. If you do not respect your elders, your life will be miserable."[24]

This passionate recommendation to treat elders with deference needs to be read against the context of the 1990s, when many Kwawu *mpanyinfoɔ* (elders) were no longer granted respect by the younger generation. Further, the statement reveals not only the importance Marfo attributed to senior masculinity but also his own self-perception as a "traditional" elder, drawing legitimacy and continuity from his admired father's advice, stretching back for almost a century. Urged to reveal more about their special relationship, Marfo reacted with proverbs:

> SM: Why did you want to become like your father?
> MA: The reason is because my father knew herbs. If I want to talk about that, I would talk and talk and talk. . . . There is a saying that *"Obi mfa ne nsa benkum nkyerɛ n'agya amamfo so"* (Nobody shows his father's abandoned village with his left hand). Yes, my father was so powerful that nobody was above him. When it comes to worship, to medicine and healing, he was outstanding. Therefore all my goals were to become like him.[25]

This proverb draws on the Akan convention of not pointing with the left hand, since this hand, used for personal hygiene, is associated with "filth, uncleanliness, disgrace, disrespect, and vice."[26] In Marfo's answer the proverb not only closed the discussion but also informed his audience, a Swiss historian, Douglas Asomani, and other bystanders, of his reservations about revealing too much about his father. In the proverb, the deserted village represents undisclosed knowledge; its existence is acknowledged but its location remains secret. Marfo might have had an additional reason for his silence. Since his mother was a stranger in Kwawu, he had become part of his father's *abusua*. This made him even more hesitant to speak about his father's past.[27]

Unlike Marfo, retired trader E. K. Addo (born 1904) was highly ranked in his *abusua*. Still, he talked much about his father and paternal brothers. Addo's childhood recollections feature an important shift among Kwawu traders' economic activities in the early twentieth century. As a small child, like Wahyee, Addo stayed with his mother, Adwoa Agyeiwa, in his father's house in the old section of Abetifi. Father Kofi Safo, a brother of the Abetifi ruler, was a prosperous trader who frequented the northern "transit-markets" of Atebubu and Salaga, purchasing beads and items like brass basins to be sold in the south. At the age of six Addo was taken to his mother's home at the town of Nteso. There he lived with his *wɔfa* who, as a member of the Bretuo "royal house," had aspirations to become Nteso chief. Addo helped to weed around the cocoa trees and served his *wɔfa*'s mother, who took a liking to him.

> The old lady . . . said, I would be a chief one day. So they should not play
> roughly with me. When they were going to farm, I was just carrying water for
> drinks.[28]

Significantly, a few years later, two of his father's older sons, J. K. Kwakye
and J. E. Sampong, took Addo under their wings. The brothers had reoriented their trading toward the south by establishing themselves as itinerant traders in the original cocoa-growing area of the Eastern Province in
the first decade of the twentieth century.[29] Addo accompanied Kwakye to
the mining town of Obuasi where he lived during World War I. Vividly he
recalled the outbreak of the influenza epidemic in October 1918. He believed
that returning soldiers who handed out cigarettes from train cars spread the
disease. As a nonsmoker, he remained healthy.

> I was the only boy nursing the people in the area. You smash pepper, raw
> pepper, for them to drink and sweat, and they would get all right, some of
> them got cured by that. Because medical aid was very poor at that time.

The same medicine was recommended in newspapers for symptomatic relief.
Although about one hundred thousand people died across Ghana, Addo and
his immediate family were lucky. Those "affected by the influenza were
cured."[30]

In 1920 Addo returned with Kwakye to the Eastern Province. Four years
later they moved to Accra where brother Sampong had opened "Mmodenbo
Stores" in Lutterodt Street with a capital of £3,000. As a child Addo was
fascinated with traders, especially their "beautiful clothes" and "big houses."
The brothers and their commercial world were the *focal* points of his early
memories. First his father, then his brothers acted as models of senior masculinity. While the former represented an older generation with limited resources, the latter became modern big men with increasing economic power.
Addo decided to follow in their footsteps.[31]

The father was also an important presence in the early childhood of
Ɔkyeame Kwabena Asante and Emmanuel Frempong Opusuo, both of Pepease. Ɔkyeame Asante, born in 1911, grew up with his father, George
Anim, a shoemaker, in Nsawam. Although Asante shared few childhood
recollections, he emphasized his father's discipline. He was not permitted to
leave the compound during the day but had to weed behind the house or
do other domestic work.[32] Opusuo, born ca. 1923, was the last child of his
mother Abena Nyama. He had more to say than Asante. Abena Nyama's
first husband was a policeman working in Accra. After his death, she was

married by levirate to his brother, Opusuo's father, Kwaku Adu. Opusuo was named after his paternal great-uncle who, at that time, occupied the paramount stool of Kwawu. As a child, Opusuo stayed first with his mother in Pepease. At the age of six he went to live with his father. After Abena Nyama's divorce, she was relieved that her former husband took care of their son. By then, Kwaku Adu had remarried and moved to Adonso, a cocoa village now inundated by Lake Volta. Kwaku Adu had earned enough capital for launching a cocoa farm while working in the gold mines of Obuasi. He left Obuasi around 1920, when the booming cocoa industry was the mining industry's main competitor for labor. Cocoa farming offered an attractive alternative, enabling him to settle within reach of his hometown. Kwaku Adu welcomed Opusuo since he depended on labor performed by his wife and children, supplemented by a few migrant laborers from Burkina Faso (Upper Volta).[33]

Today Opusuo considers Kwaku Adu's influence as crucial in developing his work ethic, and credits him as a role model representing an older form of senior masculinity. Opusuo expressed pride that his father, as an *ɔmanheneba* (a child of a paramount chief), had a close connection to the ruling *abusua* of Kwawu.

> OP: My father did not like drinking and smoking. He always advised his children against drinking and smoking, so I wasn't brought up drinking and smoking, so I hated it. . . . When I became a teacher, I did not like people who smoked. . . .
> SM: So you were against drinking . . . ?
> OP: I drank only during Christmas and funerals, ah yes, I was not a regular drinker.

Although Opusuo left his father's village to attend school, he frequently returned for the cocoa harvest.

> My father liked me more than any of his other children, because I was hard-working. I helped him whenever I was on holiday; I helped him to do his farm work. . . . I was not big [physically]; I was just tiny and smallish, but I was hard-working. . . . I knew how to weave baskets, so he did not need to buy baskets to carry his cocoa. . . . Because of this, he liked me more than any of his other children.[34]

Opusuo's upbringing was distinctly different from that of his sisters who stayed with their mother and did not develop a close connection with the father. The *wɔfanom* (maternal uncles) were not an important presence. Because of their poverty, neither uncles nor mother was in a position to support

27

him. There was a gender fluidity in children's living arrangement. Boys were more likely to reside with fathers to learn their skills. As long as fathers provided for their children, they had rights over their children's labor. Yet when maternal relatives had greater means to support nephews, fathers retreated into the background, made fewer demands on their sons' labor, and were less prominent in childhood memories.[35]

Working for the *Abusua* (Matrilineage)

Three of my interview partners, Akasease Kofi Boakye Yiadom, Rev. E.K.O. Asante, and Kofi Ankoma, stressed the influence of maternal relatives during their childhood. Working and learning took place within the fold of the *abusua*. In these cases, the *wɔfa*, either the mother's brother or her uncle, became a crucial figure taking an interest in the child's life and making demands on his labor. The *wɔfa* was not only involved in decisions about the training of his *wɔfase* (nephew, niece) but also expressed expectations and acted as a role model, a reference point of senior masculinity. A. K. Boakye Yiadom was born in 1910 in Apedwa, Akyem Abuakwa, the child of a cross-cousin marriage. His mother, Afua Ntoriwah, belonged to a secondary branch of the royal Bretuo *abusua*. His father, Moses Kwabena Somua, had a store in Akyem Abuakwa. Like E. K. Addo's brothers, Somua had joined Kwawu traders moving south to the prosperous market towns along the railway of Akyem Abuakwa and Akuapem to profit from the expansion of the cocoa industry. In 1923 the father was forced to leave Akyem Abuakwa by order of the paramount chief, Nana Ofori Atta I, expelling all Kwawu traders. He returned to Kwawu and started his own cocoa farm at Ankoma behind Kwawu-Tafo.[36]

Boakye Yiadom lived first with his parents in Apedwa, then was sent home to stay with his maternal grandmother, Adwoa Antie, in Abetifi. At age ten he was taken to the smaller town of Akwasihu, soon a railway stop. There he served his maternal grandfather and local chief, Nana Kwasi Ampomah, a big man who had fathered seventy-five children. Wealthy and respected, Ampomah was considered an *ɔbarima pa*, a valiant and successful man. Ampomah was of unique importance for Boakye Yiadom. Since his grandmother, a stranger to Kwawu, had married Ampomah, she and her children had become part of her husband's *abusua*. Ampomah was not only Boakye Yiadom's maternal grandfather but also his *abusua* head. Staying with Ampomah exposed Boakye Yiadom to life at the *ahenfie* (chief's palace). He learned drumming and playing praise names on the elephant tusk horn. He was responsible for fetching water, sweeping around the house, and helping with farm labor. In Akwasihu, he feared the powerful grandfather and dared not play in the evening. Whenever he had the chance he visited Abetifi on the ridge where he was less supervised. There he stayed with his *wɔfanom*, Kwadwo Opong and Kwabena Mensa Opong, who had done apprenticeships as tailors. Mensa Opong was making a living as a petty trader, while Kwadwo Opong had found employment as an agricultural officer. They became models of progressive men involved in new economic activities and were instrumental in providing their *wɔfase* with a formal education.[37]

Similar to Boakye Yiadom, the *wɔfanom* were also important figures for Rev. Edmond Kwaku Osafo Asante, born in 1911. Asante resided with his mother, Ohenewaa, who lived with two daughters and two sons in an Abetifi house built by her brother, Kwabena Adofo. Asante's father, Kwadwo Osafo, a trader, came from the Kwawu town of Obomeng and traveled across French West Africa purchasing beads which he sold in the markets of southern Ghana. Whenever the polygynous father visited Abetifi, he stayed with his first wife, Ohenewaa. Kwadwo Osafo named his son Asante after his own father; he died before Asante was ten years old.[38]

Asante emphasized boys' and girls' different responsibilities. Again, children's worlds became gendered at an early age. This not only applied to the production of food, with girls following their mothers to the fields and boys helping their fathers or other male elders, but also applied to food consumption.

> SM: Did boys and girls eat together?
> AS: No, the girls ate with their mothers, but the boys were separated to join the men. They ate differently, not from the same dish. They were given their share, and all boys sat together to eat from one dish.
> SM: From one big bowl?
> AS: From a big bowl, next to the men. But the men used tables, seats, while the boys were squatting.

In the morning, Asante recalled, they had porridge made out of corn or cocoyam and plantains which were either cooked or roasted. The cost of oil made fried foods a rarity. In the evening fufu was prepared from plantain and cocoyam and sometimes with yam. Although the same dishes were cooked for men and women and for boys and girls, differences in portions and eating order reflected age and gender. Asante noted:

> In the family the men would be served the food first, then later the children and the mothers. That's how it is shared. The women will see to it that the

men's food is properly set before [the men] are invited to come [in]. Not that [the men] sit [start eating] and later ask for water, for a piece of salt and so.[39]

Anthropologist J.W.A. Amoo, writing in the 1940s, interpreted this gendered eating arrangement as a sign of "the [male] child's dependence on the father," stating that "until marriage the son [would] dine with [the father]."[40] I found instead that the shared meal was a moment of intimacy between a male elder and his son or nephew, when the senior could express appreciation of his junior. Nana Atta Daaku, an *ɔpanyin* at the Abetifi *ahenfie,* explained that he would share food, often a piece of meat, with his son to reward him for completing a task. When Asante was invited to comment, he added that this practice was "an incentive for the children to behave properly. If you [didn't] behave . . . they [would] refuse to give you meat." Since husbands and wives did not live together, these eating arrangements could be further complicated. According to Asante:

> And if a woman is living in a house, in a different house from her husband, then, after finishing the meal, it is the children, or the mother herself, who carry the food to the husband's house. Then the boys may follow the mother to the father's house, set the table, and wait until after he has finished the meal. The boys will then finish the remaining food and wash the dish, the table, everything, clean the place, and carry the empty dish back to the mother.[41]

Such practices were not only part of children's domestic duties toward mothers and fathers but were also moments when boys (ob)served fathers, uncles, and other senior men. Eating was part of learning about senior masculinity, the distinct habitus of elders.

Male elders of Asante's maternal Adoako *abusua* became role models. His *wɔfanom* were engaged in trading and farming. They had stores in Wenkyi in the Western Region, where they sold cloth. On their occasional visits to Kwawu, they invested in cocoa, becoming pioneers during the second decade of the twentieth century. The older *wɔfa,* Dwamena, farmed cocoa in the village of Okrakyei, now flooded by Lake Volta. The younger, Kwabena Adofo, helped to found Ankoma, a small cocoa village behind Nteso. Asante's recollections about his uncles' enthusiasm for cocoa farming confirm that "more money appears to have flown *from* trading *into* cocoa farming than in the reverse direction."[42] His memories were most vivid about Kwabena Adofo. Around 1920 this *wɔfa* used his cocoa profits to built a house. Its spatial organization reflected the needs of senior masculinity and indicated Adofo's hopes of becoming a big man. The compound house was

arranged around an open courtyard that featured a raised, three-walled platform, *pato,* for the elder to sit and hear cases. The largest rooms, with
chamber and hall, belonged to the *wɔfa;* smaller ones, whose verandas
opened to the courtyard, were for *abusua* members like Asante's mother and
her children. In the 1920s about twenty people shared this house. It still
stands today in *Manem,* Abetifi's old section. Adofo succeeded in his aspirations and later, as *Akwamuhene,* occupied the family stool.[43]

Another towering figure was his great-uncle Adaakwa, then Abetifi's
Akwamuhene, who taught Asante about local history and customs. Asante
witnessed his great-uncle's skill in settling disputes. Learning often meant
serving. In 1918 there occurred one of the rare occasions when Kwawu chiefs
celebrated *afahye,* their version of the *odwira* festival. During *afahye,* chiefs
assembled in the capital Abene to pay respect to the *ɔmanhene* (paramount
chief). The "long procession of chiefs" walking up the sacred mountain,
Ampon Agyei, outside Abene, is deeply engraved in Asante's memories. He
recalled how the chiefs first celebrated "in their respective towns" and then
gathered in Abene for one week, where he witnessed much "drumming and
dancing." Asante carried his great-uncle's stool when they climbed the steep
mountain, covered by thick forest, for the final *afahye* ritual.[44] The first ruler
of Abene, Nana Ampon Agyei, had migrated to Kwawu from Mampon, and
hence the name (M)Ampon Agyei. According to a widely told story, he
never died but disappeared in an opening of a large *odade* tree on the sacred
mountain. A hunter found Agyei's cloth hanging from the *odade* tree; a hand,
grasping Agyei's sword *Danfosan,* stretched out from the trunk's hollow. A
voice told the hunter that Ampon Agyei had flown away: there was no need
to perform funeral rites, because Ampon Agyei would continue advising the
Abene people. Since then, Ampon Agyei's spirit continues to be venerated
under the same *odade* tree on the sacred mountain, especially during *afahye.*[45]

The eighth man in the cohort, Kofi Ankoma, born in 1914, takes us to
Obo, Kwawu's largest town and bustling market center early in the twentieth
century. Visiting in 1906, Decima Moore dismissively referred to Obo as the
"queen of rabbit warrens," an area under a quarter of a square mile "crammed
with over 1200 rotten-thatched, irregular-shaped mud-huts and compounds"
and more than 9,000 inhabitants. Unlike Abetifi, Obo resisted the encroach-
ing British influence and the presence of Basel missionaries. By the second
decade, Obo's population had declined due to out-migration of cocoa farmers. Others relocated to the new commercial centers, using their skills as
artisans to acquire capital for trading. By the 1930s wealthy traders had

erected storied buildings that transformed Obo's appearance. These characteristics, Obo's migrant traders and resilience against Christianity, are reflected in Ankoma's recollections.[46]

During Ankoma's childhood, *abusua* elders were more present than his father who was a poor farmer and unable to look after his son. Ankoma stayed with his mother, Abena Dapaa. Originally from the Bretuo *abusua* of Pepease, she had moved to Obo after her mother married there. Dapaa was well known for her spiritual power, helping women to conceive, and her skills as a midwife. Talking about her *adwuma*, I asked:

> SM: Did she have a day in the week when she stayed at home and people were coming to see her?
> KA: Yes, it was Fofie [a ritually important Friday]. Every Fofie she would be at home. She would go to the shrine's room and sit down, while you [the visitor] entered. Anything you needed, you would tell her, you would tell the shrine. Then, she would see if she could do it for you. If she couldn't do it, she would tell you: "I am sorry, I can't meet."[47]

Dapaa's religious work as an *ɔkɔmfo*, with spiritual power based on secret knowledge about local deities, made a lasting impression on Ankoma. When she had passed her childbearing years, Dapaa embodied a form of female masculinity: she acquired the status of a man, someone who could "wear [his] cloths in a male fashion, drink liquor, and pour libations."[48] Being the son of an *ɔkɔmfo* was crucial to Ankoma's self-presentation. He deplored the growing strength of Christianity in Kwawu and never joined any of the new churches. Rather, he emphasized his attractions to shrines like Tegare. Ankoma's reference point for senior masculinity was his *wɔfa*, Kwadwo Adofo, a wealthy Obo trader, who represented the proverbial big man. Adofo saw Ankoma as a potential successor. Although Adofo was illiterate and not a Christian, he came to the conclusion that the future generation of traders needed the advantages of literacy. When he summarized his childhood recollections, Ankoma underscored close supervision. His *wɔfa*, as well as the more distant father or the beloved mother, could exercise harsh punishment for any small misdemeanor. Therefore Ankoma was eager to leave Obo.[49]

In their accounts the eight men each identified individuals, either fathers, paternal brothers, or maternal uncles, who dominated their childhood memories and had become role models, representing ideas about senior masculinity. All role models were powerful people who provided leadership and settled disputes in their hometowns and *mmusua* (matrilineages). As children, my interview partners watched these elders perform their responsibilities. At times their relationship was one of intimacy rather than one of discipline or hierarchical order. In this view of senior masculinity, authority was tempered by the desire to pass along and to acquire knowledge rather than a respect invoked by force. Moreover, all interviewed men, at least briefly, connected these role models with their own childhood aspirations. Wahyee, Marfo, and Addo were quite reverent when speaking of their fathers or brothers; they considered them spiritual mentors to be emulated. Reverend Asante and Opusuo presented their role models as inspirational although their own lives took different directions. Okyeame Asante and Ankoma expressed an ambivalence toward some childhood elders. Boakye Yiadom shared this ambivalence concerning his grandfather but welcomed his *wofanom*'s influence. Ankoma felt a deep spiritual bond with his *okomfo* mother. Forms of imitation rather than direct instruction were frequently the mode of connection with elders. Yet these connections across generations were always intertwined with a strong sense of obligation to provide key elders with labor and serve them.

Gendered Games

Although the men interviewed had to work hard for these elders, they talked with joy about their activities during *afoofi* (leisure), a term translated by Christaller as "keeping at home resting or doing domestic work; refraining from plantation work." As elsewhere in early-twentieth-century rural Africa, Kwawu people experienced time as task-oriented. *Afoofi* started when work was completed, not at a specific time on the clock. Yet in the Akan calendar, organized around *aduanan,* a forty-day cycle, there were a series of *nnabone* (bad days), considered sacred and ritually important, when no farming was permitted but lighter work like domestic chores or communal labor could be performed. Among Akan people, in particular, there was a clear opposition between work and leisure on *nnabone*. On these bad days children had more time for play than on days reserved for farmwork.[50] Those who entered mission schools or migrated south seeking industrial employment in gold mines or those who worked in the coastal cities had to adjust their sense of time to a modern, urban understanding ruled by the clock and organized around a six-day workweek. The boundaries between play and work were more fluid in Kwawu than in colonial cities where people were "gradually . . . caught in a 'net' of urban time," and "leisure" emerged as concrete activities opposite to work like watching or playing sports, dressing well and going to bars, meeting in recreational clubs, and gathering informally with family and friends.[51]

In Kwawu during *afooft*, childrens's *agorɔ* (games) were organized by age and gender. Boys usually played with other boys of the same age group. In his seminal essay about the connections between play and culture, Johan Huizinga defined play as a "voluntary activity" conducted during free time "outside the immediate satisfaction of wants and appetites" with its own rules; play happens "within certain limits of time and places," absorbs players' full attention, remains "distinct from ordinary life," and is frequently surrounded by secrecy.[52] While Huizinga argued that play can be studied as a foundation of human cultural production, I suggest that local gender systems are represented, reproduced, and at times even challenged in play. This is embedded in a historical context. The interviewed men remembered games played by boys after finishing their work. Reverend Asante listed *atetaate* (hide-and-seek), *aguma* (wrestling), the board game "draught," and one in which "a heap of leaves" were thrown into the air and caught with a rope.[53] Some games sharpened mental abilities while others tested muscle strength and agility; all (re)produced male hierarchies. Concerning *aguma*, Akan scholar J. B. Danquah noted that "two opponents meet to wrestle arm to arm, leg to leg, and body against body, in a rather violent but artful manner [until] one of them succeeds in conquering the other by sending him down."[54] While some girls' games were also competitive, like the popular clapping and jumping play *ampe*, others focused more on mutual trust and support. In *asɔ*, a group of girls formed a circle. While clapping and singing, the girl in the middle falls back and is caught by the nearest member of the group who swings her around. The girl in the middle is moved from side to side until the end of the accompanying song when she is exchanged. Other games prepared girls for motherhood. Since these games happened in the separate spheres of boys and girls, such group play was crucial in preparing children for adult life.[55]

In group games, boys imitated men's activities like hunting and warfare. Edmond Perregaux, a missionary stationed in Abetifi from 1891 to 1901, reported that "children" (meaning boys) made their own arms "resembling the bow or the gun," and set traps catching birds and fish "in the bush."[56] Many of the interviewed men talked about the "drill" or "soldier game," widespread during and after World War I. According to Reverend Asante, boys, organized into military groups, exercised with "dumbbells and some sticks." This game gave them a forum to compete with one another, stake their territories, and show their physical prowess. Boakye Yiadom remembered his participation with pride. When visiting Abetifi, away from his grandfather's supervision, he took part in mock military parades:

> BY: There were outside games, [we played] with our friends, we called it "army." We tie our cloths and hang it over the shoulder (gets up, calls his wife, and uses her cloth to demonstrate it) and put some stones into the cloth and tie it. Then we march in the night, let's say from seven o'clock going, we march from street to street. (starts singing) *"Pii, pii, yɛnsuro obiara, pii, pii, yɛnsuro obiara, yɛrekɔ Asante yeato tuo, poo . . ."* [Piff, piff, we don't fear anybody, we don't fear anybody, we go to Asante to shoot, bang . . .]. So, we march, when we meet other children from this side and go to the end of the street, then those boys there also march. When we meet them, we take them [stones wrapped in cloth] and start beating up one another.
> SM: That can be painful.
> BY: Yes, very painful! And sometimes those other boys run away, or we will run away, being defeated.[57]

Wahyee, who was ten years older than Boakye Yiadom, emphasized the violence of the soldier game. Elected leaders, called "Captain" and "Assistant Captain," commanded the band of boys. Wahyee explained:

> We looked for somebody who is stronger than everybody else and who is able to "command" us all. He may say: "All stop!" And we all stopped. "You all come!" And we all came. If somebody was "rough," he [the Captain] may order somebody else to beat him. And he will beat him mercilessly and we all hoot at him.[58]

In Abetifi, children of one *borɔn* (ward) fought against those living in other *mmorɔn* (wards). Sometimes, as Wahyee recalled, it turned "into a real fight" and players were "injured." The youths of *Kubase* competed with the boys of *Dome,* or the *mmerantee* (young men) of *Dwenease* beat those of *Ɔkyemase.* Yet children living in *Aberem* (the Christian Quarters) were excluded from the soldier game. Both Boakye Yiadom and Wahyee emphasized that they "were afraid" of the European missionaries and dared not enter the Basel Mission settlement. Moreover, church elders would not permit Christian children "to go to town."[59] T. E. Kyei referred to the soldier game as *ntɔmaa* (cloth fighting). He grew up in the Agogo Basel Mission Salem where, unlike Abetifi, he and other children of Christian parents participated in this game. In his published autobiography, Kyei explained the game's formal structure. Only those who did not obey its rules "put sand or, in some cases, stones at the looped ends of their cloths to hit an opponent." Striking an opponent in the "head and in the belly" was not permitted; unruly teams "were shunned and boycotted till their misbehaved player had been excluded."[60] In their more spontaneous oral recollections, Boakye Yiadom and Wahyee conveyed a different impression by focusing on the competitiveness, the violence, as well as the selection of heroic leaders. These two accounts reveal different understandings of the game's role in shaping boys into men. The Abetifi men evoked an artful competition that permitted violence among the players from different *mmorɔn*, while Kyei insisted that strict rules tamed this warrior game, making it quite benign and harmless.[61]

Like the more formalized stick fighting practiced by South African male youth, the soldier game provided a space for "ritual reproduction of gendered age hierarchies," where male youths could develop an identity and a self. Yet, as Ann Mager has noted for a later period, such games "did not . . . foreclose the exercise of new options or prevent instability in individual or group identities."[62] Rather, the games reflected historical change and other boys' and young men's organizations such as urban gangs and colonial militaries. In Boakye Yiadom and Wahyee's recollections, titles like "Captain" echoed the structure of the colonial army. This was only an indirect reference since the Gold Coast Regiment lacked a strong presence in Kwawu. Prior to World War II, soldiers were recruited in the Northern Territories and in Muslim *Zongos* (stranger quarters) at the edge of southern towns.[63] The soldier game closely reflected the local militias, particularly *Asafo* companies which were a dominant and at times violent factor in Kwawu politics during the first third of the twentieth century. The success and influence of the *Asofo* companies that revolted to oppose and destool unpopular chiefs were watched by children and reflected in their *afoofi* activities.[64]

In retrospect the men's dominant impression was that children were too busy to engage in group games during the day, as Ɔkyeame Asante stressed.[65] Still, the dividing line between work and leisure, between work and play, was not always sharply drawn. The laborious chore of fetching water inspired boys' creativity. Boakye Yiadom and Opusuo mentioned the "toy lorry" they used to gather water at the well. As Opusuo stated:

> You know the water is far away, so we had a toy lorry to fetch water, a long stick with a round tire, we call it "tire" [in Twi], a round object we used to push. When you push it, it goes like a truck, we used it for fetching water.

And Boakye Yiadom:

> When I was a child, I was too fond of making this wheel. It was a long pole, and you fix it to some tires, and you put it under your shoulders. I used to carry [tin buckets of] water with that long wheel with a pole. You see.

The "lorry" did not have rubber tires. The wheels were either cut from a wooden board, or from the round roots of the *onina* tree. This water-fetching device was only driven by boys. Opusuo recalled going to the well even if there was plenty of water—just for fun. Boakye Yiadom commented:

> So one day, if say Saturday or Sunday, if I don't go to farm or church, I can fill a bucket of water, ten buckets of water into the house, because I like wheeling, making the wheel. Because of the wheel, I say it is not me who goes to the water [well or stream], it is the car, the car goes to the water.

This toy is still in use, although the material has changed. For the 1950s, Kaye reported that Ga boys "of about six" made " 'lorries' out of sticks and cigarette tin lids" in Central Accra. Today old cans or cut-out boards are mounted as wheels in Kwawu.[66]

During *afoofi* boys and girls also played together. J. A. Wahyee, his nephew Kwadwo Donkor, and their neighbor E. V. Osei Addo fondly talked about *di ahen-ahen,* a form of mock marriage in which players engaged with adult gender patterns. Wahyee explained:

> In the olden days, when many children did not go to school, these games were very popular. This is how it was done: some boys could meet some girls in one place, about ten boys with ten girls. When they meet like that, they will say: "Today yɛdi ahen-ahen, we are playing marriage." The boys will be at one side and the girls on the other. This game took place at about seven in the evening. At that time everybody had finished their house work. The boys sit down and wait for the girls to come one after another to be picked. When the girls go, they look at the boys for the one they like. Then they touch with their hands the top of his head gently which means he is chosen. She has gotten her man, they get up and move to the side. In the meantime the other boys wait for their turn. When one girl has made her choice, another will follow. This continues till all boys are chosen. That means she is your wife. But this did not mean you had really married the girl in the customary way.[67]

Boys and girls did not follow their parents' example in choosing their marriage partners. Instead, girls had more agency. In Kwawu a man customarily selected his future wife with the assistance of his father, mother, and other family members. This role reversal in which girls chose not only created a space for children to experiment with gender conventions but sparked adult opposition. *Ahen-ahen* was forbidden among Basel Mission congregations. For the Agogo Salem, Kyei recalled his parents' concerns about the "delicate matters" of marriage: children "ought not be permitted to toy with them however innocently they were conducted."[68] Yet among those children playing husband and wife, the game included a mutual exchange of favors that did resemble their parents' practices. As Wahyee recalled:

> In the olden days, if the boy needed to have something done [washing his cloth] he could inform her, and she would do it for him. When it was time for clearing the land, he would come with his friends to help clear the land for her mother. When she needed something, she could also tell him.[69]

In this game children's work and play overlapped. Mock spouses assisted each other in work responsibilities, a mutual help modeled after the division of labor among adult men and women. A girl who needed help tilling her farm could not only expect her "husband" to help but to bring his whole group of male friends. In turn, the "wife" could count on the assistance of her female friends in performing a laborious task such as washing his cloth. These mock marriages encouraged "work sociability" organized across gender boundaries.[70] They reflected an older gender system in which marriage partners had provided mutual assistance in cultivating food crops on land belonging to each spouse's *abusua,* as long as both partners were free commoners. This form of conjugal labor changed with the introduction of cocoa when wives traveled with husbands to launch farms on their lands without sharing in the profits during these men's childhood.[71]

Anansesɛm (Storytelling)

Storytelling was an important vehicle of instruction among Akan people as in other African societies. Rattray suggested, "A large part of a child's training is derived from listening to the *Anansesɛm* [Spider Stories] and later reciting them."[72] *Anansesɛm* presented normative ideas about men and women. Many feature as protagonist the spider Kwaku Ananse who moves between animal, human, and supernatural worlds. This male figure is a trickster, full of wit and eloquence but also selfish and lazy. Ananse seeks ways to enrich himself and to satisfy his immense appetite for food at the expense of others, frequently his wife Yaa Asɔ and his children. Although he is clever in gaining an advantage, occasionally Ananse gets entangled in his own net. Usually justice is done and Ananse fails in his mischievous endeavors. Ananse represents adult masculinity: married man, father, and farmer. This is a male-centered world; the female characters are girls learning to accept paternal authority in the selection of husbands, to become helping wives and nurturing mothers, and the old women are evil witches.[73]

The interviewed men talked about storytelling as a favorite leisure activity that brought boys in contact with girls, as well as with adult women and men. Recalling village life, Opusuo noted that "after work, in the evening the stepmother would collect us [children] together and would tell us nice stories." Ɔkyeame Asante commented on the advice in *anansesɛm*:

> The elders did not allow us to go out at night. They made us sit down and told us *anansesɛm*. They taught us everything about life, what they had seen and experienced, they showed us. So we may not do anything bad against somebody.

Anansesɛm were full of magic that captivated the imagination. Ɔkyeame Asante remarked:

> When darkness fell and we were going to the latrine that was in the bush, we had to go in groups because we were afraid due to the stories we had heard.[74]

Mothers encouraged children to share their knowledge about Kwaku Ananse's adventures. When children were by themselves, they told them to one another. Yet, when listening to men, they remained silent. As Opusuo described it:

> From time to time, even the old men gathered at night, they lit a fire, and around the fire they were sitting, telling stories to . . . I mean we were just listening. They were telling stories to themselves.

Asked to recall any of these *anansesɛm*, Opusuo hesitated.

> OP: Mm. There are so many, Ananse stories.
> SM: One which really impressed you?
> OP: There is this story (pause), Ananse and his son, I mean Ntikuma, the gathering of wisdom into a pot and the hiding of it (pause). Ananse thought he could collect all wisdom into one pot, and then hide it that there would be no wisdom in anybody's head, so he alone would have all wisdom. He . . . got a pot, and attempted to collect all wisdom in the world, put in that pot and then covered it. He wanted to hang the pot up, high up in a tree. Instead of putting the pot behind him, he put it in front of him, and used a cloth to tie it. He wanted to climb a tree, to hang it up in that tree. While he was attempting to climb the tree, he could not climb it, because the pot was in front. His son Ntikuma . . . was watching his father. When he saw that the father was unable to climb . . . because the pot was in front of him, he called: "Father, why don't you put the pot behind, so you can climb the tree." When Ananse heard this, he said: "Oh, I thought I had collected all the wisdom in the world, so there is some wisdom in somebody's head left." He became so angry that he dropped the pot. It broke, and all the wisdom was shared, so everybody got some. (laughs) That is one of the very interesting stories about Ananse and the wisdom, the wisdom-pot.[75]

In this tale Kwaku Ananse's son, Ntikuma, surpasses his selfish father. This motif does not describe Opusuo's life, since he had deep respect toward his own father who, unlike Ananse, was known for hard work. Still the larger message—that no one could have a monopoly on knowledge—was poignant for the former teacher. These days, the practice of *anansesɛm* belongs to a remote past, since insights drawn from tales about animals who act like humans do not fit Opusuo's self-presentation as a modern educator.

> OP: I stopped telling these stories a long time ago, so I have forgotten a lot.
> SM: You should tell them to your children, if you don't, who will?
> OP: (laughs) Well, when I was teaching in the middle schools, I did not teach the primary schools, so I did not tell, there was no storytelling in the curriculum. . . . If you did anything, you told the children: "Write a story!" But storytelling was not on the timetable, that's why I was not telling the children any stories. It made me forget most of the stories. But storytelling in those days was very interesting, we learned a lot, a lot of wisdom. You see, you compare life with a story, the life we led. And, in fact, it opened our mind.[76]

Missionary education succeeded in reconstructing *anansesɛm* as belonging exclusively to the world of small children; for Opusuo, the stories have been relegated to the curriculum of primary school children. The infantilization of folktales has parallels elsewhere. In early-nineteenth-century Germany, the Grimm brothers not only committed their collection of folktales to writing but cleaned them of any erotic content and made them "suitable" for children. In the South African countryside, German missionaries followed the Grimm brothers' example when selecting local stories to be included into the primary school curriculum.[77]

Ɔkyeame Asante also associated *anansesɛm* with his primary school experience. Pupils met in the evening for homework. When tired, they would tell each other *anansesɛm*. Soon this turned into a public event; children *and* adults took turns as narrators:

> Old people even came to tell us some of the stories, so that we would learn.
> . . . It was not just us [children telling stories], we learned some from the elders as well.[78]

As these memories show, narrating *anansesɛm* was a communal performance not restricted to a particular gender or age group. Rather, children, inside and outside schools, as well as adult men and women both told and listened. *Anansesɛm* could be heard in many places: the evening fire, the *pato* (three-walled room) where elders conversed, and even the classroom. When they presented a tale about Kwaku Ananse, narrators and audience assumed roles, played the characters, and frequently broke into song with solo and chorus. They engaged in a dialogue.[79]

Since most tales close with a moral statement that sets out a norm or explains the status quo, *anansesɛm* were oral entertainment with a didactic function. Donkor emphasized the teaching he received through *anansesɛm*, since he grew up without modern innovations like the radio, concert parties, or school. *Anansesɛm* transmitted ideas about masculinity and femininity. Ghanaian philosopher Kwame Gyekye has linked instruction of *anansesɛm* and proverbs to the Akan concept of personhood. Since elders define a person's *suban* (character) "in terms of habits," *suban* becomes the "configuration of individual acts." It is believed that "narratives are one way by which children acquire and internalize moral virtues" in their process of reaching full personhood.[80]

Gambling and Dancing

In his 1925 ethnographic report, District Commissioner A. J. Walker identified "dancing and drumming" as "favourite pastimes" among Kwawu people. The "most popular" games were *ɔware* (a board game), *ntɛ* (spinning marbles), and *ɔdame* (a form of draught), games that the interviewed men mentioned as part of their childhood *afoofi*.[81] *Ɔware* is a board game with two rows of six cups. At the beginning of the game, each cup is filled with four seeds. Two players, placed at opposite sides of the board, seek to capture each other's seeds. In this game of calculation and capture, the loser is expected to compensate the winner. *Ɔware* is popular all over West and East Africa, and, in a slightly different form, known as *solo*, in southern Africa.[82] Wahyee was fond of *ntɛ*.

WA: We erected a platform, covered it with a mat, and sank the middle a bit. I spin my marble, then you spin yours so they both turn very fast on the mat. If I am able to knock your marble off the mat, then you have to pay me something.
SM: Did you use money?
WA: Yes, we charged 40 [4 pence?]; sometimes we used groundnuts for payment. If I knock your marble off, you pay me one *kyɛnsen* [measuring tin] of groundnut. We make a very big platform, so that many people can spin their marbles at the same time. One will start, another will follow, and so on. They all keep spinning on the mat. All of a sudden there will be a crushing noise. If you are lucky, you are able to knock two or three marbles down. The player of these three marbles will pay you one tin of groundnuts each. They all will give you groundnuts. The marbles we used were all weighed, so one is not heavier than another.[83]

Beeswax and lead, poured in small holes, were used to achieve marbles of equal weight. Only after all players were "satisfied" with the marbles could the game begin. Gambling was gendered; men played by themselves. When asked about reasons for excluding women, Wahyee and Donkor responded, in slightly different phrases, that women could not bear the consequence of potential debt. As Wahyee said:

> It amounts to gambling. If one takes part in this game and he loses and has no money to pay, his attire would be taken off him, or his whole cloth may even be ripped off.

And Kwadwo Donkor added:

> In this kind of game a big amount of groundnuts are brought beside the *ntɛ* players and a *kyɛnsen* is placed on it. Whoever wins receives one *kyɛnsen* full of groundnuts. In another form of this game, two peanuts are split into halves, and each of the players puts one six pence down. When the nuts are spun, the winner takes both coins. When I spin and I don't win, and the other spins and wins, he takes the whole calabash of groundnuts and adds it to his own stock. That is why people can end up in debt gambling.[84]

There was resistance to gambling in Kwawu, particularly from the Basel Mission. Congregation members who were caught gambling faced sanctions like temporary exclusion from communion.[85] Marfo, who as the son of an *ɔkomfo* never joined any church, also spoke against it. He recalled that his father, Kwasi Nyame, did not allow him to play either *ntɛ* or *ɔware*. Only *ɔdame*, a game resembling draught, considered more suitable for children, was permitted, since it stimulated cognitive abilities. Nyame told his son that whoever plays *ɔware* "becomes too talkative, and, as a result, you never get your work done."[86]

Gambling places conveyed ideas about adult masculinity, since boys could watch older men play and observe how they interacted. When they were old enough to play themselves, they learned directly from their seniors. It took years of playing *ɔware* to acquire the crucial ability to calculate the next move quickly. Since such skills developed with age, older men continued their dominance over younger and physically more able males. Thomas Reefe argued that games like *ɔware* reflected men's notion of "rights in people." When men accumulated gambling debts and did not have the resources to pay them, they fell back onto their lineages, among Kwawu people the *abusua*. Before ample cash or individual land was available to serve as a loan guarantee, an *abusua* faced with debt was apt to pawn its female members. While watching gamblers and hearing about players who lost their cloths, houses, or even female *abusua* members, as missionary Perregaux lamented, boys not only learned about masculine behavior but encountered gender asymmetries.[87]

Men had more leisure time for gambling. This is well expressed in the proverb *"Wonni adagyew a, wonto ware"* (If you don't have spare time, you don't play *ɔware*). Because wives, supported by daughters and nieces, were responsible for domestic chores like cooking, cleaning, and gathering firewood, as well as engaging in agricultural work such as cultivating food crops *and* helping husbands in weeding and harvesting cocoa, they were less free for leisure activities. Although none of my male interview partners commented on this imbalance, women did. Recalling her childhood in the 1920s, Paulina Ago Acheampong noted that "boys had more time to play" since they "did not do any house chores."[88] From a Geertzian perspective, the gendered underpinnings of gambling, in which senior men dominated juniors and women were absent, symbolically reveal Kwawu's gender and age hierarchies. These hierarchies were performed, promoted, and reproduced in public spaces like an elder's *pato*, the palm-wine bar, and the market square where men played *ɔware*. This reading misses social contestation and historical change. Gender norms based on seniority *were* contested in the opening decades of the twentieth century. Migrant men challenged elders' domination and reformulated gender ideals, which were acted out in new dancing styles.[89]

Watching dance parties was another childhood leisure activity of the interviewed men. In Twi *agorɔ* means "games and play," as well as "dancing and singing." Ritual dances were performed at a chief's palace, at a funeral, at a shrine, and also as entertainment. As spectators, children witnessed how new dance styles became popular. Wahyee mentioned the *ahyiko* (or *ashiko*) as the "first *agorɔ*" that was introduced to Kwawu from coastal cities early in the twentieth century. He elaborated:

> The *ahyiko* dance was brought by some people from Monrovia [Liberia] who came to Accra and Sekondi, and then it spread to this area. Those who had traveled to such places saw it and brought it here. Male and female *akwantufoɔ* (travelers) brought the *ahyiko* dance. The accordion was played, women sang, and men responded in beautiful harmonies. They had some metal rod hanging from their neck and rubbed over it with another metal stick making a nice sound: *tɛtɛ tee, tɛtɛ tee . . .* (making the sound of the instrument). I saw it, I was then a young boy.[90]

Ahyiko was danced to an early form of highlife music, a fusion of indigenous musical styles and rhythms with European instruments and harmonies that was first popularized in the coastal centers of West Africa. Originally the urban poor coined the term "highlife" for the elite social activities that excluded them, such as brass band performances and ballroom orchestras. In a second phase a new hybrid popular culture formed, when a less respectable highlife, so-called palm-wine guitar music famous for songs like "Yaa Amponsah" and new dance styles like *ahyiko*, spread inland.[91]

Participation in *ahyiko* was restricted by age and status: *ahyiko* was the dance of "people with money." Dancers were expected to dress in expensive clothes showing off accessories like hats, shoes, handkerchiefs, and ladies' bags, and also needed access to cash. *Ahyiko* dancing was popular among Kwawu men and women who had traveled south for employment and trading during the period of economic growth before and after World War I. They encountered *ahyiko* and other new dance styles at the sites of its creation—in the coastal cities of Accra, Cape Coast, and Sekondi—or in the commercial centers of the cocoa-growing areas like Koforidua and Nsawam where it spread from the coast. Migrants were called *akwantufoɔ* (travelers) or *gentlemanfoɔ* (gentlemen). Donkor remembered watching an *ahyiko* dance performance in the early 1920s, when he was about ten. As an *ɔkɔba* (a child born following siblings who had died in infancy), he wore long dreadlocks and carried a *bɔtɔ dua* (little calabash containing spiritually powerful black powder). Marked as a child kept alive with the assistance of an *ɔkɔmfo*, and hopefully considered too ugly to be taken by the gods, he was quite a contrast to the well-clad and polished dancers. According to Donkor,

> Both men and women participated: while women were singing and clapping their hands, the men were dancing. They used their handkerchiefs to wipe the faces of the men. If somebody had some money, he pasted it to the dancer's forehead or on other parts of the body. That was a way of showing appreciation and recognition.[92]

Wahyee was unable to understand all the lyrics of *ahyiko* songs, since many words were in Kru *borɔfo*, the pidgin English spoken by Liberian migrants. But he remembered well listening to and watching the musical impact of *ahyiko:*

> (sings) *Mokolɔmi yɛn terɛma, mokolɔmi yɛn terɛma* . . . [meaning not clear] They sing and dance; the drums go like this: *Pim-pam-pam, pim-pam-pam,* they [the men] dance and play the accordion while the women sing and clap. They also play the tambourine—a wooden frame with a skin covering one side; the frame is square like a frame for a picture with some battering fitting to it. On the skin, they can make all kinds of musical sounds.[93]

These dance performances took place in Manem, Abetifi's old section, where each *borɔn* formed its own dance company. Embracing different styles, the *akwantufoɔ* of Dwenase danced to rhythms of *ahyiko,* while those of Ɔkyɛmase chose the *ahima*. Like the *ahyiko,* the *ahima* dance was solely for adults, mainly married people who had the money to acquire the proper wardrobe. The instruments accompanying the *ahima* dancers were different from those of the *ahyiko:* the former was accompanied only by drums. As Wahyee recalled: "a small one for calling the rhythm to be danced . . . the big one for the melody, and a medium one."[94]

Wahyee and Donkor were born too late to participate as adults in these performances. Still as children admiring the dancers—their clothing and their movements—they were introduced to new styles of masculinity. Between the 1890s and 1919 an increasing number of migrant men from Ghana's interior moved to the mining towns of Obuasi and Tarkwa, and to coastal centers like the railway hub Sekondi where they entered into wage labor. With a distinct "leisure time" on Sundays as opposed to "working time" during the week, urban workers participated in an emerging popular culture that included new forms of dance, music, and social drinking. They also challenged traditional and colonial authorities, particularly the authority of *abusua* elders and chiefs. Returning to their hometowns, these migrant workers and traders promenaded their new money and status by wearing possessions like clothes and shoes. In the streets of Kwawu towns, and especially during dance competitions, they literally performed their new gender identity.[95] Senior masculinity no longer depended exclusively on age and locally acquired status but was now linked instead to migration, wage labor, and the new cash economy. These urban workers evoked older notions of *abirɛmpɔn* (big men) who had publicly displayed their riches, while they redefined the meaning of big-man status. Children like Wahyee and Donkor observed the purchasing power of the *akwantufoɔ* and learned how such migrant men entertained themselves. They quickly noticed who was considered the most popular dancer and what made somebody successful and attractive. They heard bystanders' judgments about the public comportment of dancers and audience members; they saw the public appearance of older big men in the audience. Watching adult and senior men perform their gender identity in public spaces was an important and always fascinating part of children's *afoofi.* Dance competitions were sites where children as spectators witnessed both older notions of masculinity and more recent challenges.[96]

Conclusion

There was a sharp divide between children living in the old sections of Kwawu towns and those residing with their parents in Christian settlements established by the Basel Mission. European missionaries, as well as African presbyters and pastors, closely supervised not just the adult congregation but also their children. The latter were not permitted to participate in certain games outside the Christian Quarters. Instead, they were expected to attend school which freed them from some daily chores. Missionaries criticized the workload of non-Christian children. The *Gemeindeordnung* regulating the daily life of congregations contained extended guidelines about raising children. Following a "bourgeois" notion of childhood, which had become prevalent among certain classes of Western Europe since the late eighteenth century, the *Gemeindeordnung* stipulated that children were in need of individual attention; parents "should not regard their children as playthings to serve their pleasure, nor as a means of income." Rather, parents were advised to provide their children with a Christian education at home and to send them to school. This view of childhood affected those who attended Presbyterian schools during the interwar period.[97]

The interviewed men and women's recollections show that children's spatial realms were not always clearly separated from those of adults. Rather, in Kwawu, during the first third of the twentieth century as well as today, children were *omnipresent* in most gendered locations. Boys observed men's activities from the sidelines: overhearing conversations among elders, closely following a game of ɔware, or watching men and women dance to the rhythms of *ahyiko*. They often acquired their ideas of masculinity by extrapolation from observation rather than from direct instruction. Girls remained with mothers and aunts, listened to their stories, and witnessed crucial events within female spaces like preparations for childbirth, child rearing, and girls' nubility rites. During most adult activities the presence of boys and girls was tolerated as long as the younger ones were willing to serve, showing deference. Frequently children were left to themselves and formed their own groups engaged in work and play. While boys created their world by organizing themselves as soldiers fighting against other boys, girls did their additional domestic chores or gathered for a game of *ampe*. Occasionally boys and girls participated in games together such as forming mock marriages as described above.[98]

All narrators, male and female, agreed that they had to work hard as children, especially when comparing their experience to that of the younger generations. This sentiment was even stronger among the interviewed women who noted that boys had the pleasure of more *afoofi*. The notion of a carefree childhood, with much attention paid to a child's development, was distinctly absent. Instead, after the age of six, boys and girls moved into worlds of work and play that were increasingly separated. Children learned about obligations and comportment that would be expected of them as men and women, the dominant notions of masculinity and femininity. The cohort of men whose lives are foregrounded here recalled elders representing forms of senior masculinity as decisive role models. Elders featured prominently in their childhood stories. These elders exercised different forms of power, rooted in spiritual knowledge, political office, and increasingly in economic resources. Whatever the power, in remembering their role models, the interviewed men found in that power not a source of fear but an example born of intimacy. My interview partners witnessed how men who had migrated south had improved their social status within hometown communities, expressed in clothing and dancing styles, as well as in investments like launching cocoa farms and erecting buildings. Boakye Yiadom's and Reverend Asante's *wɔfanom*, who had traded outside Kwawu, exposed their nephews, through stories and commodities, to new economic opportunities. During his childhood Addo experienced a shift in trading activities from his father to his older brothers. His brothers introduced him to new markets and commercial practices in the south. Such childhood recollections bear witness to larger socioeconomic transformations unfolding across southern Ghana early in the twentieth century. These changes were reflected in new ways of reaching senior masculinity and claiming big-man status. As elsewhere in early colonial Africa, when economies became monetized, men's access to cash became an increasingly important way to attain senior masculinity.[99]

FORMS OF EDUCATION: APPRENTICESHIPS AND SCHOOLS, 1919–1947

3

In colonial Ghana European forms of education were dominated by mission societies, particularly the two Protestant churches, Presbyterian (former Basel Mission) and Wesleyan Methodist, as well as the Catholic Church.[1] There is a broad consensus in gender studies on the importance of missionary activities, especially the introduction of formal education, in shaping notions of masculinity and femininity among Christian converts across colonial Africa. Schools were sites where gender values were "produced and disseminated."[2] Scholars have focused on missionaries as agents in reconstructing African men and women, and have tended to neglect the contributions of teachers and catechists of African descent.[3]

Most scholarship has been less concerned with local forms of instruction like apprenticeships *outside* the structured context of mission schools, or Islamic education.[4] There is little documentary evidence about such apprenticeships. Yet, for many in Ghana, particularly in rural areas where school education was not as available or as compelling, the relationships between apprentice and master proved important to the formation of the masculine self. As the men at the center of this study engaged with their masters and teachers, they perceived norms of behavior and expectations for men which they weighed against their familial and precursory influences; that most of these figures were African gave greater weight to their examples, even when the values were colonial or foreign.

Akan ideals of senior masculinity were conveyed in formal and informal apprenticeships; ideas of "Presbyterian masculinity" were dominant in a mission church and its schools. These notions of masculinity were decisive influences for the interviewed men. Whether undertaken by choice, compulsion, or economic necessity, these educational experiences transmitted by both individuals and institutions during this formative period when they were first learning what constituted masculinity covered great societal and personal change. What they learned here remained strongly present throughout their lives. As childhood gave way to greater responsibility of work and formal education, the need for some resolution among contested ideals became more urgent. For instance, according to Presbyterian masculinity, pupils were expected to become monogamous husbands who privileged their wives and children over their *abusua* (matrilineage), and to become men guided by strict discipline expressed in regular work, Christian devotion, and deference to secular and religious authorities like the colonial state, local chiefs, and the church leadership.

Apprenticeships

In her pioneering history of Ga women in Accra, Claire Robertson suggested that most apprenticeships "were informal between relatives," daughters learning skills of housework, child care, or trading from their mothers or grandmothers or stepmothers, or even from more distant relatives. A few apprenticeships were formally organized involving fees along with nonrelatives as mistresses, particularly in the crafts of sewing, bread baking, and bead polishing. Such arrangements gave the mistress the right to exploit the labor of her apprentice, who was not permitted to keep any profit and could only work with the mistress's tools. Some girls also apprenticed in mission schools.[5]

Apprenticeships were sites where young men and young women became aware that certain crafts and occupations were gendered. In precolonial Asante, as in other Akan areas, most pottery was made by women, while men engaged in crafts like goldsmithing, weaving, and wood carving. Skills were usually handed down either from mother to daughter or from father to son, often at an early age. Despite the matrilineal descent practiced among Akan people, male patrilineal succession existed and included offices at the *ahenfie* (chief's palace) and occupations like drumming and hunting.[6] R. S. Rattray reported an informant's observation of early-twentieth-century Asante: "If you have any *dwumadie* (profession), e.g. are a hunter, weaver, drummer, or blacksmith, you will train your son to be that too, and this without his uncle's permission." But, the informant added, should the son not obey, the father could "send him away to his uncle." Rattray considered this an "ex-parte" statement reflecting the father's point of view, since an uncle could remove his *wofase* (nephew, niece) if the father was "too poor to bring up the child properly."[7]

In the course of the twentieth century these practices changed. In Asante a father could not only apprentice his son in his own craft but could "pay to apprentice him to someone else," a paternal cash expense expected of a father. Mechanized transportation, urbanization, and cash-cropping brought a series of new occupations to southern Ghana, like carpentry, bricklaying, tailoring, shoemaking, and motor mechanics.[8] As fathers invested to apprentice their sons, the younger generation moved from agriculture to self-employment, from "peasant to artisan," as Sara Berry noted for motor mechanics in southwestern Nigeria.[9] Since the market for these occupations existed mainly in the commercial centers of Ghana's cocoa belt and larger coastal cities, apprenticeships frequently resulted in migration. For Kwawu, Sophy Osafo recorded new boys' apprentices as "drivers, fitters, shoemakers, and tailors." Still, most men were traders expecting "their sons [to] help them in store keeping."[10]

The interviewed men's recollections document these shifts. They provide insights into apprenticing crafts, as well as the inculcation of gender values outside the classroom. J. A. Wahyee and Kwaku Marfo never attended schools. Although E. K. Addo and Ɔkyeame Asante received some schooling, they considered their apprenticeships to be their formative learning experience. Some men entered formally arranged apprenticeships involving a contract. Usually they left Kwawu, moved to commercial towns, or traveled with their masters while acquiring new skills. After reaching puberty, Wahyee was placed in the care of two Abetifi bead traders hand-picked by his father. They were not kin. Called Asare and Adu, they both lived in *Manem,* Abetifi's old section. Wahyee explained the arrangement:

> My father asked them [Asare and Adu] to take me along and teach me the bead trade. They charged me some money for that. The charge was quite high for those days.

There was another form of "contract," the English term used by Wahyee:

> Other people would not charge you money as such. But rather would ask for some capital from your father to trade with. When you have finished your apprenticeship with him [your master], then he will return the capital he got from your father and keep the profit for himself.[11]

After completing his training, Wahyee started his own trading, accompanied by his *wɔfase* as apprentice.

In the early twentieth century bead trading was lucrative; in Kwawu it was the specialization of Abetifi traders.[12] Wahyee traveled with his masters, then with his nephew, over long distances. They walked through French territory to Bamako where they purchased beads to sell in the markets of southern Ghana. These trips were full of dangers and were considered inappropriate for women. Wahyee remembered being harassed by French border guards when reentering the British Gold Coast. Some soldiers not only took beads but physically molested a trader who was glad to keep his life. Beads had to be polished. (According to Robertson, this was women's work. Wahyee, however, recalled performing this task himself.) He told of buying old beads, "precious stones," with names like "*bota, teteasɔ,* nnyaane, and others such as *bɔdɔm* and *nyeewa.*" He categorized customers along ethnic lines: Ewe and Krobo people preferred beads to gold. Occasionally he sold one string for one hundred pounds, a tremendous sum of money during the 1920s. He invested his profits in a spacious house, built with his brother, in Abetifi's Christian Quarters. Yet bead trading was only a brief period in Wahyee's life; he switched occupations in the early 1930s. Robertson noted that bead trading declined, as imports were affected by world wars and fashion changed. Wahyee mentioned none of these reasons. Rather, he took up cocoa farming since he had accepted responsibilities as an *ɔpanyin* (elder) and wanted to stay closer to Abetifi.[13] Serving his masters, Wahyee had learned about respecting elders, the ability of elders to settle disputes, and elders' obligations toward *abusua* (matrilineage) and other communities. Although these ideas about senior masculinity never lost significance for him, Presbyterian expectations became more important after he converted to Christianity.

For Marfo, as for Ɔkyeame Asante and Addo, apprenticeships had a more immediate and enduring impact. Marfo was informally apprenticed to his father, Kwasi Nyame, who, as an *ɔkɔmfo* (diviner), was well-known for his medicinal knowledge. Marfo accompanied his father on his travels throughout Kwawu and Asante. Pepease people often called Marfo *aduro owura* (medicine person), an informal title inherited from his father.

> SM: Why did your father give you this name?
> MA: Because he, as Ɔkɔmfo Kwasi Nyame, was also given that name; so he passed it on to me. If you are the *nsumankwaafoɔhene* in the palace, all your children become *nsumankwaafoɔ*. If you are the *afonakitafoɔ* (sword bearer), all your children become *afonakitafoɔ*. Therefore, if your father is called *aduro owura,* you are also called *aduro owura.*[14]

When Marfo talked about children, he only referred to sons who acquired skills and social positions from fathers. When Marfo became *Nsumankwaahene* of Kwawu, an adviser at the *ahenfie* "with varied forms of power" that populate the Akan spiritual universe, he again followed in his father's foot-steps.[15] The latter had taken care of a *suman* (charm, amulet) at the Asan-tehene's court in his younger years. Throughout Marfo's life, his father re-mained the undisputed model of senior masculinity. Kwasi Nyame represented the qualities of respect, deference, and accomplishment in com-munity standing which Marfo sought to emulate.

Ɔkyeame Asante's apprenticeship resembled those of Wahyee *and* Marfo. Initially his father sent him to Catholic school and he became the first among his siblings to become literate. In 1929 Asante began a formal apprenticeship as a tailor. He moved to Kraboa Coaltar, a cocoa town in the forest of Akyem Abuakwa west of Nsawam. A verbal contract stipulated that Asante would work exclusively for his master, Agyena, his father's younger brother, who provided him with room and board. Upon successful comple-tion two years later, his father paid some money and presented drinks. Asante remained in Kraboa Coaltar working on his own as a tailor until he joined the army in 1939.[16]

Already in Kraboa Coaltar, Asante started another, informal apprentice-ship as an *odunsini* (herbalist), an occupation that was predominately male. This long apprenticeship shaped his sense of self. On visits to his hometown of Pepease, he helped his *wɔfa* (maternal uncle) Kwasi Prɔnkɔ, an established *odunsini*. His learning entailed performing errands:

> Whenever he needed some herbal medicines like roots, he would ask for me and send me out to find them for him. When I brought them back, he told me that he did this or that with them. For example, this [plant] cures this disease and that one cures that illness.

After he enlisted in the army, Asante continued this training. He was sta-tioned in Bombay and assigned as "wireless" (radio) operator to guard a large hospital. There he became friendly with an Indian physician who cultivated herbs and trees in the hospital garden.

> The doctor liked me very much and so he taught me. He had many trees planted and he used them to make his *nnuru* (medicines). So he gave me a big book with all herbs in it, which ailment each herb can cure. So, I look at the book to make my *nnuru*.

Asante copied these herbal remedies. When he returned to Ghana, he brought along his notes as reference to prepare his *nnuru*. Asante noticed that the medicinal trees planted by the doctor in Bombay could be found in the Afram Plains.[17]

Asante's second apprenticeship involved a third person. He was discharged in 1946 and moved to Nkawkaw, Kwawu's new commercial center and main railway station, in order to support himself by tailoring. He became involved in a local Tegare shrine and soon was appointed ɔkyeame (spokesperson). Making a living as a tailor was difficult in the postwar period. In 1947 Asante found employment as a forest guard, an occupation preferred by ex-servicemen. For this position as sɔfea prosi (surveyor police), he moved to Kwawu-Tafo, where he continued his involvement with Tegare. He also tailored and made nnuru on the side.

> When I stayed with him [Ɔbosomfo Kwame Bruni, Tegare priest of Kwawu-Tafo], he had an elder who was an herbalist. This elder taught me some medicine in addition to mine. I got some herbs from him to add what I knew to make them three [masters].

Following his retirement from the forest service in the late 1970s, Asante returned to Pepease to complete his informal apprenticeship as odunsini with a fourth master.

> Even when I came here, one elder taught me more about herbs and medicines saying that he had become an akwakora (very old man) and would not be able to practice anymore, so I should succeed him. I agreed. . . . When I got a sixpence, I sent him some of the money to buy tobacco and "drink."[18]

The elder, Asim Kuma, had acquired his herbal knowledge from a big-game hunter, Obɔfo Konadu.

Asante's informal apprenticeship as odunsini thus stretched over a period of more than forty years. This journey had a strong spiritual dimension. Asante turned away from his father's Catholic Church, then from the Presbyterian Church, to become an ɔkyeame and odunsini at Tegare shrines. He explained:

> Everybody has something God has given him to do, and so I was interested in the herbs. All the medicines have also been created by God. If the sun shines [during the dry season], all the plants die. If it does not rain, what would the plants do to grow again? So it is all God's work. So all the spirits and the herbs are from God. The same way the herbs can grow, tells us that the spirits and the power of the herbs are given by God. So, when you are doing it and you pray to God, when you give the medicine to someone, it helps cure. It is not possible to do the medicine and to forget about God. If you forget about God, your medicine will not work. Is he not the one who created the medicine? If he is the one who created the medicine, and you forget about him, how will your medicine work?[19]

Asante not merely cured his patients but sought to heal them, which entails among Akans a complicated interaction of "human beings, the community, and above all the intervention of God."[20] His extensive training in the art of herbal medicines is crucial to Ɔkyeame Asante's self-understanding. During his informal apprenticeship he considered himself an *aberanteε* (young man), serving masters who represented senior masculinity. In a different context, however, Asante would have qualified for adult masculinity once he had been married for several years. Yet, only after completing his training did he claim the social position of an *ɔpanyin* (elder).[21]

Retired Abetifi trader E. K. Addo recalled how his senior brother, J. K. Kwakye, organized his apprenticeship. First Addo assisted Kwakye. Then, ca. 1914, the latter decided that Addo should acquire clerical skills. He placed Addo in the house of William Hanson, an accountant from Akropong, Akuapem, who worked for the Obuasi gold mines. Although briefly sent to school there, Addo did not learn much. Instead, he worked as Hanson's houseboy and studied with him:

> He was an *ɔnimdefo,* a man of special knowledge. And so at night, when he did his accounting, I sat next to him, and he explained things to me. So, if I told you that I did not even get to ABC at the Methodist school, you would not believe me.

Addo expressed pride in acquiring literacy outside the classroom:

> Now, if I need to write anything in a language which is not familiar to me, I would not use the "dictionary." Except when I am writing something new. I have not hired anybody to write anything for me, except when there is an *amannenya sεm* (court case).

Staying with Hanson, Addo was exposed to a new world. He became familiar with the environment of a successful *krakye* (clerk) who had close contacts to his European employers. This experience helped Addo in his career as retailer for the United Africa Company. He noted that Hanson "never married a woman" during the years he stayed with him.

> *Eyε anwanwasεm;* it is surprising. But because he was my master, I was not able to ask him why he did not marry a woman. He was very liked by the Europeans, because he was not like other Africans. He had a very big dog in his "bungalow." No one dared to go to his bungalow.[22]

While Addo worked for Hanson, his brother, Kwakye, traded in and around Obuasi. In 1920, when his business was not flourishing, Kwakye relocated

[margin note, handwritten: master is a form of masculinity encountered]

54

with Addo to the cocoa-growing area of the Eastern Province. For the next eight years Addo continued his apprenticeship by accompanying Kwakye, all the while gaining more business experience. They lived in Mangoase and traded in commercial centers like Koforidua and Nsawam along the railway line from Accra to Tafo, which was built to transport cocoa.[23] Addo recalled staying for a while in Ɔpanyin Sakyi's village; Ɔpanyin Sakyi was an Akuapem cocoa farmer from Larteh with "plenty of children." From there they went to Nsawam-Adoagyiri where Kwakye and his senior brother, J. E. Sampong, had constructed a house to serve as their "base" for trading. In 1924 Addo and Kwakye joined Sampong in Accra. Sampong, who had joined the Basel Mission Abetifi congregation in 1904, made a crucial contribution to Addo's education. He encouraged his younger brother to become Christian and enroll in baptismal classes at the Scottish (former Basel) Mission, which had just been reorganized as the Presbyterian Church. In 1926 Addo was baptized and confirmed by the most senior African pastor, Moderator Rev. William A. Quartey. Addo's formal apprenticeship came to a close in 1928, when Kwakye opened a "branch store" in Nsawam, about twenty miles north of Accra, and invited Addo to manage it. Commenting on Kwakye's influence, Addo exclaimed, "he is the one who trained me for commercial purpose."[24]

Different apprenticeships were crucial in shaping these men's professional identities and constituting their male subjectivities. As part of their training, they left their Kwawu hometowns and were exposed to new environments. An apprenticeship could last a few years like Wahyee's, or several decades like those of Marfo and Asante. This experience distinguished them by occupation, status, and—in the case of trader Addo—wealth not only from women but from male contemporaries who had received different forms of education. In the 1960s social scientists examining socialization in Africa's "traditional societies" argued that local education was "primarily a homogenizing process," viewed as "contributing to social consensus and cohesion."[25] The recollections of these Kwawu men demonstrate that local ways of formal and informal education were not homogenizing; indeed, apprenticeships created and sharpened gender differentiation.

For Wahyee and Addo, involvement with the Presbyterian Church meant exposure to new ideas about masculinity. Other men spoke at length about their experiences with European education, often Presbyterian schools, modeled on those created by the Basel Mission. This meant another form of gender differentiation, in keeping with the mission society's educational objectives and institutions.

Schools in Kwawu

Since the mid-nineteenth century the Basel Mission established an elaborate educational system for boys and, to a lesser degree, for girls: six years of primary school (infant primary included Classes I to III and junior primary consisted of Standards I to III), either as *Gemeindeschulen* (day schools) or *Erziehungsanstalten* (boarding schools), and four years of middle school (senior primary—Standards IV–VII—were organized as separate boarding schools for boys and girls), followed by a seminary for training male teacher-catechists; some were later ordained.[26] These schools offered domestic training for girls and academic and vocational training for boys. Initially the colonial government had little interest in mission schools. In the 1880s education ordinances created an education board and stipulated conditions for government aid, conditions such as admitting children regardless of religion and providing instruction in English. The Basel Mission seminary, middle schools, and some primaries qualified. Unlike its main competitors, Methodist institutions, the Basel Mission situated most of its schools in rural areas and provided instruction in Twi or Ga, on the grounds that Christians should read the Bible in their native language. As a Swiss and German organization, the Basel Mission was expelled during World War I. Yet, its educational legacy had an enduring impact.[27]

The establishment of Basel Mission schools in Kwawu offers a good account of how its gendered educational program was disseminated. The support of African teachers and catechists was crucial. In 1877 Eugen Werner reported that teacher Emmanuel Dako had organized a primary school in Abetifi with fourteen boys from the ages of eight to fourteen. The following year the school was transformed into a boys' boarding school. During the 1880s missionaries placed catechists outside Abetifi to establish additional congregations. Other towns were regularly visited in order to open small schools staffed by indigenous teachers. Still, the introduction of European education was a slow process, since children were expected to provide labor for fathers, mothers, and other *abusua* members. Boys and girls assisted with domestic chores, farming, and as carriers; some stayed with relatives in need.[28] Children, especially girls, were subject to pawning. In 1890 Friedrich Ramseyer, head of the mission station, reported:

> It is really sad, that our Okwawu people do not show more desire to send their children to school although we have been working here for fifteen years. Part of the reason is their system of handling debts and security. People consider their children and nephews as part of their property that is at their disposal in

case of need; and how often does this happen as a result of disorderly lives & "*coutumes*" [customs]—funerals. How much have I fought against this falling into debts & against pawning, but unfortunately with "little" success.[29]

The notion was widespread that giving children to missionaries meant a loss for the *abusua*. Kwawu people quickly noticed that "going to school and becoming a Christian were identical."[30] Yet African teachers and catechists, dressed in European clothing, were powerful images of a different life. The Ɔdekuro (headman) of Asakraka explained that schoolchildren not only acquired "wisdom" but became the missionaries' *asonoma,* or "decoy birds." To Ramseyer's dismay, teachers were compared "to decoy-parrots" placed "on trees in order to call the others in the forest to come and get captured on the glue!" In the local perception there was a fine line between pawning a child and sending a child to school. The practice of placing children as house servants in mission homes and lodging them in the boarding school reinforced this idea. Some guardians demanded money before sending a child to school. Johannes Tschopp mentioned a claim of four pounds, the cost of a male slave.[31]

Missionaries developed various strategies to recruit students. In 1888, after Kwawu chiefs signed the protectorate treaty with Britain, Ramseyer emphasized the advantage of literate subjects. He warned reluctant chiefs that the mission would refuse to handle correspondence unless school enrollment increased. Ramseyer also relied on his familiarity with colonial officials to pressure Kwawu chiefs. These efforts led to rising enrollments, although the mission stopped paying allowances to boarders. No longer convinced that children attracted with money would evolve into diligent pupils, Ramseyer hoped to attract them instead by converting their parents.[32] If a Christian father failed to enroll at least some of his children, he was sanctioned. Missionaries were aware of fathers' limited authority toward claims by mothers and their children's *abusua* and tried to strengthen paternal powers. Over the first forty years the number of schools and students rose. In 1877 there were 14 pupils in one school; by the turn of the century the number had increased to 420 in seventeen schools; and by 1916 there were almost 600 pupils in sixteen schools.[33]

What did pupils study? What notion of masculinity and femininity were they exposed to? The Basel Mission attempted to transform pupils into Christian men and women with a distinct gender ideology. As elsewhere in colonial Africa, girls were introduced to the arts of domesticity with activities such as needlework, cooking, hygiene, and motherhood in missionary homes that became "emblems of evangelical domesticity."[34] But, "as a marked feature," the Basel Mission also founded boarding schools for girls already in the 1850s.[35] Boys received both academic and industrial training in crafts like carpentry and masonry. Missionaries sought to shape male students into hard-working, moderate, law-abiding colonial subjects, as well as monogamous husbands who showed primary allegiance to wife, children, and church, and only secondarily to their *abusua*. Schools were instrumental in promoting this *Presbyterian masculinity*.[36]

According to the principle *"durchs Christentum zur Arbeit"* (through Christianity to work), manual labor was crucial to a Basel Mission education. In 1891 Ramseyer reported that Christians living on mission land had finally accepted the idea that his regime of "hard work" was good for boys. Ramseyer ordered pupils to clear land for a coffee plantation.[37] This introduction of cash crops was welcomed by the colonial government. Friedrich Jost identified the Protestant goal of shaping pupils into "Christians, pious, but also industrious and diligent members of the people." There were challenges. Jost complained about male pupils who saw themselves only as future "scholars," detesting any manual work.[38] Frequently school attendance was irregular because pupils had to work on fathers' and uncles' farms or carry a load on a hunting or trading expedition. In 1883 Gottlieb Dilger recorded that two students had left the boarding school, one after "seducing" his maid. African teachers, so indispensable to the missionary project, were blamed for pupils' lack of "discipline" and "attentiveness."[39] Jacob Haasis wrote about the failure of teachers to comprehend the difference between *"Schulung,"* which meant the instruction of reading and writing, and *"Erziehung,"* which meant character training: punctuality, cleanliness, tidiness, obedience, diligence, and so-called moral behavior. While many teachers succeeded in *Schulung*, they rarely understood the scope of *Erziehung*.[40]

In 1916 the first government school opened in Obo, competing with the mission schools. According to Hermann Henking, Obo was not the ideal location since even the "able" Basel Mission teacher had only assembled twenty to thirty pupils.

> The people of Obo do not want to learn anything, many of them live most of the year on their plantations [farming villages] and are not ready to send their children to school. Obviously it was only the wish of a few clerks to get a Government School, the people of Obo were not asked. The Chief of Obo even sent his son to the school of Nkwatia last year, and the Chief of Aduamoa (only one hour distance from Obo) gathered over thirty children and requested from us a teacher, because he prefers our school, if he has to have one at all.

Basel Mission schools did not lose many pupils. Henking noted with satisfaction that "among heathens there were men who preferred if their children did not only study English, but also Twi."[41] Government schools were known to offer instruction only in English. Despite this competition, the two schools joined for Empire Day celebration.

School inspector Arthur Jehle interpreted local wishes for government schools as a sign that people were refusing the mission's "strict discipline." This demand for government education followed the spread of the cocoa industry across southern Ghana. Cocoa was launched in the closing decade of the nineteenth century in Akuapem and Akyem Abuakwa, and reached Kwawu after the boom of 1907; the planting of cocoa trees rapidly increased following World War I.[42] Many scholars have argued that cocoa farmers invested a substantial amount of their earnings into their children's education, envisioning them as future clerks. The missionaries lamented that cocoa led to "secularization," a lowering of morals combined with an unwelcome desire for material goods.[43] The correlation between the spread of cocoa and the demand for education reflects only a larger trend. The year the Obo school opened, cocoa prices actually plummeted. Cocoa farmers in remote areas of Kwawu and Asante-Akyem were unable to sell their crop, because transportation costs of carrying beans to the coast had skyrocketed.[44] Yet missionary hopes that the Obo school would falter did not materialize. In fact, student enrollment increased steadily. In 1924 a government middle school was added. During the 1920s the Methodist Mission also opened its first Kwawu school at Atibie, on the outskirts of the district capital Mpraeso.[45] Census data for Kwawu, although not very accurate, indicate new educational opportunities during the interwar period. In 1921 an estimated 2.1 percent of the population was literate. By 1948 this figure had risen to 5.2 percent. Literacy was equated to having at least a Standard III or IV education. Educational centers like Abetifi saw more pupils complete primary school than did other towns. According to the 1931 census, 4 percent of the Abetifi population had received no less than a Standard IV education; in 1948 this figure had climbed to 13 percent.[46]

Among the cohort of Kwawu men discussed here, five attended school during the interwar period: Rev. E.K.O. Asante, A. K. Boakye Yiadom, Kofi Ankoma, Ɔkyeame Asante, and E. F. Opusuo. Three enrolled in Presbyterian schools, established by the Basel Mission and continued under the auspices of the Scottish Mission. Reverend Asante and Opusuo went straight from primary to middle school and then to teachers' training college. Boakye Yiadom did not have the chance to continue beyond middle school until later in life. Although none of them encountered Basel missionaries directly supervising their schools, their teachers were all products of the original Basel Mission institutions. As decisive role models, these teachers passed on Basel Mission ideals of masculinity. Two men took different paths: Ankoma enrolled at the Obo government school and Ɔkyeame Asante only attended Catholic school up to Standard IV, one year beyond primary school, before apprenticing as a tailor. Recollections of Abetifi women who attended school also provide insights about the gendered nature of Presbyterian education.

Primary Schools

Reverend Asante entered school at the age of seven, younger than the other men interviewed. From 1919 to 1925 he was a day student at the primary school in Abetifi's Christian Quarters. He emphasized that his *wɔfanom* (maternal uncles), as well as his father, had learned about trading from their fathers. He should have apprenticed in bead trading like his father. This anticipated career path changed when his *wɔfanom*, Kwabena Adofo and Dwamena, enrolled him in school and then covered the expenses of his education.[47]

Boakye Yiadom was sent to the Abetifi primary school after his older brother had received some school education. Despite fifty years of missionary presence, it was still quite unusual for a child to become a pupil in 1926:

> During our time we did not go to school in time. I stayed home for sixteen years. . . . I was accepted, because they wanted children to come to school. Our parents did not understand schooling, so they let the children stay at home to serve. But they were begged by missionaries, they came to your house and they ask you: "What is this boy doing here? Let him come to school tomorrow."

The European missionaries' request for children is probably more a topos than an actual occurrence in Boakye Yiadom's case. From 1924 on, missionaries only occasionally lived at the old Basel Mission station. Still, as a child, Boakye Yiadom must have witnessed missionaries, accompanied by the African pastor, evangelist, and presbyters, going from house to house, engaging in street preaching. Striking their omnipresent bell, at times supported by a brass band, missionaries gathered the people of Abetifi, and encouraged them to attend church and to send their children to school. Later, Boakye Yiadom corrected himself and spoke about "teachers and ministers [who] used to go from house to house."[48] Probably Rev. C. M. Adu, local pastor and school manager, convinced the *wɔfanom*, Kwadwo Opong and Kwabena Mensa Opong, to send Boakye Yiadom to school. They went to see Kwasi Ampomah in Akwasihu and pleaded with the old man to let his grandson go. Further, the *wɔfanom* had to overcome reluctance from Boakye Yiadom's father who demanded his son's labor. But the *wɔfanom* insisted, "This is our nephew and we have the power over him." They succeeded and paid his school fees. Looking back, Boakye Yiadom emphasized the importance of his late start and declared that these days children enter school too young. There were thirty-six pupils in his class, and he was "truly . . . the first," as he wrote in his "Autobiography: My Own Life." After one year, he was able to skip one class, which gave him much pride.[49]

The European education of E. F. Opusuo began differently. He started school in 1933, at about the age of ten, in the cocoa village of Adonso where he was living with his father, Kwaku Adu. He recalled the intervention of the Pepease ruler.

> OP: When [Nana Owusu Mensa] came to the stool, he made it compulsory for every elder of the chief to send at least one child to school, whether you liked it or not. Every stool [subchief, head of a local *abusua*] must send one child to school.
> SM: Was he literate?
> OP: He was literate, but he did not have much education; I think up to Standard III. But he was interested in education. It was during his time, that all these school buildings were put up. He encouraged the people to put up students, when he came here, the school was up to Class III. . . . He died in 1950.

Since this small "bush school" with one teacher only offered instruction to Standard I, after two years Opusuo relocated to his mother's home at Pepease. Daily he walked the few kilometers to the Abetifi primary on the new lorry road, recently built by survey school students.[50]

Ascending the hill to Abetifi Christian Quarters removed these boys from their previous surroundings not only physically but culturally. They were introduced to norms guiding the lives of the congregation. Although the Presbyterian Church went through a phase of growth during the interwar years, the original Basel Mission settlements maintained their distinct character and elaborate rules. Presbyters, under the pastor's leadership, supervised the daily conduct of church members and settled disputes.[51] Becoming a pupil in a Presbyterian school created a sense of separation and produced a new identity, especially for those who were not born into Christian families. Opusuo mentioned how schoolchildren "were admired," since even in educational centers like Abetifi only a minority of children attended school. Those who were not enrolled had ambivalent feelings: envy of schoolchildren as well as fear of teachers' discipline. Teachers examined homework and also pupils' physical appearance and personal hygiene. On Sundays students were expected to attend church. If they stayed away, or if their clothes were considered dirty, teachers used the cane or sent them home. Corporal punishment was not alien to Akan culture; however, the principle that teachers had the authority to beat children regardless of their *abusua*'s status was foreign. Wearing khaki school uniforms and being exempt from work on parental farms on weekdays, pupils were constantly reminded of their new status.[52]

Moving between non-Christian parts of Kwawu and schools located in Christian Quarters created mixed feelings. Opusuo was "afraid" to cross by himself the "four hundred yards between town," where he stayed with his mother, "and Pepease Christian Quarters." Yet, in the company of his friends, he did enter "to steal oranges." It was strange to him how Christians disregarded local taboos and kept goats forbidden in town by the *ɔbosom* (lesser god) Tano.[53] Reverend Asante was clearly attracted to this new world. In the morning he left with a sense of eagerness to cross the forest that separated Abetifi's Manem from its Christian Quarters. In the evening he returned to his *wɔfa*'s house with an enhanced sense of self, excited to share his new knowledge about Christian songs and games with his barely clothed age-mates. Asante and Boakye Yiadom emphasized the fascination of Bible stories and missionary tales like Bunyan's *Pilgrim's Progress;* they enjoyed passing them on to those outside the classroom.[54]

In the interwar period Presbyterian primary schools were coeducational. Most female students came from Christian families, making education for them less a break from their former environment than it was for the interviewed men. At school, pupils from Manem, like Reverend Asante, met Christian girls who rarely ventured into town. Elizabeth Ntim (born 1912) noted that girls attended school through Standard III. Some had to leave earlier "because people said that girls' education was not profitable."[55] In older Christian families there was more support. Attending the Abetifi primary school, Adelaide Opong (born 1919) lived with her *wɔfa*, the headmaster of the boys' boarding school. She followed in the footsteps of her mother who had attended school for thee years, then "stayed with German missionaries as a maid servant" and learned about European cooking.[56] Opong's cousin, Paulina Addo (also born 1919), attended school in Duanyaw-Kwanta (Brong-Ahafo) and commented on the gendered curriculum in vocational subjects: girls learned pottery, boys basket weaving. The teacher's cane enforced discipline for boys *and* girls:

Once I was late, and the teacher gave me twelve lashes. A certain teacher, whipped us, he was a Krobo man, and he was called teacher Tete. During those days, people did not recognize the importance of school. So, the day the teacher whipped me, my parents confronted him. They said they would not allow a teacher to beat their only daughter.[57]

After the confrontation with her parents, the teacher just ignored her.

Kofi Ankoma did not attend Presbyterian schools. Once a government primary was established in the merchant town of Obo, its chief, Nana Kwasi Nyarko, became "very keen on this school," as District Commissioner A. J. Walker reported. Since classes were not well attended, Walker complained about a "shortage of infants" during his Empire Day address in May 1926.[58] Ankoma's *wɔfa*, Kwadwo Adofo, a wealthy trader, was subsequently urged by the Obohene to send his *wɔfase* to school. Ankoma recalled:

We had one chief by name Kwasi Nyarko. He beat gong gong that elders around the chief, each of them should send his son, his nephew, or grandson, or granddaughter to school. Most elders in town, everybody who was grown up [had a certain status] sent somebody [of his *abusua*] to school.

In 1927 Ankoma enrolled at the government school. He explained that only a few pupils attended a secular school, since secular institutions were rare. As an *ɔkɔmfo*'s son, he explained his preference:

KA: Formerly, during colonial days, when you were a member of the Presby Church, you were sent as a child to school, the Presby one, and automatically you became a Christian. Methodist the same, Catholic the same. . . . It is only recently that Anglican came. Well, when I was attending school, there was no force that I should have become a Christian, or be a "heathen."
SM: Is that why you went to government school?
KA: Yes! The only place I wanted to go to school.

Still, discipline in government schools could be harsh. Ankoma narrated an episode when corporal punishment received his *wɔfa*'s endorsement. After failing to answer his teacher's questions, Ankoma received "four lashes" and was dismissed for the day.

KA: When I came home, my uncle was inside [and asked,] "Kofi, have you finished school?" I said: "No." "Why?" "I have been beaten by the teacher, I won't go back to school at all." "Look, I told you to go to school so the teacher would teach you; I did not tell the teacher to beat you. I will go and fetch the teacher." I was very happy. . . . So, I followed my uncle (laughs), I followed my uncle to a friend who was called D. K. Asante; then we moved to the government school. [The uncle explained to the friend:] "This teacher is very stupid, why should he beat Kofi? Let's go and see this teacher, the headmaster. If necessary, we will fight them." I had such a swollen head [felt triumphant]. The teacher, the headmaster and my uncle went to the office, leaving me outside. I was waiting to hear the result. . . . The result was that I should be beaten again! (laughs)

SM: How many lashes?

KA: Twelve! (laughter). I had four, I was not pleased with it, they had to give me twelve. Now the headmaster had something to say: "The twelve is plus one, that is thirteen lashes." I was laid on the table; he beat me. I had six lashes here, and I had seven lashes there (pointing to his buttocks). My uncle then asked me whether I would still refuse to return to school. "*Wɔfa*, I will go to school, I will go!"

Looking back, Ankoma considered this punishment appropriate. He deplored the fact that children of the 1990s were no longer subjected to such beatings; instead, they dared to take teachers to court. Ankoma felt that he had deserved this treatment because of his challenge to the authority of his teacher, as well as that of his *wɔfa*.[59]

Ankoma's school experience was significantly different from that of the other interviewed men. Becoming a pupil was less a departure from the ideological world of his parents and *abusua*. In the rather low-key government schools he encountered fewer attempts to reshape schoolboys through an education that promoted a specific notion of masculinity. This is reflected in his recollections. Unlike those attending Presbyterian schools, he did not dwell on his experience nor emphasize how being a pupil changed his sense of self.

In the final year of primary school, pupils sat for the Standard IV entrance examination. Boakye Yiadom noted how the Scottish school inspector, Rev. J.A.R. Watt, administered this exam. Boakye Yiadom did well; out of seventy-three candidates from Kwawu towns, he placed third.[60] In the Presbyterian system successful pupils graduated to boys' and girls' middle boarding schools, leading from Standard IV to VII. Among the interviewed men, only Ankoma pursued his education at a government middle school; he remained in Obo. Since Presbyterian boarding schools were a prime site for conveying gender norms, and feature prominently in the recorded recollections, they deserve close attention.

Boarding Schools

Boarding schools had been a principal strategy of Basel Mission education. They guaranteed the isolation of pupils from unwarranted influences.

The first boys' middle boarding schools were established at Osu in 1863 and at Akropong in 1867; others followed. After World War I the Presbyterian Church continued these schools, supervised by Scottish missionaries. The Abetifi Boarding School opened in 1920. Upon inspection District Commissioner (DC) Walker rated it "above average" and "situated in very fine grounds," located next to the church and old mission house. Since "accommodations for boarders [were] rather limited," the DC urged "townspeople" to provide labor to construct new buildings, completed in 1926.[61] Boarding schools had about 160 to 170 pupils, 4 class teachers, a head teacher, and a school manager, usually the local pastor, "all of whom took a very keen interest" in the boys' "character training."[62] Government officials agreed; one emphasized how teachers' "intimate relationship" with pupils afforded a "greater scope for moral development than in the day school."[63] Reverend Asante, Boakye Yiadom, and Opusuo had vivid memories of the boarding school. This was an institution of discipline like those analyzed by Michel Foucault, and it is where they became fully immersed in ideas of a Presbyterian masculinity.[64]

Life at the Abetifi Boarding School was strict and regulated. Students were introduced to a new concept of time, since every hour of the day was parceled into a rigid schedule. Opusuo recalled:

> Early morning, the work bell rings at 5:30, at 5:30 you have to rise up [and go to morning service], and [then] you have to go to see your plot. Part of the compound is allotted to you as a plot; if it is weedy, you have to weed. Between six and seven, it is clearing the compound, and after seven, we take our bath, and at eight o'clock, there will be roll call. From there we go to the class rooms and start the classes. . . . At twelve o'clock, there is a break for lunch, at quarter to two, we start the afternoon class and end at four o'clock. . . . [Then] we go for games and sports, and we close at five o'clock, and you can take bath, and . . . supper at six o'clock. And after supper, you have night studies till nine o'clock, 9:30. At 9:30, we went to bed.

It is striking how closely this timetable in the 1940s resembled the *Schulordnung* printed for Basel Mission middle schools in 1869.[65] The clock imposed a schedule and was instrumental in creating separate entities of physical work, academic studies, games and sports, meals, personal hygiene, religious service, sleep, and rarely some free time. The local distinction between *adwuma* and *afoofi*, work and leisure, was altered. Similar to industrial workers across twentieth-century Africa exposed to the discipline of "colonizing time," pupils were introduced to modern work rhythms. Yet unlike the dockworkers of Mombasa, these former pupils explicitly remembered the boarding school's rigid schedule positively as part of the elaborate program of self-improvement that shaped them into hard-working men, devout fathers, and monogamous husbands, that is, Presbyterian males.[66]

The spatial organization of the Abetifi Boarding School underscored the importance of African teachers who were not only in charge but served as main agents in transmitting gender ideals. The new buildings formed the sides of a quadrangle around an open courtyard, at the center a flagpole with the Union Jack. At two sides of the quadrangle were two-story stone buildings with classrooms and dormitories upstairs, at the other sides the teachers' quarters. In one corner, the headmaster's bungalow indicated its importance through size and proximity to the church. Although modeled after older Basel Mission schools, there was a major difference. Usually the mission house, a two-story bungalow with veranda upstairs under a large roof (see Fig. 1.2), had occupied one side of the quadrangle. As supervisor, the missionary, from his veranda, had "a bird's eye-view [sic] of the entire school—teachers and pupils, as well as outer parts of the school—the garden, water-pump, the kitchen, wash-house and other out-houses."[67] This pattern was broken at Abetifi. There the school, staffed by Africans, maintained a distance from the former mission house where only occasionally a European school inspector resided under the new Presbyterian regime. The recollections also reflected a correlation between space and teachers' importance. Reverend Asante, at the boarding school from 1925 to 1928, narrated how pupils created "Asoba Road" which connected quadrangle and church. This short lane was named after the initials of four teachers and the school manger. Among them, teacher I. O. Sampong and Rev. E. M. Asiedu, characterized by Asante as "disciplinarians," had the most enduring influence. In his own teaching, and later as pastor, he emulated them.[68] How much Sampong embodied the values of Presbyterian masculinity was expressed after his untimely death in 1943. Asante's paternal relative, E. K. Addo, eulogized Sampong as "one of the most disciplinarian teachers" who was "hard-working, conscientious, very studious, friendly and sympathetic, very stimulating and God-fearing."[69]

The classroom buildings were divided into two sections, organizing pupils into four "houses," numbered 1 to 4 and distinguished by the colors blue, red, green, and gold. Each boy belonged to one house with its own hierarchies and group identity, under the authority of a Standard VII student as "prefect." Similar to the "fag system" in English public schools (actually private institutions), junior pupils served those in Standard VI and VII, fetching water, gathering firewood ("faggots"), preparing bathwater, and cleaning classrooms and dormitory rooms. Reverend Asante remembered the rivalry between houses, displayed in sports, that occasionally led to fights. To emphasize personal achievement, pupils sat in classrooms according to rank. They were taught to compete against classmates not just in academic subjects (English, Twi, history, geography, math, and Bible studies) but also in sports and in planting the most productive plot of cassava and corn. When they sold these crops, they split profits with the school.[70]

The boarding school, like other missionary institutions, was not just a place to acquire literacy and Christianity but became a training site for particular regimes of domesticity, cleanliness, and order. The "school prospectus" detailed the clothes and other items pupils had to acquire, ranging from a Bible, hymnbook, cutlass, bucket, and sweeping broom to consumer products like a pressing iron, white trousers and jacket, bedsheet, pillow, towels, and sponge. Reverend Asante commented on how he used soap. Prior to enrollment

> Soap was made locally by our mothers and grandmothers. So we did not need to buy European soap. And even, not long ago, there were some locally made soaps by some traders. The ingredients were not very good, acid and all these things which made the soap look rather poor (laughs).

Yet, as a boarder, industrially produced Key Soap became an important item in his "chop box," since pupils did their own laundry according to school standards.[71] Punishment was ubiquitous. Those who fell below a certain mark in examinations feared to be "caned in public and warned to show more diligence in their studies."[72] Pupils were only rarely permitted to leave the school grounds and reenter the town. Opusuo explained:

> If you are found on the way to town and a teacher met you, he asked you, "Who gave you permission?" And if you were not able to tell, you would be punished, when you come back you would be punished, even on a Saturday, every day. I think it was on Sundays that we were allowed to go to the town to buy perhaps soap.[73]

Any contact with girls, including the writing of letters, was forbidden and could cause severe sanctions, even expulsion. This was a major change for pupils who had participated in intergender games like mock marriages prior to their enrollment.

Religious training dominated the curriculum; schooling was "the model for conversion."[74] Those from a non-Christian background, Reverend Asante, Boakye Yiadom, and Opusuo, joined the church at the boarding school. Overseeing Presbyterian schools, Scottish Mission director Arthur Wilkie maintained the Basel Mission practice of "fostering the evangelical character of education" and seeking to convert students; any teacher who "neglected his work as catechist of the church would be subject to dismissal or to reduction of salary."[75] Reverend Asante recalled this religious training, organized on a fixed schedule:

> Monday Bible history, Tuesday catechism, Wednesday Bible history, Thursday hymns, Friday Bible history. So three times Bible history a week, and Tuesday is for catechism and Thursday for hymns.[76]

Regular praying sessions not only structured the school week but provided headmasters the opportunity to set "the 'tone' of the school," as worship guidelines advised. In their prayers headmasters should convey the "Christian way of life . . . bringing their pupils face to face with life problems and temptations." Serializing these addresses, the headmaster exemplified character development in the biblical story of Joseph, featuring the "Parable of Jesus" or "The Life of Livingstone."[77] Singing was popular and was another way of teaching. Pupils had to recite and sing a selection of Twi hymns. Asante developed a special fondness for the hymn "*Fa wo kwan hyɛ wo Yɛfoɔ, wo Nyame*" [Commit thy way unto thy Maker, thy God], to accompany him for the rest of his life.[78]

For many, baptism and confirmation fell on the same day. This was an important marker that not only indicated their new Christian faith but also demonstrated to the "heathen town" that they had broken away from the world into which they were born. New Christian names were widely adopted in mission schools across colonial Africa and became an outward sign of personal transformation. On Christmas Day, 1926, as a Standard V student, Reverend Asante was baptized and confirmed. He commented on the preparations:

> You see, the class would attend baptismal or confirmation classes in the evening with the pastor or the catechist; this would continue for about three or six months; then at the end of the term or year, this class would be baptized and confirmed.

In his sermon Rev. C. M. Adu addressed the candidates "with particular emphasis on [their] good behavior" and exhorted them to strive for "the life of a good Christian." Asante was given a certificate that included the text of Psalm 23, one of his favored Bible quotes, "The Lord is my shepherd, I shall not want." He took the name Edmond, in honor of the late missionary

Edmond Perregaux. (Although his *abusua* continued calling him Kwaku (Wednesday-born male), his classmates and teachers referred to him as Edmond.[79]) Boakye Yiadom and Opusuo experienced similar ceremonies in Standard VI. Boakye Yiadom vividly recalled his confirmation in December 1933, described in his second autobiography as "an especially wonderful occasion." But he hardly used his Christian names, Winfried Erasmus. Opusuo chose Emmanuel, "the name of Jesus," at his confirmation in 1942.[80]

The decision to attend boarding school was frequently a matter of money. Many gifted pupils were encouraged by teachers but lacked support to pursue their studies. Unlike Reverend Asante and Boakye Yiadom, whose *wɔfanom* covered expenses, Opusuo was not so fortunate. His *abusua* was poor, and he depended on his father, Kwaku Adu. In 1941, one year after entering the boarding school, the father withdrew his support. Opusuo recounted:

> When the school reopened . . . I stayed home. So my teachers, my headmaster sent [somebody] to ask me why I was not coming. I told him: "My father said he would not pay." So they asked me to come there. . . . They told me: "If you can get somebody to buy books for you, then we shall pay your school fees."

After his brother agreed to pay for the books, Opusuo returned to school:

> My teachers decided to report the matter to the State Secretary [G. P. Johnson]. So the Kwawu State Secretary reported the matter to the Ɔmanhene of Kwawu. And, I don't know what happened, but my father was asked to take up my education.

From the 1930s the Kwawu Ɔmanhene (paramount chief) Akuamoa Acheampong, himself a former member of the Abetifi congregation, was well disposed toward Presbyterian schools. As a son of a former ɔmanhene, Opusuo's father paid attention to the palace's wishes. After two months he agreed to pay. Opusuo continued:

> Not that he did not have any money, he had money. But he did not know the importance of education (laughs). And also, if I became somebody in the future, I did not belong to this family, I belonged to another family.[81]

The father was reluctant to invest in his son's education, since, as a well-to-do cocoa farmer, he had commitments toward his *abusua*. He considered his paternal responsibility fulfilled by having provided his son with a Standard V education. Opusuo's struggle reflects a larger shift in paternal obligation among matrilineal Akan societies during the middle decades of the twentieth century. Based on his extensive Asante survey of 1945–46, Meyer Fortes maintained that "nowadays it is strongly felt that a child's schooling, which is widely regarded as the most important preparation for gaining a living in the modern world, is the father's responsibility."[82] Sophy Osafo conducted research in Kwawu around 1950 and found that this shift was far from complete. She noted that "both the father and the maternal uncle are responsible for the children's education." While some fathers helped with school fees, others would not "pay a penny."[83] For colonial Asante, Jean Allman and Victoria Tashjian have forcefully argued that a father's increased expectations meant "greater rights of use in, even paternal ownership of, children."[84] For the interviewed men who succeeded in their education, such paternal demands were not heavy. Opusuo merely provided labor for his father during holidays from training college but became free of obligations upon launching his own teaching career. He completed the boarding school only because of his teachers' intervention. Therefore Opusuo and other graduates developed lasting relationships with their teachers who became decisive role models, replacing fathers and *wɔfanom* as advisers in career choices. This led to a change in relations among men with shared school experiences. Opusuo and his successful classmates tended to embrace a Presbyterian notion of masculinity, including monogamous marriage and privileging their children over *abusua* members, particularly in terms of educational support.

During the interwar period girls' middle boarding schools transmitted ideas about "Presbyterian femininity." Young Kwawu women, especially daughters of teachers and other senior church members, profited from the opening of the Basel Mission Girls School at Agogo, Asante-Akyem, in 1931. This school sought "to educate girls as Christian wives and mothers."[85] The Basel Mission director summarized its objectives as "training for marriage, for home life, and for the instruction of their own children." He emphasized "classroom subjects that prepare girls for all tasks of their lives: cooking, sewing, hygiene, and all other domestic work."[86] Felicia Asante (born 1918), granddaughter of the Abetifi senior presbyter Okra, first attended school at Bompata where she stayed with her father's brother, teacher Ntim. In 1933 she enrolled at Agogo. Unlike the boys' middle schools in the 1930s and 1940s, Agogo and the girls' boarding schools at Aburi and Odumase were still dominated by European missionaries. Felicia Asante recalled the strong presence of three "German" women (the first two actually Swiss): Gertrud Goetz, Helen Schlatter, and Elisabeth Ackermann.[87] Asante and Adelaide Opong, who, as a teacher's daughter, attended Agogo from 1934 to 1937, both emphasized the strict discipline at the school. Opong explained:

> By "discipline" I mean, they [European teachers] looked after us very well. They
> did not want us to be *basabasa* (disordered) as young people are roaming around
> town these days. When you met a student, and he spoke to you, she would
> use expressions like "please," but today, when you meet somebody, this is not
> done anymore.[88]

Opong lamented that today's youth disregard missionary discipline, which
leads to dangerous disorder and confusion, implying sexual improprieties.
The gendered curriculum included academic subjects like English and math,
in addition to the focus on domestic training. A few industrious girls were
assigned to serve the European staff. Opong elaborated:

> I had to tidy some of the European teachers' houses, in their rooms. They used
> to send me to town to post letters and to fetch mail, I became the "post-girl."
> They also called me, instead of Adelaide, "Heidi." . . . Heidi Kwakye, my fa-
> ther's name was Kwakye. . . . And I had to respond to their calls.[89]

Receiving her Standard VII certificate, Adelaide Opong had hoped to continue her education at the two-year Presbyterian women's training college at
Agogo. But, as in the case of Felicia Asante, there was strong parental pressure for marriage.

These forms of education, in apprenticeships and in European-style
schools, shaped the lives of men and women. Among the interviewed men,
those in apprenticeships learned much about senior masculinity from their
masters and took them as role models. Those in schools, especially in Presbyterian institutions, experienced their education as a turning point. Becoming a pupil, particularly after enrolling in the boarding school, gave them a
new sense of self as *krakye* (clerk, scholar). In mission schools they were not
only introduced to Christianity and eventually converted, but they also
learned about the Presbyterian notion of masculinity that stipulated a different set of ideas concerning marriage, fatherhood, and *abusua* relations.
Boarding school graduates recalled with pride the rituals and stages of self-
improvement witnessed in their training that influenced their attitudes toward their age-mates outside school, work discipline, and authorities.
Thereby teachers, most of them from outside Kwawu, became their role
models. Further, the interwar years saw increased government interest in
education, as Presbyterian schools introduced organized sports and scouting.
These became focal points in debates about masculinity: educational policies
launched by the colonial government and fostered by a Scottish school inspector.

Pursuit of Manliness: Sports and Scouting

In 1925 Governor F. G. Guggisberg presented his "Fifteen Principles of Education" as part of his annual address to the Legislative Council. In this, the most complete policy statement on education of the interwar period, Guggisberg proclaimed that "organised games should form part of the life of every school."[90] This proposition was part of a fresh government commitment to education, funded by the booming cocoa industry. At the lower level of a new, two-tier system, vocational and technical training should overcome the "bookishness" of existing schools; for a small minority, higher education would be available in secondary schools, reflected in the founding of the elite Prince of Wales College at Achimota. The government raised standards by closing African-run "bush schools," creating a registry of teachers, and by increasing supervision of subsidized mission schools.[91]

These initiatives were directly influenced by the Phelps-Stokes Commission, which had toured the Gold Coast and other parts of Africa in 1920–21. Across colonial Africa, the commission supported secular tendencies in mission schools. T. Jesse Jones, author of its report, noted that European education had been transplanted from metropoles, neglecting African conditions and harming "Native people." The commission embraced the controversial philosophy of Booker T. Washington who had advocated a separate curriculum for African Americans, emphasizing industrial training wrapped in Christian ethics at the expense of academic subjects.[92] Lauding the example of Basel Mission schools, Jones urged the creation of an educational system concerned with the "development of the individual and the community" by focusing on "health, hygiene, gardening, soil cultivation, husbandry, handicrafts, and domesticity." The report identified "character development and [Christian] religious life" as crucial objectives to be achieved through "perseverance, thoroughness, order, cleanliness, punctuality, thrift, temperance, self-control, reliability, honesty, and respect for parents." Jones suggested that sports and games, which required "skill and mental alertness and cooperation," should replace leisure activities and amusements that could be "physically or emotionally enervating." Sports would help curb "sex indulgence and wild forms of emotion," considered "too general in the life of primitive peoples."[93] Although it was praised in missionary circles, the commission did not win approval from all sides. In a scathing review, W.E.B. Du Bois attacked the report not only for promoting a second-class education but also for advocating "co-operation" among colonizers and colonized, thereby perpetuating Europe's exploitation of Africa.[94] A similar critique appeared in the *Gold Coast Leader* which praised Du Bois's review as "the finest bit of work he had done for black Humanity." The newspaper was deeply offended by the notion of Africans being "on a different level of advancement" and thus in need of a different curriculum.[95]

Still, the Phelps-Stokes report had a strong impact. In 1925 the Colonial Office released a major statement on education, compiled by a special Advisory Committee, followed ten years later by a memorandum on education in rural communities. Both echoed the priorities of the Phelps-Stokes Commission. Throughout the Advisory Committee's recommendations, as in most contemporary writing, boys and men were taken as the norm. According to the committee, education should shape a man's character through the "formation of industry, of truthfulness, of *manliness,* of readiness for social service and of *disciplined co-operation.*"[96] Manliness evoked the late Victorian ideals of self-restraint, robustness, perseverance, and stoicism. James Mangan, in his study on the diffusion of manliness across the British Empire through team sports, argued that this ideal had two dimensions implying "dominance *and* deference"; thus "its inculcation promoted not simply initiative and self-reliance but also loyalty and obedience." Mangan, however, did not explore how boys and men across the diverse cultures of the empire responded to this ideal, whether it was accepted, resisted, or mediated and adapted to local conditions by the colonized.[97]

The interviewed men confirmed the importance of sports in school and how they participated in popular games, especially football (soccer). Reverend Asante explained how sports at the primary school contributed to the pupils' redefinition of self and separation from those outside the classroom:

> When we attended school, we had different things to play. There, you have the opportunity to play football and other games, hand ball. . . . The children outside the school had their own traditional games. . . . We started [playing football] from the primary school. There, it was almost compulsory.[98]

Recent scholarship has explored the spread of football as part of a new leisure culture in urban settings of colonial Africa; less attention has been paid to football's popularity in rural areas like Kwawu.[99] In Abetifi, when football was played outside the schoolyard, it took a different format. "Sometimes it was not an organized one like football teams," as Reverend Asante noted, "just the football is provided and everybody can join and play here and there."[100] Opusuo, ten years younger than Asante, talked about propagating football among boys who did not attend school. They had to be inventive:

We used tennis balls, sometimes oranges, if there were no tennis balls. We used everything, we used rubber to make dry balls, and used them to make a football. Whenever we had a chance, we played with the younger, I mean older children, but it was rare [since they went to farm].[101]

At the boys' boarding schools sports became more serious. With their "plethora of rules" and fixed "time-frame," organized games like football were a marker of modernity, reflecting the industrial society where they had been invented.[102] Pupils competed against one another in "cross-country" and "one hundred yards," as well as in teams representing their "houses" in games of football and volleyball. As a member of the football team, Reverend Asante played against the other houses and occasionally against the government-run Obo middle school, which could be reached through the forest in half a day's walk. In Asante's account Abetifi usually won, benefiting from its additional practice time. Schoolboys who excelled in sports received "high respect."[103]

Incorporating organized games and sports into the curriculum, former Basel Mission schools began to resemble English public schools. Protestant missions, as part of a "muscular Christianity," popularized their cult of "athleticism" across British Africa. For adolescent boys, playing sports provided a way to prove their physical skills and prowess. They were confronted, at least implicitly, with the idea of manliness, its high value of fair play, perseverance, and respect of rules. Team sport and manliness found their way from England not only to government schools like Achimota but also to the rural setting of the Abetifi Boarding School in Ghana's hinterland.[104] Yet African footballers and European administrators had different motivations. In colonial Brazzaville, Africans played "for fun," whereas Europeans "were interested in the inculcation of values."[105] Although games were supervised by African teachers at Abetifi, there was still a discrepancy between conflicting views of this sport. Pupils engaged creatively with games and their accompanying modes of behavior. Their nicknames reflected playing styles. As goalkeeper, Boakye Yiadom was a preferred teammate. For him, rules were not fixed but instead were to be adapted by a clever mind:

We played this netball, and we had volleyball too, and football and other games. I was always leading, I liked it in school, because I was sharp. So I learned to keep the goal. . . . Even if I could not get the ball to catch, I was in the goal pit and I could not get the ball to catch quickly, I could ask one of my back keepers to make foul. And when they made foul, they have to make penalty to see that I catch; and penalty, I catch easily. Yes (laughs), I was very sharp, very smart, so even I was called Kofi Smart in the school.[106]

In the 1930s eagerness in sports counted as a qualification when Boakye Yiadom was seeking employment as *krakye*, following his Standard VII examination. His teacher wrote in a letter of recommendation:

> [Boakye Yiadom] was diligent and of very good conduct while he was at school, that he was versatile and therefore very useful in many of the school outdoor activities, that his zeal in games and other athletic sports was exemplary being a captain of his school section, and his sportsmanship was a copy or a model of his section.[107]

Playing sports in the Presbyterian boarding schools was not just a leisure activity but increasingly became a "test of masculinity."[108] Similar to the introduction of football elsewhere, its organization and competitive nature "resonated" in Kwawu with existing forms of recreation like dance and singing competitions.[109] Both were public entertainment and spectacles, as well as sites for boys and young men to prove themselves as senior men to be. Yet, there were differences. Abetifi dance competitions could only be performed in Manem. Competitive sporting events, like those during Empire Day celebrations, were held on the playing fields of the Abetifi Boarding School. Unlike dance parties, they had the blessing of colonial officials and the leadership of the Presbyterian Church, African pastors, and European missionaries.[110]

Scouting was another school activity prominent in the advocacy of manliness. In 1908 Robert Baden-Powell launched the scouting movement in Britain to shore up the virility of Britain's youth, particularly lower-middle- and working-class boys living in overcrowded cities. During the prewar years Britain experienced a "crisis in masculinity," a range of concerns about the feminization of British young males, unprepared for the next war, and fears about national efficiency compared to other emerging imperial powers like Germany and Japan. Baden-Powell promoted scouting as a way to "develop character, manliness, honour, endurance, patriotism, and good citizenship in boys" by organizing outdoor activities.[111] Scouting quickly spread to the British dominions, the United States, South America, South Asia, and, in the 1910s, to Africa. In 1914 a branch was founded by Samuel Wood at Cape Coast, and the Gold Coast became the first colony to embrace the movement. After World War I the movement enjoyed "considerable success" among Africans in the Gold Coast as elsewhere in British West Africa.[112]

W. H. Donald, appointed as chief scout commissioner in 1923, expanded scouting in schools and advocated activities like those in Britain. In an article for the *Gold Coast Teachers' Journal,* he praised the "ideal of service" as a form of "practical Christianity." Through "woodcraft, nature study and camping," a scout should "acquire qualities of self-reliance and resource, bodily health and energy, technical skill and handicraft, and a sense of service to the community." This catalogue of personal and vocational skills prevented a school leaver from joining the "great army of the unemployed."[113] The governor acted as chief scout enforcing the colonial hierarchy. During the interwar period policy makers considered scouting to be another avenue of redirecting the focus in education from producing literate clerks to supplying skilled labor. The *Gold Coast Handbook* characterized scouting as "officially encouraged" but not as an "official movement . . . invaluable in the character training of the Gold Coast youth."[114] But Donald offered a contradictory message. On the one hand, he urged teachers to provide leadership "in the interests of the young manhood of the Empire," cementing the status quo. In a "self-less effort" they created the perfect "men of the future" with qualities of "right doing, straight living and clean thinking," the ideal of manliness. On the other hand, he argued that this "wonderful brotherhood" should transcend the social barriers of a racialized colonial society, implicitly challenging the status quo.[115]

Opusuo recalled that participation in scouting was "not compulsory." He and his classmates were attracted to outdoor activities and male camaraderie. Teachers recruited leaders among Standard VII seniors. Scouts had to walk in "military formation," but, as Opusuo stated, "marching like the military was a very common activity," especially after the outbreak of World War II.[116] More than team sports, scouting had a pronounced individualistic bent. Scouting created a venue to acquire discipline and practical, marketable skills, and prepared a boy for a life as a productive, as well as loyal, colonial subject. Boakye Yiadom linked a career in education with scouting: for example, E.V.C. Darko was a prominent Abetifi teacher who served as scout master while rising to the post of general manager of schools. Boakye Yiadom's first scouting adventure was a campaign to promote hygiene as a Standard V student. They went to Manem and Abetifi's surrounding villages to "clean houses and compounds." With pride, he recalled his promotion to senior scout commissioner, crucial to his self-presentation. He requested that I include a photograph sporting his old scouting uniform (see Fig. 0.4 in the prologue).[117]

Presbyterian Training College

Upon completing middle school, gifted students had two options. Either they enrolled in one of the few and expensive secondary schools or they sat for the competitive training college entrance examination.[118] Leaving the boarding school in 1928, Reverend Asante wished to attend a secondary school, but his *wɔfanom* and teachers convinced him to seek more financial security as a teacher. Unlike secondary school students, those in training colleges paid only nominal fees, since their education was subsidized. Instead, they were bonded to teach for five years for the sum of £100.[119] Fifteen years later Opusuo was also encouraged by his teachers to attend training college. Prior to the education reforms of 1951, only those sponsored by wealthy family members had the opportunity to enroll in a secondary school with the hope of attending a university overseas.[120]

During the 1920s the organization of the Presbyterian Training College at Akropong went through changes stimulated by government policies and a transformed leadership. Although the Scottish Mission continued to run the college to train teachers as church agents, a less dogmatic and more practical theology was adopted, criticized by the Basel Mission as too "liberal-modern."[121] The training college introduced team sports to complement academic courses, renewed an interest in African languages, and expanded teachers' training from three to four years, with an optional fifth year for instruction in catechism. By 1928 the college opened new buildings, financed by a government grant of £20,000.[122]

College students further developed their social position. Parading their woolen suits, shoes, and ties, they distinguished themselves from farmers and elders who dressed in the toga-style cloth of Akan men. Following frequent complaints about students overdressing, the college introduced uniforms, which caused an uproar. Under the new dress code, students were required to wear khaki shorts and shirt during the week, and on Sundays a "white twill suit" with tie and shoes called "brogues." The dress code marked them as future teachers.[123] As in the (middle) boarding schools, students lived in hierarchically organized houses. Opusuo, who attended the training college from 1943 to 1947, recalled how daily chores were performed according to rank:

> When you came into the first year, you do a lot of work in the house. . . . The second year was carrying kitchen rubbish; and the first year, was carrying urine (laughs). In our dormitory there was a piss can . . . when the whole house urinated at the end of the day, you have to carry it, the first year has to carry it.

> And we did it in turns. If you carry this week, next week somebody else will
> do it. And the third year, we were not doing much work, we were [just] working
> in the kitchen. And in the fourth year, you are a senior, and therefore, your
> burden is only a little work. Anyway, in the fifth year, in those days, there was
> a catechist course. . . . When you are in the fifth year, you are not doing any-
> thing, you are a senior.[124]

Male students with little seniority were expected to clean bathrooms and
perform kitchen chores, jobs that had been the duty of their sisters and other
female household members in their hometowns. Asked whether such work
was difficult for him, Opusuo gave a surprising answer. He explained that,
since his college days, he had "always swept his room" to guarantee cleanliness to his "satisfaction."

> Nobody wants me to do that. . . . Even when I see that the kitchen is not clean
> enough, some of the children will be sweeping there. But when I go and see
> that it is not well, I take a broom and sweep again. . . . (laughs) . . . I always
> clean my bathroom and my toilet.

When I wondered whether any male elders in Pepease did such work, he
replied:

> They don't do it! Even, if they see me, people see me doing that, they would
> think that I am doing my wife's job (laughs). But I feel pleasure doing that.[125]

Other men confirmed this domestic work at the college but said they were
relieved when they could pass it on to wives or house servants. Only Opusuo
incorporated these cleaning standards into his daily habit, performing domestic chores that challenge Kwawu perceptions of appropriate tasks for
adult men and, even more so, senior masculinity. The Presbyterian education
succeeded in radically altering Opusuo's gendered behavior. As Opusuo himself maintains, the cleanliness of his personal space has become a marker of
his transformation as an educated man embracing Presbyterian masculinity,
as well as an expression of his reconstituted self.

In early 1929, with the occupation of the new buildings, the Presbyterian
Training College opened its own kitchen to cook for students and staff. Until
then, each student had made arrangements with a female caterer in town,
paid from his allowance. The college disapproved, since "a series of young
girls" delivered food twice a day, providing ample opportunities for "little
chats" and at times even more, as Wilhelm Stamm noted. On Sundays students ate at their cooks' homes, where they could hide "forbidden things like
certain books, cameras, and clothes."[126] The caterers' carriers also tended to

disrupt the college's rigid schedule by delivering food either too early or too late. In order to limit such unwanted contacts and establish the practice of common meals, the college replaced the caterers with a staff of male cooks from Liberia. This sparked resistance. On May 13, 1929, students went on strike owing to the "poor quality of food."[127] They objected to Kru men as cooks, because they were unfamiliar with local dishes. This conflict is deeply ingrained in the memories of Reverend Asante and his classmates. Food intersected with gender, authority, and ethnicity. After the failure of a settlement attempt by the Akropong pastor and presbyters, the principal suggested that students should ask their guardians for an additional fifteen shillings to improve the food. Students abandoned the college and either returned to their hometowns, if close by, or stayed in Akuapem with friends. Meeting in "an uncompleted house" at Akropong's outskirts, students agreed to return in eight days for talks.[128] While Stamm's and Asante's accounts of the strike's organization are almost identical, they differed about the negotiations. Stamm reported that the synod clerk, Rev. N. T. Clerk, and Reverend Martinson convinced class leaders to ask Principal Ferguson for forgiveness but the majority of strikers disapproved.[129] According to Asante, committee members of the synod (the church's governing body) gathered at the principal's bungalow and demanded to speak with the strike's initiators.

> But we said no, we refused to accept that, because they wanted to get him and punish him. Then they said: "How did you all unanimously refuse it?" We replied: "We went to the dining hall, sat at the table and tasted the food, then we saw that it was not the kind of food we liked, so we refused taking the food and threw the food out." "Then, why did you throw the food away to destroy it?" We said: "We didn't like it, so well, we refused and went pushing the plates on the table, some fell, but not all the food was thrown away." . . . "Then what exactly do you want?" We said: "We don't like to have the male cooks, they should be dismissed at once, we don't like them. The Kru men from Liberia, who had been employed at the bungalows by the Europeans, we don't like them. They don't know how to prepare African meals."

As an illustration, Asante described a dish prepared by the Kru cooks:

> They did not know how to prepare cassava *ampesie* [boiled cassava] for instance, they just filled the pots with water (laughs) with pieces of cassava, some were bad, very hard, you could not take it. They just shelled them, together with the good one. And we said: "No, we don't like it."

Akan students objected to the preparation *and* the choice of cassava as a staple dish, since this root crop was considered "food for pigs" and other ethnic groups, especially for "Ewes." Students insisted on a choice of food. As Asante related:

> We said: "We were not allowed to buy food from outside. Now we like that we choose what we like and eat what we can get." So, they said: "What?" "Akropong women are ready to give us good food, so either we buy from them occasionally on some days during the week or they cook for us. We employ them as cooks at the college." It is alright, they noted that; then, they said: "Now what else do you want to change?" We said: "That's all, these are the main causes of the strike."[130]

The strikers succeeded. The male cooks from Liberia were dismissed; no student was punished. The college staffed its kitchen with local women and permitted students to buy food in town on Wednesdays. Objecting to "Syrians" supplying bread from Accra, students convinced the college to buy locally baked bread, bringing additional business to Akropong women.[131]

Observers disagreed about the strike's implications. The *Gold Coast Independent* opined that many "innovations introduced in the name of progress and advancement of our educational system, [were] not by any means as good as [they] should be." Regretting this waste of money, the newspaper lauded the "erstwhile Basel Missionaries" for their "simple way of dealing with these matters," since the catering "by the women of Akropong at very cheap rates [had] proved entirely satisfactory."[132] Stamm, the Basel Mission representative, supported the introduction of in-house catering and expressed concern about the strikers' "state of mind." Their opposition resulted from secular influences, indirectly nurtured by the Scottish leadership which privileged "education" over catechism and spiritual growth.[133] Stamm's superiors in Basel were "seriously worried" about this lack of religious training and urged Stamm to provide a corrective in the catechist course.[134] Although strikes at mission schools were quite common, the home board tried its utmost to hush their occurrences, with some success. There is no word about this strike in the official history of the college published for its 125th anniversary.[135] For Reverend Asante and his classmates, the strike showed that students were unwilling to accept college policies unconditionally and that they had the collective power to resist, if necessary. Although students were willing to adapt their behavior in many ways and to embrace a Presbyterian notion of masculinity, they indicated their limits when they insisted that food preparation remain gendered. This work should not be performed by men, especially not by foreigners. The college made no further attempt to alter this practice.[136]

The Presbyterian Training College was formative in shaping identities as teachers. The interviewed men developed a sense of belonging to a social group, a sense that altered their own self-understanding. In his senior year Reverend Asante posed for a photograph with classmates, carefully dressed in suit and tie. They gathered in front of a new building beautified with a box of flowers. In this staged appearance they showed that they had become different men as teachers and were elite members of colonial society, at least educationally (see Fig. 3.1). Although students at the college remained in contact with hometowns by spending holidays there, they considered themselves above their peers. Even their former boarding school colleagues were now below them, and not only in educational matters. The Presbyterian Training College, with its high value on "character training," had turned them into teachers who became self-proclaimed "disciplinarians." The notion of a "German discipline," identified by Opusuo as physical work, strict rules,

Fig. 3.1. Rev. E.K.O. Asante, seated second from the right, with classmates at the Presbyterian Training College, Akropong, ca. 1933. The others are, standing (*left to right*), S. L. Akyemang (Aburi), M. D. Kumi (Mamfe), and H. T. Dako (Begoro); sitting, E. A. Aboakye (Akyem Abuakwa), E. Mensah (Peki), and E. S. Adu (Adukrom). Photo, Rev. E.K.O. Asante's Papers (Abetifi, Ghana).

close supervision, and severe corporal punishment, is crucial in the men's recollections. They proudly incorporated this discipline into their teaching and made it a cornerstone of their professional identities. Evaluating the work of younger colleagues, they lamented its disappearance.[137]

Conclusion

Education, either in apprenticeships or in schools, was a crucial experience for the eight men, since they were exposed to, and absorbed, distinct notions of masculinity. This could be challenging: masculinity ideals common among Kwawu elders and those promoted by school authorities were often contradictory. Ɔkyeame Asante and Marfo identified their masters as not only teaching them skills but also serving as role models who represented the ways of senior masculinity. Such ideals were rooted in religious authority and (older) Akan norms of a man's achievements, his obligations as a member of his *abusua*, his roles as husband and father, and his social position. Although Wahyee formally apprenticed in bead trading, his involvement with the world of the Abetifi Christian Quarters became more important. Wahyee, like the trader Addo who apprenticed to his older brothers, came to embrace a notion of masculinity promoted by the Presbyterian Church.

The other four men enrolled in European schools. Kofi Ankoma, who reached Standard VII in a government school, consciously maintained his distance from the moral and religious ideas of mission schools. Instead, he embraced an Akan understanding of masculinity closer to that of Ɔkyeame Asante and Marfo. Reverend Asante, Boakye Yiadom, and Opusuo were deeply influenced by Presbyterian masculinity. This comprised a set of norms and expectations of how to behave as men, fathers and husbands, and colonial subjects. Its genesis goes back to the mid-nineteenth century, when the Basel Mission introduced a program of gendered education that advocated specific goals for male and female converts. Separate *Erziehungsanstalten* (boarding schools) for boys and girls sought to reshape individual personhood. Although this mission society was forced to leave the Gold Coast at the end of World War I, its school system had a lasting impact.

The interwar period brought innovations. While Basel Mission senior schools had been managed by Europeans staff, African teachers and pastors took charge of boys' (middle) boarding schools within the reorganized Presbyterian Church. Africans became the main agents in transmitting ideas about Presbyterian masculinity, except for a continued European presence at the Presbyterian Training College and at girls' (middle) boarding schools.

With an increased government involvement in education, mission schools became more secularized and adapted to educational standards dominant across the British Empire. Educational policies stressed individual character development for boys *and* girls, combined with academic *and* vocational training. Presbyterian schools incorporated organized games, team sports, and scouting—all vehicles in the dissemination of the ideal of manliness. Yet students—and even some teachers—did at times challenge such expectations. Sporting rules were reinterpreted; the imposition of objectionable or subverted social rules, like the importing of foreign male cooks at the training college, created resistance from students. These paths of education were not without interconnecting crossroads. Addo, who received little schooling while apprenticing, later became literate and joined the ranks of *akrakyefoɔ* (scholars), influenced by Presbyterian masculinity.

The years spent in apprenticeships and schools altered these men's sense of self and their understandings of masculinity. This period laid a foundation and provided guidance for further challenges they encountered, for example, in their work and employment, in relationships with women in marriage, and in finding their position as elders within hometown communities.

THE EMPLOYMENT OF MEN: CLERKS, POLICE, SOLDIERS, AND TEACHERS, 1930–1951

4

In colonial Ghana of the 1930s and 1940s male students who had passed the Standard VII examination were called in Twi *krakye* (pl. *akrakyefoɔ*). The word is derived from the English word "clerk" and is often translated as "scholars." *Akrakyefoɔ* were mainly trained in mission schools to work as clerks, cocoa brokers, storekeepers, pupil teachers, and, if they pursued their education, as certified teachers and pastors. They had "a high prestige in the community due to their wealth, occupation, or literacy" and exercised "an effective influence in the political and social life of the community corresponding to their enhanced status."[1] The subjective meaning of belonging to the *akrakyefoɔ* affected these men's selection of employment and self-presentation. *Akrakyefoɔ*'s habitus, their "systems of dispositions" rooted in individual and collective experiences of hometown *mmusua* (matrilineages) and education, not only structured their work but shaped their notions of masculinity and its enactment.[2] As pivotal middle figures in colonial encounters, *akrakyefoɔ* maintained a balance between home and host communities, between employers, government officials, church leaders, and salaried colleagues and friends. These men shared the following characteristics: literacy, a community of peers, ambivalence about politics, and consumption of certain goods. Different forms of employment, such as clerks, soldiers, policemen, and teachers, placed them into intermediary positions, which affected their social, economic, and political standing, as well as their individual experience.

As members of intermediary classes, *akrakyefoɔ* experienced a double social exclusion. Most of them were neither part of the older and established chiefly elites who as "traditional rulers" were in charge of local administration under indirect rule, nor did they belong to the highly educated and financially secure intelligentsia. This was the lawyer-merchant class, who controlled an increasing number of African-owned newspapers and gathered in exclusive social clubs in cities, while waiting to inherit the colonial state. Still, *akrakyefoɔ* had political, social, economic, and cultural aspirations. Many hoped for a share of power and sought to be part of a modern and increasingly urban world.[3] They were not unique to Ghana. In colonial Tanzania they were "true medial figures" who stood educationally, economically, and culturally betwixt-and-between modern European and traditional native culture."[4] Or, as Nancy Hunt's sophisticated analysis of the Congo shows, they were "hybrid middle figures," crucial players in the intricacies and translations of colonial encounters.[5] Yet, in Ghana as in other locations along the West African littoral like Freetown or Lagos, they had a longer history reaching back to the nineteenth century.[6]

Prior to World War I *akrakyefoɔ* were in a privileged position. Gold Coast historian C. C. Reindorf, himself a product of Basel Mission schools, reported in 1895 that middle school leavers had "no difficulty in obtaining an apprenticeship in a mercantile business or in the Government office." Reindorf commented that these young men reflected the "honour of our schools, but not so much on our congregations."[7] He was concerned about *akrakyefoɔ* who did not live up to missionary expectations about masculinity. Missionary reports increasingly criticized "fallen" *akrakyefoɔ* for their extramarital affairs, for excess in dressing habits, and for religious shortcomings, like seeking advice at an *aberewa* shrine, a common anti-witchcraft cult. Although enrollment in boarding schools grew, most graduates looked for well-paid employment in government offices and European trading houses, and not for work as teachers and catechists. The economic opportunities created by the cocoa industry had led to their secularization.[8]

In 1917 Emil Nothwang gave an overview of the professional career of *akrakyefoɔ* trained at the Akropong Boarding School over the last fifty years. He calculated that, of fifteen hundred graduates, "hundreds found employment with the colonial government or with trading companies, and about five hundred entered into the seminary preparing them as teachers out of which 28 were ordained as pastors."[9] Some graduates were also hired as clerks in such distant places as the Congo and Sierra Leone. *Akrakyefoɔ*'s favorable economic position changed during the crisis of World War I and worsened in the 1920s, despite the postwar economic recovery. In 1925 Governor Guggisberg deplored that the Gold Coast produced annually four thousand Standard VII leavers, most of them "only suitable for clerical work," while merely five hundred clerks were required "to replace the normal wastage."[10] Educators proposed policies to redirect the curriculum, widening school leavers' vocational qualifications. Following the Depression, *akrakyefoɔ*'s employment options further declined. After the Second World War the Watson Commission considered school leavers' unemployment and lack of educational opportunities as one of the reasons for the political disturbances of 1948. By the 1950s, although the self-rule government of Kwame Nkrumah implemented an "Africanization" of the civil service, nevertheless not all *akrakyefoɔ* were assured of clerical employment. Their ranks continued to swell because of growing school enrollment.[11]

Akrakyefoɔ claimed a special socioeconomic status. In the 1930s Standard VII certificate holders looked for wage labor appropriate to a literate *krakye*. In middle school parlance, they entered "the world."[12] But during the post-Depression years they faced difficulties securing clerical employment with the government, with banks, or as a shopkeeper for a European company. Some *akrakyefoɔ* sought to join the police force, the railway or sanitation department, or the less secure job of a tribunal registrar. All were positions that required literacy, preferably a Standard VII certificate.[13] Others looked for employment as teachers; only a few continued their education at a secondary school or a teacher training college. All these jobs, except primary school teaching and some clerical work, were reserved for men since women's education emphasized domestic skills. In becoming a *krakye* men looked for professional careers that were privileged compared to women's options in wage labor. Colonial education was "reinforcing" women's "subordinate position."[14] In newspapers, literate men expressed an ambivalence about women "taking the place of men as clerks," and warned about "the competition for employment between the sexes."[15] In her women's column, "Marjorie Mensah" (pseud., Mabel Dove) noted that "many a girl would like to take up a business course in book-keeping, shorthand and such subjects that would engage her to get a job and earn good money."[16]

Joining the ranks of the *akrakyefoɔ* meant a new notion of masculinity. Because they became part of a migrant social group while remaining connected to their home communities and extended families, they were subjected to conflicting expectations. They had to redefine their selves within work environments and create a professional identity that was also meaningful to their wider network of social relations. Many of these middle figures left a paper trail; a "tin-trunk literacy" that has been overlooked by Africa's social historians.[17] Trader E. K. Addo and teacher-catechist A. K. Boakye Yiadom wrote about their experiences as clerk and storekeeper during the 1930s.

Akrakyefoɔ and Writing

In 1935 the *Gold Coast Times* published a letter deploring the "Plight of the African Mercantile Clerk." The writer, himself a clerk, referred to *akrakyefoɔ* working for European firms like the United Africa Company (UAC), the United Trading Company (UTC), or the Société Commerciale de L'Ouest Africain, whose stores were run by an African manager. Unlike clerks in the African civil service or working for a bank, mercantile clerks had a "precarious existence" without a standard grading system, regular increments to salaries, or security for old age. Rather, their wages fluctuated "like shares on the Stock Exchange." In the "slump" of the 1930s, mercantile firms were "understaffed and their overworked clerks underpaid," while European employees departed for their vacation "with clockwork precision."[18] Still, many school leavers with aspirations as *akrakyefoɔ* envisioned themselves in clerical employment or as shopkeepers.

Graduating from the Abetifi Boys Boarding School in 1935, Boakye Yiadom wrote in his "Autobiography: My Own Life" that he now had entered the "life of the world." He traveled to the Central Province where his *wɔfanom* (uncles) Kwadwo Opong and Kwabena Mensa Opong worked as tailors. He hoped they would provide the capital of at least one hundred pounds to become a store manager for one of the European firms. Failing to receive support, Boakye Yiadom went to stay with his mother, Ntoriwa, who had married Kwasi Obeng, the *Ɔdekuro* (headman) of Kurofa. As a "well-known cocoa broker," the stepfather introduced him to W. F. Neizer, a cocoa buyer for UAC, "the commercial colossus of West Africa," in nearby Konongo.[19] After examining his arithmetic skills, Neizer presented Boakye Yiadom to the *oburoni panyin*, the senior European. Having attended "a good school," he was hired as Neizer's second assistant cocoa-weighing clerk in 1936. The UAC manager considered Abetifi a "good town" because of its Presbyterian schools; Boakye Yiadom's Standard VII certificate counted as reliable qualification for clerical employment.[20] Following standard procedure, Boakye Yiadom did not receive any pay during the first year of training. By 1937 he earned one pound a month, increased by ten shillings in each of the following three years. This salary enabled him to buy some furniture, as well as shoes, clothes, a hat, toiletries, and writing paper. Such goods, reflecting new needs, aided in the public display of his *krakye* status.[21]

Boakye Yiadom began exchanging greeting cards with his literate male friends, clerks and teachers, some of them relatives. In 1938 he had his photograph taken in Konongo; part of it was inserted into a Christmas card (see Fig. 4.1). The card, decorated with large roses, depicts in a European aesthetic a three-quarter portrait of Boakye Yiadom wearing the *krakye* "uniform," white pleated shirt, light-colored jacket, and dark bow tie. His carefully groomed hair is parted above the left temple, a style then popular among *akrakyefoɔ*. The card, addressed to his "beloved younger father Mr. D. B. Bruce Preko" of Abetifi, a former classmate, featured the poem "Christmas Thoughts":

> One time is as good [as] another
> By sending to friendship's call
> And yet if you think about it
> This time is the best of all![22]

Understanding the card's symbolic language required some knowledge of popular European iconography. The horseshoe that framed Boakye Yiadom's head referred to good luck, the roses to friendship, renewed at Christmas time. The exchange of greeting cards among *akrakyefoɔ* became a marker of their membership in this social group. Sending them to extended family members, such as Bruce Breko, served as "kin work" to maintain relations between literate men. The exchange of holiday cards by *akrakyefoɔ* in 1930s Ghana was the reverse of the "female world of cards" of the late-twentieth-century United States.[23]

Writing cards and letters, or keeping a diary, was common among *akrakyefoɔ*. Boakye Yiadom started his first diary together with classmates, including Bruce Breko, at the Abetifi Boarding School.[24] E. K. Addo kept a written record of his work as a storekeeper. Unlike most *akrakyefoɔ*, Addo acquired literacy outside the classroom. In 1928 his older brother, J. K. Kwakye, had set him up as a store manager in Nsawam, a market center twenty miles north of Accra. Influenced by J.E.K. Aggrey's motto that "any person who wishes to learn can learn," Addo sought help from Achimota teachers to improve his written and oral English skills.[25] They frequently came to his Nsawam home at weekends or during holidays. As part of writing exercises, Addo began keeping a journal. Among his papers are two diaries covering the years from 1932 to 1934; one appears to be a draft of the other. Addo followed a practice introduced by Pietist missionaries and popularized in Presbyterian schools. It resembled the "station diaries" kept by Presbyterian pastors and catechists. Addo wrote daily entries of at least a few lines, at times covering more than one page. Unlike the Pietist model, his entries were seldom introspective but rather served as a logbook. They

Fig. 4.1. A. K. Boakye Yiadom as *krakye*, Kanongo, December 12, 1938. Photo, A. K. Boakye Yiadom's Papers (Abetifi, Ghana).

provide a rare window into the everyday life of a storekeeper during the Depression and show how Addo embraced Presbyterian masculinity.[26]

The diaries document Addo's activities as a trader. From Monday through Saturday he opened his shop as early as 6:40 A.M. and closed after 5 P.M., "when the sun sank to the horizon." The early 1930s were difficult years. Complaining about "very poor sales," Addo was greatly concerned about "the world depression."[27] Since cocoa prices had plummeted, not reaching the level of 1930 until 1946, his Nsawam clients, all connected to the cocoa industry, suffered. Addo considered his sales "fair" as long as he made two pounds a day. They picked up toward the end of the year, when cocoa farmers started selling their crops; they peaked in the days before Christmas, reaching twenty pounds in December 1933.[28] Addo shared profits with brother Kwakye who had provided the initial capital. Seeking to improve returns, Addo hired two itinerant traders from Kwawu; one woman, Adjeiwah, was particularly successful.[29] Addo had a keen ability to acquire items not available from his competitors. When he made six pounds, he attributed this to offering "nice clothes that people desire most." Still, sales remained dependent on local economics *and* social activities. One Saturday he noted that "the only goods sold were collars and ties because dance is to take place tonight."[30] Addo did not attend the dance but went straight to his residence. In the evening he usually "stayed indoor to study." Unlike other *akrakyefoɔ,* who frequented the recently opened "Mikado Picture House" at Nsawam, Addo disapproved of the moral content of movies. The only leisure activity he permitted himself was watching a boxing tournament, "occasionally" staged at the Mikado.[31]

Addo's devotion to the Presbyterian Church is well represented in the diaries. He attended church service on Sundays, sometimes twice, and then recorded the Bible texts and commented on the preaching, which was usually in Ga for Nsawam's multiethnic congregation. Echoing the proverb *"Asɛm pa tiawa"* (A good message is brief), Addo preferred short sermons, which "did not waste time of the listeners" but "inspired hearts." He participated in preaching journeys and joined the Easter Monday picnic. When traveling, Addo attended Presbyterian services. On a journey to Kumase, he not only praised a "very short and inspiring" sermon by Rev. I. Bellon of the Basel Mission but visited Mmofraturo, the new Methodist kindergarten and women's training college, which prepared students for Christian motherhood and womanhood. Impressed by this school, Addo attended his first Methodist service the following Sunday. Reverend Acheampong "preached very well," invoking metaphors like "Bible is best [*sic*] than Gold and Silver." Still, Addo remained faithful to the Presbyterian Church.[32]

The entries permit a reconstruction of Addo's perception of *akrakyefoɔ* and his network with other "gentlemen" and "scholars." After "Dr. Aggrey Day Celebrations," Addo observed that contributions were "very, very poor," even though the local pastor acted as "introducer." Addo explained: "Many gentlemen were presented but because of the world depression and scarcity of money they could not do their duty." They failed to donate according to their rank. On a Sunday he strolled with two teachers, "Messrs. Dako &

Wiredu," through Nsawam. By the late afternoon, "Mr. Wiredu went out for Tennis at the Teachers' Tennis court" without Addo.[33] His records reflect the increased mobility of *akrakyefoɔ* who maintained relationships between one another at a distance. When his friends traveled south, Addo entertained them for one hour while their trains stopped at Nsawam. On his own journeys he stayed with them. In Agogo, where the Basel Mission had just opened a hospital and girls' school, Addo spent an evening in the company of three *akrakyefoɔ* at the house of a teacher, Ntim. For five hours they "debated on many subjects concerning our country." One might have been public health. The following day Addo portrayed Agogo as the "the filthiest town of the colony." This characterization corresponded to press reports about sanitation, hygiene, and town improvements during the 1930s.[34]

The outbreak of World War II had an impact on many *akrakyefoɔ*. With the Gold Coast serving as military hub for the Allied war effort, trader Addo saw his business volume rise. In 1944 he managed to return the capital of 150 pounds to brother Kwakye. The latter declared in a written statement that his "heirs, executors, administrators, or assigns have no claim or interest whatsoever in the above named business."[35] Having established himself an independent businessman, Addo aspired to big-man status. Others like Ɔkyeame Kwabena Asante and Boakye Yiadom enlisted in the Gold Coast Regiment (GCR). Becoming soldiers affected their sense of self; the uniform strengthened their *krakye* identity since literacy qualified them for certain positions in the regiment.

Akrakyefoɔ in Uniform

With the beginning of World War II the GCR of the Royal West African Frontier Force aggressively recruited soldiers to secure the borders in West Africa and to fight for the empire. By the end of the war more than seventy thousand men had served in the GCR in various theaters of combat: against Italians in East Africa, as laborers in North Africa, and in the Burma campaign of 1943–45. The prewar army had been a small infantry force consisting of recruits from the Northern Territories, some of them from the neighboring French colonies, led by British officers. Very few southerners had joined the army, taking positions as clerks and signalers. In 1940 the army was more equipped with technical services and required a larger number of clerks and skilled artisans. Extending recruiting to the Colony and Ashanti, the GCR looked for volunteers to fill the ranks of technical corps like "Signalers, Medical, Ordnance, Pioneers, and a Service Corps for transport and supply work."[36] Male school leavers looked to the army for adventure. In June 1941 the colonial government passed the Compulsory Service Ordinance, initially applied to the Colony but extended to Ashanti and the Northern Territories in the following year. Forced conscription was common, and drivers and artisans frequently resisted, especially throughout southern Ghana. Among the 340 ex-servicemen interviewed by Wendell Hollbrook, 27 percent had entered the GCR "as a result of indirect coercion or direct conscription."[37] Yet the men I talked with had volunteered. Ɔkyeame Asante recalled, "I joined the army on my own initiative. I was not forced into it."[38]

When Ɔkyeame Asante enlisted with the GCR in September 1939 he responded to an old desire. As a child, seeking to emulate his *wɔfa* who had fought in East Africa during World War I, Asante proclaimed, "When I finish school I want to go to the army." After learning about signaling for six months, Asante became a "wireless operator" (radio engineer). Reminiscing about his service, he mentioned exact dates as if they were not only recorded in his military papers but imprinted in his memory:

> 1941, I went to Gambia. I left Gambia June 17, 1941, and I went to Sierra Leone and Nigeria. On November 18, 1941, I returned to Ghana. From Ghana, I went back to Nigeria, from Nigeria I went to Burma. So in Ghana I did not stay long.

In Burma Asante participated in combat against the Japanese for "three years and seven months," holding two types of equipment: "the wireless on my back, the gun in my hand." Asked about suffering, he quipped, "it was no joke."[39]

Attracted to uniforms, Boakye Yiadom also fulfilled a dream. In middle school he told teachers and friends about his desire to become a soldier. He had "two aims": he "wanted to be a soldier" and "to be called master [head teacher]."[40] In January 1940, when a train filled with GCR soldiers stopped on its route from Accra to Kumase in Konongo, Boakye Yiadom closely observed the spectacle.

> My house was very near the railway station, so I went there to watch them. The train waited there for about thirty minutes, and they made a parade at the railway station . . . in Konongo, wishing to get more soldiers. Every big station they stopped for about thirty minutes and then they paraded. So I watched them, that parade. They were blowing their whistles, singing, marching, then I said, well, I will go to the soldiers, too.

Joining the army, Boakye Yiadom made a break with three responsibilities: his employment, his marriage, and his engagement with the emerging Presbyterian Church of Konongo. According to "My Own Life," leaving his job for UAC came as a great relief. He noted that "owing to the hard and strict discipline of my master" he was more than willing to quit his clerical work. He was living with his customary wife from Kurofa, Yaa Ntiri Frempomoah, who had borne his first child in 1936.

> So I came home and made all my preparations. During that time I was staying with this woman, Yaw Obeng's mother, so I told her to go to Kurofa and go to collect some food. I did not tell her that I wanted to join the army, otherwise she would [have] cried and [not] let me go. So I told her to go to Kurofa and collect some food stuff and come [back]. She went there on the 17th of January, 1940.

As in Okyeame Asante's case, the exact dates are ingrained in his recollections:

> So on the eighteenth I made all the preparations in my room and put them there and I locked the room. I wrote a letter on the table, and I wrote another letter to the house owner, so when my wife comes, he can tell her I had gone to Kumase to the army and I would not come back. So on the eighteenth, I left for Kumase. On the nineteenth, we were taken to the senior officer, the commanding officer of the army, and we were sworn in. So, I wrote another letter to my wife that she should marry, because I was going overseas. That's all. I did not come until we were [discharged]. . . . So, it came to me as a man going to the front to fight. So it was in my power to go, it came to me as a dream.[41]

Boakye Yiadom was quite willing to exchange his commitment toward wife and child for the life of a soldier. He was driven, at least in his memories, by a romantic notion of going to war in order to prove his masculinity, his bravery as a warrior in the all-male environment of the GCR. It meant living his boyhood fantasy. There was no room for marriage in this endeavor.

In making the transition from a weighing clerk to a GCR signaler, Boakye Yiadom acted as a *krakye* and wrote letters. This allowed him to communicate with his wife and landlord without directly confronting them. Instead, the literate landlord was to read the letter to Boakye Yiadom's illiterate wife, informing her that he had decided to leave the marriage. In this communication the landlord, as the interlocutor, became the crucial link. If a translation from English into Twi was required, would he elaborate certain parts or omit a section? Although Boakye Yiadom had acquired literacy and distinguished himself by using it professionally, his letter to his wife still went through the filter of orality.[42] This practice of writing explains Boakye Yiadom's surprising recollection of dates. He *wrote* them, first composing letters, then recording them in "My Own Life," rewritten in 1946, and finally, some fifty years later, reminiscing about military service in his short autobiography, "My Life History." Being a *krakye* altered his sense of time. Certain events did not happen in some distant past but could be located as specific instances on the time line of his life. These moments, connected to a precise date, were recalled and contextualized with other events. In retrospect, Boakye Yiadom emphasized his missionary zeal for the Presbyterian Church, helping to found a congregation in Konongo. Curious about his writing habits, I inquired whether the Church also received a letter.

> BY: No, [I left] without saying anything to the mission, because they were not paying me. . . . So I went without their knowledge. One day they heard that their missionary had gone to the army. The one they got [as replacement], came from Abetifi, this man, Mr. Donko. . . .
> SM: When you left did they blame you?
> BY: No, no one blamed me. Because I was establishing the church, I was caring for the church for five years. So if I go, well, another person will come to control the church.

Since there was no employment, Boakye Yiadom did not feel obliged to inform the church authorities. His relation with the UAC was different. In Kumase, dressed up in his new uniform, he informed his boss, Mr. Neizer.[43] Despite his enthusiasm for the male world of the military, Boakye Yiadom failed to become a hero on battlefields in faraway countries. After six months of basic training, divided between Kumase and Accra, Boakye Yiadom qualified as a signaler.[44] Three months later he was discharged because of a suspicion of tuberculosis. Although rejection on medical grounds was common, the sudden end of his military career came as a disappointment. In his second autobiography, "My Life History," he did not indicate any reason for leaving the GCR but emphasized that he had been decorated and extended the duration of his service to more than two years. His love for uniforms was later fulfilled by his career as a boy scout leader.[45]

Serving in colonial armies had gendered implications. World War II veterans in Mali developed an "alternate masculinity which combined local ideas with those learned from other African and French cultures such as command of linguistic and technological skills and access to consumer goods," as Gregory Mann has suggested. Upon returning, they asserted a particular masculine identity by promenading their uniforms, exploiting the colonial state's patronage, and emphasizing "their differences from civilian peers."[46] The same applies to Gold Coast veterans like Ɔkyeame Asante who served abroad. Their identity as ex-servicemen became crucial in their sense of self. In his old age Asante not only received a small military pension but was widely known as an ex-serviceman. When I took his photograph, he dressed in his old uniform with decorations (see Fig. 4.2). Yet even Boakye Yiadom with his limited time of service claimed membership in this group. In 1948 he unsuccessfully applied for a program offering employment and teachers' training to two hundred ex-servicemen.[47] When he attended St. Andrews' Presbyterian Training College, he and other ex-servicemen demonstrated their group identity by sitting for a photograph with their British principal, a former army chaplain, in uniform. By 1953 his teacher's salary was slightly adjusted as a result of his "275 days of War Service." Recently, in his request for field ordination, he listed his military service as an important qualification.[48]

Kofi Ankoma, who had become a store clerk in the mid-1930s, was also drawn to male society and uniforms. Although his business was profitable and "easy," he was not happy. Determined to join the police or military, Ankoma secretly left the career path laid out by his *wɔfa* Kwadwo Adofo. In 1942, under a false pretense, Ankoma traveled to Accra to enlist with the Gold Coast police. A *krakye* friend provided guidance.

> The only man I met in Accra was an ex-policeman from Mpraeso here, Mr. Donko. When he met me, he asked: "Eh, my friend, what do you want here?" . . . I told him: "Well, I want to be a policeman." "Have you got your [school] certificates? Alright, let's go home." We sat down, and he gave me lines to write on my application. I wrote the application in my handwriting, attached the certificate [and took it] to the police depot. They were tossing me up and down, up and down, up and down before I [enlisted on] August 30, 1942.[49]

Following medical examinations, recruits needed to purchase goods like a cutlass, blankets, cloth, knickers, and a mat. For six months Ankoma was in training at the Accra police depot, located at the city's edge. This spacious facility, which had opened in 1928, contributed to the "attractiveness of the Police as a career."[50] Training included rifle drill and firing and "some inculcation of nationhood"; instructors "stressed the need for impartiality."[51] Passing "small tests," Ankoma was sworn in.

> You swear, that you stand in the name of God, of everybody, be a policeman, trustworthy. When they tell you to go to any place, you go, whether dark, whether rain or shine. . . . Then we were transported to Cape Coast.

While recruits received four and a half pounds per month, Ankoma's pay rose to five pounds, five shillings, upon leaving the depot. Although he did

Fig. 4.2. Ɔkyeame Kwabena Asante as "an ex-serviceman," Pepease, 1993.
Photo, R. Lane Clark.

not earn more than a storekeeper, his income was more consistent. Since the police housed its ranks and permitted one wife, Ankoma wrote his spouse to join him. She reported at a Kwawu police station and traveled to Cape Coast "on government expense." Yet, unlike his colleagues, Ankoma did not allow her to stay in the barracks but rented her a room in town. He explained:

> Because the police wives . . . create havoc, troubles between wives and husbands. Somebody will go and tell her . . . "My husband gave me about one pound to go to the market," whilst she has only received, say, five shillings. That creates big havoc, so when my wife is staying away from the police station, nobody would know whether I gave her money to go to the market, or I did not give money.

Ankoma sent Kwadwo Adofo a letter, instead of informing the *wɔfa* personally. When he joined the force, he challenged the authority of the most senior man of his *abusua*. Adofo was "very, very sorry." He died the following year, succeeded by his younger brother Kwame Asiama.[52]

Literacy was crucial in Ankoma's new occupation; he was assigned a clerical position as "station orderly." Literacy organized the force into two divisions: the illiterate escort police and the general police, the latter limited to Standard VII certificate holders.

> KA: As a policeman, formerly with the black uniform, you know how to read and write. [The escort police] with khaki, with patis [bandages wrapped around the calves of the leg], he does not know his left from right. That's all, bring this man, they usually go to night duties.
> SM: So the escort police did easy things where there was no decision making?
> KA: Yes, "Go to this bungalow, go and guard the bungalow." When you go there and you are fortunate, you will be exchanged, if you are not fortunate, you stand there from six to six in the morning.
> SM: And a regular constable would not have to do such work, he is too educated?
> KA: Not at all, you be in charge of writing, taking statements, reporting all such reports that come.[53]

Contemporary observers emphasized additional distinctions. General policemen wore boots and came from the south. Easily spotted in their red fez, escort policemen marched barefoot and were "natives of the Northern Territories or other Hausa-speaking tribes."[54] They were, according to the colonial ethnic stereotype, more martial and formed "the bulk of the mobile reserve unit."[55]

Serving as a policeman outside Kwawu, Ankoma remained concerned about his reputation and prospective status of senior masculinity in his home-town.

> I wanted to be a *good policeman*. Because a good policeman, that is a man who has served without any trouble in the police force and without any trouble when he comes back to his civilian site. [Upon achieving this] people will give you a good name [and say], "This man is good; this man is good." But when you come back from force, either from army or police, and you start to molest people, well, you create a bad name for yourself and the family.

Ankoma did not always reveal his profession during hometown visits:

> If you do not wear uniform, let the thinking [happen] in your mind, don't tell anybody that you are a policeman. If somebody knows you at all, and you see him, just make a sign (makes hush sound) for him that he will not disclose your identity, [then] you are a good policeman.

Still, Ankoma's new identity became a source of pride. He cherished a special quality among those who had served in uniform,

> When I see people who have come back from force, and you see them very quiet, but they have got something in their mind, you see. He will not tell you, "I am a policeman, or an ex-serviceman," . . . no, no, no. You have to be very quiet. If somebody wants to tell you something, you have to sit down quietly and listen to what he will say. Well, good or bad, if you know you can give him some answer, you reply, if you don't, then you go away.[56]

This notion of keeping a deeper truth hidden was at the core of Ankoma's understanding of his alternate masculinity as a man in uniform. His tenure in the Gold Coast police not only strengthened his *suban* (character) but redefined his sense of self. This all-male hierarchical organization with its esprit de corps became a key experience in his aspiration for senior mascu-linity. To his chagrin, however, in his view, qualities of modesty and thought-fulness are disappearing among younger generations. Asked about women in the Ghana police force of the 1990s, he welcomed them. He emphasized women's underestimated potential for bravery and cited Yaa Asantewaa who instigated the Asante rebellion against the British in 1900, showing exem-plary leadership after the forced exile of the *Asantehene*.[57] Nevertheless, An-koma recognized a fundamental difference:

> A man has got a higher thinking than a woman, because a man thinks twice. . . . If she wants to fight you, she comes straight to you and fight. But a man will sit down and think, if I fight with this man, and wounds me, or if I wound

him, who is going to be held responsible for that? But a woman, if she gets up, she comes straight to fight you, that's it.[58]

Male and female policemen do not respond identically. Men show more deference of hierarchy and status, even in rage, while women tend to react more impulsively.

Frequent transfer characterized Ankoma's police service. After his clerical position in Cape Coast, he guarded an "aerodrome" during the final years of World War II. The Allied forces had built and upgraded airports across southern Ghana to support fighting in North Africa and the Middle East.[59] Ankoma was briefly stationed in Asikuma and then received a desk job again in Cape Coast, working on criminal investigations. He narrated an episode in which his ability to remain quiet became part of the assignment. When a woman was murdered in Saltpond the police suspected her boyfriend but lacked evidence. "On duty as a detective," Ankoma had to investigate the boyfriend of whom he was given a photograph. Wearing plain clothes, he followed the suspect to Kyebi, the capital of Akyem Abuakwa, and stayed there as a migrant farmworker. Finally, the suspect confessed while drunk and Ankoma had him arrested. To his dismay, he was not adequately compensated. Ankoma remained a first-class constable, slightly above the lowest rank. Promotion depended on seniority and less on merit. All gazetted officers, however, were Europeans. As intermediary figures between colonial employers and their host or hometown communities, *akrakyefoɔ* were exposed to the political tensions during Ghana's nationalist awakening. In 1948, shortly after the "Gold Coast Disturbances," Ankoma quit the force.[60]

Akrakyefoɔ and Politics

Ghana's historians have highlighted the participation of *akrakyefoɔ*, as well as school leavers with less education, in nationalist politics in the interwar and postwar periods. Jarle Simensen explored the challenges by commoners who were organized as Asafo companies (originally for military purposes) and confronted chiefs in rural politics during the 1930s. In Akyem Abuakwa, an "educational sub-elite," consisting of primary school leavers employed as traders, teachers, and clerks, "played a key role as a connecting link between coastal elite and the protesting commoners." The protesters resisted new taxes and the authority of the powerful paramount chief, Nana Ofori Atta I, who directly blamed *akrakyefoɔ* for the unrest.[61] In Kwawu,

Asafo companies demanded constitutional reform. They boycotted native tribunals for eighteen months and destooled the ɔmanhene and his major divisional chief, the Adɔntenhene of Kwawu (chief of Abetifi), in 1931. This uprising was led by the asafoakye (leader) Eugene R. Addow, locally known as Kwame Mossi. A krakye by training, Mossi had worked as a tribunal registrar and wrote about Kwawu history and customs.[62] Between 1939 and 1947 railway workers and miners engaged in a series of successful strikes led by new unions that demanded higher wages and better working conditions. School leavers who had opted out of clerical jobs were crucial in this resistance. The Labor Railway Union was "the creation of a dynamic, elementary-school educated, labor elite of artisans"; they were mainly literate Fantes who looked to skilled technical work as "a suitable alternative to clerical work."[63] The Gold Coast Miners Employees Union was established by "literate artisans" from the Colony. Its president, J. N. Sam, was "a Fante carpenter"; its secretary, S. M. Bissah, "an Nzima electrician." Both had previously worked as teachers.[64] Yet, the akrakyefoɔ discussed here were more ambivalent toward these political struggles. Their attitudes resemble those of clerical railway workers who, even after unionization in the early 1940s, continued "to display a marked moderation, even humility, in their approach to grievance representation."[65]

E. K. Addo occasionally referred to political events in his diaries. When the Asafo leader Kwame Mossi had to appear in the High Court of Accra in a case against the Obo chief Kwasi Nyarko, Addo went "with intention to make an appeal for his case." At the time he must have felt sympathy for this fellow krakye, although in retrospect he considered Mossi an "agitator."[66] In 1934 Addo attended a meeting at the Mikado, Nsawam, to discuss the "condition of the proposing Bills of the Gold Coast Government." Choosing religion over politics, he left the meeting early for a Presbyterian Church service and "did not know how they concluded the matter." Quite likely the Mikado gathering focused on the controversial Criminal Law (Amendment) Act, locally called the Sedition Bill, pushed through the Legislative Council by the governor in 1934 and widely discussed in the press.[67] As a migrant labor force, akrakyefoɔ organized themselves according to their ethnicity and hometowns. On a Sunday, Addo traveled to Suhum to participate in a gathering "in regards to Kwawu State Scholar to be discussing with Scholars of Mpraeso." Again, he rushed off "to attend the Lord's Supper in the evening." In the 1940s, influenced by the nationalist movement, such scholars' organizations and literary clubs became increasingly politicized. Addo was supportive of the United Gold Coast Convention (UGCC) and at times participated in their activities.[68]

During Boakye Yiadom's clerical employment, the cocoa industry was brought to a standstill by the "cocoa hold-up" of 1937–38. Cocoa producers, in a coalition with brokers and chiefs, challenged a buying agreement among major European firms. The hold-up was a reaction by cocoa producers and their allies to falling prices which they ascribed to market manipulation by the large buying firms. Farmers sought to improve the conditions under which their product was sold. The hold-up, accompanied by a boycott of European goods, was so successful that Governor Arnold Hodson asked the secretary of state for the colonies, W.G.A. Ormsby-Gore, to appoint an independent commission to inquire into the marketing of cocoa and the grievances that had led to the hold-up. The commission, chaired by William Nowell, found evidence that local African brokers had engaged in "trade abuses." The report stated that the agreement between European companies hindered "competitive buying" and infringed on the "legitimate interests of the sellers." Subsequently the commission suggested a "drastic" reorganization of cocoa marketing by the establishment of a farmers' cooperative to be charged with marketing the entire cocoa crop of the Gold Coast. Although the Nowell proposal was never implemented because of the outbreak of World War II, its recommendations set a precedent in official thinking about state regulation of the economy.[69]

This is not the place to reevaluate the cocoa hold-up and its impact on various social groups. Yet, Boakye Yiadom's memory of the event reveals a great deal about his identity as *krakye*. He took an intermediary position between cocoa farmers and buying companies. Although he expressed a certain admiration for the "brave" farmers who were destroying their crop, he did not share their cause. Rather, he was unaware of their agenda.

> SM: Did you understand why the farmers stopped bringing the cocoa?
> BY: No, *we* did not understand.

Here he spoke for the group of *akrakyefoɔ* employed by the buying firms. Then, changing perspective, he explained the farmers' strategies:

> But what the farmers would do, they would go to a meeting, a special meeting, and write resolutions to the cocoa factors, and through the factors to the cocoa head office of UTC, UAC, Ollivant and the cocoa buyers that . . . cocoa should be increased to this price. If we . . . , you don't do that, say in two or three months, but the farmers did not do that. They just said, "We don't want to sell our cocoa."

Assessing the attitudes and power of Europeans, Boakye Yiadom described why the producers were forced into the hold-up:

[The farmers] said: "We are not bringing you our cocoa." So the farmers . . . the factors, the agents of the cocoa dealers, they did not mind, they [just] kept it.

In Boakye Yiadom's analysis, the cocoa farmers lost the struggle for higher prices since they were stuck with their crop that spoiled.

So [the farmers] came forward to sell their cocoa; they got about one shilling and a sixpence for a load of cocoa . . . [prior to the boycott] they were paid about five shillings.

The cocoa farmers had also called a boycott of imported European goods. Boakye Yiadom recalled respecting the boycott but added that he had done so more out of necessity than political solidarity, since he himself "had no money" at the time.[70] Although Boakye Yiadom's oral recollections were vivid about how the hold-up placed him in the middle, he did not mention the disruptions caused by the cocoa hold-up in his diary-like autobiography "My Own Life." During the late 1930s and early 1940s the farmers' political action was not his principal concern, or at least he did not feel compelled to write about it. Instead, he noted his "grand luck" in receiving a salary increase and, the following year, a promotion to first assistant weighing clerk.[71] Perhaps the silence in "My Own Life" concealed his tension over conflicting loyalties. He was close to cocoa producers, since many members of his *abusua* made their living in the cocoa industry, and he was impressed by the farmers' bravery in resisting the power of European firms. Later in the conversation he explicitly identified bravery as an important male virtue.[72] Yet, as a *krakye*, he had moved away from farm labor. He depended on his employers' goodwill and on an uninterrupted cocoa industry in order to receive his salary and consume material goods appropriate to the habitus of a *krakye*. This discrepancy between Boakye Yiadom's autobiography and his later accounts points to internal conflicts, uneven layers of his subjectivity that were crucial in organizing his life and negotiating his *krakye* identity.[73]

Commenting about the political violence of 1948, Ankoma also took a middle position, despite his misgivings about the racial discrimination he encountered in the Gold Coast police. On February 28, 1948, members of the Ex-servicemen's Union and their supporters gathered for a demonstration in Accra to petition the governor about unfulfilled financial promises and a lack of employment opportunities. The protesters changed the prescribed

route and attempted to march to Christiansborg Castle, the governor's residence. They were halted by a police detachment, and a tumult broke out.
Police Superintendent C. H. Imray opened fire, killing two protesters and
wounding four or five others. Following these shootings a crowd gathered
in the center of Accra, set UAC offices on fire, and looted European stores
leading to more deaths and injuries. The next day protesters opened the
gates of Ussher Fort and released prisoners. From Accra, the riots spread to
commercial centers across the Colony and Ashanti.[74] Declaring a state of
emergency, the government arrested the UGCC leaders. In April a commission arrived from England, chaired by Aiken Watson, "to enquire into
and report on the recent disturbances." The Watson Commission conducted
its investigation publicly, followed closely by the press.[75] In its influential
report, the commission stipulated constitutional reforms that led to self-rule
within less than three years. Identifying the "underlying causes" of the crisis,
the commission noted political, economic, and social factors. Foremost, the
commission listed the ex-servicemen's "political frustration," the slow pace
of the Africanization of the civil service, the disintegration of chiefly powers,
the impact of India's and Burma's independence, and a "general suspicion of
Government." As economic factors, the commission mentioned high prices
for imported goods, the campaign of cutting cocoa trees affected by swollen
shoots, the Cocoa Marketing Board's control over reserves, and the lack of
government initiatives that promote "development" in industry and agriculture to facilitate local consumption. Finally, the commission identified as
social causes limited educational opportunities, a housing shortage, an increasingly "landless peasantry," and the government's inadequate legal powers
in dealing with the nationalist movement.[76]

Ankoma was not directly involved in the events of 1948. Still, his recollections show his ambiguous position as a former member of the police
force. He absolved both the ex-servicemen and the police from any wrong-
doing:

> The thing was, it was not the fault of the soldiers who made this demonstration;
> and it was not the fault of the officer who gave the command to cause trouble.
> They [police] did not understand what the soldiers were doing at the dem-
> onstration. They [soldiers] were fighting for their rights that after the war they
> should be given something. But they never, nobody gave them the right route
> to pass. And the police force who shot these people, he [the officer] did not
> get any good information that these people were fighting for their rights. They
> were thinking the ex-servicemen, who were rushing to the Castle, [would] do
> some bad things to the governor.

A misunderstanding between the involved parties caused the riots. Ankoma did not foreground the calls for self-government voiced by protesters and elaborated in the published statements of the arrested UGCC leaders. Rather, he emphasized the ex-servicemen's "right" to improve their predicament. Only indirectly did he link the crisis with anticolonial resistance.[77]

Ankoma's account of the 1948 riots, Boakye Yiadom's recollection of the 1937–38 cocoa hold-up, and Addo's diary entries of the early 1930s reveal how some *akrakyefoɔ* took an intermediate position in political struggles. They identified with both sides, Ankoma maintaining his loyalty with the police force while understanding the ex-servicemen's actions, and Boakye Yiadom sympathizing with cocoa farmers and cocoa buyers. Occupying this middle ground did not preclude them from supporting Nkrumah and the Convention People's Party (CPP), founded in 1949. As a teacher at Adumasa, Boakye Yiadom did clerical work for the CPP before enrolling in a training college. Ankoma never lost his admiration of Nkrumah and eagerly defended his record, blaming "his subchiefs" for the 1966 coup.[78] Although Addo was critical of the CPP, he offered transportation during Nkrumah's release from prison. These accounts suggest that school leavers, identified in the nationalist historiography as "youngmen," were a diverse group not speaking in one voice.

Dennis Austin divided Ghana's political players into three categories, "intelligentsia, chiefs, and youngmen," for the 1940s and 1950s. Youngmen included "farmers, petty traders, drivers, artisans, school teachers, clerks, and letter writers—among whom were the growing number of elementary school leavers."[79] Emmanuel Akyeampong distinguishes between "chiefs—and their allied educated elite—and the young men and women," and identifies the "urban young men" as "the only coherent group capable of directing the Accra riots" of 1948.[80] In fact, not all youngmen were political activists, and this category must be disaggregated. Among *akrakyefoɔ*, school leavers with a Standard VII certificate, an individual's perception of the political events depended on his education, his religious affiliation, and especially on his place as *krakye* within colonial society. If he had found employment, he tended to move toward the middle, thereby protecting his own status and distancing himself from the unemployed and from those with less prestigious jobs. This intermediate space was the site for negotiating conflicting expectations from European police officers and employers, as well as from fellow policemen, *abusua* members, and political activists like the leaders of new mass parties. Moreover, as middle figures, similar to the ones studied by Nancy Hunt in the Belgian Congo, members of the *akrakyefoɔ* could evolve and maintain contradictory positions, resulting in shifting and unstable alliances.[81]

Since the 1920s, the colonial government was concerned with different groups of *akrakyefoɔ*: clerical staff, tribunal registrars, and particularly teachers. Officials developed strategies to professionalize their work by establishing rules and channels of control.[82] Teachers in government and government-assisted schools were targets of campaigns that sought to alter their professional status as well as their subjectivity and understanding of masculinity.

Teachers

As part of the 1925 Education Ordinance, a central register and improved salaries strengthened teachers' professionalization and prestige. Although the number of trained teachers increased during the 1930s, still only a minority of primary school teachers were certified college graduates. The vast majority of trained teachers were men; female teachers worked in co-educational primary schools and the few girls' middle schools.[83] *Akrakyefoɔ* with a Standard VII certificate could seek employment as pupil teachers in village schools, most of them run by mission churches. Becoming a teacher distinctively altered their identities. Boakye Yiadom, after his discharge from the army in late 1941, was hired as a pupil teacher, first for the African Universal Church in Abetifi, and then for the Presbyterian church outside his hometown. Leaving training college, graduates like Rev. E.K.O. Asante and E. F. Opusuo were posted to small villages. Based on their performance they hoped for promotion to teach in larger towns or at a middle school, segregated by sex. It was considered a "unique honour and privilege for a teacher to be appointed to the staff of a middle boarding school."[84] An uncertified teacher like Boakye Yiadom did not have these options.

Within small rural communities, teachers were in an ambivalent position. Because of their literacy, they enjoyed status while being scrutinized by villagers. Remaining clear outsiders, they represented church authorities and often acted as mediators, "enabling traditional community elders to communicate with or gain access to external sources of wealth and power," as Sara Berry noted for southwestern Nigeria.[85] The Colonial Office identified male teachers as the "chief agency through which new ideas" reached villagers.[86] The *Gold Coast Teacher's Journal*, published by the Department of Education, featured articles on public health promoting hygiene and sanitation, as well as on sports and village mobilization.[87] In the waning years of colonial rule, education officer Francis Austin reflected on the relation between teacher and villagers. He noted that the latter considered the former as "raised above them," expecting "inspiration and guidance." The teacher became the "center of attraction"; his comings and goings were "closely watched" and "private comments [were] passed on him." Austin urged readers to renovate dwellings, clean their compounds daily, and plant "flowers and shrubs." Teachers should induce "young men" to form sport clubs and influence chiefs to improve public health, by maintaining "a small clean market," by digging and maintaining "a pit latrine suitable for both men and women," and by erecting "a good school." Teachers' unique status is reflected in the village practice of calling them "teacher" in lieu of proper names.[88]

When the interviewed men narrated their experiences, they commented on the pressures and expectations they felt from colonial and missionary authorities, as well as the burden of acting "properly" as male teachers in the perception of the local community. While school inspectors showed up occasionally and unexpectedly, local opinion was always present. Opusuo, who completed training college in 1948, remembered:

> When people saw you drinking, going about drinking, becoming intoxicated, going in bad company, in fact drinking outside, they would not respect you. So if you make friends, you have to make friends who are well behaved, friends whose characters are not questionable.

According to Opusuo there were financial benefits to an unblemished reputation, since villages provided teachers with food.[89]

"Having a good character" (ɔwɔ suban papa) is an important concept in Akan culture. The Ghanaian philosopher Kwame Gyekye stated that suban is expressed in a person's habits and conduct: "deeds and actions" signify his or her status.[90] Teachers, fearing loss of respect, maintained their distance from villagers. Boakye Yiadom had few friends outside the profession. Stationed in a remote Asante village, he felt isolated. In his autobiography he recalled his loneliness after the death of his wife in 1944. He only knew one person in Kumawu, his former teacher from primary school. His personal life did not always match the expectations of village elders and church authorities. After an accusation of adultery, he left the Presbyterian Church and looked for other employment, first teaching in a Catholic school, and then briefly working as a clerk.[91]

In 1950, at the age of forty, Boakye Yiadom returned to the Presbyterian educational unit and enrolled in the recently opened St. Andrews' Presbyterian Teacher Training College. This institution was established to strengthen the qualifications of untrained primary school teachers. Deliberately placed in a "genuinely rural environment," it focused on practical subjects, such as hygiene, gardening, agriculture, and citizenship, besides more academic ones: English, arithmetic, history, geography, religion, and one local language.[92] Although Boakye Yiadom received a government scholarship of twenty-five pounds, he struggled to raise the additional twelve pounds needed for his tuition. He secured some help from his older brother, Ampoma; then, finally, his "College Friend" W. A. Badu granted him a loan. Although his academic performance was rated "below average," he received praise for his interests in "Scouting and Preaching."[93] After two years Boakye Yiadom became a certified B teacher, profiting from the expansion of education in the postwar period. Attending the Presbyterian seminary at Abetifi for one year, he was consecrated with eight other students on December 7, 1952, joining the approximately six hundred Presbyterian teacher-catechists. A dark blue blazer with a patch marked his new status. Basel missionaries in Abetifi considered these English-style uniforms "irksome" but noted their popularity among students.[94]

Reverend Asante, who started teaching in 1935, praised the "good cooperation among teachers" in his first station at Adukron, Akuapem. After training college, teachers had to pass a series of exams in order to be fully certified. Asante found support among his follow teachers.

> We had our own private studies, sometimes invite the school manager [district pastor]. You have to sit for a bar examination, so through that we were able to learn the subjects. . . . You sit for the first examination, second class, then [you sit for the] first class. If you get your first class degree, then you are finished. It is then that you have to prove your work.[95]

Opusuo felt lonely teaching in a Methodist school. Engaging with colleagues, preferably from the same church, reaffirmed a group identity, recreated bonding experiences of the boarding school and training college, and helped in the forming of a teachers' union. Such collective representation was needed in order to be heard by church officials and education inspectors. The inspectors were almost exclusively Europeans until the 1950s.[96]

The Colonial Office emphasized "outside help" from missionaries and government officers to raise up rural communities.[97] Teachers, however, recalled with bitterness how overpaid European inspectors ignored them and declined to pay respect. As college graduates the teachers did not consider themselves inferior to such officials. Clashes with superiors resulted in transfers, hindering promotions.[98] Teachers in government-assisted schools first organized themselves in 1932 when "threatened with a drastic cut in salaries." In 1937 the organization took the name Gold Coast Teachers' Union and included teachers in government schools. The union also demanded unified salary scales and pensions.[99] The Gold Coast Teachers' Union was the only one recognized by the education department and had affiliates representing teachers of various units like Presbyterian and Methodist schools, as well as secondary schools. Yet union participation did not provide protection from inspectors. The narrator in Kofi Awoonor's novel, *This Earth, My Brother,* adeptly observes, "The history of colonial education is one long war between the arrogant white school inspector and the teachers."[100]

The Gold Coast Teacher's Union promoted nationalist ideas. During its second conference at the Palladium Cinema in Accra, speakers urged teachers to brighten pupils' outlook and "foster the spirit of good citizenship." Nigerian journalist Nnamdi Azikiwe impressed the audience the most. He proclaimed that "the time had come for teachers to aid in the intellectual emancipation of the youth of the new Africa." Addressing the current theme of "co-operation," he argued that "Africans had been doing all the 'co-ing' while the other races had been doing the 'operating.'" Teachers' critique of colonial rule became pronounced after Italy's invasion of Ethiopia in 1935.[101] However, only after the 1948 riots did the colonial government become concerned about political activities in schools. In a confidential statement the Central Advisory Committee on Education noted that a "decline in manners and discipline" had been much accelerated because of "political and racial feeling stirred up by propagandists working through teachers in the school." According to the committee, "the deep and widespread demand for self-government" should not be "under discussion," since politics were "for adult citizens" who were not "in *statu pupillari*." The committee suggested the mobilization of "right-disposed people" to work on "small groups of teachers, parents and others." Through informal social contacts, they could initiate discussions to strengthen the "right attitudes" and evoke "a proper understanding of the implications of political teaching in schools and of the dangers to the children."[102] The director of education instructed that each visiting education officer should submit monthly confidential reports on "behavior of pupils but also on the attitude, spirit, conduct example of teachers."[103] In a widely circulated confidential memorandum, education officers were urged "for a renewed vigilance" to protect schools from political infiltration and to work "for the final liquidation of the lamentable, long-established tradition of 'strikes.'"[104] Nongovernment teachers were warned that "continued indiscipline" would lead to "disciplinary action."[105] Even subtle signs of resistance were reported. After visiting the Presbyterian senior primary (middle school) of Pepease, the education officer recorded that the Standard VI teacher had written "tactless remarks" on the blackboard "during a Vernacular lesson." Not without humor, the teacher had noted,

> *Aberante kɔkɔɔno aba. Onipa hunu no aba. The black man is dead.* (The young white person has come. The unimportant person has come. Therefore, the black man is dead [meaning in trouble]).

Assuring his superiors that he had dealt with the culprit "adequately," the officer added, "The school requires watching that this sole instance does not spread."[106]

Unlike the files in colonial archives, stories about clothing were just as prominent as the political events of the late 1940s in teachers' recollections. While education officers enforced a dress code, teachers themselves regarded their clothing as crucial for their professional identity. During the week male teachers wore the obligatory nickers, and on Sundays suit and tie. To wrap themselves in a *ntoma*—a toga-style cloth, the "traditional" outfit of Akan men—was not considered appropriate for a teacher-catechist in church. Professional dress demanded economizing on salaries. Teachers recalled proudly when they had saved enough money to purchase a tailor-made suit. Opusuo, of humble means, ordered his first woolen suit from London "for seventy-five shillings" after several years of teaching.[107]

Dress standards were intensively debated in the Gold Coast as elsewhere in colonial Africa. In 1931, when Ephraim Amu, music master and teacher-catechist at the Presbyterian Training College, preached in "native cloth" at the Akropong chapel, he created a scandal. The Akropong session, the leadership of the local Presbyterian congregation, interpreted Amu's choice of dress as an act of the "devil." The session ruled:

> Since our mentors the Basel missionaries came here in 1828 they did not allow their teachers and ministers to wear native attire in public. It is never done. A church worker—teacher, catechist or minister—should always appear dressed modestly as a servant of God.[108]

This meant, according to Amu's biographer, "invariably . . . a European black woolen or alpaca coat and trousers, black shoes, white shirt and black tie and black hat."[109] Amu was suspended from preaching and urged to reconsider his conduct. Amu had a broader agenda to Africanize the Presbyterian Church. He encouraged his students to exchange their European dress for cloth, hence reorienting themselves in closer alignment with their African origins. In his compositions of choral music, he drew on local harmonies and rhythms. Amu and his students established an African drumming ensemble and performed his songs in Presbyterian churches of Akuapem. After witnessing a graduation at the Akropong training college, trader Addo recorded in his diary that "Mr. Amu and company . . . rendered a very inspiringly African songs [sic] to cheer the new teachers."[110]

Amu's choice of dress led to discussions among other akrakyefoɔ in the Presbyterian Church. Diarist Addo noted that Reverend Damptey had preached against "wearing of native attire" in the Nsawam Presbyterian Church.[111] Then the Amu case became a national affair. In March 1933 Amu and his choir were invited to sing at the residence of the colonial secretary "in the presence of the cream of African society." This private concert, widely reported in the press, was followed by a public performance in the Palladium.[112] Yet the press did not only hail Amu's revival of African music but launched a debate about educated men's appropriate clothing. In an editorial the *Times of West Africa* asked whether Presbyterian Church elders were "race conscious" by expressing a "preference of European dress to the accustomed dress in the Gold Coast worn by our Kings and superior persons."[113] Understanding the conflict in generational terms, a "Young Presbyterian" argued that Amu's decision "to appear in the pulpit in African attire (kente cloth)" did not create "a serious departure from the essence of the Bible or Christian teaching." Rather, he recognized the irony of "White Ministers" endorsing Amu's ideas of "Native Dress," while presbyters (church elders) insisted on European garb, distancing themselves from their own African past. Elders were warned about "pull[ing] down the originality and modernity of youth."[114] For akrakyefoɔ in the Presbyterian Church, "traditional cloth" became an expression of modernity and nationalism. Kwaku Okae wrote that "Jesus did not dress in European or any formal attire."[115] He provocatively asked whether the Christian God would only listen to those dressed like Europeans. Another reader, J. Kwesi Ansah, took a different position. Pointing to the connection between dress and social and professional identities, he opined that every chief donned "his superb native attire suitable to his rank" and every "fetish priest" his "white shirting cloth." Members of the legal profession had "their respective wig and gown" and military, police, customs, and sanitary officials their uniforms. Therefore Amu should "sacrifice his national pride for obedience to his superiors, the Presbyterian Church." Participants in this debate directly linked Amu's choice of dress to notions of gender, status, modernity, and aspirations for nationhood.[116]

Yet the leadership of the Presbyterian Church was prepared to accept neither Amu's African garb nor his Africanized church music. Amu insisted, in a letter, that he was not questioning the authority of the Church. Instead, he argued that his "preaching from the pulpit in African attire" was a "genuine result of the influence of the Spirit of Christ." He did not wish to break with the "glorious and rich inheritance" of his church but to purify and preserve aspects of the African past that were not evil.[117] Since Amu refused to comply, he was sacked from the Presbyterian Training College. His unemployment was brief; the principal of Achimota College invited Amu to join its prestigious faculty. There Amu launched a long academic career as a composer and musicologist. The Amu episode and the interviewed teachers' recollections exemplify Hilde Hendrickson's argument about clothing being "critical in the representation and reproduction of society," clothing differences serving as a "critical link between social groups across space and through time."[118]

Becoming a teacher meant consuming certain goods. Teachers surrounded themselves with material objects that marked their new status. Reverend Asante told how he ordered furniture from a local carpenter at his first station; one chair, still in his possession, "cost five shillings."[119] A lack of furniture was a hardship. Opusuo gave a vivid account of his embarrassment during his first year of teaching. Unlike his wealthier classmates, his family had not set him up properly.

> I went to my station with my trunk and one blanket and one pillow. . . . I had to buy a mat, I did not go with a bed, I did not go with a chair, just my room was empty. . . . Because of that, you see, as a young man, you were interested in women, and women would be visiting young teachers. And so, when I heard a knock (knocks on the table), I just ran out to meet that person so she would not come to see that my room is as poor as if I was not a teacher (laughs). But in those days, teachers were respected, because they appeared to be enlightened people in the society. And so, if a teacher's room is just empty and poor, it is discouraging.

Opusuo explained that only *akrakyefoɔ*—teachers and "scholars, clerks for commercial firms, storekeepers, and people working in government offices"—owned furniture in the late 1940s. A teacher needed "a table, writing desk, cupboard, and chairs, table chairs, and arm chairs." The arrangement of his personal space shaped his identity.[120] Other possessions indicated a teacher's social position. Reverend Asante purchased books as a training college student and acquired a small library on anthropological, historical, and theological subjects. When he was posted to Abetifi in 1937, he commissioned a cabinet with carved doors to protect the books from humidity. Displaying his library in his parlor underlined his literacy and "bookish" knowledge.[121] Boakye Yiadom bought books on teaching, scouting, and theology. He also purchased a gramophone and highlife records by some of the musicians from Kwawu when stationed in Adamsu, Brong-Ahafo, in the early 1960s. Before transistor radios became available, a teacher's gramophone entertained groups of villagers.[122]

Like other *akrakyefoɔ*, teachers were subjected to conflicting expectations. Not only did the education department, church authorities, and local communities stipulate rules of conduct, but teachers' extended families made demands as well.[123] A hometown posting was often problematic. While many teachers used the opportunity to invest in their own future by building a house or starting a cocoa farm, others hoped to improve standards of education in their home communities. Reverend Asante was stationed in Abetifi from 1937 to 1945. Opusuo served in Pepease for four years in the 1950s. Members of Opusuo's *abusua* demanded that his loyalty toward them should take priority over his professional ethics. They requested school fee reductions and could not understand his refusal to guarantee that relatives would write satisfactory exams. Opusuo deplored a lack of respect. Local elders still saw in him the young boy who had just grown up; they denied acknowledging his new role and authority as a head teacher. Opusuo was relieved when posted to another station.[124] In 1951 the education department was concerned about abuses in primary schools. In a confidential memorandum the education director listed a "number of allegations of dishonesty," particularly forms of bribery paid by parents and extortions demanded by teachers: charges for admission and testimonials, "desk fees," and pupils' compulsory work "in teachers' private gardens." While the director sought to persuade parents to refuse paying bribes and to report teachers' illegitimate demands, he was unaware of pressures teachers faced when working in hometowns.[125]

Conclusion

Akrakyefoɔ formed a distinct group that considered itself different, at times superior, from men and women with less or no schooling. The *akrakyefoɔ* enacted this difference in dress, in leisure activities, in the organization of space, in the consumption of goods, and in the practice of reading and writing. Boakye Yiadom and Kofi Ankoma looked for employment during the 1930s, the former as a mercantile clerk and the latter as a storekeeper. Trader Addo managed a store with capital provided by his brother. Upon completing the Presbyterian Training College, Reverend Asante and Opusuo worked as certified teachers. Attracted to uniforms, Boakye Yiadom and Ɔkyeame Asante enlisted in the Gold Coast Regiment; Ankoma joined the police force. In spite of brief periods of service, their time in uniform had a profound impact on their sense of self and understanding of masculinity. Identifying as ex-servicemen (Ankoma as a former policeman), they sought government privileges and community status.

For *akrakyefoɔ*, literacy meant more than an employment qualification. Literacy skills enabled them to participate as members of the reading public, contributing to political and moral debates in the Gold Coast press, or, as Stephanie Newell has shown, engaging in "paracolonial networks" of literary and social clubs.[126] Some, like Addo, preferred involvement and leadership in their church over the increasingly politicized scholars' unions. In rural settings village teachers and tribunal registrars had less access to such clubs. Instead, they maintained informal networks with other *akrakyefoɔ* by exchanging letters and greeting cards, and by hosting a traveling friend. Writing altered modes of communication. Letters created intimacy but also enhanced social distances, since illiterate recipients depended on others to transmit written messages. *Akrakyefoɔ* wrote for personal usage, too. In their diaries and autobiographies, Addo and Boakye Yiadom produced detailed records that allow a reconstruction of their everyday lives. Literacy placed *akrakyefoɔ* in a position of authority, since others, regardless of their status and wealth, depended on their services.

As middle figures, village teachers served different constituencies. Some acquired power as scribes and advisers to native authorities; they acted as interlocutors between colonial officials and chiefs. The colonial government sought to implement regimes of professionalization to improve these middlers' job performance. Concerned about political affiliations, the government introduced mechanisms of control, particularly in the aftermath of the 1948 crisis. *Akrakyefoɔ* not only negotiated between different concepts of masculinity—those dominant in their hometowns, those acquired at school, and those advocated by employers—but also dealt with conflicting loyalties: toward employers, other *akrakyefoɔ*, religious institutions like churches, chiefs, elders, and other hometown communities. A mercantile firm like UAC demanded from its African clerks an unconditional commitment during cocoa hold-ups, while the clerks' relatives, as cocoa farmers, expected support from their literate *mmusua* members. This intermediary space allowed some *akrakyefoɔ* to assert authority; others faced ambiguity, their intermediary position turning into a liability.

The analytical category "youngmen," widely deployed in Ghana's historiography, needs to be disaggregated. According to this literature, all *akrakyefoɔ* belonged in that category and had common class interests. In reality, their politics and actions were shaped by their specific subject positions, determined by education and employment, as well as by *abusua* connections and hometown status. Exploring individual life histories and foregrounding these men's gendered subjectivities not only complicates such histories but opens a new window onto the political struggles leading to Ghana's independence.

In order to develop a fuller picture of how the social position and aspirations of *akrakyefoɔ* affected their understandings of masculinity, we need to look more closely at their relationships with women, particularly wives and concubines. How did different notions of masculinity influence their sexuality? How did men organize their marriages and understand their responsibilities and obligations as husbands and fathers?

THE MARRIAGES OF MEN: SEXUALITY AND FATHERHOOD, 1930–1970

5

Since the colonial period, multiple forms of marriage have existed in Akan societies. Some men lived monogamously, others in polygynous marriages. Most couples entered customary marriages, involving an exchange of marriage payments between lineages. A small minority contracted marriages regulated by statutory law. Members of Christian congregations had their customary marriages blessed in church. Some men cohabited with girlfriends. The colonial state, Christian churches, and matrilineages sought to regulate marriage. Chiefs' courts enforced customs that stipulated men's responsibilities toward wives and children, and set fees for adultery and divorce. In Kwawu towns most married couples kept separate residences and pursued their own economic activities. Members of mission churches were under pressure to follow a different set of marriage practices, many of them contrary to Akan practices, such as conjugal co-residence, monogamy, and privileging children over the matrilineage. Colonial institutions like the education department or the police force established additional rules about their employees' marriages.

Such multiplicity of requirements, rules, and customs understandably engendered an atmosphere of shifting conjugal relations in twentieth-century Ghana. Normative frameworks drawn from ethnographies and court records provide a base from which to explore the interviewed men's recollections about sexuality and marital arrangements, accounts which are then juxtaposed with comments by descendants, spouses, and other women. Contradictions often emerged in the men's subjective portrayals. Narratives of their youth, showing how they dealt creatively with marriage by mixing and matching elements of different marriage styles, were set against the examples that followed later in life, as they sought to live closer to established norms with an eye toward achieving senior masculinity. At the same time, agreements about what constituted a marriage were transforming in Kwawu and society at large.

Marriage Forms

In Twi the verb *ware* (to marry) refers to the act of marrying, "to take in marriage," and to any form of open cohabitation, "to live together as husband and wife."[1] Although the meaning of *ware* is broad, the older ethnographic literature, with its male perspective, presented a coherent marriage system that included "any legitimate union of the sexes."[2] Marriages were not just arranged between husband and wife but involved their *mmusua* (matrilineages) and fathers. In the 1920s R. S. Rattray distinguished between "at least six forms of marriages in Ashanti."[3] Each stipulated specific payments, conferring rights and responsibilities onto the spouses. Marriage was forbidden between members of the same *abusua* (matrilineage), the ideal being a cross-cousin marriage of either side, preferably from one's hometown. Twenty years later Meyer Fortes observed few changes to the marriage customs described by Rattray, except the "substitution of money payments for most of the gifts in kind," an increase of "shortlived illicit unions," and a decrease in cross-cousin marriages.[4] Fortes's research assistant, T. E. Kyei, identified five ways for a man to acquire a wife: *mpena twee* (courting and wooing); *asiwaa* (early childhood betrothal); *dɔ-yere* (offered wife); obligatory wife, that is, *kuna yere* (inherited wife) and, in the case of a chief, *ayetɛ* (customary stool wife) and *ahen-nyerɛ ntaa* (female twins as customary stool wives); and *awowa-yere* (a wife married when given as a pledge). He listed "seven consecutive formalities" of gifts and payments from husband to wife's family that led to the "consummation of a lawful customary marriage."[5] Although couples may never complete all formalities, their unions were still legitimate. Kyei was the first to recognize the "fundamental fluidity in Asante marriage" in which the participating lineages decided the precise marriage status, regardless of which ceremonies were performed.[6]

Marriages in Kwawu resembled those in Asante, with some differences. During a short research stay Rattray commissioned a local *krakye*, Eugene Addow, to write ethnographic notes, including a section on marriage. When Addow explained a free wife's enduring ties to her matrilineage and her husband's obligations, he connected marriage customs to a historical person. He stated that "all marriages in Kwahu are regulated by what is known as *Kwabena Atia Mfea* [Kwabena Atia's regulation]." Quite unique, his comment warrants quotation.

> A certain man named Kwabena Atia lived at Ankesepon who had so many daughters and nieces. He was the head of his family. This man is reputed to have been so cunning that he would not grant the hand of any of the young

women in [his] family to any body in marriage until the suitor had agreed to his (Kwabena Atia's) terms. The terms were to the advantage of Kwabena Atia and his family and all against the suitor: e.g. the suitor had to agree to bear all debts of the woman, farm for the woman and otherwise do everything required by the wife for the advancement of Kwabena Atia's family; at the same time if the woman came into possession of any valuable property the husband was bound to hand the same to Kwabena Atia. All children of the marriage were to be brought up at the expense of the father but they were the absolute property of Kwabena Atia's family. If the woman committed theft or any serious offence or swore the Oman Oaths the husband had to bear all the expense of the litigation but if any money came as a result it went to Kwabena Atia's family. All other families eventually adopted Kwabena Atia's regulations, and to-day at the solemnization of any African marriage, the words, "Kwabena Atia Mfea" is repeated by the parties handing over the wife and the husband raises his right hand, which means the terms are accepted, before other formalities are gone into.[7]

Although Rattray also noted a husband's responsibility for his wives' debts and torts, it was Addow who presented this custom as introduced by a historical figure whose rules were evoked in Kwawu court proceedings as a precedent.[8] This shows not only how "traditional customs" might have been instituted but how they were memorized and legitimized.

Addow presented the steps that led to a free customary marriage. When a man and woman agreed to marry, implying the possibility of a secret relationship, he informed his mother, who made inquiries about the "pecuniary and social standing of the girl's family," prevalent disease, and her "temper, manner, industry or laziness." The mother reported her findings to her brothers and *abusuapanyin* (lineage head). Following approval, the groom's father was invited "to marry the girl for his son." He sent messengers to her father, who informed her mother and family. After their consultation and the bride's consent, her father had the authority "to give her away." The agreement was marked by a bottle of gin and some money, called *akɔbo ɔpon* (knocking fee), a recent, coastal innovation.[9] From this moment the groom offered "presents of meat, cloth and money" to his bride. Addow added that "sometimes engagements keep long before the marriage takes place," thus indicating the stages in marriage formation. A conjugal union became fully legalized when the groom presented *tiri nsa* (head-drink), "two large pots of palm wine or demijohn-fuls [*sic*]," to the bride's father and her lineage, and some money according to her rank. On the wedding day the groom provided additional gifts, reflecting his wealth and her status, such as "wearing apparel, beads, trinkets, brass calabashes, tin or wooden boxes, silk headkerchiefs and other trifles." The bride also received foods to cook a splendid meal for the groom, his friends, and relatives. "Recently," Addow noted, another fashion had been "adopted from the coast": offering one pound, *Anyame-dwan* (God's sheep), to the bride's father after payment of *tiri nsa*.[10] Finally, the groom presented *tiri adeɛ*, or *tiri sika* (head-money), ranging from two pounds to sums as high as forty pounds. Her family could request *tiri sika* for debt payments at any stage, even years after the marriage had been legalized.[11] In case of a divorce, *tiri nsa* was irrecoverable, while *tiri sika* had to be returned, including all the husband's gifts to his wife.[12] Fulfilling these marriage rites could extend over years and might never be completed.

Kwawu marriage regulations were contested and changed. In 1917 commoners recorded the Asafo Laws that curbed chiefly power, particularly court fees, and de-monetized some marriage rites. Chiefs were no longer permitted to "contract infant marriages unless the child happened to be a twin or rufus (red-haired person)." Without *tiri nsa* no marriage was valid; the groom should not offer money "to either the girl or to her parents." Instead payments were replaced with ancestral gifts like "salt, meat, tobacco, shea-butter."[13] In 1950 Sophy Osafo noted that "nowadays" a young man and young woman frequently enter a *mpena-twee*, an unofficial relationship initiated by a small payment of "eight shillings to the girl," known as *ketɛ-asehyɛ*. Their arrangement may last "for a long time without the knowledge of both the parents." *Tiri sika* of approximately eight shillings to two pounds had become the norm.[14] Other marriage forms, like *asiwa* (betrothal), mentioned by Addow, had lost importance. Instead, more Kwawu couples had their marriage blessed in a church. By the early 1970s Wolf Bleek wrote that it was "no longer possible to speak of *the* Kwahu marriage system." He found a "variety of types of marriages and sexual unions, not only within one society or sub-division . . . but also within one family and even within one personal life-history." He distinguished between "temporary sexual unions" and "recognized marriage relations," the former subdivided into lover relationship and free marriage, and the latter into customary and Christian marriage.[15]

Based on these ethnographic accounts, we can distinguish five marriage forms. First, a man could cohabit with a woman without formally entering a marriage contract. In such a *mpena* (concubine) relationship, the distinction was between clandestine and open, depending on whether a woman cooked for her partner and whether the relationship was known. While a clandestine affair was denied any recognition, a known concubinage had little difference in practice from a formally contracted marriage. Second, a man and a woman could enter a customary marriage, performed by their fathers and *mmusua* (matrilineages), involving various ceremonies over a period of time. Third, as Addow stated, a man could "please himself with any other woman." Yet he had either to conduct such a relationship in secret or pay a pacification "aggregating the value of a few dozen eggs, or a fowl or two" to his senior wife (wives). Fourth, he might formalize an open concubine relationship, including payments to senior wives, since polygyny was "the rule rather than the exception."[16] Fifth, a church could bless a monogamous customary marriage. Sixth, a few couples opted for a union under statutory law and entered an "Ordinance marriage."[17] Legal disputes in marriage forms of the first four types above were subject to customary law and mediated by fathers, *abusua* elders, and chiefs; conflicts in Christian marriages were settled by individual churches, in the Presbyterian Church by the session (body of pastor and presbyters). Only Ordinance marriages fell under the statutory law that restricted divorce and altered inheritance rules.[18] Thus most marriages were "not a state of being but a series of multiple, often overlapping processes."[19] A man and a woman could initially have a secret *mpena* relation and then cohabit, with his and her parents' approval, before fully formalizing the marriage by performing at least some of the marriage rites. Later on, their marriage might be blessed in a church.

Jean Allman and Victoria Tashjian suggested that women in rural Asante perceived marriage along a continuum described as "degrees of knowing." Women became increasingly bound to their husbands because of the "expansion of cocoa, the monetization of the economy, and the 'customary' interventions of indirect rule" during the first half of the twentieth century.[20] While Allman and Tashjian focused on the relations between marriage and changing economic conditions for the first colonized generation of Asante women, exploring the triad of marriage forms, masculinities, and subjectivity, mainly from a Kwawu male perspective, provides a useful parallel. Furthermore, the colonial state and mission churches caused conflicts by strengthening "the marital bond in opposition to the lineage bond."[21] Showing how people engaged marriage forms advocated by a mission church brings into the foreground both the necessity and difficulty of negotiating various constituent realms.[22]

Playing and Dancing for Courtship

Although there is a rich literature on changing forms of marriage in twentieth-century Africa, less attention has been paid to practices and rites of courtship.[23] In the 1990s Kwawu elders asserted that premarital sexual relationships had become more frequent. In their youth they lived under close supervision of *wɔfanom* (uncles), parents, and other elders who prevented them from being sexually active. Ɔkyeame Asante from Pepease did not know the "meaning of having a girlfriend."

> But these days, while going round, a woman will leave and come back married. Even if you are sitting here [at his house], he [a young man] will pass by with his girlfriend, and go to his room; even a girl will take a man to her room! These days, [young men and women] do not respect anything, they are not afraid of anything. . . . The way they hang out together in town everywhere, oh no, right in front of their fathers and mothers![24]

Ɔpanyin Marfo, also from Pepease, blamed women for new excesses:

> Today, the women are mostly money conscious. How women behave! If God would help the men to open their minds. . . . If they [the men] invited a young girl, she would not hesitate to come. She is not afraid, she does not think that she has never done it before. Because of money, if you invite her she will come. Because of toffees [candy], if you invite a small girl she will come. Because of this, if you are not careful, you disgrace yourself, you soil your name.[25]

Asked about his first encounters with women, Ɔkyeame Asante recalled attending Catholic school in Nsawam at a time when young men "were afraid to go out and speak with a woman."[26] Others referred to games and dance competitions as sites of courtship, yet had mixed recollections about premarital sexuality.

In Kwawu, as elsewhere in southern Ghana, "make-believe games in which children play[ed] 'fathers and mothers'" were widespread (see chapter 2).[27] Acting as husband and wife, boys and girls exchanged favors and helped each other with daily chores. Mock marriages were not restricted to prepubescent children but included *mmerantee* (young men) and *mmabawa* (young women before giving birth). Still, Abetifi elder E. V. Osei Addo noted that mock marriages should not become an opportunity for sexual experimentation.

> Some were 15, others were 14 or even younger. So, they stayed together. It meant if your cloth or your *ntadee* (clothes) were dirty and you gave them to the girl, she would go and wash them nicely for you and bring them to you. His father and mother would all know about it. In those days, my apologies, we did not have any bad intentions—*enti na yenhyia*, so we did not meet [we did not have sex].[28]

Parents' knowledge of playful arrangements meant that a relationship was in the open and permitted. Osei Addo narrated playing *di ahen-ahen* (mock marriage) at the age of twenty in Koforidua. As "husbands," Osei Addo and his friends provided their "wives" with food. Lacking cash for *adidi sika* ("chop-money"), they gathered snails "in the bush." Fulfilling their duties, the wives cooked a meal. Although cooking for one's husband had erotic overtones, in the evening, as Osei Addo insisted, "she slept at her house," and he at his. Yet, Osei Addo admitted that some of the players "were quite grown" and had sex that might lead to marriage. Osei Addo, supported by J. A. Wahyee and Kwadwo Donkor, regretted that "all these games have stopped." Thus mock marriages were not only an institution of work sociability organized across gender boundaries, as noted above, but also the site of a sexual youth culture.[29]

Dance performances were another occasion for courtship. In his ethnographic notes, Addow observed the popularity of dancing in Kwawu. Held in open places, male musicians played on "drums, gong-gongs, and often with small pieces of sticks knocked together," accompanied "by clapping of hands by female participants." He described a dance party:

> The drummers and singers stand or sit at one end, a circle is then formed by the members of the dancing club beginning from one side of the drummers' position and finishing at the opposite side. Inside this ring the dance takes place and behind the circle of members the general public stand and look on.[30]

Dance styles came in waves. During the first two decades of the twentieth century, *ahyiko* was most popular. By the 1930s *bontuku* arrived, the dance of "bachelors and young girls in their prime," as Donkor recalled.

> The *bontuku* dance was played with a big band and a side drum that is used in playing highlife tunes. It was accompanied by a flute. When one player gave the tune with the flute, two or three others responded, or joined in with a gong sounding in the background. The young men and women enjoyed dancing to it. They made a big circle and while they were dancing, a loved-one such as a mother, father, or brother or sister may have come over to dance with you to congratulate you and wipe the sweat off your face. They may also have pasted some money on your forehead or sprayed some nice perfume on you to show their appreciation.[31]

In Abetifi dance companies distinguished themselves by their dress and only permitted men and women from the same ward into the ring. Wahyee:

> Bontuku ... was played by both [wards] *Dwenase* and *Ɔkyɛmase*. [Company members] put on uniforms like a police band. The *Ɔkyɛmase* group had one made of "khaki," and the *Dwenase* had theirs out of *chico* [cotton material] with

red spots. So this group had their dance with their women, and the other group had their own with their women.[32]

During the 1930s *bontuku* was rivaled by *konkomba,* another "neo-traditional music" influenced by brass bands.[33] Ɔkyeame Asante remembered *konkomba* dance in Nsawam after sunset, accompanied by an "orchestra" of local percussion and a side drum, bugle, or other brass instrument.[34] A. K. Boakye Yiadom talked about *konkomba* in Abetifi. As schoolboys, neither Asante nor Boakye Yiadom participated often, since pupils spotted among dancers or in the audience "would be whipped by [their] headmaster."[35]

During the 1930s and 1940s E. F. Opusuo witnessed dances performed in Pepease. "[A]*bera* that was for boys and girls . . . between twelve and fifteen"; couples "between eighteen and fifty" danced to the rhythms of *accra, adakem,* and *ɔdanu.* Different wards adopted their own styles and competed "just like politics." *Konkomba* was performed by dancers of ages ranging from twelve to fifty.

> Older men were just like patrons, and the young men and women were dancing *konkomba,* and they dressed neatly, they dressed very neatly. . . . *Konkomba* at Pepease went to face *konkomba* at Abetifi, a competition to see who was better. They [the winners] were given a silver cup.[36]

Dance parties served as a forum for young men to show off their physical skills when looking for a concubine or wife. Since male dancers struggled over women's attention, their gatherings were loaded with passion and desire, and could become violent. As Wahyee explained:

> We did not want men from the other wards to marry our women. If there was a woman who was very beautiful, getting her married was a big problem. Everybody fought over her. We liked to marry and keep her on our side [in our ward] of *Dwenase,* but the *Ɔkyɛmase* men also wanted her. Thus, we met them, and it resulted in *kitikiti* [small] quarrels. Some may even stab one another with a knife! There was one man called Kwasi Mampong, he was stabbed. He came here to *Dwenase* [to get a woman], but being from *Ɔkyɛmase,* he was attacked and hurt with a knife by the *Dwenase* people.[37]

Although Wahyee denoted such flirtations with *ware,* dancers did not enter a formal marriage. Rather, in this dating game, some encounters remained casual, whereas others became sexual and could result in marriage. A man who was seriously seeking a wife was not limited to women in his ward.

Missionaries predictably had a less favorable impression of these dances. In Abetifi church leaders prevented dances from taking place in *Aberem*

(Christian Quarters). They urged congregation members not to participate, preferably not even to watch.[38] Initially this prohibition referred to religious dances performed by *akɔmfoɔ* (diviners) possessed by their *ɔbosom* (lesser god) but later extended to secular ones as well. Missionaries tied dancing to the assumed uncontrollable sexual desires of Africans. Edmond Perregaux characterized dancing as "*jeu par excellence* of the Akans, one they would never abandon." Although Akans created an infinite amount of varieties, dancing supposedly led to illicit sexual liaisons. The accompanying songs were so "lascivious" that a "native" refused to repeat the lyrics because they were unfit for missionary ears.[39] G. L. Schmid referred to *ahyiko* as "obscene" causing "damage" among "heathens and Christians." He complained that "carnal Negroes" turned *ahyiko* performances, which could last for two weeks, into popular imitations of the annual church harvest. A catechumen even considered *ahyiko* "sweeter" than church service.[40]

Colonial officials shared these concerns about the morality of the dances. In 1908 the commissioner of the Eastern Province, C. N. Curling, worried about his domestic servants being corrupted by "a lewd dance named Ashiko."

> While District Commissioner of Accra, I came in contact with it in Christiansborg, and owing to its effect upon the health of the servant boy community, I refused to grant passes for any dances unless assured that the dance was not Ashiko. The lewdness of the dance varies with the rank of the dancers, but it is customary that when a woman has consented to be a man's partner for the dance, she stays with him for the night. In Okwahu they have in almost every town organized two companies, each with a fenced off dancing place which are invariably at the opposite ends of the Town.

Curling had observed similar dance groups in Koforidua and other towns of New Juaben. There, he noted, "quite recently it has become fashion for the members of the two companies to change wives for a particular night's dance."[41] He wanted to prohibit *ahyiko* and have the fences around the dancing places destroyed. But since his enquiry in Kwawu had the purpose of addressing political and religious problems, he refrained from these actions. Curling saw a direct correlation between *ahyiko*'s "increased popularity" leading to permissive sexuality and the "increase in the number of compensation cases for adultery." Only recently the *Ɔmanhene* (paramount chief) of Kwawu had raised adultery fees causing objection among members of the Asafo company. To ease tensions, Curling suggested the complete prohibition of *ahyiko*, together with a "similar dance called Osibi Saba."[42] This policy was not carried out.

I confronted Wahyee and Donkor with Curling's negative representation of *ahyiko*. Their response is significant. Neither agreed with the commissioner but emphasized the supervision placed on young people.

> KD: In those days young people respected their parents. One could not conduct him- or herself indecently in public, in front of our fathers, mothers, or any family members. If your father or mother saw you misbehaving like that, you could be in big trouble.
> WA: If my children misbehaved, I wouldn't allow them to participate in it [in these dances] again.
> KD: When the dances were over everybody went home to sleep. But if one does not go home, but stays out over night, your father and mother will question you.

They acknowledged, however, the importance of dance parties as sites for courtship. Donkor suggested that "most people met their life partners at such dances, but the marriage had to be contracted well." Wahyee explained:

> As you know, some people are good dancers, others are just dancing along the rhythm. A particular girl may dance so beautifully that you may be attracted to her. If you fall in love with her, then the next thing to do is to go to her father to ask for her hand in marriage. You could also tell the girl yourself and, if she agrees, then you could prepare to get married.[43]

Perhaps a bit tongue-in-cheek, Wahyee, Donkor, and Osei Addo insisted that only others breached these norms and experimented sexually. Since our conversations were public with younger men listening, these stories were not only addressed to my research assistant, Joseph Kwakye, and me, but, rather, were also ways of conveying to those listening how courtship *should* be conducted. Reluctant to acknowledge their own noncompliance, they sought to set an example of how a man should enter marriage and reach adult masculinity.

Adult Masculinity and Customary Marriage

In Kwawu, adult masculinity was signified by marriage. As in other Akan societies, men reached adult masculinity by taking "the role of material providers and protectors of families."[44] Kwawu elders expected a married man to "look after the health of his wife, to clothe and feed her and to farm for her and house her." As a father, he should "rear [his children] till they come of age" and find them suitable marriage partners; he could demand that they work for him, even after divorcing their mother.[45] A man's responsibilities extended to the well-being of his own *abusua,* since he would be succeeded by his *wɔfase* (nephew).

Of the eight men interviewed, three entered customary marriage without having their unions blessed by a Christian church: Kwaku Marfo, Ɔkyeame Kwabena Asante, and Kofi Ankoma. Telling stories about selecting a wife, they mentioned the importance of older relatives, particularly fathers. They echoed Fortes's assessment, "A father should provide his son with a wife," and Addow's observation, "It is the duty of the father" to arrange the marriage.[46] Some scholars have interpreted this paternal intervention assisting the son to reach adult masculinity as a *rite de passage.* This transition from boyhood to manhood was a minor equivalent to the more elaborate initiation rites for girls once practiced by Akan people. In Kwawu a father used to usher his son into manhood "by providing the young man with a musket and a wife, combining puberty and marriage in the same rite."[47] By the early 1970s this practice was no longer performed. Instead, young men preferred to make their own conjugal arrangements. But fathers "harangued" their sons to marry and settle down, if they had spent "too many years in bachelorhood."[48] None of the interviewed men experienced this.

The interviewed men were less concerned than the ethnographers with details and content of successive marriage rites. Rather, they emphasized *who* covered their marriage expenses. Some expected fathers to pay; others noted sons should raise their own funds. The former driver Kofi Ankoma of Obo commented:

> When you decide to marry a woman, your father will ask you your financial position. And you tell him that you can look after the woman, then you go and marry her.[49]

Ankoma's father only assisted him with expenses for the first wife. Ɔkyeame Asante argued differently:

> You see, in those days it was your father who would marry for you. If he saw a woman and realized that it was good to marry from that house, and if you were an adult, and it was time for you to marry. "I am going to marry this woman for you." Her *abusuafoɔ* (lineage members) had [already] consented and you would also agree. You would give money to your father, and he would go to perform all the necessary things. Then, she became your wife.[50]

Yaw Mensa of Nkwantanan saved money working on his cocoa farm. Since his father was deceased, he asked his younger brother to play the father role and to make the marital arrangements. I asked whether the father's successor provided him with a cutlass and gun. With a smile, Mensa remarked, "If I had been able to get money to marry, then I surely had enough money for a cutlass."[51] Yet, for some, elders' advice was decisive.

Ɔpanyin Marfo of Pepease presented himself as an elder who had lived according to norms lost to the present youth. He reported how he followed closely his father's wishes and *wɔfanom's* counsel concerning marriage:

> When I grew up, I married. I married late because of my father's advice that I should have patience, lead a good life and see, when I marry, that I can take care of my wife.

Marfo did not choose his first wife himself. Rather, after his mother had died, his *wɔfanom* from Fanteland came to Pepease for the funeral celebrations. They convinced him to marry a woman from his mother's hometown, so he would "remain eager to visit." His second wife also hailed from Fante. Later in life he married a woman from Mankesim-Dominase. His three wives gave birth to eleven children. Marfo emphatically denied having *any* children outside marriage. Instead, addressing me, my research assistant Douglas Asomani, and others gathered, he deplored that women do not "respect themselves" anymore:

> But today, what we see is that men know married women, they will go ahead and call them. Excuse me, if a woman calls a man a fool, the man will not stay but leave, since this humiliates the man. If a man proposes to a married woman, and the woman tells the man, "Don't you know that I have a husband," the man will not continue. But if a man calls a woman and she smiles, it encourages him to go ahead.[52]

Women should fend off unwelcome advances by men. For men, Marfo advocated an ideal of polygynous marriages with many offspring. Yet he respected the parameters defined by elders. Condemning extramarital sex, he exhorted juniors to conduct themselves according to elders' expectations and not to rush into unwarranted adventures. Marfo in his self-representation did not dwell on lived experience but turned his life into an idealized script to be emulated by young men seeking to reach adult masculinity.

The recollections of Ɔkyeame Asante and Ankoma diverged from Marfo's normative statements. Initially Asante stressed that he and his agemates did not have premarital sex. Then, eventually, he talked about his first concubine. After his apprenticeship in Coaltar, Asante met a Fante woman from Apam near Winneba in the mid-1930s. They started a *mpena* relationship; the woman became pregnant.

I looked after her till she delivered. When I decided to perform the marriage rites, her *wɔfa* [maternal uncle] did not allow me to do that. His reason was that I am a native of Kwawu.[53]

Asante providing for his pregnant girlfriend complied with expectations of a man to look after the woman who carried his child, and engage with her sexually in order for the child's *ntɔrɔ* (patrilineal spirit) to develop well, a view expressed in the proceedings of the Abetifi Native Tribunal.[54] Although the woman's parents accepted the marriage, her *wɔfa* objected because of Asante's ethnicity. Negotiating with the *wɔfa*, Asante relied on two senior men from Akuapem: the Mampong chief working as a cocoa purchasing clerk in Coaltar and an *ɔpanyin* (elder) from Obosomase. Their efforts proved to no avail. His former girlfriend, however, refused to enter another marriage. When she delivered this promise, she stated that "her daughter should bear all the children she did not have born." Asante added:

True to her word, she never married. I was there when she died and was buried. . . . My daughter had ten children; five males and five females. She took care of them till they grew up. Some of the children of my daughter are overseas, three of them. . . . She said she would not like to have children with different fathers.[55]

More than fifty years later Asante was still puzzled by his girlfriend's decision. Hearing this story, Kwame Fosu, my research assistant, concurred, considering it "a little strange" for a woman with only one child to decide against marriage. Yet "opting out of marriage" was not that unusual among women in rural Asante during the 1930s and 1940s, although there is scant evidence.[56] Native authorities were concerned about young unmarried women, suspecting them of prostitution, and sought to introduce bylaws that coerced them into marriage. In Kwawu, there appears to have been a practice of rounding up "spinsters resisting marriage" since 1916. In 1943, the state council proposed the "Kwahu State Unmarried Women Movement Control By-Laws" that were rejected by the colonial government.[57]

Following his military service during World War II Ɔkeame Asante married Akua Tanoa, a Kwawu woman from Obomeng. They had one child. Then he entered another marriage that remained childless. A third marriage produced six children; three of them survived into adulthood. Another woman whom Asante referred to as wife lived in her hometown of Kwawu-Tafo. They had no children; nor is it clear which marriage rites, if any, they had performed. Asante provided for his children and paid school fees, the obligation of a twentieth-century father. Asked whether he also assisted his nieces and nephews, he responded that he only "provided for some" since most were supported by their fathers.[58]

Kofi Ankoma also entered several marriages. In the late 1930s he married his first wife who followed him to Cape Coast after he had joined the police. They had no children. Returning to Kwawu in 1948, he launched a transportation business. Ankoma gave two different accounts of their divorce. When he discovered his wife stealing money, he did "not make any palaver." Rather, he informed her father that he would no longer stay with her. In the second account, he recalled driving the route Obo–Accra–Obo.

> I often brought her chop [food], then I would eat with her. So the woman was seeing that I was becoming all right. She started picking on me, "I will never stay with you . . ." Then, I started some "hanky-panky" with her . . . [in the end] she was not prepared to marry again [any longer]. I said, "All right, thank you very much." I went to the father and told him that I could not marry again. He asked, "Why?" "If your daughter tells me she is not marrying me any longer, I cannot force her to marry me. So she can go."

In this version the wife took the initiative. His authority questioned, Ankoma felt threatened and terminated the relationship. He married another Obo woman; they had two sons and one daughter. As a driver, it was never difficult to find a concubine. Access to cash allowed him to shower girlfriends with rare items like bread or consumer goods from Accra. Ankoma attempted to prevent pregnancies.

> You may not know whether she got another boyfriend. . . . And, if she is conceived, she comes to tell you that she got conception by you, and automatically, you have to abide the law [and support her].

Ankoma had learned about women's menstrual cycle from a hygiene book as a middle school student. Thereafter he asked girlfriends about their menses, only visiting them "one week before their time."[59] Nevertheless, three of them gave birth to a child. Without formal marriage, he accepted paternity, paid school fees, and hoped that these children would support him in his old age. Ankoma spoke with some nostalgia about being young, mobile, and desired. This ready access to sexual partners added to the attractions of driving, probably a reason for quitting the police. Once, after some drinking, Ankoma boasted how he had a *mpena* in almost every Kwawu town.[60]

Unlike Ankoma, Ɔkyeame Asante did not elaborate about girlfriends. He only alluded to such experience while discussing proverbs, providing contexts to possible meanings. The proverb *"Obi rennya sɛ wɔde ne mpena abesi ne na awowa*" (No one rejects when one's concubine is brought to one's mother as a pawn) is advice to a man who fears maternal disapproval of his concubine. Asking her to serve the mother allows him to be close to her without suspicion. Another proverb addresses a man's responsibility toward his girlfriend: "*Obi mfa osigyafo na n'apɛde nka mu*" (No one goes to bed with an unmarried woman without giving her something).[61] In a sexual relationship an *osigyafo* (unmarried woman) can, and usually does, claim gifts or financial support.[62] Asante argued that the man should inform "her father and *abusua* members" about the gifts. Should she stop their liaison, he could reclaim his expenses. Asante warned, "If you take her secretly, then it becomes a trap. . . . In this case, if you divorce her you cannot do anything." When nobody knows about payments, the suitor will lose. But Asante added, "If you have taken her [to bed], and you failed to give her anything, she can still send you to court. Even her father can issue summons against you." Commenting on another proverb, "*Awareɛ rebɔ wo a, wonhwehwɛ mu yɛyere*" (If you are almost going to remain without a wife, you don't look for a favorite wife), Asante opined that an unmarried elder does not have the luxury of looking for a *yɛyere* (favorite wife). Defining *yɛyere*, he evoked mutual conjugal support.

> She is a woman you have married who is obedient to you. She does whatever you expect her to do for you. She helps in any work you do. She is your *yɛyere*, your special wife. Because she does whatever you expect her to do, you also will do whatever she expects from you as her *ɔbarima* (man). So, the minds of those two become one.

Asante elaborated that, in such a relationship, should the man take a second wife "and the new one wants to spoil the senior wife, he would say, 'she is my *yɛyere*; I don't want anybody else to disturb her.'"[63]

Ɔkyeame Asante's recollections and exegesis of proverbial lore reflect his understanding of how men should organize marriage and relations with girlfriends. Reaching adult masculinity, Asante abandoned the ideas of his Catholic upbringing about monogamy. For him, polygynous arrangements were not problematic but rather jealousy and hidden relationships were. He embraced the ideal that *mpena* relations should lead to marriage or be in the open, transparent to all involved parties. A man is expected to provide for his wives *and* girlfriends but can insist that gifts be returned if the woman "stops marrying him."[64] Asante advocated a father's obligation to look after his children, including education, while also supporting, if needed, his nephews and nieces. Both Ɔkyeame Asante and Ankoma, who came of age in the 1930s, used their travels to enter relationships with non-Kwawu women. Yet eventually they married Kwawu women known to their families and followed more established marital conventions.

Akua Nimako's account provides a female perspective. In recounting her marital history, she expressed her expectations for adult masculinity. After her mother's death, Nimako took care of her younger siblings until she married in 1930 at the age of seventeen. She noted:

> If you stay humble, as I have been advising my grandchildren here, not playing around with any boys, not indulging in sexual relations with boyfriends, and if you are a good girl, if they [the town] see you, and somebody is looking for a girl to marry, they will say, this girl is good, go to that house, she is a good girl. Go and marry her. If you marry her, she will be a good child. And if you marry her, you will have a good life with her. That is how I did it.

M. J. Opoku Yao, a *krakye* who hailed from the neighboring town of Ad-uamoa, was stationed as a police constabulary in Koforidua. He looked for a wife in Abetifi, his father's hometown.

> When they brought drinks to my father to perform the rites, they only told me: "Today you have been married, you have got your husband. A certain man has come to marry you. He is coming from Koforidua, for you to see him." And he came to see me and said he would like to marry me. And I also said, "I like him."

Ready "to give birth," Nimako immediately accepted. When she arrived in Koforidua, she learned about Opoku Yao's senior wife. Although she tried to "humble herself," the relationship with her *kora* (co-wife) proved difficult.[65] Both wives occupied the same house and shared cooking facilities causing tension, since rivalry for sexual attention was linked to food preparation.[66] Nimako sought to accommodate her husband's wishes, "When he told me to sleep here, I said hmm [yes]. When he told me to sleep there, I agreed." Still, the *kora* was "aggressive," at times "violent."

> She went to the extent of acquiring medicine from a medicine man to kill me. . . . My husband told me not to be bothered by her, and I agreed. The co-wife continued in her wild behavior so that the man's eye turned away from her.

In Koforidua, without access to farmland, the wives depended on Opoku Yao's salary. The distribution of "chop-money" and the assignment of daily chores reflected the wives' status. When they went to the market, Nimako carried the metal tray on her head, while the *kora* "bought things and placed them into the pan."[67] Nimako's experience refutes the observation by a 1940s

130

anthropologist that women in Akan polygynous marriages "cannot but appreciate the lightening of the burden of work."[68]

After six years Opoku Yao was discharged from the police. They returned to Kwawu. In Abetifi Nimako stayed again with her *abusua*, following Akan practice: separate residences in hometowns, a co-residence while sojourning.[69] Soon Nimako was sent to work in a cocoa village owned by her well-to-do father-in-law, Yao Annor, whom she remembered for his numerous wives and children. Although they harvested "plenty of cocoa," they failed to sell any because of a boycott. The crop had to be burned. Nimako lived through hardship after delivering her second child; "I really had to live with severe poverty; I was left alone with God." Since she worked for her husband, Nimako's dependency grew, causing her much grief.

> All I did was to help him on the farm. He had a very big palm plantation, and so we made a lot of oil palm-nuts. We made many barrels of oil every year. Some days we were able to make three or four *grawa* [container of about four gallons]. While *we* made the oil, *he* sold it, and from that he gave us chop money.[70]

In addition to cash crops they planted yams, plantains, and cocoyam. Nimako's memory of laboring for her husband without remuneration shows how the advent of cash-cropping replaced the custom of conjugal mutual assistance—working on each others' farms—and did so at the expense of women.[71]

Marriage troubles continued. Although Opoku Yao had divorced Nimako's co-wife, he continued seeing other women. At one point he had six wives. When Joseph Kwakye, my research assistant, reacted with surprise, Nimako responded, "Are you from here? Don't you know Opoku Yao? If you had known him . . . you would say, 'Woman, you have really tried hard.'" Nimako felt ignored. Sometimes for six months, Opoku Yao did "not set foot into [her] house nor come close to [her] bed." These days, she added, "no woman would live in such a marriage."[72] After his dismissal from the police he was hired as a tribunal registrar, first in Abetifi and then in Aduamoa. In 1940 he was accused of being responsible for the disappearance of a "considerable amount of money" and was fired.[73] Briefly he joined the Gold Coast Regiment. Since he did not provide for Nimako and their four children, she initiated a divorce.

> Because I was hungry, and I could not get money to buy food to eat, and I had a husband, so I could not [look] elsewhere. . . . Finally, he came one day. . . . from Accra to Mpraeso for a football match. When [a group of men] came,

> I saw that my husband was among them. But he stayed overnight at Aduamoa.
> . . . I cried, and cried and cried. So I told my father's brother, my real father
> had died. And so I told my father's brother what my husband was doing to
> me, and that I cannot continue marrying him, and that I would leave him. My
> father's brother sent someone with me, and we went to Aduamoa, and he broke
> with [performed the divorce ritual].[74]

Opoku Yao was an *ɔbarima* (valiant man) who boasted his sexual prowess
and played an important part in Kwawu politics. He was feared by his opponents and admired by his supporters, a man who succeeded in achieving
big-man status. He became one of the first literate chiefs of his hometown,
remembered for his modernizing efforts. Nimako recalled:

> He was chosen *Kurontehene.* Then, Aduamoa was in the bush. But Opoku Yao
> went there, he forced them to make it into a real town, that is why he was
> chosen *Kurontehene.* So he died on the stool. When he died he was given a
> royal funeral.[75]

Nimako described how Opoku Yao should have conducted himself as a husband. She requested capital so that she could trade and keep the profit; she
expected to receive a regular supply of meat, and occasionally a piece of cloth.
Finally, a husband should clothe his children and pay for school fees. She
was aware of marital changes and noted that in her parents' generation a
wife was content with "a token amount of money." But in her case, if a
husband refused to purchase her "cloth for the body and the head," she would
"not be willing to remain in the marriage."[76]

A few years after her divorce Nimako married Yaw Mensa, who, to her
delight, sold smoked bush meat in Abetifi. At that time men still controlled
the meat market; "only recently," as Nimako commented, "women have
started." Since Mensa treated her well, she was not unhappy to become a
kora again. Asked to compare the two husbands, Nimako responded quickly
that Yaw Mensa "was far better."

> SM: Did he give you "chop-money" and a big piece of meat?
> NI: Yes, he even gave me cloth. He gave me a *duku* (head scarf), he gave me
> everything, he gave me *toma* (waist beads). When everybody has something to
> eat until he or she has enough, then there are no worries. If you have cloth to
> wear, you have no worries. I ate to my satisfaction, and I could do whatever I
> liked. He also entertained me all the time and made me happy.[77]

In the late 1940s Yaw Mensa acquired the Tegare *aduru* (spiritual medicine).
Since there were already four Tegare *abosomfoɔ* (priests) practicing in Abetifi,
they had to move to Juaben, Asante.[78] When the shrine failed to provide an

income, they relocated to Yaw Mensa's hometown in Akyem Abuakwa to launch a cocoa farm on land granted by his *abusua*. Breaking with their past, they joined the Pentecostal Church and burned the Tegare. Yet, by the 1950s, the cocoa industry had declined rapidly across the Eastern Province, mainly because of swollen shoot disease and soil exhaustion. Farmers suffered from poor yields and lost trees. In the 1960s, having given birth to eight children, Nimako returned without Yaw Mensa to Kwawu to start an onion farm on her *wɔfanom*'s land. It is unclear whether she formally divorced Yaw Mensa or whether the physical separation ended the marriage.[79] In retrospect, Nimako remained bitter. Although promised a part of the cocoa farm they had started, she received nothing. After her departure, Yaw Mensa sold the farm to an *ɔkɔmfo* (diviner) who never paid the agreed-on price. Nimako and her children "had toiled for nothing."[80] Disappointed in marriage, she noted that none of her husbands lived up to the obligations of adult masculinity by providing for her and their children. Her choice to opt out of marriage fit with patterns identified for rural Asante since the 1940s. Many wives who were not compensated for their work "began to weigh the relative benefits of marriage."[81] Women contemplated divorce strategies "to invest in their own enterprises, most commonly a farm of their own or small-scale trading."[82]

Unlike Akan customary marriages, mission churches advocated marriage forms that privileged the nuclear family over the *abusua*. How did such "Christian marriages" differ in organization and practice from customary marital arrangements?

Christian Marriages

Most of the interviewed men and women who entered Christian marriages were members of the Presbyterian Church whose 1929 regulations recognized two forms of marriage: "Marriage under Ordinance," legally performed only by a minister "in a duly licensed building," and "marriage according with native customary law," blessed in any church building. In the latter form the parties had to profess to be married "in accordance with customary law," witnessed, if possible, by two presbyters (church elders), before they could have a Christian ceremony.[83] According to Presbyterian rules, the only accepted place for sexuality was a monogamous marriage; pre- and extramarital sexual relations were frowned upon and could lead to suspension or exclusion.[84] Within Akan societies there was more flexibility. Although premarital sex was not encouraged, a man who had fathered a child acted properly as long as he supported the mother during pregnancy. After delivery, he should either marry or compensate her, and pacify her father or guardian.[85] Because men with many children were well respected, those who could afford it married more than one wife.[86] Akan customary marriages, to the dismay of the Presbyterian Church, could easily be dissolved. Although a father was expected to name and look after his children and their mothers, men often failed to provide for all their children. They focused instead on nephews and nieces of their *abusua* who would inherit and succeed them. It was problematic for many men in Presbyterian congregations to live with different concepts about marriage and sexuality.

Marriages were highly contested in Kwawu. The Abetifi Native Tribunal frequently heard cases about adultery, broken marriage promises, and inheritance disputes in which spouses, children, and lineage representatives argued about marriage forms. In one case, in 1936, trader Salome Owusua engaged the tribunal to prevent her husband, Charles Gyeni, from leaving their Christian marriage. Gyeni, a cocoa farmer, had taken another wife because of Owusua's alleged barrenness. He even accused her of prostitution. He claimed that his wife had sex with his close male friends, men with whom he ate regularly. Such an act would "destroy a man." Owusua admitted her affairs. Still, she insisted that Presbyterian regulations would not permit Gyeni to divorce. The tribunal accepted her argument and required Gyeni to compensate her. The case was sent back to the presbyters for intercession.[87]

The marriages of Wahyee and retired trader E. K. Addo represent the two types endorsed by the Presbyterian Church. Wahyee married twice. In the early 1920s, before converting to Christianity, he met his first wife. His father, Kwaku Frempong, played a significant role negotiating with his wife's parents.

> I found her myself and informed my father. Then, my father sent some people to go and inform the woman's father. They told her father, "Kwaku Frempong's son would like to marry your daughter, and so his father is here to marry her for him." After the girl's father had agreed, he asked for his daughter's agreement; then he allowed the customary rites to be performed. He then said to the boy's [Wahyee's] father: "Come and marry her, bring me my drinks and come for her."

Wahyee and his first wife had one child. The marriage did not last. When Wahyee became interested in the Presbyterian Church, his wife threatened to leave him. Seeing her "moving with another man," Wahyee became so "jealous and offended" that he divorced and "forgot about her." After his conversion, Kwaku Frempong advised the son to marry a Christian woman and chose a bride for him. Although blessed in the church, the same "procedure was carried out" as in the first marriage.[88] Kwaku Frempong sought the consent of the bride's parents and followed Presbyterian regulations that prohibited "intoxicating spirit . . . given or shared at the proposal for engagement" but allowed the exchange of money if "custom requires a present."[89]

Trader E. K. Addo was one of the few who had his customary marriage recognized by a magistrate, and thus entered an Ordinance marriage. Although introduced in 1884, this marriage form, stipulating monogamous and lifelong unions, remained unpopular throughout the colonial era because it made divorce difficult and costly, subject to a British court decision. The Marriage Ordinance restricted the customary "family"—in Kwawu the *abusua*—in matters of inheritance.[90] Most Christian couples were reluctant to enter such marriages, causing disappointment among pastors and missionaries who had hoped that the Ordinance would strengthen Christian marriages.[91] However, senior members of the Presbyterian Church were strongly encouraged to marry according to the Ordinance. As was often the case in Addo's life, his brother, J. K. Kwakye, was the driving force.

> I myself did not stay with a woman for one day, not one week, nor one month [before marriage]. It was my elder brother who told me, "You are grown, you have reached maturity, it is time for you to marry! And so, we have chosen this young girl for you to marry her. Whether you like it or not, you have to marry." I agreed with the marriage, but I was not able to do my own [choosing]. My elder brother . . . said . . . "She has a good *suban* (character), she fits you, so marry her." I did not disagree.

The bride, Beatrice Ohenewa Preko, came from Abetifi. Addo is still proud of his lavish wedding in 1931. As a successful trader, managing his own store in Nsawam since 1928, he took the opportunity to publicly demonstrate his recently acquired wealth and big-man status. He recalled spending the sumptuous amount of seventy pounds on the festivities that became "the highest and grandest wedding ever held in Abetifi."[92] There was an abundance of food. After the church service a crowd witnessed the spectacle of "throwing rice and powder." This gesture of appreciation combined European and Akan protocols, since throwing rice is an ingredient of European weddings and throwing powder, in Akan practice, is an expression of joy, the latter a feature during a chief's enstoolment.[93]

Although Addo emphasized his *Christian* marriage, his wedding did not fully conform with Presbyterian rules. Since Presbyterians should have "renounced pride and vanity" in baptism, they were to "celebrate a joyful feast such as marriage in simplicity without worldly and idle display." Regulations stipulated that "all unnecessary expense for feasting and all extravagance in clothing or ornaments should be avoided."[94] Rather, Addo's wedding, with its visible splendor, echoed a procession of an Akan chief or the precolonial performance of honoring a successful man for his riches and contributions to the state with the title of *ɔbirɛmpɔn* (big man). An *ɔbirɛmpɔn* publicly displayed his wealth in front of the *Asantehene* (king of Asante) before he was granted the title.[95] Considerations about status and prestige influenced Addo's decision to enter an Ordinance marriage, the form preferred by lawyers, pastors, and senior civil servants. Because he was self-educated, the lavish wedding became an occasion to show Abetifi people, within and beyond Christian Quarters, that he not only knew how to conduct himself as a *krakye* but that he had become both an educated and wealthy coastal trader. The elaborate wedding underlined his claim for big-man status. Kristin Mann observed for early colonial Lagos that "Ordinance marriage clearly defined persons' status as educated Christians. Moreover, it enhanced their social standing, because most Europeans and many members of the élite regarded Christian unions as more prestigious than customary unions."[96] This link between the choice of marriage form and personal status also existed a generation later in a Kwawu town of the Ghanaian hinterland during the early 1930s.

Both Wahyee and Addo in conversation expressed pride in fatherhood. After divorcing his first wife, Wahyee took his oldest son along to the Christian Quarters and sent him to school. He had four children with his second wife, three sons and one daughter. All received a Standard VII education, some even going on to attend college. Wahyee not only cared for his own children; in 1932, after his brother's death, Wahyee adopted the brother's children and paid for their education. These children lived in the house built by their late father and Wahyee. Further, Wahyee also provided for some of his nephews and nieces. Wahyee succeeded to his brother's cocoa farms and became a successful farmer despite many obstacles, including sinking prices and the cocoa hold-up during the 1930s, the swollen shoot disease, and enforced cutting of trees during the 1940s. Since cocoa farming was lucrative, his children were not expected to do agricultural work. Instead he hired laborers, usually three, from Ghana's Northern Territories or from colonial Burkina Faso. These laborers assisted Wahyee and his wife in the weeding and harvesting.[97]

Addo had seven children who feature prominently in his recollections and writings. He reported in his diary about the well-being of his oldest daughter, Edna (1932–1998), and described the "christening of our babe boy, a second born," called Andrews (1934–1992); the guests, entertained "with mineral waters, wine and Biscuits," presented Andrews with a few shillings.[98] Unlike an older generation of Kwawu traders, Addo strongly believed in Western and gendered education. According to his son, he encouraged his children and close relatives to succeed in school.[99] Addo highlighted his children's educational and professional achievements: three became teachers, one a veterinarian doctor, and at least two found clerical employment. With pride, he saved documents like Edna's primary school certificate, passing examinations in English, arithmetic, domestic science, and needlework with distinction, and Andrews's "School Leaving Testimonial" from the Abetifi Boarding School.[100]

In the 1950s wealthy Kwawu men started to send children (particularly sons) abroad for further study; many stayed away. By the second half of the twentieth century the Kwawu population was dispersed. At the time of our conversations, three of Wahyee's and two of Addo's children lived overseas.[101] Addo narrated how his son, Andrews, had studied medicine in Edinburgh in the early 1960s and then settled in the United Kingdom, working as a veterinarian until his death in 1992. His oldest daughter, Edna, followed her husband to the United States in 1961, eventually living in Seattle where she raised their daughter after her husband's death.[102] Addo's correspondence documents the social network that assisted these migrants studying and living abroad. Addo assisted them financially, especially Andrews, on whom he spent up to six hundred pounds per year.[103] His letters express the anxieties about whether payments might fail to arrive, and contain veiled threats to stop the allowance should the son "disgrace" the father. Andrews's letters show his deep gratitude and concerns.[104] By the 1990s, having children abroad had become a distinct sign of status in Ghana. They are expected to send their loved ones remittances, and to assist with building houses and purchasing expensive consumer goods like a radio or television set. Yet, for Addo, children overseas were less a matter of financial support than personal pride. This is echoed in my research assistant's comment after a visit to Addo's house, "He has done well and he is an accomplished man, because he has children abroad."[105]

Addo took responsibility for a wide circle of paternal relatives. When Rev. E.K.O. Asante attended the Presbyterian Training College at Akropong, Addo provided support. In his diary he noted witnessing Asante's consecration as a teacher-catechist in 1933; "I proceeded whilst raining because I do not fail my promise made to him." Addo purchased Asante a dark suit; later he helped him to study at the seminary.[106] When his senior brother's daughter was in training, she sought Addo's assistance in acquiring "a midwifery bag."[107] Most prominent, Addo supported the nine children of his late "brother," in fact his father's brother's son, I. O. Sampong, who died at the age of forty-three in 1943. Addo's correspondence vividly conveys not only the Sampong children's requests for clothing and school fees but also their profound appreciation.[108] Addo's obligations included supporting *abusua* members in their education. In 1965, when he withdrew from his Nsawam business, Addo chose his nephew as a successor and left him his security deposit without interest.[109]

There were other women in Addo's life. After his wife, Beatrice Preko, died in 1991, he married Susanna Anyema and adopted her daughter. When Paulina Acheampong of Abetifi heard about my frequent visits with Addo, she revealed that she had once been his concubine and bore his child. When I asked Addo about additional wives, he changed the subject.[110] Throughout our conversations, he emphasized that he had lived in a Christian marriage. Perhaps he expected me, a European, to share the marriage ideal promoted by missionaries and the Presbyterian Church, and to be someone who would not condone polygynous marriage arrangements. Yet his son Kwaku Addo Darko, conceived with his "outside wife," is well known in Abetifi. After Addo's death, Paulina Acheampong explained that their relationship "was not a proper marriage." Addo wanted to marry but "his wife did not permit." Acheampong was pleased about Addo's sense of fatherhood. Unlike her first husband, who did not look after their children following divorce, Addo provided for his son, leaving him a house in Abetifi.[111]

How do Addo's and Wahyee's marriage arrangements relate to ideas about masculinity? On the one hand, Addo followed Presbyterian rules that a man should focus on his conjugal family at the expense of obligations toward his *abusua*. On the other hand, he used specific events like his wedding or his contributions to the town of Abetifi to present himself as an *ɔbirɛmpɔn*, the quintessential local big man. The big-man role had space for relations with other women, whether or not customary marriage rites were performed. Wahyee emphasized his roles as father, husband, and *wɔfa*, and presented himself as somebody who lived consciously within the fold of the Presbyterian Church, embracing Presbyterian masculinity. His second marriage of more than sixty-five years was stable and monogamous, following Presbyterian regulations. He settled "upon Church land" where he lived with his wife under one roof in the "sense of the strict unity of Christian married persons."[112] Yet, while Wahyee embraced Christian ideas of the conjugal family and provided his children with formal education, he also respected his obligations toward his *abusua* and supported at least some nephews and nieces, even if they stayed outside the Christian Quarters. Wahyee was fortunate that his relative success as a cocoa farmer allowed him to fulfill these diverse social and financial responsibilities.

Marriages of Presbyterian Teachers

Although Presbyterian norms concerning sexuality and marriage applied to all members, teachers were under particular scrutiny. Presbyterian regulations stipulated that prominent members "should make it a duty to give a good example" to their communities "because of their special influence."[113] Teachers were obliged to have their marriages blessed in a church or enter an Ordinance marriage. Any pre- and extramarital sexual relations could have serious personal and professional consequences. Church leaders expected teachers to arrange marriages according to the ideals of Presbyterian masculinity. Still, living with different concepts of marriage was problematic for men in the Presbyterian congregation.

The interviewed retired teachers insisted that they did not have sex with women before finishing school. In a 1926 newspaper an open letter to "young manhood" advised a certain Patrick that "pre-marital commerce with opposite sex" is "both shameful and wrong." Instead, Patrick was urged to "make a friend or two of your own sex, who share your desire to be clean and manly," in the sense of exercising self-restraint. Surprisingly the writer alluded to a homoerotic potential in such male friendships.

> It is quite possible and practicable to find among members of your own sex such fervour of friendship (camaraderie in its highest sense) as will satisfy the nervous demands of the system. I need not more openly refer to this aspect of what many stigmatise as a vice. The world with evil mind is always ready to misconstrue what is really the most innocent fellowship.

Such homosocial relations should not preclude marriage when "manhood is fully developed."[114] During the 1940s Opusuo experienced this rigid situation. If a college student was seen "with a girlfriend" and somebody reported to the principal, he "might be sacked." Fearing the consequences, he became "afraid of women." Asked about homosexual relations in all-male educational institutions, Opusuo responded that he had never heard of it but doubted if there was much "opportunity to do that, unless perhaps in the holidays."[115]

Teachers were pressured to marry since Akan men who were single had not reached adulthood. Teachers were expected to embody the model of a Christian family life. The education department preferred that teachers seek brides who have a comparable education. A 1935 memorandum stated that teachers should be encouraged to create a "modern" household that exemplified "health" and "hygiene" to be emulated by villagers. And, according to the Colonial Office,

> [a teacher] can do little to teach the community . . . without effective help from a married woman, and his work will always be crippled if his wife is entirely uneducated and unable to carry out even in her own home the rules of health which her husband is trying to teach in the school.[116]

Unmarried teachers could not be promoted to the position of head teacher. These colonial policies were supported by mission churches. In 1931 the Basel Mission, on behalf of the Presbyterian Church, founded a girls' boarding school in Agogo to train "brides of young teachers" with skills essential for Christian motherhood.[117] Reverend Asante explained:

> This school was a special one for Christian parents to see that their children were well educated; they sent them to Agogo. The children, the girls, they learned one special quality: they are not so ostentatious, [instead] they are hard working, you (pause) . . . the German training, modest, very modest. So they [the church] recommend many teachers to marry someone from the Agogo Girls' School.[118]

In Presbyterian congregations teachers were popular marriage partners. Elizabeth Ntim (born 1912) recalled her "ambition of marrying a teacher" who would look after her children and guarantee her support, including house servants for fetching water and firewood.[119] Adelaide Opong, an Agogo graduate, narrated meeting her groom, a teacher and the son of E. K. Addo's older brother:

> I did not know this man at all; but once my father had agreed, and my mother had agreed, I had no choice. Excuse me to say, I had never slept with a man before. When it was all arranged, they came to perform the customary rites in front of my father. . . . In 1939 we returned to Abetifi to have a wedding service in the church.[120]

In 1937, four years after leaving college, Reverend Asante married Felicia Animaa, who had been selected by his mother. Felicia Animaa, a granddaughter of Abetifi's senior presbyter, Okra, recalled how she learned about her future husband while a student at Agogo in 1936. Although she did not know Asante, she was "obedient" and accepted the spouse chosen by her stepparents. She emphasized the difference between a Christian wedding and a union formed in Manem, Abetifi's old section. While the former was a public event "for everybody to see," the latter was merely an agreement between two lineages, the groom presenting drinks and money, followed by the bride cooking a meal "for the husband's house."[121] Asante and Felicia Animaa's wedding was celebrated in Abetifi. A photograph captured them standing on the steps of the Abetifi Presbyterian Church, both dressed in white (see Fig. 5.1), the Akan color of joy, purity, and victory. Asante wore a three-piece suit in white appropriate to his rank. This photograph surfaced in E. K. Addo's album; he had provided "all the refreshments" and "many other things."[122] These experiences confirm Carol Summers's argument for southern Rhodesia: teachers pursued "strategic" marriages with educated Christian women to achieve "adulthood, parenthood, and success within African communities" and to manage "missionaries' fundamental discomfort with the autonomy of individual African men."[123] Yet, in colonial Ghana, decisions about ideal marriage partners did not rest solely with teachers. Frequently mothers played crucial roles. Presbyterian marriage ideals were formulated by missionaries *and* senior African pastors.

Adelaide Opong and her husband had ten children, of whom only one had died. For the first twenty years of marriage, she followed the husband from station to station where he was teaching. Although her marriage was not always easy, she praised his commitment to fatherhood, emphasizing that he took "good care of his children."[124] Reverend Asante and Felicia Animaa also had ten children, eight daughters and two sons. Four of their daughters, following their mother, attended the Agogo school. All the children received a higher education. In 1994 five of their daughters lived abroad, two in the United Kingdom, two in Germany, and one in Nigeria. Asante named his children to honor the memory of his older relatives. Two were named after his father, Osafo; one after his mother, Ohenewaa; one after his *sewa* (father's sister), Effa; one after each *wɔfa*, Dwamena and Adofo; two after his wife's mother and grandmother; one after E. K. Addo; and the last child after his friend, Akyeampong, a senior presbyter of Agogo.[125] Calling Asante an *agya pa* (a good and exemplary father), his wife commented on his discipline and vulnerability as a teacher and later a pastor:

> When his children were young . . . when they did something wrong, he punished them. And then, he keeps them on his lap [brings them again close to himself]. He also shows them the right path to walk on. When they grew up, he continued to show them the right path . . . that they don't learn bad things

141

Fig. 5.1. Rev. E.K.O. Asante and Felicia Animaa after their wedding on the steps of the Abetifi Presbyterian Church, Abetifi, 1935. Photo, E. K. Addo's Papers (Abetifi and Accra, Ghana).

to disgrace his name. Because, if you are pastor, your children should have good names, otherwise your own name will be soiled.[126]

Reverend Asante also assisted nieces and nephews who stayed in his house and provided domestic labor in exchange for some education.

Although Presbyterian rules demanded co-residence, married couples did not share finances. My female interview partners stressed the importance of having their own source of income. Felicia Asante referred to herself as "a housewife" but one who "was not just sitting around."[127] In home science classes at Agogo, she had learned to bake bread. Further, she sold *ɔfam*, pounded ripe plantains with roasted corn flour, ginger, pepper, and palm oil, baked in an oven. Baking was a common occupation for a teacher's wife. When Adelaide Opong received some capital from her husband, she started baking. Bread was sold to pupils and teachers. Felicia Asante also fried cocoyam, ripe plantains, and *banfo bese* (corn fritters), and, for some time, she traded with cloth for tailoring. Both women reinvested their profits or bought small luxuries like earrings and beads. Felicia Asante helped with school expenses. When her daughters attended Agogo, she sewed dresses and purchased some of the required items. This recollection forms a striking contrast to Mrs. Helen Haegele's assessment who complained that Felicia, the "young teacher's wife," did not enjoy sewing.[128] Agogo was expensive. In 1953 tuition was two pounds, eight shillings, and boarding fees twenty-four pounds per year; pastor's children received a two-pound reduction.[129]

Adelaide Opong urged a younger generation to privilege the "children's welfare," since parents would eventually "profit from such investments." She cautioned against "practicing the European method" of pooling resources. To illustrate her point, Opong recounted that her daughter Margaret had moved to Brooklyn, New York. There Margaret saved with her husband until they could buy a "deep-freezer and a car." After the husband left, Margaret lost everything. Although Opong was a senior member of her church, she insisted on a wife's financial independence, explicitly rejecting the Presbyterian model of a male-dominated household. Instead, she reminded her listeners:

> European customs are different from African customs; as for us, our mind is different. European men do not marry a second wife, so it's easier for them to pull their resources together. . . . We should take what is good for us Africans, but not try to copy their practices.[130]

In her study of Akan senior civil servants, Christine Oppong observed that few couples jointly owned property and shared finances. Her explanations are relevant here. A husband's continued responsibility toward his matrikin affected property ownership and inheritance; civil servants' "higher living standard, in terms of spending power and accommodation," created demands by relatives.[131] Therefore a civil servant's wife desired a separation of resources to protect herself against her husband's matrikin, particularly should she survive him, even if they had entered an Ordinance marriage that provided some legal protection. Husbands who had children with outside wives caused further drain on conjugal resources.

Not all teachers conformed to Presbyterian expectations, much to the dismay of senior church officials and Basel missionaries. The Abetifi Native Tribunal records include many court cases in which fathers complained that their daughters had been seduced by teachers.[132] E. F. Opusuo talked about his strategies of hiding "many girlfriends" from church superiors. Premarital sex was risky, since an unwanted pregnancy could jeopardize a teacher's career.

> When we were young, there was no family planning as such, but people were using contraceptives. For instance, when you were a teacher . . . and you made a woman pregnant and you are not married, you could be suspended. First, it was nine months. You were suspended for nine months without pay; later on they reduced it to three months. Because of fear of that, young men were using contraceptives. There was something [called] Gyanomin, then Rendex . . . tablets used to insert into the vagina.[133]

Contraceptives reached Ghana in the postwar period. Interviewed men who became sexually active in the 1930s had not heard about them. Ten years later anthropologist J.W.A. Amoo called them "practically unknown."[134] Opusuo and his teacher friends shared information about female contraceptives, since none of them liked condoms. Although Opusuo considered them "common" and available in "drug stores" by the 1950s, not all young men had access.[135] While advice columns in newspapers had much to say about marriage in the 1950s and the early 1960s, questions about contraception were not really addressed.[136] Some men sought help elsewhere. John Akoto, an eighteen-year-old secondary student of Akropong, asked the London Family Planning Association "how to satisfy [a girl] with sexual intercourse and how to have intercourse without conceiving." Since Akoto "hate[d] using rubber barrier or anything worn on the penis," he asked for "another method." The Family Planning Association secretary forwarded his letter to the International Planned Parenthood Federation to give "this young man some advice," adding that "his girlfriend will have to take the precautions!"[137]

Despite Opusuo's familiarity with contraceptives, in 1955 two of his girlfriends became pregnant. In a settlement with their families he agreed to provide support until his children were born and offered a few pounds of compensation. Disregarding Presbyterian rules, Opusuo considered his decision adequate as long as he educated his children. He strongly disapproved of church interference into teachers' personal lives. He recalled with sadness female colleagues who had abortions by "crude methods" because they were "pregnant without marriage." He added that missionaries "thought they were doing good, but they caused a lot of harm."[138]

In order to save money, Opusuo delayed marriage until he was in his mid-thirties. Reflecting a generational shift, Opusuo did not rely on his father or other relatives when looking for an "educated girl" as a fitting spouse for a teacher. In 1956 he met Ester Dankyi from Akyem-Oda. Since she had not completed her education, Opusuo volunteered to pay the remaining school fees.

> [Her] parents were not interested in education . . . they did not find importance in educating the girl, so at the end of Standard V, she was asked to stop school. Because I was interested in her, in fact, the [her] uncle was my friend, so I was visiting [him], I was very regular in the house, the family knew me. When I decided to marry her, I said, I will allow her to continue to Standard VII, before I [marry].[139]

They had three children; two sons lived to adulthood. By about 1965, while stationed at Begoro, Akyem, Opusuo divorced Dankyi under dramatic circumstances. As an education officer, he traveled on weekdays. One evening, overhearing a conversation between his "Ewe house girl" and a "schoolboy," Opusuo learned that Dankyi was sending letters through her servant to a man in town. Curious, the servant asked the pupil to read the letter, in which Dankyi requested her lover to purchase female contraceptives. Immediately Opusuo called the servant and made her confess that his wife "had a lover staying for the night while [he] was on trek." When confronted, Dankyi denied it. Opusuo, accompanied by a friend, visited the culprit who also insisted on his innocence. When Opusuo pretended that he had received his wife's confession, the man broke down. Later, Ester Dankyi admitted the affair, too. Opusuo did not ask her parents to return marriage payments, as was common in Kwawu when seeking divorce. Instead, he demanded a twenty-five-pound adultery fee from her lover.

> It pained me a lot when my first wife became unfaithful. Because of her, I sent two women away [his girlfriends and the mothers of his first two children],

and I paid for her school fees. . . . This wife wanted to come back, but I refused. She is still not married today.

For five years Opusuo refrained from marriage. Ester Dankyi had so deeply challenged his sense of self that he "feared women." Yet his second marriage followed a similar pattern. He helped the new wife complete her studies at a training college before they had three children. Upon learning about her unfaithfulness, he divorced her. In 1981, after another interval, Opusuo married his third wife, "the best of the three . . . in spite of the age difference." Affectionately he added, "She really loves me." They also had three children.[140]

Even more so than Opusuo, A. K. Boakye Yiadom struggled to accommodate conflicting marriage expectations. Since he shared his autobiographical writings and spoke freely about his involvement with sixteen women who gave birth to his twenty-seven children, we can reconstruct how he negotiated between different notions of masculinity. These narratives provide a window onto how he recorded events at the time, and how he presented them later to different audiences. According to Presbyterian rules, he usually lived with one woman with whom he had performed customary marriage rites. With five of them, sequentially, their unions were consecrated by the church. They became "inside wives." He sought to prevent church officials from learning about "outside wives" and concubines.[141] This arrangement was for him neither problematic nor contradictory to his life as a devout Presbyterian, since he claimed to have compensated the extramarital mothers of his children and paid his offsprings' school fees. Yet there are discrepancies in Boakye Yiadom's representation of his marriages. In his autobiography, which is addressed to his Presbyterian congregation and presents a flawless life of a teacher-catechist, Boakye Yiadom only mentioned two of his Christian wives.[142] In his other, more intimate autobiography, written like a diary, as well as in our interviews, he revealed different layers of his sexual relationships as he navigated through and around church regulations.[143] In the 1940s he encountered accusations of sexual misconduct and was once forced to leave Presbyterian schools. Eager to enhance his qualifications, he returned and enrolled at the Presbyterian Training College in 1950. In the hope of conforming to the college's expectations, he presented himself as a single man without children.[144]

Fatherhood is important for Boakye Yiadom. His numerous children demonstrate that he fulfilled a central aspect of adult masculinity. He noted, "When you beget, you become a man yourself. I have become a man."[145]

146

This is reflected in his self-presentations. During our interviews he spoke at length about his children. In "My Own Life," he meticulously recorded the birth dates of his children, sometimes adding comments about their conceptions and the fees of midwives. He noted his children's expenses and his grievances when they failed to live up to his expectations.[146] His position as father was supported among his non-Christian relatives, as long as he had named his children. This recognition applied whether he had entered customary marriages with their mothers or only compensated them. Boakye Yiadom was expected to provide for *all* his children. If he failed to do so, this caused serious tensions. Because of his moderate salary, he struggled to pay school fees. It appears that he was more generous toward those whose mothers he had married. He also supported "two nieces and three nephews," some of whom stayed with him as "houseboys."[147] Jean Allman, documenting a shift from reciprocal obligations to paternal rights over children in colonial Asante, has suggested that school fees became "a never ending source of conflict between mothers and fathers."[148] From the interwar years, she argues, fathers increasingly resisted paying the rising costs of rearing their children. Boakye Yiadom's case supports this view.

In our conversations about marriage, Boakye Yiadom mentioned two important attributes: entering a "Christian marriage" and finding a wife "at home."[149] Both wives included in his short autobiography met these criteria. In 1943, selecting his first Christian wife, Alice Safoaah, he did not rely on mediation by his father or other relatives. They met during a funeral service in Bukuruwa, a town close to Abetifi. Preaching from the pulpit, he spotted a "particular woman" whose presence "touched" him. When he learned that she also hailed from Abetifi, he considered their meeting to be divine intervention.[150] Soon they were married with their union blessed in the church. In his writing, Boakye Yiadom added "Christian" whenever referring to Alice Safoaah. In 1944, upon the birth of his fifth child, he rejoiced that his "real and beloved only Christian wife delivered a well symmetrical child, called Grace Ankomaah Yiadom."[151] Reflecting Presbyterian regulations, Boakye Yiadom stressed the importance of husband and wife living under *one* roof:

> In Christian Quarters here, it is the law, Christian law, that every person stays with his wife so you can cooperate with your wife and everything. It is not good when you are living here and your wife is living in the town.

Then he added all the inconveniences, should husband and wife not reside together.

Your wife would come to this place in the night to sleep, she would have to take water from town for you to take your bath, and even, if she wants to consult a small matter with you, she should not have to travel up from the town. So, it is better if you stay with your wife.[152]

He emphasized economic disadvantages in marriages with spouses from different hometowns, including higher costs attending funerals. Following his own death, he expects matters of inheritance to be easy since his *abusua* and that of his wife and children know each other.

In 1964 Boakye Yiadom entered what he thought to be his final marriage. By letter he contacted his mother from his work station in Adamsu, Brong Ahafo, to find him a suitable spouse from Abetifi's Christian Quarters. In reply his mother sent him a photograph of Susana Ansomaah. Since Boakye Yiadom liked the picture, he mailed his own and instructed his mother to initiate marriage negotiations. Because he was twenty-five years older than Susana, he posted her a ten-year-old photograph. When they met for the first time, his real appearance came to her as quite a surprise. Later, commemorating the event, the two anachronistic pictures were enlarged and mounted together (see Fig. 5.2).[153] Exchanging photographs among potential marriage partners echoes the missionary practice of requesting a "picture bride." Fifty years earlier Arthur Jehle, a Basel missionary in Abetifi, asked his parents to search for a suitable and healthy *Missionsfrau* (missionary wife) who could do without luxuries. Jehle and his bride became acquainted by exchanging letters and photographs prior to her arrival on the Gold Coast.[154] Boakye Yiadom praised the quality of this marriage since it was "properly arranged by his relatives," who guaranteed that his wife had come from a "good house," not from one of "thieves or robbers." He deplored the fact that such scrutiny is being neglected by the younger generation who are, instead, following their "hearts."[155] Later, when he gave me access to "My Own Life," I learned how Boakye Yiadom at the time had highlighted Susana's Presbyterian credentials. The marriage payments included expenses for "Abetifi Presby Church Box Marriage Fee" and the Presbyterian "Women's Fellowship," each ten shillings sixpence. To what extent all participants knew that Susana became the co-wife of Agnes Fodwoo, whom Boakye Yiadom had married in 1961 according to "Native Customary Marriage Law and in respect to the Presbyterian Church of Ghana," is not clear.[156] According to Akan custom, his second marriage was not unusual; church officials, however, would have objected.

The pages of "My Own Life" provide a detailed record of how Boakye Yiadom arranged these two marriages while occupying his position as head

Fig. 5.2. A. K. Boakye Yiadom and his wife, Akosua Ansomaah; Boakye Yiadom's photograph was taken ca. 1950, Akosua Ansomaah's ten years later. The photographs were mounted and framed together after their wedding in 1964. Photo, A. K. Boakye Yiadom's Papers (Abetifi, Ghana).

teacher and catechist at Adamsu and Amuana-Praso. Since Agnes Fodwoo studied at the Agogo Training College, she only stayed during vacation with her husband who paid tuition. When Fodwoo was in Agogo, Susana Ansomaah could visit. Graduating in 1967, Fodwoo returned "for permanent stay," while Ansomaah resided with her brother in a cocoa village nearby where she traded with capital provided by her husband. Following several conflicts in which Boakye Yiadom accused Fodwoo of infidelity, their marriage was dissolved in 1971. During divorce negotiations, Boakye Yiadom first insisted on reimbursement of 316 pounds for her education. Later he settled for much less.[157] Still, reconstructing his relationship with Ansomaah in 1993, the existence of his senior wife was omitted. Rather, the story of his marriage to Ansomaah had become a formulaic description of how Christian marriages *should* be performed and emulated in contemporary Ghana. After taking liberties of arranging marriages and relations with a multitude of wives and concubines, he suggested that this marriage was precisely conducted according to Presbyterian rules, fitting his self-image as a devout teacher-catechist. In retrospect, Boakye Yiadom no longer foregrounded the fluidity of his previous marriage arrangements. Instead, thinking of his legacy, he promoted the Presbyterian ideal he sought to achieve for which he hopes to be remembered. In 1999, quite unexpectedly, Susana Ansomaah passed way. Two years later Boakye Yiadom had remarried.[158]

From 1930 to 1970 the implementation of Presbyterian rules in teachers' marriages was not static. Particularly the 1950s, the beginning of self-rule under Kwame Nkrumah's Convention People's Party (CPP), brought many changes. The Accelerated Development Plan in Education of 1951 promoted a rapid expansion of primary schools and gradually removed all differences between government and nongovernment teachers. These policies "inexorably altered" the relationship between churches, schools, and government.[159] Although churches retained their own disciplinary codes, they became increasingly difficult to enforce. Presbyterian teachers ceased to be church agents; instead, they became government employees. This shift is ingrained in the memories of the interviewed men. Opusuo recalled how suspension for "immoral behavior" was reduced. He no longer felt obliged to have his second and third marriages blessed in the church. Boakye Yiadom emphasized that an education officer was more interested in his classroom performance than marital activities, now considered "private matters."[160] Yet his correspondence reveals that, at least by 1971, his polygynous arrangements with Agnes Fodwoo and Susana Ansomaah had come to the attention of Presbyterian officials. Although Boakye Yiadom emphasized that the marriage with his senior wife was no longer valid, he was still transferred from Amuana-Praso, Kwawu, to Dwerebease, closer to Abetifi, thereby losing the positions of head teacher and catechist, the latter for two years.[161] As long as the appearance of following the expectations of Presbyterian masculinity remained intact, teachers could carve out their own spaces to accommodate relations with women outside the boundaries of Christian marriage. If tensions were brought into the open, sanctions could still be applied but these were less harsh than earlier in the twentieth century.

Conclusion

In Akan societies marriage occurred in stages, involving different payments and rites between the involved parties. In the twentieth century mission churches and the colonial state advocated marriage forms that privileged the conjugal bond and patrilineal descent over ties to matrikin. This led to contestation. When arranging their own marriages, the eight men operated within these different normative frameworks with flexibility. Their experiences demonstrate the importance of Christian marriage ideologies, here explored within the fold of the Presbyterian Church and understood as the expectations and obligations of Presbyterian masculinity.

The recollections confirm the trends in the changes of Akan marriages suggested by scholars; these include an increase in marital payments, a far-reaching monetization of conjugal relations, and "the transformation of marrying processes into a single act of marriage."[162] While the interviewed women, Akua Nimako, Felicia Asante, and Adelaide Oppong, entered arranged marriages, men increasingly ignored parental wishes, especially those belonging to a younger generation like Opusuo and those with spatial mobility, Ɔkyeame Asante and Ankoma.[163] Fathers' responsibilities and obligations changed as well. By mid-century men from southern towns, which had a strong presence of educational institutions, were expected to pay their children's school fees up to Standard VII. In rural areas men engaged in the cocoa industry expressed increasing demands on their wives and children's labor, as Allman and Tashjian have noted.[164] This situation does not fully correspond to that of the interviewed men. Only Wahyee was a cocoa farmer but sufficiently well-off to hire laborers; Marfo as an herbalist did not farm. Ɔkyeame Asante, Reverend Asante, Opusuo, and Boakye Yiadom had salaried employment; Addo as trader and Ankoma as lorry driver ran their own businesses. Boakye Yiadom, however, relied on his sons to help with his cocoa farms in Kurofa. Still, accomplishments in fatherhood remained crucial to adult masculinity. Those without children were not perceived as full adults and could not aspire to senior masculinity.

In exploring the relations between masculinity and marriage, it is particularly interesting to look at those who navigated between different normative frameworks. Presbyterian converts, among them many teachers, had relations and obligations both in *and* outside their congregations. Teachers belonged to a new social group of literate men—*akrakyefoɔ*—who shared the experience of education, material desires like specific clothes and furniture, and a salaried income. They were under greater scrutiny to follow the norms of Presbyterian masculinity than ordinary congregation members. In these men's lives there was a coexistence of different forms and expectations. They sought to create their own conjugal arrangements without following any given model. Thus they deployed different strategies. Some, like Marfo, used their stories to remind their audience about what he considered appropriate practices. He took conversations about marriage as an occasion to lament the loose morals of today's youth, no longer listening to their elders. Yet there were cracks in such presentations, like Ɔkyeame Asante's elaborations about proverbs and Wahyee's reminiscing about courtship games. In this meta-discourse, they provided glimpses of other experiences that challenged expectations and, in doing so, revealed deeper layers of their subjectivity. Unlike the men, the women were more prepared to address the hardship and disappointments they encountered in marriage; they spoke about husbands who seldom lived up to their expectations of adult masculinity.

Wambui Karanja's notion of inside and outside wife is helpful to understand the marriage arrangements of those who lived in a supposedly monogamous Christian marriage and yet had other relations.[165] While Addo came close to the elite setting presented by Karanja, Boakye Yiadom's accounts show that even a village teacher, living away from the urban setting, operated within a similar model that identified only one marital union to church and educational authorities. Boakye Yiadom's autobiographical writings and the interview transcripts demonstrate an unevenness between his oral and written self-representations, while illuminating tensions between conflicting notions of masculinity. They delineate a precise historicization of his self-representations, of his subjectivity. These texts show how he remembered certain episodes in his life, how he wrote about them for specific audiences, and how he presented them in retrospect. An examination of these accounts indicates his choice of strategies to balance conflicting expectations while developing subjective, social, and professional identities. His extensive written documentation reveals the limits *and* possibilities of oral history. Oral narratives do not tell "how it really was." Rather, they portray how it should have or could have been. Oral history is less a factual representation of the past than in its rendering a reflection of the past's meaning for the present and thus a reflection of the speaker's subjectivity.[166] Although Boakye Yiadom's life is better documented than other accounts, we can extrapolate that his changing views of marriage and sexuality are somewhat typical of the group. All seemed to experience the conflicts and struggles of shifting marriage ideals and different ideas of masculinity. Yet not everybody was willing to address these complexities and offer access to a documentary trail.

In the final chapter I broaden the chronological framework by looking at the long twentieth century, the period from the 1880s to the 1990s. This allows us to deepen the focus on the central question of how, and under what circumstances, men achieved elderhood. Could those with access to wealth take shortcuts to senior masculinity? And what legacies did these men leave behind?

SPEAKING SENSIBLY: MEN AS ELDERS IN THE TWENTIETH CENTURY

6

Ideals of elderhood and big-man status have formed a continuity in Akan societies since the nineteenth century, although responsibilities and expectations of elders and big men have changed. Ɔbirɛmpɔn (big-man) status means not only disposable wealth but also incorporates values like generosity, the commitment to share one's riches. Big men replaced an older ranking system based on lineage and chiefly office. Such social categories were formulated, contested, and renegotiated in a dialectic response to historical transformations like migration, cash-cropping, salaried employment, and monetization. For the eight men I studied, reaching senior masculinity was decisive. By senior masculinity I mean not age so much as the qualities embodied in the social position of ɔpanyin (elder), expressed by a person's comportment, reputation, and ability to speak well. The changing articulations of senior masculinity and big-man status of twentieth-century Ghana are reflected in these men's recollections.

Becoming an ɔpanyin was a process that could extend over years. Since elderhood is not self-ascribed but granted by society, hometown communities—most prominently the abusua (matrilineage)—played an active role in the making of an ɔpanyin. While living outside Kwawu, migrants sought ways to establish physical markers, such as building a house, which would remind hometown communities of their aspirations. Returning to Kwawu, potential elders volunteered or were recruited for community service in their abusua, at the ahenfie (chief's palace), in shrines and churches, in Asafo companies, or in new political institutions like local councils and district assemblies. Those who conducted themselves well might receive the desired honor and public recognition. During their final years the interviewed men were preoccupied with social obligations like funerals, as well as their own strategies of leaving a legacy. Yet, going against community expectations, even if one was a trusted and respected ɔpanyin, could confuse matters and alter wishes for funeral rites. Although, with modernity, individualized selves have become increasingly important for elders and big men in twentieth-century Ghana, communitarian ideals remain crucial for attaining personhood.

Discussing Ɔpanyin

In Twi the term ɔpanyin incorporates a broad semantic field. J. G. Christaller distinguishes between two groups of meaning: age ɔpanyin, "an old person, an adult," as opposed to a child; and status and achievements ɔpanyin, "a gentleman, [a] respectable man, [a] person of rank." The second definition refers to an ɔpanyin as a figure of authority, either a chief or belonging to a chief's council of elders.[1] My question in Kwawu about the meaning of ɔpanyin triggered lively discussions. Ɔkyeame Kwabena Asante, spokesperson of the Pepease Tegare shrine, stressed age. Jokingly he added that somebody needed to be at least "eighty years or older" to be called ɔpanyin, referring to himself as aberantee (young man).[2] Rev. E.K.O. Asante emphasized maturity and animonyam (honor). He explained that the term ɔpanyin stems from the expression "wanyin, he or she has grown up."

> If you are an ɔpanyin you should act as an elder, or an experienced person. It depends on your behavior and attitude. But, when somebody of that age behaves like . . . a child, we say you are not fit to be called an ɔpanyin. . . . We don't give him respect. But as an ɔpanyin, you speak sensibly. You act like an experienced person. . . . But if you are an elderly person and you misbehave, they say, "ɔpanyin kwasea, a foolish elder" (laughs).[3]

In Reverend Asante's assessment, an ɔpanyin's position is not permanent. People recognized as ɔpanyin need to continue proving their worthiness. Conduct, behavior, and speech are considered decisive. People lose respect for misbehaving elders. Every occupant of a stool is ex officio an ɔpanyin. His or her misconduct reduces the office's honor and might lead to de-stoolment. This reflects J. B. Danquah's understanding that "the Opanyin is made, discovered, and not born." One who loses dignity or honor, suffers disgrace, animguase, meaning: "face descending baseness" or "debasement of the person."[4]

The retired teacher-catechist A. K. Boakye Yiadom claimed the status of ɔpanyin for himself. For him, an ɔpanyin embodies the essence of a man's achievements in reaching senior masculinity and thus personhood. He must marry, support a wife with capital, provide children with an education, and fulfill financial and social obligations toward the matrilineage. An *ɔpanyin* should mediate conflicts. It is significant that Boakye Yiadom stressed an *ɔpanyin*'s responsibilities toward his wife and children, as well as toward his matrikin. His Presbyterian training emphasized the Christian (nuclear) family privileging patrilineal ties at the expense of the matrilineage. Boakye Yiadom sought to combine norms of his church *and* the matrilineage, equal attention to wife and children, and to nieces and nephews. He indicated the contentious relationship between these competing notions of masculinity. Again, Boakye Yiadom struggled to fulfill these expectations because of his limited resources.[5]

Fatherhood was important in reaching adult masculinity *and* senior masculinity. A man without children could not aspire to become a respected elder. Early in the twentieth century Akan societies ridiculed married men who did not father children. In Kwawu there was a specific ritual to out an *ɔkrawa* (barren man). E. F. Opusuo recalled:

> When I was a child, when I was in school, in the village where I attended school, there was a man who was impotent, he was not fertile . . . he was not producing any children. So they said a certain custom must be performed for him so that he would be able to produce children. It was a queer thing. It was organized publicly, even children were there slapping him (laughs), they got out to slap him.

The story had a happy ending. "Fortunately for him," Opusuo continued, "when all these things happened . . . he began producing children."[6] By the 1970s this ritual was no longer performed in Obo. Phil Bartle heard accounts of the practice. An impotent man could be "caught, slapped, and decorated with food, plantain leaves . . . and a cat's skin." In a mock ceremony the *ɔkrawa* was enstooled as *ɔkrawahene,* "given a wooden toy, and made to swear an oath to all other old men with numerous progeny that he would father children." An *ɔkrawa* received less to eat; "food would make him too sleepy at night to engage in intercourse."[7] He was the antithesis of the *ɔpanyin:* a man not publicly respected and honored but instead ridiculed, despised, and the subject of gossip, laughter, and contempt.

Sjaak van der Geest interviewed Kwawu men and women about their understandings of *ɔpanyin.* His informants remarked on the fluidity in the transitions between the stages of life that followed adolescence: *aberanteɛ* (young and approaching middle age), *ɔpanyin* (getting old), and *akwakora* (old man). The female equivalents are *ababawa, ɔbaa-panyin/ɔpanyin,* and *aberewa.* He suggested that "*ɔpanyin* and *akwakora/aberewa* do not so much

represent a chronological order—but a moral one, a difference in appreciation of old age."[8] He drew on a fascinating discussion about proverbs to
distill an ɔpanyin's virtues: wisdom, ability to advise people, ability to keep
secrets, mutual respect with dependants, self-restraint, and honor. Van der
Geest did not historicize the ɔpanyin ideal nor did he analyze it in terms of
gender, although he did note the possibility of a female ɔpanyin.[9]

(Many of those I interviewed thought that both men and women may
act as elders, but that male and female elders should act differently.)When
Ɔkyeame Asante discussed the meaning of the proverb "Akokɔbere nim adek-
yee, nanso ɔhwɛ onini ano" (The hen is aware of daybreak, but she watches
the cock's beak [waits for the cock to announce it]), he elaborated on distinct
gender roles:

> Some women are very intelligent. They have the mind to settle cases for peace
> to prevail. . . . We might meet at a public place, you see, a certain woman and
> many elders may meet to discuss a case. She knows and wishes to say, but she
> would prefer that you, as the man, speak first. She can get closer to you and
> whisper, she can make a sign with her foot, or she can get up and go outside.
> . . . The man also leaves informing the elders that he needs to urinate. . . . [He]
> goes to listen to her and returns to announce her opinion. That's why whenever
> cases are heard, we suggest that we go and ask the *aberewa* [old woman].[10]

The proverb indicates that if a female elder acts as an adviser in the chief's
palace, her input should be less public than that of her male colleagues. She
should use her influence from behind the scene, playing the *aberewa* who is
consulted.[11] How have ideas about ɔpanyin evolved in the course of the
twentieth century? What were the experiences of those who sought to live
up to expectations of senior masculinity in the past? The biographical portrait
of John Yaw Atta, an early Basel Mission convert in Kwawu, offers an excellent case study.

The Afflictions of Ɔpanyin John Yaw Atta

In 1915 Ɔpanyin J. Y. Atta died after two decades of service as senior
presbyter (church elder) of the Basel Mission congregation in Abetifi. After
his death the Abetifi pastor, Rev. D. E. Akwa, wrote an account of Atta's
"life and death" for his superiors. Reverend Akwa followed the conventions
of a conversion story, outlining Atta's development from a "heathen" youth,
born in 1854 into the ruling Tena *abusua*, to his successful integration into
the congregation.[12] Reverend Akwa described the trajectory of a noble man
who became a prominent member of the Abetifi Christian congregation,

achieving wealth and status while remaining trapped in his ties and obligations to his non-Christian relatives. Atta's remaking as a Christian man is reflected in his transformation from a member of the "royal family," who "dislik[ed] farm work," to becoming "the most celebrated farmer in the whole district." In 1876 Atta started working as a "houseboy" for the Abetifi missionaries who had given him a loan to pay for court debts. As elsewhere, the missionaries encouraged their domestic servant to enter baptismal classes and divorce his three wives. In 1878 he was baptized as one of the first four Abetifi converts. In the 1890s Atta was elected presbyter to assist the missionaries with the supervision of the congregation.[13]

Reverend Akwa presented Atta as "lover of civilization and improvements." Farming "became his favourite occupation at the middle of his age." As a royal, Atta used his connections to obtain a substantial piece of land for "Christians" and founded farm villages on it, launching the Kwawu cocoa industry. Subsequently he owned an "extensive cocoa plantation" but, as Reverend Akwa noted, wealth "did not ruin his Christianity, as it has affected many other Christians." In 1907 Atta tried his luck with trading by selling cocoa to European merchants who paid him with imported goods. This entrepreneurial spirit was, for Reverend Akwa, most evident in Atta's ambition to improve commerce. He led "Abetifi Christians" to build a road that later accommodated motor lorries "along [the] river Afram from Pitiko down to Mankrong," connecting Kwawu to the Volta River traffic. In 1913 he lobbied the visiting governor for a railway extension.[14] Atta played an important role in the mission church and among Kwawu chiefs. Reverend Akwa emphasized his performance as senior presbyter. Atta participated in the state's "civil cases" as "excellent councillor, witty juror, and faithful judge." The ɔmanhene (paramount chief) and mpanyinfoɔ (elders) did not settle major disputes without consulting him. Atta was known for his generosity: he paid debts for his abusua and served as "benefactor and kind-hearted Christian to the Mission workers" stationed in Abetifi. He became a respected ɔpanyin within the congregation *and* among chiefs, taking responsibility and sharing his wealth with both groups. In so doing he acted as a cultural broker, one of the "middle figures" so crucial in colonial encounters.[15]

Yet Atta's biographer found his multiple responsibilities problematic and characterized them as "afflictions." Reverend Akwa suggested that Atta died as a troubled man and that his skills in negotiating between different contexts were a sign of failure. In Akwa's perception, the world of Christian Quarters, created by missionaries in collaboration with middle figures, was incommensurable with that of the ahenfie. These settings reflected opposing expectations of elders and competing forms of senior masculinity. Atta, although baptized, continued to acknowledge his obligations as an ɔdehyeɛ (royal). According to Akwa, "he suffered too much about the affairs of his relatives," meaning their financial and dynastic troubles. Whenever an emergency occurred, Atta was "the only man who [bore] the yoke." On his deathbed he recalled spending more than six hundred pounds on his relatives' debts and "the improvement of the District" without receiving a word of thanks. Reverend Akwa did not understand why Atta decided to assist during stool disputes and other crises, why he sought to fulfill his abusua's and the mission's wishes.[16] Another affliction was based in gender expectation. Atta lacked a Christian marriage, the "true unity which is to exist between himself and family." This caused "the hardship" of his life and made him die of "broken heart." His wife was "not submissive, and not a good helper to the husband." His sons, belonging to their mother's abusua, "disobeyed their father." Atta had confessed that his children were not a "blessing to [his] marriage, but misery, or punishment from God." For Reverend Akwa, the lack of proper domestic arrangements made Atta vulnerable to other afflictions. A life closer to the missionary masculinity ideal, like closer conjugal bonds, would have enabled Atta to overcome his abusua's insatiable demands.[17]

These conflicting expectations culminated when Atta was elected to serve as Ɔmanhene of Kwawu, "the most troublesome time of his life." In 1898 the crowd carried him toward the ahenfie to be enstooled.

> [According] to the native fashion, he was caught, daubed with white clay from head to foot, sprinkled his feet with the blood of a sheep, carried on the shoulder of one of the king-carriers, and applauded after him from one end of the town to another; which bespeaks of his being a Chief. He told them . . . "if you will be in position to carry me always on your shoulder, and head, and will never descend me, then I will always be your Chief. But mind that as soon as I am descended, I will leave your quarters to the Christian quarters, where you will never be in a position to retake me." [When] John Atta was eventually descended, he bent his steps to the Christian Quarters, where no one dared to recall him.[18]

Atta's life in the Christian Quarters lay beyond the reach of those who wanted him as ɔmanhene. Still, at least in Reverend Akwa's account, Atta was tormented that he could not help his abusua by serving as ɔmanhene during a period of instability. In 1905 the stool was again offered to him, but he refused. The last time he was nominated, half a year prior to his death, the mission leadership in Abetifi informed him that "kingship is not a violation of God's commandments." He was encouraged "to rule as a Christian, resist all the stool temptations in his old age, and die as a Christian," and especially to "draw the heathens to the service of God." Atta confronted the king makers with a list of conditions, among them his insistence on living in the Christian Quarters and not marrying any stool wives. He demanded that all "subjects" cease libations and other rituals, and instead attend church. He also planned to terminate the "Chief's oath" for initiating a court case. The ɔkyeame, speaking for the delegation, could not accept conditions that must have sounded outrageous. Although Atta was a devout Christian, a "lover of civilization," "generous," "plain-speaking and truthful," who abstained "from all appearances of evil," he did not break away from his previous environment. Atta failed to embrace Christianity fully and live by its rules like the missionary version of senior masculinity. He was caught in the predicament of seeking to be a "good father," in the sense of an elder, "to both heathen[s], and Christians of Okwawu country, outwardly and inwardly."[19]

In 1993, almost eighty years after J. Y. Atta's death, I had a conversation with J. A. Wahyee about the early history of the Basel Mission congregation in Abetifi. Wahyee was full of memories and stories about Atta who was his wɔfa (grand-uncle), his grandmother's twin brother.

> He had power in Kwawu! And so when the chiefs brought up something, which would go against the church, he went straight before them to tell them, "What you are doing is not good; you should stop." And they stopped, because he was an ɔdehyeɛ [member of the ruling lineage] in Kwawu.[20]

These days Atta is celebrated as one of the founding heroes of the Presbyterian Church in Abetifi. People remember him as a model Christian with no mention of the ambivalence expressed so eloquently by Reverend Akwa. Frequently I heard the story of Atta refusing enstoolment as ɔmanhene, exclaiming, "My kingdom is not of this world."[21] In his version Wahyee emphasized how Atta acted like an ɔpanyin.

> He was held and was going to be enstooled. The Nkwatiahene was a very strong man; he lifted him on his shoulders and took him to the ahenfie to be enstooled. Seeing that they were really taking him there to be enstooled, he slapped him [the Nkwatiahene] and this one let him down. Later, he went to Nkwatia to kneel before him and apologized.... Further, he gave his niece to the Nkwatiahene to marry. The woman died recently, it is not even two months ago. So, that man was really brave, nebo yɛ duru [literally, his chest was heavy].[22]

Using the expression *nebo yɛ duru,* a synonym of *ɔyɛ barima* (he is a brave, valiant man), Wahyee referred to Atta's masculinity, emphasizing his reputation. This locution is related to *ne sunsum yɛ duru,* having a strong personality, referring to one's character.[23] Unlike Reverend Akwa, Wahyee thought that Atta succeeded in accommodating competing expectations as *ɔpanyin.* Atta conducted himself effectively in both settings, in the Christian Quarters and among the *mpanyinfoɔ* at the *ahenfie.* This shift is important. While Reverend Akwa considered the formation of multiple masculine identities among senior members of the Basel Mission congregation problematic, two generations later this predicament had become normal, almost ordinary, for Wahyee. Since the 1930s members of the Presbyterian Church have gradually moved into the ranks of elders and stool holders, especially in Abetifi.[24] Ɔpanyin Wahyee did not encounter the challenges faced by his grand-uncle. Following Luise White's argument, it appears that both Reverend Akwa and Wahyee were reflecting on their own experience while presenting aspects of Atta's life. Their stories about Atta served as vessels to reveal and historicize their own selves.[25]

Becoming an Elder

In his social history of alcohol in Ghana, Emmanuel Akyeampong has argued that "the status of elderhood is the desired goal of all."[26] Particularly the first generation of male migrants to the coast anticipated temporary migration in the hope that urban wage labor would help to achieve elderhood. Most of my interview partners talked about migration and addressed the following themes: preparations to returning home, community recognition, and the creation of a legacy. These reminiscences provide an entry into individual processes of becoming an *ɔpanyin* and can be read as a catalogue of one's accomplishments. For men and women who worked outside Kwawu, returning to their hometown was a crucial transition in their lives. In his study of Obo, Bartle suggested that "at the final stage of the life cycle, the migrant return[ed] permanently to the hometown or satellite village and eventually live[d] off the produce of his investments: his children, his farm, his savings, his property."[27] This might happen early in life as in the case of Wahyee. Hometown stays could be interrupted by additional sojourns outside Kwawu, as in Kofi Ankoma's experience. The preparations for the final homecoming—launching a cocoa farm, building a house, and providing children and relatives with education—relate to the process of becoming an *ɔpanyin.*[28]

Bead trader Wahyee returned to Abetifi in the early 1930s to take over his late brother's cocoa farms and focus on domestic responsibilities. This marked his transition to becoming an ɔpanyin.

> The reason why I stopped [bead] trading was that I [and my wife] then had given birth to many children, and I needed to stay home and look after them going to school. My older brother had also died, and this house was entrusted into my care. I had many children, nephews and many other family members under my care. Here is one of them (pointing to his nephew Yaw Apea).[29]

After returning to Abetifi, not only did Wahyee take a senior position within his *abusua* but, at the age of thirty-five, he was elected presbyter and became responsible for supporting the local pastor "in the oversight of the Christian life in the congregation, especially the family life and the upbringing of children."[30] Wahyee served on the building committee and organized "communal labor" to maintain and erect new school buildings. He played an active part in settling marriage disputes and "enforced the laws" of the church.[31] Basel missionaries, resident in Abetifi during the 1950s and 1960s, recalled Wahyee's stature and dedication as presbyter.[32]

The records of the Abetifi session, the congregation's governing body of presbyters, survive only from 1960 on. The minutes provide further evidence of Wahyee's influence. In 1963 he informed the session that Florence Adoma, suspended for becoming a junior wife, knew well that her husband "had so many wives." The session decided to re-admit her only if she ended her marriage. At the same meeting Wahyee admonished the headmasters of Abetifi's Presbyterian schools about "the mischief school children have been doing in bush destroying farms or crops" when fetching firewood.[33] Other business featured Wahyee negotiating with the Swiss contractor A. Lang about "paving around the chapel," and with the *Adɔntenhene* (Abetifi chief) who "placed a fetish groove [*sic*] Dente on part of our Mission land."[34] Wahyee served as the session's messenger. He traveled to Accra to inquire why a new Kwawu map only showed "part of the land originally acquired by the Missionaries"; he spoke with a man whose daughter had "gone astray" and entered an adulterous relationship.[35] Frequently Wahyee's intervention closed the case, a sign of his persuasive eloquence.[36] The session minutes show that the separation between the Christian Quarters and *Manem* (Abetifi's old town) lasted through the 1960s; Wahyee advised a new communicant "against unnecessary visits to the town."[37] If a congregation member challenged a presbyter, there were consequences. Yaw Opoku, "seriously sick in bed" and seeking reacceptance, had to "render apology to Op. J. A. Wahyee whose authority and advice he had thwarted."[38]

As a presbyter and cocoa farmer, Wahyee lived close to Abetifi. Although forced to plant new trees because of soil exhaustion and loss to government policies intended to fight swollen shoot disease, Wahyee continued to farm in Kwawu, at times on church land. Whenever needed by the session, or by his *abusua*, he could reach Abetifi within a day.[39] Because of his distinguished record of mediating cases, Wahyee's reputation as *ɔpanyin* grew beyond Abetifi's Christian Quarters. By the 1990s, when he was bound to his house as an *akwakora* (old man), people still sought his advice. For Ɔpanyin Wahyee, elderhood had become permanent.

Kofi Ankoma was less successful in reaching senior masculinity. Like Wahyee, he returned to Kwawu in his mid-thirties. Quitting the Gold Coast Police in 1948, he relocated to Obo to be closer to his mother and to accept *abusua* responsibilities. With the help of an Anglican bishop, he bought a Morris van for four hundred pounds and started a transport business driving to Accra.[40] Establishing himself in his hometown was Ankoma's first attempt to become an *ɔpanyin*. He left Kwawu twice. He did not explain his decision, merely saying that he "felt like traveling." In 1956 he sold the Morris for three hundred pounds and became a "licensed driver" with Swiss Motors in Accra. Four years later he was back in Kwawu with a new Bedford truck with a wooden top. Ankoma resumed his transportation business, driving within Kwawu and occasionally to Accra. In 1968 he left Obo, first delivering Club beer for the Swiss company Accra Brewery. Eight years later he worked for International Tobacco. In 1984 a doctor diagnosed high blood pressure, and Ankoma retired at the age of seventy.[41]

His investments in cocoa farms behind Kwawu-Tafo did not bring the expected returns. Soil exhaustion, drought, and fire during the 1980s destroyed his trees. In 1992 Ankoma finally succeeded his *wɔfa*, Kwame Asiama, and inherited several buildings in Obo and in the commercial centers along the Nkawkaw-Kumase railway line. Kwame Asiama's older brother, Kwadwo Adofo, was a wealthy trader who had financed Ankoma's education. Because Asiama lived to be one hundred years old, Ankoma waited for decades to gain access to Adofo's properties. Still, Ankoma served as an elder for his *abusua*, his children, and particularly for a Tegare (Gare) shrine. As long as his health permitted, he traveled to Pepease every forty days for Anwona, the main Gare ritual coinciding with *Fieda Fofie*, ten days before *Akwasidae* Sunday. There he sat among the elders watching the *agorɔ* (ritual performance). Frequently he was called into the shrine house for a drink, to renew his pledge, and to receive Gare's protection.[42]

Akrakyefoɔ, like Reverend Asante, E. F. Opusuo, and Boakye Yiadom, mainly worked outside their hometowns; their final return home corresponded with retirement. If possible they made preparations early in life, thereby initiating the process of becoming an *ɔpanyin.* Reverend Asante served as primary school head teacher in his hometown of Abetifi from 1937 to 1944 where he had a close relationship with the pastor, Rev. E. V. Asihene. The outbreak of World War II provided Asante with the challenge to prove himself as *ɔpanyin,* acting as leader for the church. In late 1939 the colonial government decided to deport all German nationals. On a Sunday the district commissioner arrived with policemen in Abetifi to arrest school supervisor Eugen Haegele and his wife, both of German nationality.[43] Asante recalled:

> The tension was so great that people were always alert to hear something from Europe and Hitler. Then, after the service, the presbyters were invited by the minister to hear some information about the war. . . . While we were there, the district commissioner and some policemen came and arrested them [Haegele and his wife]. Yes, a very sad scene.

Asante closely witnessed the drama that unfolded for the missionaries, pulled out of their domestic setting.

> They were given one hour to pack (laughs), and even it was difficult for them to take their meal. The wife was shaking like this (demonstrates her shaking), so the district commissioner ordered the policemen to let her be free, not to molest her. . . . The man started packing his personal properties, sorted out from the church properties. So, his personal properties were packed in the car with them and sent away to Koforidua [regional capital]. Since then we never saw them again. Then, they asked one policeman to watch, to take charge of the bungalow. They locked all the rooms and took the keys.[44]

This description reveals Asante's sentiments toward the missionaries. He had affection for the Haegeles, terming this "a very sad scene." He also laughed involuntarily at the irony: the missionary couple, despite their European privilege, was forced by the colonial authorities to pack and leave without advance notice. The sacred Sunday meal, in which missionaries exemplified Christian family life, was prevented by the DC's intervention. The missionary couple's sudden disappearance made a deep impression on the congregation.[45]

Since the pastor was on leave, Asante had to take charge. Although other Abetifi teachers and the presbyters were older and more experienced, the mantle of leadership fell on Asante's shoulders because of his qualification as a trained teacher-catechist. Presiding over Sunday services and looking after the Presbyterian schools, Asante became an ɔpanyin for the Abetifi congregation at the age of twenty-eight. Most presbyters had authority owing to their advanced age and experience, qualities Asante lacked. The senior presbyter Joseph Okra, John Yaw Atta's successor, had served for more than twenty years. Asante's successful performance contributed to his admission to the Kumase theological seminary in 1945, recommended by his mentor, Reverend Asihene. Two years later he was ordained.[46]

Reverend Asante had a distinguished career as a pastor and became a respected ɔpanyin. His personal papers and other archival sources allow a detailed reconstruction of how he established himself as senior pastor. In 1948 the Presbyterian Church decided to expand its activities to the less developed Northern Territories (NT) and appealed for volunteers at the synod. Working in the north was unpopular, since this area was considered backward and lacking in modern amenities. In print Asante recalled:

> [There] was a long deep silence. I looked around and felt a strong urge in me that God was speaking to me. I then asked a friend . . . to give me a piece of paper. I wrote down my name on the paper and presented it quickly to the Synod Clerk, Rev. C. H. Clerk, who in turn passed it on to the Moderator, Rev. S. S. Odonkor. He rang a bell on his table and announced my name to the big gathering. This was followed by a loud applause. All the delegates were asked to stand up and sing. . . . After the singing, the Moderator offered a short prayer asking God's blessing on my work. Friends and many well wishers came forward to congratulate me. That was the proudest moment in my life.[47]

Asante's volunteering became "the positive high point of the synod," otherwise dominated by political tensions, reflecting the strong nationalist sentiment after the 1948 riots. As the first "missionary pioneer" to the NT, Asante gained instant fame in Ghana and abroad.[48] For eighteen months he worked in Salaga, leaving his wife and children in Abetifi. As an African missionary, Asante did not enjoy the same privileges as the resident Basel missionary, Otto Rytz. While Rytz and his wife were permitted to stay at the government rest house, Asante had to be satisfied with more modest accommodations. In a characteristic understatement, he wrote that he and his "houseboy" Kofi were taken to the government rest house "only to see that [there] was no room for us." Instead, they were given a room elsewhere with "no ventilation" and "found it too hot to sleep inside."[49] His tasks were numerous: learning the Hausa and Gonja language; preaching in villages around Salaga, the town dominated by Muslims; teaching literacy to cate-chumens; and offering first aid to villagers. He traveled on a secondhand bicycle purchased by Rytz for ten pounds. Moreover, he had to conduct fund-raising. On his visits south he gave speeches about his missionary work, copies of which were distributed. In one address he asked the audience for contributions toward the seventy thousand bricks needed to build the Salaga mission house and the purchase of a water tank.[50] The mission house was completed in 1950, with major assistance from the Union Trading Company (UTC), and was offered to Rytz and his family. Asante supervised the work, which included digging holes for fifty-three citrus trees.[51] Fund-raising ef-forts continued to be called "Salaga brick fund." Asante tapped into his personal connections. He wrote to his benefactor, trader E. K. Addo, plead-ing for 150 pounds to buy an old "kid car" from the NT chief commissioner, who was planning to replace it with "a grander touring car." Addo imme-diately sent the requested amount.[52] At Asante's funeral in 1997, Addo praised Asante's missionary work and recalled the "jalopy sort of car" he bought, commenting that "unfortunately the car did not last because of the bad nature of our roads."[53]

In 1951 Asante relocated to Tamale, the NT administrative center, and was joined by his wife and children. He led the United Church, serving the Presbyterian and Methodist congregations of southerners, and did evangel-ical work, reaching villages by bicycle (see Fig. 6.1).[54] His wife organized a women's fellowship and traded. She recalled sowing and selling cloths "for children and adults . . . because in the north, people really needed cloths." Not everybody was pleased with trading in the pastor's house.[55] Asante used his leadership skills "to build a permanent Pastor's House at Nyohene, from the Salaga Brick Fund" and from a contribution of three hundred pounds from the Basel Mission.[56] A steady stream of church officials traveled to Tamale and lodged with the Asantes; for Basel missionaries, to be hosted in an African home was still an unusual experience.[57] The inauguration of the pastor's house in 1954, attended by Moderator Asihene, the synod clerk, and the visiting Basel Mission inspector, was remarkable. It not only showed Asante's ability as an organizer but also indicated how the Presbyterian Church had become involved in the nationalist struggle. In his speech Rev-erend Clerk, the synod clerk, emphasized that this new mission field was under the auspices of the Presbyterian Church. He referred to the visiting Basel Mission inspector Fritz Raaflaub as the "grandfather" who was no longer in charge.[58] Asante had to mediate between an outspoken church

Fig. 6.1. Rev. E.K.O. Asante (left) receiving two bicycles for evangelical work, Tamale, ca. 1953. Photo, Rev. E.K.O. Asante's Papers (Abetifi, Ghana).

leadership and the Basel Mission representatives, whom he accompanied on a road trip. With some "bitterness," Clerk asked Raaflaub whether the UTC would have provided financial support for the bungalow of an African missionary at Salaga. He considered it "racial discrimination" that Rytz in Salaga drove his own car while Asante in Tamale rode a bicycle. Times were changing under self-rule; the Presbyterian Church asserted its independence, demanding an "Africanization" of senior positions and an integration of the remaining foreign missionaries. Raaflaub noted that he needed "much tact and humble reserve" in his negotiations with the Presbyterian leadership.[59] The executive synod committee welcomed Basel Mission medical and technical support but not evangelical work, to the disappointment of Raaflaub and many missionaries.[60] Yet staffing the northern expansion with African missionaries proved to be difficult. Raaflaub recorded that southerners "never stay long in the north," not even pastors, an opinion shared by one of Asante's supporters.[61] Even Reverend Asante, the big hope of the Presbyterian Church, asked to be transferred south in 1955. In our conversations he did not elaborate why. In his memoir he wrote that "after some six hectic but glorious years in the Northern Territories, he came to Bekwai Ashanti where he built the Local Presbyterian Primary School and the present chapel." It was not easy to find a replacement.[62]

In his recollections Asante presented himself not just as a pioneer missionary but also as a builder of the church, spiritually and materially. In the early 1960s he enrolled in a "one-year post graduate course in Theology at New College, Edinburgh," joining the illustrious group of senior pastors who had studied abroad.[63] Before continuing with Asante's account of his service as a Presbyterian elder, we need to look at the relationship between elderhood and wealth, particularly the changes in big-man status.

Wealth and Big Men

Throughout the twentieth century Kwawu has been well known for its wealthy traders and businessmen hailing from towns like Abetifi, Nkwatia, Obo, and Obomeng. Although most of them spent their lives in the commercial centers of southern Ghana, their presence was felt in Kwawu, their deeds toward the larger community closely watched. Their large homes, built since the 1920s, served as a reminder of their means.[64] Those who contributed generously were well regarded as *abirεmɔn* (big men) and *mmarima pa* (valiant men), while those who refrained from sharing wealth faced criticism. During discussions about the big-man status in Abetifi I frequently heard two names: P. K. Anim Addo and E. A. Saka. Although both donated buildings and had statues erected in their honor, they occupy different spaces within the local understanding of wealth and reputation. Anim Addo, who died in the late 1980s, acquired a vast real estate complex, giving him the reputation of "Ghana's most affluent man."[65] Yet Kwawu people are ambivalent about his social position. His impressive record included constructing the Abetifi technical school, a day nursery, and the "Aduana House" for his *abusua*, and making national contributions like an endowment to the University of Ghana. Still, many people recall him as stingy, lacking in true community spirit. Saka, who made a fortune in timber and then diversified into other enterprises, is seen differently. People praise him for his modesty and for constructing the Abetifi Community Center in 1978. Wahyee was outspoken about the difference between the two. Anim Addo, he noted, did not use his money "to do anything for the community"; he "was just rich but Yaw Saka, he has done better; Yaw Saka . . . we will always remember."[66] Wahyee acknowledged Anim Addo's involvement in the Kwawu Water Project. But since this ambitious project to pump water from the Afram failed to work properly, it has become symbolic of his contribution. Anim Addo's buildings are viewed as self-aggrandizing monuments, particularly his four-story palace, whereas Saka is perceived as humble and generous, effectively sharing his wealth. In 2002, when Saka died, his life as a respected big man and devout Presbyterian was much celebrated.[67] Both men were big in wealth, but only Saka was big in terms of recognition, widely consulted for advice, and thus considered an ɔpanyin.

The connection between big-man status and the communal responsibility to share wealth has deep roots. Historians of precolonial Asante emphasize the importance of wealth accumulation in measuring "societal and individual achievement."[68] During the eighteenth and nineteenth centuries, with the emergence of a centralized state, participation in state offices became crucial in acquiring wealth, measured in gold, land, and people (slaves and wives). Successful asikafoɔ (rich men) were honored for their contributions to the state with the ɔbirɛmpɔn (big-man) title, after a public display of their wealth in front of the Asantehene (Asante king). Upon death, an individual sikani (rich man) could not dispose of his wealth freely, because awunnyadeɛ (death duties) guaranteed that the lion's share of self-acquired mobile property was directed toward the state. The state acted as "custodian of the wealth of the community which also controlled its distribution," making the Asante society the ultimate benefactor of individual accumulation.[69] This arrangement strengthened the state, which "effectively retained a monopoly over access to wealth and its redistribution," and prevented the emergence of hereditary property owners.[70] By the late nineteenth century asikafoɔ contested death duties in Asante. A group of traders, akonkofoɔ, who had taken residence on the coast, embraced the British model of individual capitalist accumulation, thereby challenging the Asante state.[71] Dynastic rivalries within Kumase, leading to a decade of civil war, forced the Asantehene in 1889 to abolish death duties. The Asante state exercised this kind of wealth appropriation over Kwawu until the Kwawu chiefs rebelled in 1875.[72] Yet an independent Kwawu state was never strong enough to enforce a similar tax. Instead, a class of traders, ideologically related to the akonkofoɔ, became the principal accumulators of wealth, among them E. K. Addo's older brothers. Soon traders rivaled local chiefs, creating what Arhin called for the Fante coast "dual ranking systems, the coexistence of 'traditional' and modern elites."[73] By the third decade of the twentieth century, traders were the wealthiest people in Kwawu; their storied houses, erected in coastal architecture, outsized the ahenfie. Although the state no longer enforced a communal participation in acquired wealth, the ideal remained relevant for achieving big-man status.

Among the eight men, only E. K. Addo attained big-man status. Based in Nsawam since 1928, he frequently returned to Abetifi to attend funerals and other community events; he was soon recognized as *ɔpanyin*.[74] By 1944 Addo had become the sole owner of his flourishing business, Sober Trading Store. He built an elegant house next to his brother J. K. Kwakye's residence, "Sober House," in Abetifi's Christian Quarters and called it "Sober House No. 2." He kept a meticulous account of "money spent for building materials & workmanship," totaling more than fifteen hundred pounds.[75] Upon its completion in 1948, Addo gathered *abusua* representatives, the Abetifi pastor, and presbyters to make an official statement, namely, that because he had paid for the house, it should be inherited by his wife and children according to Presbyterian rules, and not by his *abusua* following Akan matrilineal practice. Addo sought to prevent the kind of inheritance dispute that was common in the Christian Quarters, when *abusua* members claimed that they had helped erect a building and demanded access.[76]

Addo's correspondence documents expectations of him as a big man, as well as the way he carried out the accompanying responsibilities from the 1940s through the 1990s. In 1949, when Nana Kwasi Mireku II, Ɔdekuro of Obomeng, was forced to abdicate, he approached Addo for a sum of two hundred pounds to acquire commercial real estate. He assured Addo a profit share and, should the business fail, the right to sell the properties.[77] As an autodidact, Addo enthusiastically supported the spread of Western education. In 1950 an Aburi school requested help for its band from "a few generous persons." Addo received the promise that "names of all donors will be announced publicly and will be conspicuously displayed at the School."[78] Ten years later the Abetifi secondary school had an "acute shortage of funds" leading to its "inability to pay masters for three months." A fund-raising letter was sent to Abetifi's most prominent big men, among them sixteen chiefs, the local member of Parliament (MP), and businessmen like Anim Addo, Saka, and Addo.[79] In times of economic crisis the Abetifi secondary school headmaster shrewdly reminded big men of their duties. Addo was informed that, because a "Science Lab" had been named after him, this "act of immortalization" carried

> the challenge of sustaining your name so that it lives forever. It is a challenge to every great man—to live great, to die great and, most important to persist great! In this regard, therefore, we invite you to consolidate your position through MORAL and MATERIAL identification with the school.

Addo was further informed that a competing big man, Anim Addo, had already pledged fifty thousand cedis in treasury bonds.[80]

How can a big man like Addo be situated in Ghana's struggle for independence? In retrospect, Addo declared that he was not interested in politics, considering such activities "not helpful for a trader." Rather, he supported "natural leaders," the chiefs.[81] In Richard Rathbone's classification, by 1950 Addo was no longer an "aspirant businessman" but had "arrived."[82] Yet there were moments when he became engaged in politics. Although Addo was closer to the United Gold Coast Convention, he offered his services to Kwame Nkrumah's Convention People's Party (CPP). When Nkrumah was released from prison after the CPP victory in the first general election of 1951, K. A. Gbedemah, "the ablest of his lieutenants," asked Addo for the use of his Vauxhall to bring Nkrumah from prison.[83] Addo recalled:

A: Do you know why he borrowed my car? It was having a roof door.
SM: So he could stand.
A: Stand and wave the white handkerchief. My friend Anim Addo advised me not to give my car because it would be smashed by the public, the crowd. I said, it doesn't matter. If it is smashed, I can buy another one tomorrow from UAC [United Africa Company].[84]

The photograph of Nkrumah standing in Addo's car, greeting the masses after leaving James Fort and on his way to become leader of government business, published in Nkrumah's autobiography (see Fig. 6.2). Addo was not only proud to provide his Vauxhall for Nkrumah's "journey from prison" but used the opportunity to let his audience know about his wealth, the fact that he could easily replace his vehicle.[85] His son, narrating the same story, embellished the ending. Addo and Anim Addo were debating the wisdom of lending the car, when "they heard a crowd approaching, cheering its leader." Coming closer, they saw that "Gbedemah whispered something into Nkrumah's ear. The car stopped, Nkrumah greeted them."[86] The car was returned, unharmed. In the 1950s having good connections to the CPP was good business practice. Later Addo sought Gbedemah's help to secure a training college for Abetifi.[87]

One "early policy obligation" of the CPP government was the reform of local government, ending indirect rule.[88] The Local Government Ordinance (Colony) of 1951 established forty-nine local and six urban councils. In Kwawu three local councils replaced the native authority: Kwawu North, Kwawu South, and Kwawu West. Addo ran for and was elected to the Kwawu North Local Council and served for nine years as its chairman. The

Fig. 6.2. Kwame Nkrumah riding in E. K. Addo's Vauxhall car on his "journey from prison," February 12, 1951. Photo, *Ghana: The Autobiography of Kwame Nkrumah* (Courtesy Library of Congress).

Ordinance established fourteen district councils in the Colony, the Kwawu council being the first inaugurated.[89] The Kwawu District Council consisted of seventeen elected and nine appointed members, the latter representing the chiefs; the local councils delegated all elected members, among them Addo.[90] The chief regional officer opened the Kwawu District Council with much pomp: a brass band played martial music, a church choir sang, and Boy Scouts paraded. At the end the assembled dignitaries gathered for a "Sherry Party." Addo did not make the guest list, but the recently arrived Basel missionaries, Oskar and Rosmarie Tschudin-Gehr, did and later wrote a report about the "colorful crowd."[91] A district council's powers were limited to supervision of native courts, local police authorities, road maintenance, and health posts but had no influence on taxes. In Kwawu an even split between CPP supporters and "independents" blocked the council's operation. CPP members boycotted the meetings and opposed the appointed clerk,

E. I. Preko. Addo, an independent like the majority of Kwawu North, supported Preko against the CPP, which was not very popular among leading Presbyterians in Abetifi.[92]

The new local administration was not only hindered by the CPP's effort to establish a secure footing in Kwawu but was paralyzed by a paramount stool dispute that prevented revenue collection.[93] For the next two years the regional officer, supported by the Kwawu government agent, tried to suspend the district council, but the CPP minister of local government did not follow his recommendation, much to the regional officer's dismay. Too much prestige had been invested.[94] Only after the paramount stool dispute had been resolved, coinciding with the second general election that gave the CPP a clearer mandate, did the "efficiency of the Kwahu Local Authorities" improve "greatly."[95] The local councils succeeded in gathering revenues and realizing public works programs, like the district council hall outside Mpraeso and new police stations.[96] Addo had little to say about the political conflicts so richly documented in the archives. He only alluded to a personal struggle with E. I. Preko, later MP and CPP minister. In Addo's recollections his chairmanship was reduced to his building projects: the construction of the local council hall, market sheds in Abetifi and Hwehwee, public latrines, and, most prominent, the Abetifi post office, an impressive concrete structure.[97]

Addo resigned from the local council in 1961 but participated again in a public project eight years later. He served on the Kwawu Water Project committee with Anim Addo, Saka, and other Kwawu big men. A group photograph depicts eleven big men wearing *ntoma* (cloth), the dress of chiefs and elders, gathered around Anim Addo, the chairman. For the 1994 *afahye*, Addo paid for the restoration of the aging post office. He did not want "to embarrass the *Adɔntenhene* before the many expected national dignitaries."[98] In a letter to the postal service, he requested to "send payment cheque to the New Adontenhene Nana Asiedu Agyeman III Adontenhene of Kwahu Traditional Area for the full settlement of the arrears of rents [for many years]." He announced a rent increase and stated his credentials, "I am one of the pioneers who helped to put up the building in question and handed it over to the occupant of the stool. As of now, I am the one who did the renovation and paid the costs on behalf of the New Chief."[99] The new chief depended on big men like Addo for large-scale expenses and revenue collection.

By 1994 Addo was no longer spending much money on himself. Unlike the typical Kwawu big man who arrived in his hometown in his own Mercedes Benz, Addo rode public transport on his trips from Accra to Kwawu, having sold his vehicle in the 1970s. Instead, he dedicated his resources to building projects like the expansion of the local clinic. He constructed a bungalow in the hope that a medical doctor might be attracted to work out of Abetifi. Criticizing the Presbyterian Church, the clinic's patron, for inadequate maintenance, he stated, "We don't plan, we don't plan, I have to repeat we don't plan, and if we have plans, they are very shallow"[100] The following year the *Adɔntenhene* publicly acknowledged Addo's community service by presenting him an award "in recognition of your distinguished Services and Selfless devotion to duty to Abetifi."[101] Yet despite such public recognition, highlighting his community spirit and success as a big man, Addo's final years were saddened by the death of his two older sons. Building provided a way to deal with these losses. When his son Browne Addo Kwakye suddenly passed away in 1990, Addo insisted that the house should be inherited by the son's widow and children, and not claimed by the *abusua*. He explained that he had learned from his father, though not a Christian, to privilege children over *abusuafoɔ* (members of matrilineage). He added, "if I had not allowed the woman [the son's widow] and her children to own the house, I would have acted against my principles."[102] This episode shows that not only were inheritance practices challenged by Christian churches in Kwawu but that matrilineal descent could also be subjected to negotiation even in Abetifi's old section. Addo reiterated, in a letter, his belief about the importance of building to commemorate the dead.

> You will love to hear that I arrived from Abetifi yesterday when it was raining heavily then. I went to see new extra rooms I am putting up in the house for the memories of my late son, A. A. Addo, Surgeon of Veterinary, who died in London last two years. It is a storey building and if all being well, I would finish it before the end of the year, 1995. Please, pray for me to be able to finish according to plan. I think it is one of *what man can accomplish in this world*.[103]

In the months prior to his death Addo was still asked to contribute to building funds. He was invited to the "inaugural meeting of the Ɔmanhene's Palace Building Committee." Rev. Felix Maafo, director of the Ramseyer Training Centre, confirmed receipt of fifty thousand cedis, "a donation toward purchase of minerals for dedication of mission house phase 2."[104] In the twentieth century, money, and not people and wives, has become increasingly decisive for big-man status. Money must be shared. Addo commented, "If you have something in your possession, and you see that your brother needs some of it, give him if ever possible. Don't just look for yourself."[105]

Tegare and Big Men

Businessmen like Addo were not the only ones who became big men in postwar Kwawu. Since the 1940s Tegare (Gare) priests like Kwasi Fofie of Nkwantanan, Yaw Tawiah of Abetifi, and Kwasi Mawu of Pepease acquired wealth and gathered adherents. A Tegare shrine provided a sense of community centered around the ɔbosomfo (priest) who promised spiritual protection and material well-being; the ɔbosomfo acted like a big man. Ɔkyeame Asante, Kofi Ankoma, and Kwaku Marfo participated in Tegare shrines. They and others spoke at length about the importance of the one in Pepease, established by Kwasi Mawu.

On July 21, 1993, Ɔbosomfo Kwasi Mawu died. Already a legend in his lifetime, the eighty-year-old was not only a respected ɔbosomfo but also a wealthy cocoa farmer with six wives, fifty children, and numerous followers in the towns and villages of Kwawu (see Fig. 6.3). Kwasi Mawu was a controversial figure: some people sought his advice and asked for protection from the Tegare aduru (medicine); others considered him a charlatan and saw his popularity as a threat to the Christian congregations of Kwawu. Tegare offered protection from evil forces. Such anti-witchcraft cults have a long history in southern Ghana.[106] Kwasi Mawu, the son of an ɔkɔmfo (diviner), worked as a sandal maker before becoming the ɔkyeame (spokesperson) of Kwasi Fofie in Nkwantanan.[107] Nana Okyere Ampadu II, an age-mate and relative of Kwasi Mawu, recalled that "it became necessary to expand the base of the Tegare cult in Kwawu and so the Ɔhene of Pepease, Nana Owusu Mensa [his predecessor], decided that a delegation be sent to the original source of the Tegare aduru at Ypala to acquire a fresh power of Tegare for Pepease."[108] Since Kwasi Mawu and palace mpanyinfoɔ (elders) brought Tegare to Pepease, it belonged to the chief who therefore claimed a profit share. Unlike Akan akɔmfoɔ (diviners), most Gare abosomfoɔ (priests) were male.[109] Adherents believed that Gare's power enabled infertile women to become pregnant and helped men and women to stay healthy, gather large harvests, and have success in business. Gare had the power to identify witches, protect individuals from witchcraft and poison, and detect adultery and sickness.[110] Ɔkɔmfo Amma Yeboaa emphasized the fear connected with Tegare. She noted that "in the olden days" nobody was beyond Gare's power, not even members of Christian churches.[111] Opusuo recalled financial pressure on those who confessed their witchcraft: "If you don't want Tegare to kill you, you had to give money!" Skeptical of Gare's power, he characterized fear as the fuel of this "money making machine." Even the Presbyterian

Fig. 6.3. Ɔbosomfo Kwasi Mawu, a few weeks before his death, Pepease, 1993. Photo, R. Lane Clark.

Church, Kwawu's strongest, could not stop Gare. "Everybody was so afraid" to be killed by Tegare.[112] Missionary reports confirm Tegare's popularity. Otto Rytz lamented Tegare's attraction among Presbyterian school leavers, "scholars, clerks in European merchant houses, traders, and people living in cities like Accra, Sekondi, Kumasi . . . among those many Christians."[113] On Anwona, Gare's main festival, the ɔbosomfo offered alcohol and refreshments freely to the adherents.

Kwabena Asante became a Gare ɔkyeame at Nkawkaw in 1947. Then he worked for Gare Ɔbosomfo Kwame Broni at Kwawu Tafo. He explained his role as an intermediary:

> It is all along you will hope that people do not do any evil against each other, and that there will be peace amongst the members. Even if people bring cases before me, we also help to be able to look into the cases patiently to discover who is guilty and who is innocent; so that they could be reconciled again. . . . This is my task, the work of an ɔkyeame. If somebody wants to see ɔhene [chief, meaning the priest], he or she comes to me and we sit down and look into it. If it is not necessary to take it to the ɔbosomfo himself, we settle it here.[114]

Seeking help from Gare, a supplicant received a kola nut and pledged to return when cured or, after success, to offer thanks. Ɔkyeame Asante compared this practice to the Christian communion. Somebody "caught" by Gare, manifested in dreams and illness, had to confess. In the 1960s, when returning to Pepease, Asante offered his services to Kwasi Mawu. He worked under Mawu's senior ɔkyeame, Kwadwo Tano, whom he succeeded upon his death. He noted that "each shrine has its own rules" and how much he learned from Kwadwo Tano.[115] During agorɔ, when the ɔbosomfo, possessed by Gare, swirled across the dance floor accompanied by male drummers and female singers, Asante acted as his assistant. He poured water on the ground to clear the way and fired an old shotgun to ward off evil forces. Ɔkyeame Asante credited Gare's advice for his acquisition of land to launch a cocoa farm at Amaate.[116]

Ɔkyeame Asante, Ankoma, Marfo, and others stressed Kwasi Mawu's accomplishment not only as ɔbosomfo but as elder, community leader, cocoa farmer, husband, and father. As ɔbosomfo, Mawu was frequently compared to Kwasi Fofie of Nkwantanan, one of the most successful Gare abosomfoɔ in the 1940s and 1950s.[117] Kwasi Fofie enjoyed a lavish lifestyle and died poor in 1995. Mawu, by contrast, was careful about investments, maintaining a reputation as "very hard working."[118] While Kwasi Fofie freely sold the Tegare aduru, Mawu held on to it.[119] During Ghana's postwar cocoa boom, Mawu acquired land in the Afram Plains and launched cocoa plantations with the help of his adherents and children. Based on this cheap labor, as his critics pointed out, Mawu's enterprise was very productive.[120] His success gained public recognition when he was elected *akuafoohene,* chief farmer of the Afram Plains, in 1973–74. For his followers, this was a clear sign of how much "Gare had helped him."[121] Mawu sent his children to Catholic school and had them baptized. Because of their Catholic education and exposure to the Bible, as Mawu's nephew Kwasi Addae commented, most of Mawu's children and wives no longer attended the shrine. Further, Addae was *not* selected as his *wɔfa's* (maternal uncle) successor. Instead, custody over the Gare shrine passed on to Mawu's son, Agya Kwadwo Amoa. Addae identified a correlation between the children's Catholic schooling and being privileged at the expense of *abusua* members.[122] This shift from matrilineal to patrilineal succession at the Tegare shrine shows that cultural innovations of the twentieth century also affected the surroundings of a "traditional priest."

As a big man, Kwasi Mawu generously shared his resources. In Tease, Afram Plains, he provided transport with his car, allowed people to tap into his generator, took the initiative to start a bank, and opened a store.[123] Like other prominent *abosomfoɔ,* Mawu frequently acted like a chief, engaging in dispute settlements and appearing with a large entourage at public events.[124] Mawu, with his many wives, large numbers of followers, and dispensable wealth, indeed resembled the precolonial *ɔbirɛmpɔn.* Mawu, and other Tegare *abosomfoɔ,* helped to renew local religious practices, drawing on Christianity's "code of morals" and on Akan *agorɔ* with much "entertainment value."[125] Although he appeared like a "traditional man" with his polygynous households, he was open to social and cultural changes: education for his children, opportunities of cash-cropping, and interest in the Catholic Church.[126] With his "entrepreneurial individualism," this big man embodied a new type of masculinity that combined older cultural practices with the use of modern innovations, including electricity and machines.[127] For his followers, he represented an alternative response to modernity than the one offered by those with close connections to the dominant Presbyterian Church.

Kwasi Mawu constructed houses in Pepease and the Afram Plains, providing each of his surviving five wives with one.[128] Several carry the inscription, *"Yebisa nipa ne fie yemisa ne sika"* (The importance of a person lies in his home and not in his wealth). People inquired about the reputation of someone's home, not his riches. Yet, as Marfo opined, such noble sayings served elders well in the olden days, "but now, it does not work any longer."[129] Without money, no house.

Houses

For the interviewed men, building a house was one of the most important achievements in life.[130] Starting early was helpful. In the 1920s, before he permanently settled in Abetifi, Wahyee invested trading profits to build a Christian Quarters house with his brother. In this compound house, closed to the street, life focused on the spacious courtyard. While teaching in Abetifi, Reverend Asante acquired land in a new part of the Christian Quarters, at that time still "bush." House construction started in 1943. Two years later some of Asante's maternal relatives moved in. By allowing his poorer relations to live in the house "like a village," Asante acted as the generous ɔpanyin. With pride he noted that the same masons worked on his house as on the new ahenfie in the center of Abetifi.[131] Since Asante was stationed outside Kwawu for most of his career, the Abetifi house enhanced his stature as ɔpanyin in absentia, providing shelter for needy abusua members. It also indicated his preparedness for his final return. In the late 1950s E. F. Opusuo taught as head teacher of the new middle school in Pepease. Determined to erect a house, Opusuo had delayed marriage for eight years after college. He "put up" a building at Pepease's small Christian Quarters in 1959, thereby, like Asante, reminding everyone of his ideological move from the old town and expressing his belonging to the Presbyterian congregation.[132]

The architecture of the houses demonstrated their new position as mpanyinfoɔ and akrakyefoɔ in their hometowns.[133] Reverend Asante's house followed the model of the colonial bungalow, with a central living room, veranda, and adjacent bedrooms. Windows on three sides provided the master bedroom with ample air circulation. Opusuo chose as a design the "two-room house" with "chamber and hall," a common layout used for African urban housing in the postwar period.[134] Opusuo built three separate units, taking the form of three attached two-room houses. In the middle, the largest unit with two windows and a French door facing the yard was reserved for himself. Each unit has a sitting room or hall toward the yard and a smaller chamber for sleeping in the rear; windows at both ends allow for cross-ventilation. Opusuo added a kitchen and bathrooms across the yard. Constructing three two-room units reflected Opusuo's sense of responsibility as an ɔpanyin. He could house his children and abusua members or offer units for rent. Both houses were built with cement bricks and had roofs of corrugated-iron sheets. The windows revealed changes in materials. While Asante's windows can only be closed with shutters, Opusuo had glass windows opening toward the yard and shutters facing the rooms, separated by bars. Both men furnished their European-style sitting rooms with book cabinets and comfortable chairs, presenting their version of a Christian family home. They received visitors *within* the enclosed building and not *outside* sitting on raised, three-walled platforms in enclosed yards, as was common in homes of *mpanyinfoɔ*. The spatial organization of their houses, preferably lined with flowers facing the street, represented the changes in their lives and marked their positions as men belonging to the *akrakyefoɔ*, and as a new type of *ɔpanyin*.[135]

Not all men succeeded in building a house in their hometown. As salaried men, *akrakyefoɔ* were under pressure from less fortunate *abusua* members for help. Therefore some preferred to reside outside Kwawu permanently. Opusuo's classmate, Ofori Anyinam, had a career as a university administrator. In retirement he continued to live in Accra, although he visited Pepease regularly in his role as *abusuapanyin* (lineage head). When I spoke with him in Pepease, he pointed to a heap of cement blocks withering away on an empty lot next to the lineage house. Because of his commitments to his *abusua* and eight children, he lacked the funds to build his own house. Glancing at his relatives, he added that he could not abandon their needs.[136] Boakye Yiadom also failed to erect a building in Abetifi. Since he worked as a primary school teacher, his salary was considerably lower than Opusuo's, who reached the rank of an education officer, or Reverend Asante's. As young college graduates, Opusuo and Asante had swiftly moved into upper-income brackets. Boakye Yiadom worked as an untrained "pupil-teacher" for years. While looking after a multitude of schoolchildren, he juggled demands from his wives and their children. *Abusua* members expected support for funeral expenses.[137] In the 1990s Boakye Yiadom lived with his wife Susana Ansomaah in her sister's house in Abetifi's Christian Quarters. While the main section of the house was unoccupied except for the owner's occasional visit, smaller rooms, each with a veranda forming a one-room house, were rented out or used by family members. Boakye Yiadom emphasized that at his age he no longer desired luxuries like a *ntoma* (cloth) or a fancy suit fitting for a *krakye*. Still, he had not given up the hope "to make a building for my wife and children." He elaborated that some of his children might be in a position to support him.

> But I want to have a building. If God blesses me, and my children are also coming up and get some business. . . . What I have told them is that they have to work properly without touching somebody's property. They have to go ahead with their own money, they have to keep part of it in the post office or in the bank. As "Monkey says, softly, softly, you go ahead." They come to help me to

make a building. And when they have given [me] a building, as my wife's sister has got one, then it is all right for them.[138]

In 2000 one daughter, Felicia Abena Frempomaa, started to build a house at the edge of Abetifi's Christian Quarters.[139]

Kofi Ankoma was painfully aware that he had not erected a building. While drinking in a tiny bar opposite the *ahenfie*, he confided his plan to build a house. The bar was the front section of a narrow house that had belonged to his maternal grandmother, a wife of the *Nifahene* (Obo chief). Ankoma dreamed of replacing the decrepit structure with a new "storey-building" consisting of "two self-contained apartments," one for himself and one for me. The building was to bear our names.[140] He died in 1996 without fulfilling this wish. For an *ɔpanyin*, male or female, a building that bears one's name serves different objectives. The building may house the *ɔpanyin*, spouse, children, and other family members. Moreover, as a mnemonic device, the building becomes a monument. It will remind the deceased's descendants of his (or her) former physical existence, offering a way to transcend death by creating an afterlife in the memories of others.[141]

Elders' Community Service

By the 1990s the social position of *ɔpanyin* had not lost its importance in Kwawu. All of the eight men, except Addo, had permanently returned to their hometowns to become resident elders. Following his retirement in 1980, Reverend Asante successfully balanced expectations from his Adoako lineage and the Presbyterian congregation. Although active in mediating *abusua* disputes, Asante declined to occupy a chiefly office. He helped improve the "family house."[142] He assisted in training church workers and was instrumental in establishing the Abetifi vocational training school, funded by a German development grant. Again, he relied on his network of Abetifi dignitaries like E. K. Addo.[143] As a retired pastor, he did not want to "meddle in heathen affairs," and maintained a distance from rites involving veneration of ancestors or communication with *abosom* (lesser gods). Because he had learned about Kwawu customs and history during his youth and remained interested, in old age he was consulted about "traditions."[144] In 1994, when Kwawu chiefs organized an *afahye* festival after a hiatus of thirty years, Asante advised the *Akwamuhene*, occupant of his lineage stool, about regalia and public appearances.[145] In this invention of tradition, a Presbyterian pastor assisted in building a bridge to the past and modifying the *afahye* to contemporary needs, including a spot on Ghana's calendar of "traditional festivals."[146] At our last meeting he gave me a photograph depicting him dressed as an *ɔpanyin* with his wife (see Fig. 6.4).

Opusuo retired in 1984 from his work as an education officer and returned to Pepease. As an acting *abusuapanyin*, he dealt with requests for support and organized funerals. He also chaired the local development committee, which coordinated communal labor for building latrines and weeding. Pepease voters elected Opusuo to the Kwawu District Assembly, created by the Provisional National Defense Council (PNDC) under J. J. Rawlings in 1988. Two-thirds of the members of district assemblies were elected and one-third were appointed. Unlike the local councils of the 1950s, when chiefs sent their own representatives, the central government now appointed traditional rulers, as well as nominees of churches, market women, farmers' associations, and benevolent societies.[147] Assembly members were predominately male and "relatively well educated," drawn from "locally rooted community leaders" and activists.[148] District assemblies, according to anthropologist Maxwell Owusu, created a new democratic institution that provided more "effective 'people power' from local communities upwards on a nonpartisan basis." The assemblies constituted a system building on "indigenous political traditions of local self-government that assume the existence of shared ethical and moral values."[149] Its members should reflect virtues of accountability, service, and probity. The government-run *Ghanaian Times* editorialized:

> [The] most respected people in the village community owe their high public status and esteem to their service in the community. The most respected elder is not necessarily the one with a lot of money, a big house, a large well-educated family and so on. . . . But each owes his respect to definable services to the community. . . . In this communalist organization [the district assembly], the only reward an elder receives for his service to the community is the satisfaction of being among those whose counsel and planning lead to the progress of the community.[150]

The assemblies became a forum for *mpanyinfoɔ* to provide leadership within their local communities, not for the purpose of self-enrichment but rather to address the needs of their hometowns. Organizations like the CDRs (Committees of the Defense of the Revolution) and the 31st December Women's Movement served as watchdogs to prevent abuses of power by assembly members. Yet Opusuo did not consider these organizations as being independent but instead partisan affiliates of the PNDC government. Still, in his efforts as an assembly member, he had to rely on the CDRs to gather

Fig. 6.4. Rev. E.K.O. Asante and his wife, F. A. Asante, Abetifi, ca. 1990. Photo, Rev. E.K.O. Asante's Papers (Abetifi, Ghana).

support for projects like cleaning the Pepease market and improving the lorry station.[151] Since the inauguration of the Fourth Republic in 1993, district assemblies have become more politicized, despite constitutional language to retain nonpartisanship.[152]

Opusuo, "not interested in party politics," did not compete for a second term.[153] In recognition of his service, the Ɔmanhene of Kwawu presented him with a certificate. A photograph, commemorating the event, decorates his sitting room (see Fig. 6.5). During the 1996 afahye, Opusuo's ɔpanyin status was again acknowledged. He wrote:

> I was honoured by the Pepease Community on the 24th February for my ten years (1984–1994) of selfless, courageous, honest and dedicated leadership to the people of Pepease. I was given a beautiful wall clock as an award. I am now an adviser to the Pepease Town Council.[154]

Fig. 6.5. E. F. Opusuo receives a certificate honoring his service in the district assembly from Daasebrε Akuamoa Boateng, the Ɔmanhene of Kwawu, 1994. Photo, E. F. Opusuo's Papers (Pepease, Ghana).

The notion of an *ɔpanyin* providing leadership within his *abusua* and communities is a highly valued trait of senior masculinity, alive and respected in Kwawu. Postcolonial state institutions, such as male-dominated district assemblies and the national parliament, offer venues beyond the immediate realm of the *abusua* for a man to prove his worthiness as an *ɔpanyin* dedicated to service for the entire community.[155] Although these modern institutions are located outside the *ahenfie*, it remains up to the *ɔhene*, or at major occasions the *ɔmanhene*, to present awards of recognition within a "traditional area" on behalf of the people.

Funerals

In Akan culture funerals are the most extensively celebrated rite of passage. They serve as public events to assess somebody's life and attainment of personhood. In the 1990s, twice every month, Kwawu towns are taken over by weekend-long funeral celebrations. Migrants return to their hometown to participate in funerals of their *abusua* or their father's relatives, or to assist a friend in a burial. Those who can afford it organize wakes to display the corpse, even at the expense of keeping the body in the morgue for an extended period. Others prefer to bury their dead immediately but still partake in the next funeral weekend, receiving visitors and accepting donations to defray expenses like the coffin, refreshments, and the wake. During funerals the character of Kwawu towns changes radically. What are usually sleepy places come alive, the streets fill with people dressed in black or red cloth, and roads are congested by parked cars and buses that have transported mourners and well-wishers. Funerals are key events that strengthen ties between migrants and their hometowns.[156]

In Akan culture the size and organization of a funeral indicates the status, wealth, and popularity of the deceased. For precolonial Asante, Kwame Arhin asserted that "[death], in particular, provided occasions for demonstrating the relative importance of men of rank."[157] This has been reiterated for the colonial era by T. E. Kyei, who reported that "under normal conditions the worth and importance of an Ashanti can be estimated by the funeral and expense connected with his death."[158] The organization of a funeral was not only dictated by the deceased's rank, *abusua*, and wealth but also by the circumstance of death. People hoped to die of old age, or at least of "normal illness."[159] Unexpected and accidental deaths (*ɔtɔfo wu* [pl. *atɔfo wu*]) were troubling. This is expressed in the proverb "*Nea wahintiw awu no, wontutu' mireka nkɔ n'ayi ase*" (If somebody stumbles to his [her] death, you don't rush to attend the funeral).[160] Some deaths were (and are) considered shameful, such as death caused by suicide or accidents, by certain illnesses (tuberculosis, syphilis, or leprosy), or during childbirth. These *atɔfo wu* meant smaller, less elaborate funerals with fewer participants, regardless of a person's status. The same applied to death suspected to have been caused by witchcraft or poison. For contemporary Kwawu, however, van der Geest suggested that "the dramatic cause of the death seemed, rather, to increase the grandness to display," the shame of the death only addressed "offstage."[161] In the past, death during warfare was considered especially honorable for a man, called an *ɔbarima* (valiant man) or *ɔkatakyie* (hero), who was granted an elaborate funeral. These days, religious affiliation shapes the course and organization of a funeral. Ɔbosomfo Kwasi Mawu received two large funerals, each extending over several days with much *agorɔ*.[162] During funerals there is much discourse—informal conversations, libations, and formal speeches during church services—about the deceased's accomplishments, the circumstances of death, and potential conflicts concerning succession and inheritance. Funerals offer opportunities to evaluate a life, which may take the form of a debate over ideas about masculinity and femininity.

On August 1, 1993, Chief Kwadwo Donkor, the head of the Kwawu community in Accra, died at the age of 103. Donkor was honored with a grand funeral in Abetifi. A close reading of the rites reveals the masculinity ideals expressed in relation to this elder and big man. While his body was kept frozen in the morgue for two months, funeral announcements were broadcast and posted in newspapers. Donkor was not wealthy, nor did his title have any connection to a "stool," the symbolic embodiment of chiefly office in an Akan town. Still, his children and *abusua* arranged a funeral choreography worthy of an *ɔhene*. For weeks his upcoming funeral was the topic of conversation in Abetifi. People wondered about the funeral's organization and marveled about the guests who would arrive in their fancy cars, wearing the latest Accra fashions. An outlandish wake on Friday opened the celebration. The siren of an ambulance announced Donkor's final homecoming. His body was placed on a brass bed, dressed in Kente and adorned with golden jewelry. A steady flow of mourners, recorded by video cameras, paid respect and admired the body lying in state. Outside a crowd had gathered, entertained by a police brass band, and kept warm with hot tea, candy, and spirits. Television monitors showed the people inside promenading past the body.

In the morning a burial service was held at the Abetifi Presbyterian Church. The service, covered by ubiquitous cameras, featured not only a

185

sermon and eulogy but also an impressive list of speakers.[163] The mourners learned that Donkor, although a member of the Abetifi royal lineage, was born into modest means. He had never attended school but did an apprenticeship hawking as a petty trader in the Central Region. He moved to Accra launching a business selling imported goods. Later he opened a bar. In 1932 Donkor found his calling and became head of the Kwawu traders in Accra, a position he held for sixty-one years. Since 1922 he had been married to Maame Deda with whom he had several children; she died in 1987. The subsequent speeches, delivered by his children, the Abetifi chief's ɔkyeame, and representatives of business groups in Accra, applauded Chief Donkor's exemplary life. They emphasized his wisdom, support of his children's education, (supposedly) monogamous marriage, generosity, and skills as an impartial judge. They lauded Donkor for overcoming ethnic differences between competing trading communities. One speaker noted that both Hausa and Yoruba traders in Accra wished Donkor had taken the Muslim faith. In embellishing his life, speakers borrowed from different cultures. They evoked the saying, *"Odupɔn atutu ampa"* (The great tree has fallen), a favored metaphor for a chief's death, and cited pillars of colonial education: Shakespeare, the Bible, and Horace's famous dictum about the "monument more enduring than brass." One speaker offered an appellation in Twi, appropriate to a chief.[164]

Donkor was eulogized as a big man who fulfilled the role of a successful and effective ɔpanyin. A priestess's son in a rural town evolved into the respected leader of the modern and urban Kwawu business community. In this trajectory, Donkor found new commercial opportunities, organized the Kwawu community in Accra and Tema, and reached out to other ethnic groups. People praised him as someone who valued education and lived according to Christian morals; his life was only completed when he was baptized weeks before his death.[165] The conversion symbolized the transformation of the Presbyterian Church, which had struggled from a marginal position in the late nineteenth century to become, by the 1990s, the spiritual home of the Abetifi establishment. The Gothic stone structure of the church provided the fitting backdrop.[166] After the service Donkor's body was interred in the Christian cemetery. On Saturday and Sunday afternoon thousands gathered in front of the Abetifi *ahenfie* to make donations and to greet the bereaved family, the assembled chiefs, and other dignitaries. The *Adɔntenhene* had his drummers play the large *fontɔnfrɔm* in honor of Donkor's big-man status.[167]

Not everybody was happy about Donkor's lavish funeral. Too frail to attend, Wahyee noted that only people living in Accra had "something to remember" about Donkor.

> For those of us here in Abetifi, we are farmers and have not benefited in any way from him. He went to Accra to seek money and got some. He was also able to bring up all his children very well [providing them with an education] and look after his nephews. He also helped some other "individuals."

Still Wahyee praised Donkor's accomplishments as an *ɔpanyin,* especially his skills in dispute settlement.

> *Na ɔyɛ ɔbarima pa*—he was really a man! Any case he intervened was settled amicably. Even, he managed to withdraw cases from the government courts to his house to be settled there; as for such cases, many were brought to him. If you were involved in a case, and you asked the court to relocate the case, and take it to Chief Donkor for settlement, it was immediately granted.

Kwawu's trading community in Accra erected a "beautiful grave" with a large memorial tombstone for Donkor. This was to guarantee remembrance of his life. Although Abetifi people supported this endeavor, there was "nothing else they could do," meaning that the money had to come from Accra.[168] Former trader Addo was repulsed by the funeral. While acknowledging that Donkor had hoped for such an extravagant celebration, Addo called the expense inconsiderate as there were "poor people in his family who needed help."[169]

Chief Donkor's spectacular funeral shows how traders and businesspeople, mainly based on the coast, have become the center of wealth and influence in Kwawu. With regard to changing Akan funeral practice over the last one hundred years, Arhin noted that prior to the colonial period a ranking system determined a funeral's character, based on the deceased's matrilineage and status as officeholder. In postcolonial Ghana, this "political ranking system has been substantially replaced by status ranking on the basis of discernible or pretended wealth." Grand funerals, like the one for Chief Donkor, confirm these findings for Kwawu. Yet, unlike Asante, the material base for this ranking was produced outside Kwawu. Funerals, according to Arhin, changed into "an institution of economic and social rather than religious significance in response to changes in the economy, society and material culture of the Akan peoples over the last century."[170] To some extent this applies to Kwawu where a cottage industry has developed producing coffins and offering other services. In Abetifi one entrepreneur, Station Bar owner Akua Animaa, runs a successful business outfitting bereaved families for elaborate wakes. She provides assistance in dressing corpses and rents out golden beds decorated either with white lace or Kente, according to the religious affiliation and status of the deceased. These beds are equipped with electrical appliances to light and ventilate the body. Her bar delivers cases of "minerals" (soft drinks), mainly Coke and Fanta, as well as beer and spirits. Others rent out chairs and sound systems. The religious significance of funerals persists, especially for older people. This is one of the objections to the commodification and monetization of funerals.[171]

Many elders do not approve of these recent changes. Boakye Yiadom and Addo recalled that funerals of their childhood were modest and inexpensive; the bereaved *abusua* did not stage an elaborate wake. Yet the Basel Mission already challenged funeral practices early in the twentieth century. After John Yaw Atta died, church leaders were concerned that "heathens would . . . rush to the Station and celebrate the funeral custom in a heathenish manner." Despite the "strong resistance" of the pastor, missionaries, and "Native Agents from the Out-Stations, the heathens . . . attempted several times to break [the] arrangements."[172] Trader Addo had financial concerns about current funeral practices. While pointing to the terrible conditions of Kwawu roads in the early 1990s, Addo exclaimed, "We are wasting money for funerals!"[173] Reverend Asante noted that the basic structure of funerals has remained consistent during his lifetime, except for the commodities:

> AS: You see, things have changed, and so it has happened to the funeral. . . .
> We were using [in the olden days] drinks, but it was the traditional ones, native drinks.
> SM: Palm wine?
> AS: Yes, palm wine. This time it is different drinks, minerals, beer, and so forth. But in the early days you had only palm wine which would serve several people with little cost.

Reverend Asante, despite some amusement, deplored innovations like special clothing worn by mourners, amplified music, and hired dance groups.

> You see, when we were holding a wake keeping, we had it privately in the house, not on this large, ostentatious scale with drinking and dancing and beating of the drums. This kind of music was not used. . . . Nobody was dressed differently, just sack-cloth, black. . . . You see, it has been something introduced from the outside, I don't know [when exactly], an imitation, that's how I would

describe it. Therefore these changes have taken some time and different shades. When last year somebody died, the celebration included the people from the Kumase Cultural Centre, this is something quite strange to everybody. Because we had never, never this. . . . That was the first time in my lifetime I have seen these people at a funeral, which is a new thing (laughs).[174]

He was referring to cultural dance companies of young female dancers, scantily dressed in a few Kente strips, moving their bodies to the rhythms of *adowa* and *kete* during public rites on the Abetifi streets.[175] Asante suggested measures to cut expenses. His *abusua* acquired a "common bedstead" without "flowers or decorations" and chairs to be rented out when not in use. He also urged the *abusuapanyin* to designate one responsible person to be in charge of drinks, only offering "minerals and beer" to those who donated. Inexpensive palm wine continued to be available in unlimited quantity. After a recent funeral they reported a surplus, much to Asante's satisfaction.[176] Based on evidence from neighboring Asante, Arhin wrote that for most present-day funerals "donations generally pay for the expenditure."[177] Reverend Asante's urgency in controlling funeral costs suggests that Arhin's assessment does not represent Kwawu. The *abusuapanyin* of the Abetifi Aduana family, Ɔpanyin Opoku Annor discussed funeral expenses with me in 1997, when one female elder had just been buried at a cost of eight million cedis (then about fifteen hundred dollars) with donations of six million cedis. Fortunately her children abroad covered the deficit.[178] Funds for an elaborate funeral can only be raised outside Kwawu.

When members of the Presbyterian Church talked about their own death, they wished for modest funerals. Addo loathed the idea that scarce resources might be "wasted" on his funeral. "Don't use money on my dead body!" he exclaimed, preferring a quick burial in a simple coffin of the olden days.[179] In 1996 Addo had a barrister draft instructions "to be obeyed and carried out by the members, Elders and Head of my family."

1. There should be no wake-keeping held in my honour before my burial.
2. My body must be buried no later than 48 (Forty-eight) hours after my death.
3. The members of my family should not wait for any other members of my family who has traveled, either out of the country or to any other place to return before I am buried.
4. All persons who attend my burial service should disperse as soon as the service is over.
5. The 40 (forty) day remembrance custom which is usually performed should not be performed for me after my death neither should the annual remembrance service be done in my favour.

6. My tomb must not be cemented neither should there be any monument erected over my tomb.
7. My own coffin which I have already bought must be used to bury me. There should not be any alterations whatsoever made to it.[180]

These instructions caused a stir. Addo distributed copies to the *Adɔntenhene*, Daasebrɛ (*Ɔmanhene* of Kwawu), Ntesohene (chief of his mother's home-town), *abusua* elders, children, and the Abetifi Presbyterian pastor. Addo made sure that everybody who entered his house read his instructions, and he invited me to copy them.[181]

During my 1997 visit Addo was troubled. Reverend Asante, his close relative, had just passed away. Praising Asante's "character" and "behavior," he noted how Asante "helped, worked, sacrificed." Addo called him "one of the best citizens of Abetifi," while declaring that he had "learned all these deeds at Sober House." Addo added quickly that Asante's corpse was in the "fridge," costing fifty thousand cedis per day: "What for? It's useless." He recalled that when his wife died in 1991, her family asked for a contribution of one hundred million cedis. After his refusal, they requested twenty mil-lion; he agreed to pay one million. Addo strongly objected to high funeral costs but not to the practice of honoring a life. This became evident in his impromptu eulogy of Reverend Asante. When two boys showed up during our conversation, he gave them money to help clean around Asante's house, commenting that "many pastors" would come and "it should look nice!"[182] In our final conversation at his Accra home Addo spoke again about his own death, repeating his worry. "We don't plan well for the future . . . we are always attending funerals," there should be "free hospitals in this country for old people." To those opposing his instructions, he responded:

> If people keep criticizing my wish, I will dash my body to the medical school. I will do it! . . . I wish they will do what I have written. If there is something the family has, give to somebody in need than to put it under the ground![183]

Nine months later Addo was dead.

When his son, Kwabena Ofori Atta Addo, wanted to bury him within twenty-four hours, Daasebrɛ Akuamoa Boateng, Kwawu's *ɔmanhene* and a relative, called him. Daasebrɛ declared that "he would not permit his death to be un-noticed." Since Addo had been such a prominent elder and gen-erous donor to the people of Kwawu, he deserved a funeral befitting his status.[184] Daasebrɛ's reasoning reflected his understanding of personhood. Philosopher Kwame Gyekye wrote that Akan personhood finds "concrete expression in attitudes . . . toward the funeral of an individual member." Personhood, "defined in terms of moral achievement," is not only measured by individual, social, or economic success but also by living up to the moral expectations of the community.[185] Since Addo had done this, his death needed a public rite to reaffirm this community value. Daasebre promised to assemble the Kwawu chiefs but reminded Ofori Atta Addo that it was his duty to host them. Against Addo's wishes, his body was kept in the morgue. Still, the simple coffin was used and there was no wake.[186] On the eve of the burial his body was brought to Abetifi and placed on two benches in his room, covered only with a cloth. The door was closed; everybody went to bed. The next morning, during the service in the Presbyterian Church, those gathered heard about this big man's accomplishments as a "philanthropist." His *suban* (character) was described as "disciplinarian, selfless, honest, generous, firm, and fair, very courageous and progressive in outlook." His children addressed Addo's multiple identities, and said:

> His personal sacrifices of time and energy to family, friends and community will certainly live on in memories of all those who knew and loved him. By his *numerous roles* as husband, father and community leader, he led an exemplary life manifesting those virtues which we all seek to emulate.[187]

There were ruptures. During the thanksgiving service two chiefs "collapsed." On Sunday, when mourners gathered at the *ahenfie*, there was suddenly a heavy downpour, forcing people to seek shelter. Some, according to Ofori Atta Addo, interpreted these disturbances as signs that his father was not fully pleased with his funeral. After all, Addo had the final say. The celebrations ended quickly and rather unceremoniously, without offering all guests the cooked food. Addo's effort to set an example against lavish funerals influenced the Presbyterian Church, which decided to end the practice of wake-keeping.[188]

Legacy

The interviewed men talked about how they hoped to be remembered, although at times indirectly. Some were quite active in constructing their personal legacies. Those who had the financial resources erected buildings that would carry, as concrete memorials, their names. Others who had acquired literacy wrote autobiographies, or autobiographical portraits, to provide material for a eulogy and to influence further readings of their lives. In his personal memoir, Reverend Asante focused on his thirty-three years of service as a pastor of the Presbyterian Church. Throughout his pastoral career he renovated existing buildings or erected new ones, culminating in the "magnificent cathedral" in Koforidua. Asante replied to those who criticized building at the expense of spiritual work:

> Reverend Asante firmly believed, and rightly, too, that to be able to consolidate pastoral activities certain physical infrastructures must necessarily be provided, and hence his anxiety to see the construction of chapels, school buildings, manses, quarters, and other civil structures in almost all the stations he worked in. By this commitment he was able to build a solid foundation for the Church in particular and for Christianity in general, for which he would be forever remembered.[189]

These words sum up Asante's convictions about a pastor's role, revealing crucial parts of his religious and social identity. As a builder, Asante belonged to a long tradition going back to nineteenth-century Basel missionaries who, wherever they went, erected churches and schools.[190] In 2001, four years after Asante's death, the Abetifi congregation rededicated the small chapel, constructed by Ramseyer 125 years earlier, as the Rev. E.K.O. Asante Memorial Chapel. Elders, who were not writing, devoted time to convey skills and knowledge to successors. Ɔpanyin Marfo in Pepease received regular visits from his son, Kwasi Adjei Frimpong. Marfo instructed Frimpong about his insights as *nsumankwaahene*.[191] Ɔkyeame Asante, who recalled his opportunities to improve his talents as an *odunsini* (herbalist) by listening to his seniors prior to their death, planned to use a similar technique to pass on his insights.[192]

Boakye Yiadom was most active in shaping his legacy and promoting his Presbyterian credentials. In his autobiography, "My Life History," he emphasized his devotion as missionary and catechist. In detail, he narrated the circumstances of founding a Presbyterian congregation in Konongo in 1935. This accomplishment is framed as the beginning of his church service.[193] Notes in the earlier "Autobiography: My Own Life" do not mention his missionary activity. Only a brief entry covers his work for UAC, documenting his promotion and pay raise, and the birth of his first child.[194] This omission is striking; with the exception of the Konongo missionary work, "My Own Life" corresponds closely to "My Life History." Since the 1960s Boakye Yiadom has sought to become a Presbyterian pastor. After failing the entrance exam to Trinity College, he petitioned his superiors for "field ordination," the practice of promoting a senior catechist to the position of minister without further academic training.

BY: I wanted to be a minister. . . . I sent in my application to be a minister of the church. But according to my record, they said I was overage. They have to ordain a person at the age of thirty or forty.
SM: You did not go to training college till forty.
BY: When I went to training college, even when I came out of the training college [becoming a certified teacher], I was more than sixty. But I established the Konongo Presbyterian Church in 1935. If you go there, you see my photograph at the Mission house. When I got out of the middle school in 1934 I went to Konongo to buy cocoa, as a cocoa produce agent. I saw that there was no Presbyterian Church, and I made up my mind that God may help me to establish the church. And I did, it is now flourishing.[195]

The sudden switch from talking about being denied the ordination to his accomplishment in Konongo is significant. Boakye Yiadom considered the missionary achievement to be decisive in his aspiration to become a minister. During the fiftieth anniversary celebration of the Konongo Presbyterian Church, Boakye Yiadom made a public announcement pleading with the Presbyterian authorities to make him a "special minister without salary." "My greatest desire," he declared, "is to be made a minister and receive full ministerial burial."[196] In 1994 Boakye Yiadom appealed to the synod committee to make him an honorary minister, based on his lifelong church service and his claim of having established the Konongo congregation. He provided biographical information adapted to fulfill the ideals of Presbyterian masculinity. He suggested that the Konongo chapel be renamed after him, that a plate with his name and picture be mounted at the back of the chapel, and that he be allowed to be buried there.[197] The petition was denied; his role as first Konongo catechist would not place him "in any unique or extraordinary position for the church."[198] After reading a draft of this section, Boakye Yiadom showed me another notebook with a detailed account of the Presbyterian beginnings at Konongo. This version, recorded in the 1970s, was based on earlier jottings. Boakye Yiadom saved a program of the "Laying of Corner Stones" for a new church building in 1955. He had added by hand that "Mr. B. Yiadom" presented a "History of the Kgo. Presby. Church (15 min)."[199] In 2000 we visited Konongo. Upon our request the Presbyterian pastor produced Boakye Yiadom's framed photograph with a caption stating his founder's claim. A few days later Boakye Yiadom again expressed his hope that one day the Konongo church would be named after him.[200]

Addo's son, Ofori Atta Addo, created a museum in his father's Abetifi sitting room, initiated by his late sister, Edna Sampong of Seattle. The space displays Addo's suit, dress shoes, diaries, books, and mounted photographs with captions. They depict Addo as the local council chairman in the 1950s, his children, and *abusua* members. Photos include images of historical personalities, among them his brothers J. E. Sampong and J. K. Kwakye; his role model and mentor, teacher I. O. Sampong; King George VI; and the Prince of Wales. A vitrine contains personal objects like his glasses, driver's license, and laminated copies of receipts and letters of appreciation. A coffee table stands in the center displaying imported objects of a bygone era: white porcelain dishes with a flowery design, once used to entertain guests, and a water filter. The museum documents Addo's accomplishments as an Abetifi big man, particularly his years of public service and the recognition he received from dignitaries. Ofori Atta Addo hopes that this space will remind visitors of his father's generosity and serve as an example for younger generations.[201]

Conclusion

As a cultural ideal, the status of an *ɔpanyin* had an enduring value in Kwawu throughout the twentieth century. An *ɔpanyin* was always old in the sense of experience and maturity, but could be young in years. People related the notion of *ɔpanyin* to other social positions like a chiefly office, a presbyter, and a modern appointed or elected political official. People approached elders for dispute settlement, either within informal or formal settings; *mpanyinfoɔ* had to speak well and sensibly. The status of any *ɔpanyin* was never permanent. Elders who misbehaved jeopardized respect and effectiveness even while still carrying the title. An *ɔpanyin*'s social position was not self-acquired but ascribed, the product of accomplishments and qualities acknowledged by a larger community.

The social position of an *ɔpanyin* is not gender-specific. Women have served as *mpanyinfoɔ* and *ahemaa* (queenmothers) in the chief's palace or within their lineage and communities or, more recently, as elected officials. There were female *akɔmfoɔ* who were powerful as a result of their access to spiritual forces. Some women became "big women," like Akua Animaa, the Abetifi entrepreneur.[202] Yet, in the course of the twentieth century, women's status has decreased. Social structures and local institutions that once guaranteed senior Akan women access to decision-making processes and resources lost their relevance. Colonial rule led to a "masculinization" of the local political realm; native administration ordinances and the system of indirect rule failed to recognize female elders and their courts.[203] Mission churches, which originated as patriarchal institutions, subordinated women, leaving limited spaces for female leadership. Still, the story is more complicated. Although women were only recently admitted to ordination in the Presbyterian Church, they have long been active on a grassroots level, forming the backbone of congregations since the nineteenth century. Felicia Asante has been a leader in women's fellowships for decades, not only because of her marriage to a pastor but also because of her own accomplishments. Female elders, some as presbyters, maintained a certain amount of power and influence, although it was more hidden and frequently indirect.[204]

Senior masculinity relates to personhood, understood in terms of moral achievement. Yet what constitutes moral achievement, what qualifies somebody for the social position of *ɔpanyin*, has changed in specific historical contexts.[205] In the case of Abetifi's first senior presbyter, John Yaw Atta, his biographer, Reverend Akwa, articulated tensions, as well as competing notions of masculinities, by presenting conflicting opinions over expectations and obligations toward Atta as *ɔpanyin* among different communities in early-twentieth-century Kwawu. Atta was trapped between the demands of his *abusua* and those of his church. Reverend Akwa could not accept Atta's eagerness to continue fulfilling expectations toward his *abusua* as *ɔdehyeɛ* (royal) after he had embraced the mission church as his new spiritual and material home. For church leaders, the middle ground sought by Atta did not exist. Although Reverend Akwa highlighted Atta's afflictions, for which he died a troubled man, in retrospect Atta is celebrated as an important elder of both the ruling *Tena abusua* and the Presbyterian Church.

J. A. Wahyee resembles Atta despite the generational difference. Both were born into the same *abusua* with close ties to the Kwawu paramount stool. Early in life Wahyee decided to join and move in with the Presbyterian congregation by selecting a site for his house in the Christian Quarters. Yet Wahyee did not see the tensions in Atta's life as presented by Reverend Akwa. Rather, he marveled about Atta's power and influence at the *ahenfie* and in the church. Wahyee considered Atta a successful middle figure who skillfully negotiated between two worlds. Wahyee, as well as Reverend Akwa, in talking about Atta, referred to their own experiences; they constructed a self while talking about others. Although Wahyee never occupied the rank of a senior presbyter, he was widely recognized as an effective and influential session member. Wahyee did not elaborate on his involvement in lineage politics. But it seems that he, like Atta, was invested in the expansion of the Presbyterian Church, the former Basel Mission, in Kwawu. During the 1950s Wahyee sided with Ɔmanhene Akuamoa Akyeampong, who was, before his enstoolment, an active member of the Presbyterian Church. Akyeampong not only wished to move Kwawu's capital from Abene to Abetifi but, in addition, to create a "Christian state" in Kwawu.[206] Akyeampong faced strong opposition from Abene "traditionalists" and their allies, who were concerned about neglected stool rites and Abene's threatened abandonment, and by a rising CPP, represented most forcefully by the Kwawu Youth Association. Akyeampong's opponents succeeded in ousting him. In an ironic twist his successor, young Boateng Akuamoa, was destooled in 1962 and replaced by Akyeampong who had again become acceptable to the CPP government. In 1971, when Akyeampong finally abdicated to die as a Christian, the destooled Boateng Akuamoa came back as Daasebre Akuamoa Boateng.[207] In Wahyee's final years, and this is relevant to this discussion, he had moved beyond chieftaincy disputes. When reflecting on his life, he was no longer interested in dwelling on these political struggles. Rather, he was eager to convey his ideals about senior masculinity and the importance for a big man to share his riches communally, reenforcing moral and community values.

Reverend Asante and Opusuo, having attended training college in their youth, had career options not available to Boakye Yiadom. This training had an impact on their reaching senior masculinity. Asante and Opusuo had the means to provide support for *abusua* members and the foresight to erect houses in their hometowns in their thirties. Their houses served as reminders of their aspiration to *ɔpanyin* status. Both belonged to the inner circles of their *abusua* and were asked to take leadership upon retirement. There were also differences. Asante had an early religious calling and enrolled in the catechist course at the training college, later qualifying for the seminary. Opusuo, more ambivalent about religious faith, pursued a career as a teacher and education officer. In retirement he acted as a community leader, taking a position in the development committee and being elected to the district assembly.

Boakye Yiadom faced a harder path. Entering school late, he could not pursue his education beyond Standard VII until age forty owing to lack of funds. He was forced to accept employment as a clerk and then as a "pupil teacher." He qualified as a "Certificate A" teacher only when he was close to retirement. Like Reverend Asante, Boakye Yiadom had deep religious convictions but never succeeded in reaching the desired ordination. His position as *ɔpanyin* was more tenuous. Neither in his *abusua* nor in the Abetifi Christian Quarters did he take a center position, nor was he widely acknowledged as an *ɔpanyin*. Still, he claimed the position for himself. This was different in his second hometown of Kurofa, Asante Akyem. There his position as *krakye* and teacher-catechist remained extraordinary. Kurofa people respected him as an elder, close to the *ahenfie,* since his mother had been married to the chief. As an aspiring elder, Boakye Yiadom had been most successful as a writer, creating an unusual paper trail. Similar to Kofi Ankoma and Ɔpanyin Marfo, his limited means did not allow him to erect a house, the most effective way to create permanence in the minds of the living.

In her study on Yoruba big men, Karin Barber argued that those who were successful in modern times had spent time away.[208] This applies to Kwawu traders and businessmen like E. K. Addo. Only after acquiring wealth in the commercial centers of southern Ghana could they establish themselves as big men in their hometowns, rivaling local chiefs. While older forms of big men, the nineteenth-century *abirεmpɔn,* were measured in terms of people, subjects, wives, slaves, and other dependants providing labor, modern big men's riches consisted of money and investments, real estate, and cash crops. Houses built outside Kwawu could generate income. In hometowns, buildings served for the big man's personal use or were available to the public: Saka's community center, Anim Addo's technical school, or Addo's health clinic. Businessmen like Addo represented the "new model" of *ɔbirεmpɔn.*[209] They had diverse economic interests and were engaged in modern methods of accumulation through the cash economy. Yet big-man status remained something that was ultimately bestowed by the larger community. Tegare Ɔbosomfo Kwasi Mawu remained closer to the older model of an *ɔbirεmpɔn.* Unlike Addo, he generated wealth within Kwawu. Supplicants who sought protection and assistance from Tegare brought money to Pepease. Like the precolonial *ɔbirεmpɔn,* mechanisms were in place to guarantee the sharing of wealth since the shrine belonged to the chief. Later in life Kwasi Mawu relied on his wives, children, and adherents' labor to expand his economic base by launching cocoa farms in the Afram Plains. The monetization of the twentieth century had an effect on both big-man models. Even a Tegare shrine received cash donations for pledges made in kind like a fowl, a sheep, or a cow.

My interview partners mentioned numerous times that wealth should not matter for attaining *ɔpanyin* status. Even the PNDC government evoked the same concept when promoting *mpanyinfoɔ* as ideal members of the new district assemblies. In practice, however, it became increasingly difficulty to maintain the status of an *ɔpanyin* without money. Only Ɔpanyin Marfo expressed his skepticism about a respected *ɔpanyin* with little money. He had learned the hard way. Marfo, groomed as an *ahenkwaa* (palace attendant), refused to perform manual work needed for cocoa farming, a highly profitable activity in his youth. In the past a *nsumankwaahene's* upkeep lay with the chief and his elders, whom the *nsumankwaahene* advised and served. In modern times most chiefs are strapped for cash, and Akan spiritual knowledge has lost prestige. The position of an *odunsini,* held by Marfo and Ɔkyeame Asante, no longer translated smoothly into access to wealth. Unlike Marfo, Tegare Ɔbosomfo Kwasi Mawu also succeeded in the cash economy. He invested in cocoa and real estate for times when the shrine would no longer flourish. Money had become the "symbol of a successful life."[210]

These days money is closely tied to funerals, whose scope and expense are contested in Kwawu. Funerals are the most important events to celebrate a life, to recognize someone's status and personhood. On the other hand, the "individualism" that supposedly arrived with modernity, wrapped in the package of colonialism, Western education, and capitalism, was not all-encompassing. As the cases of Addo and Reverend Asante show, an individual ultimately remained a member of a community, especially if this community had a stake to present a person's life as successful. Therefore the Kwawu Ɔmanhene and Presbyterian Church elders, assisted by the bereaved lineages, dictated that the communal well-being stipulated a fitting funeral. The wrong message would have been sent had these accomplished elders been buried without adequate rites. In Gyekye's understanding of "moderate communitarianism," the self has become "a communal being," as well as an "autonomous, self-assertive being with a capacity for evaluation and choice."[211] Yet, in the funerals of respected *mpanyinfoɔ* and big men, higher and more pressing communitarian needs overruled the wishes of even the most outspoken *ɔpanyin* like Addo. Funerals "are more for the living than for the dead."[212] In all these complexities and changing ideals of achieving elderhood, there is *one* trait that runs consistently with little modification through these accounts: elders remained dependent on their hometown communities which ultimately bestowed the title and respect that made someone an *ɔpanyin.*

EPILOGUE: "NO CONDITION
IS PERMANENT"

"No Condition Is Permanent" is one of the popular slogans painted on lorries and buses in southern Ghana. Understandings about masculinity were not permanent either in twentieth-century Ghana but were fluid and changing. R. W. Connell has suggested that the spread of European empires and ideologies brought a "global gender order" and a "prospect of all indigenous gender regimes foundering under this institutional and cultural pressure."[1] This book refutes such an interpretation by utilizing the theoretical to situate the local. Although different institutions introduced new notions of masculinity in colonial Ghana, this did not lead to a collapse of an indigenous gender system. Rather, Akan ideas of adult masculinity, elderhood, and big-man status proved to be resilient while also subject to reformulation and contestation. Individual actors creatively engaged with old *and* new gender ideals, and adapted them to changing contexts according to their needs. Novel ideas like Presbyterian masculinity—promoted by missionaries and mediated by their African agents—went through a process of naturalization. Kwawu men and women adjusted this innovation selectively. Missionary ideas about patrilineal inheritance and compulsory education seemed at first remarkable and foreign, yet by the middle decades of the twentieth century, those living in former Basel Mission settlements had partially accepted patrilineal descent without completely neglecting matrilineal ties. An increasing demand for Western education moved beyond missionary spheres of influence.

In the early twentieth century the new social category of *akrakyefoɔ* was unusual, reserved for a few. With school enrollment growing in the 1920s, and more rapidly in the 1950s, *akrakyefoɔ*, as a social group, ceased to be exceptional. By the 1970s teachers, as well as their profession generally, had lost much of their status.[2] Nevertheless, *akrakyefoɔ* kept their aspirations. As one anthropologist reported from Larteh, Akuapem, the " 'scholar' has arrived on the social scene, established in a new role the significance of which is shown by the frequent singling out of scholars in a special category." In towns of southern Ghana with old Presbyterian congregations, Twi speakers had introduced a specific response, *"yaa owura"* (hello Mister), as the "appropriate answer to a scholar's greeting."[3] Yet, while David Brokensha focused on education as an agent of change working on society, here the objective is reversed: How did *akrakyefoɔ* reconstitute their subjectivities by narrating their experiences with Western education and their lives as middle figures, negotiating between various, at times competing, notions of masculinity?

The recollections of the eight men featured in this book speak to the grand sweep of historical forces that transformed Kwawu and, on a larger scale, the worlds of colonial and postcolonial Ghana. The changes and innovations over the past hundred years, such as increased personal mobility, expanded roads and railways, migration to urban centers, Western education, monetization, and new economic opportunities in cash crops like cocoa and trade, provide the context and are reflected in the men's stories. At times their memory privileged different occurrences from conventional histories. For example, World War II and the emerging Ghanaian nationalism led by Kwame Nkrumah touched most of these lives only at the edges. A. K. Boakye Yiadom did not dwell on historical markers like Ghana's independence in his autobiographical writing. Instead, personal challenges were more salient. He and others foregrounded individuals, events, and processes that interacted directly with their lives: childhood role models, education, marriages, and the long path of reaching senior masculinity. The objective of achieving *ɔpanyin* status remained constant throughout the twentieth century; what changed were the available resources. In these lives, hardship was not merely expressed in the worsening economic conditions of Ghana since the 1960s but in a multitude of responsibilities and expectations which the men struggled to fulfill.

The eight men's stories uncovered how they reworked notions of self in relation to personhood, understood as moral achievement and filtered through memory. These men constructed selves while narrating their engagement with ideals of masculinity at different life stages. They shared with an immediate and intended audience the experiences of their life's accomplishments and joys, as well as disappointments and pains. Reflecting on our conversations, I was less interested in reconstructing "truths" and identifying what "really happened." Instead, I looked for analytical spaces in which subjectivities come to the fore and the meaning of the past for the present can be examined. Oral historians have much to learn from exploring the power of subjective constructions of self at specific historical moments.

The narrators produced their life-history accounts in interaction with me as the elicitor and listener. Because our conversations took place over a period of years, our relationships evolved. My interview partners made direct interventions that shaped the outcome of this project. They pursued me, decided to provide access to personal papers, and arranged meetings with others from whom I had to learn. Only in retrospect did I realize that Reverend Asante was instrumental for the inclusion of two elders whose wisdom he valued: J. A. Wahyee and E. K. Addo. An increasing familiarity, as well as our evolving intersubjectivity, affected and modified the self-presentation of my interview partners. My improved understanding of local contexts revealed deeper layers of meaning within narratives. I began to recognize cues that referred to moments which the men only addressed indirectly. Such telling omissions, as well as utterances at the margins of stories, provided hints that enabled a more complete understanding of my interview partners' selves.

The colonial project denied African men and women subjectivity, reflected in early ethnographies and continued in nationalist historiographies. Although anthropologists like R. S. Rattray and Meyer Fortes produced indispensable works, they wrote about "the Asante" in general, about Asante kinship structures and belief systems, without giving adequate space to individual experience. When informants were cited, they remained anonymous, hidden behind general classifications, denied a subjective identity. Writings by African research assistants can be retrieved to great benefit for the historian.[4] Postcolonial critics have argued that scholars, relying on European teleologies like "modernity," "capitalism," and "development," too often excluded from historical reconstructions the position of the former colonized people as subjects. The historiography of colonial Africa embraced the rise of the emerging sub-Saharan nations under the vanguard of "elites" who pushed toward modernity, the forms of resistance by men and women against colonial domination, and, more recently, the "colonization of minds" by missionaries and other cultural agents of the colonial project.[5] Historians, however, paid less attention to the personal experiences of those men and women who actively negotiated with the introduction of new concepts and ideals, individuals such as *akrakyefoɔ* trained in mission schools, railway workers forming part of a newly created African labor force, and other middle figures like birth attendants.[6]

Making Men in Ghana calls for a fresh approach to the study of gender and to the analysis of cultural and historical constructions of masculinities. It advocates anthropological and historical methods in exploring oral and written sources. By combining a discussion of historicized subjectivities and constructions of masculinity, it points to a new direction for research on masculinity in colonial and postcolonial Africa, as well as outside the African continent. This book moves beyond the observation of the multiplicity and fluidity of masculinities by exploring how subjectivity and masculinity are constituted in concrete historical contexts, how different normative structures are played out in people's lives, and how people engaged with these normative structures at different times, thereby transforming them. Looking at self-presentations shows how specific sites form separate story lines in autobiographical narratives, which are then selectively articulated and amplified for various audiences.

POSTSCRIPT

The conversations that led to this book usually ended with a ritual. Some interview partners insisted on an additional drink. Others, who were spiritually inclined, offered prayers or libations, depending on their personal preference. Whenever I parted for an extended period, a formal closing became imperative. On my last visits in 1994, Ɔpanyin J. A. Wahyee prayed and Ɔkyeame Asante poured a libation. Both elders were gifted orators who took the opportunity to give me advice and to seek spiritual protection for my endeavors. In Akan societies, such public communications with supernatural forces are highly performative and provide spaces for audience engagement. During a libation the audience participates by frequently exclaiming "listen" or "go on" and, in the end, complimenting the speaker for an elaborate performance, much as Christian prayers are interspersed with "amens" from the audience, followed by an acknowledgment of a task well done.

After talking about childhood games and his work as presbyter, Wahyee offered this prayer for me, witnessed by his nephew Kwadwo Donkor and Joseph Kwakye.

> God, our Father, the God we can always lean on. We need to thank you for the good direction and guidance. You always give us the good things in life. If misfortune befalls us, then it is due to our own stubbornness. We are before you this afternoon to plead for this *ɔburoni* [European] Kofi Mensa [my Twi name]. When he came here, he gave himself to me as a father and I also took him to my fold as a good son. Please God, I entrust him into your hands. May all that he tries to undertake prosper. May he not forget what he is doing so that everything he does will bring fruits in abundance.
>
> Father, you have told us to get married and multiply and fill this earth. Please help him as he tries to get married that he may find a good, understanding and loving partner. May he find a woman who will love him and he, Kofi, can also love her, so that they can both live for you.
>
> Father God, you have taught us faith, hope, and love. Out of these three love is the greatest. So may you give him a deep love. May he love deeply all

people he will come into contact with. May he see them as dear brothers and sisters. May he live with his wife like brother and sister from one father and one mother. Have mercy on him. May he see no darkness or sickness. All throughout his life may you have mercy on him. May all the good work you have used him to do succeed so that those of us he has stayed with and walked with may also be glorified. Bless him and keep him safe. May he enter into good friendship with everybody he comes into contact with to reveal your love and word to all those who meet him. Come and hear us this evening and grant him a safe journey. Be a light to his path and feet. May you grant him a trouble-free journey going home to meet his brothers and sisters, as well as his parents so that they will have a great reunion. Please hear our prayer in Jesus' name. Amen. May you go in peace.[1]

As a Tegare *ɔkyeame* (spokesperson), Kwabena Asante was well versed in the art of libations. Always eloquent, he could adapt them to any given context. Still, a libation follows a structure which includes inviting the gods and ancestors to share a drink, informing them about the occasion, and asking for their blessing and protection of the task ahead. This libation was informal, delivered in an intimate setting, and adjusted to the presence of foreigners. Asante mentioned only a few gods and no ancestors, nor did he graphically describe the cursing of evil-doers. Instead, he incorporated Christian references. Asante poured the libation after a conversation about proverbs and questions about his life. When Asante reached for the bottle of schnapps that Lane and I had presented earlier, Kwame Fosu rose, lowered his cloth, and filled the glass. Asante said the following words while slowly pouring the schnapps onto the ground:

Ei! Otwieduampɔn,[2] the mighty one
We thank you.
You led them to come
No evil befell them
They arrived
We have finished everything nicely
We thank you all
We implore you to send them back home in peace
Let no evil person or any wild animal meet them on the way
Christmas is approaching
They are roaming about in people's towns
Soaring their work, some people are bad.

They are going to their country
When they go
Let it be said that they did a good job here.
When there is the need for something
We shall be friends with them

So that we will teach them
So that whatever we need
They will teach us
We shall also do for you then
This is what we wish
No evil spirit should cross their path
No evil spirit should get them into trouble in their undertakings
This is our plea
We beg you, Otwieduampɔn, the mighty one
Baafoɔ Gare,[3] we beg you
In these days, the world is fearful
As you walk, your neighbor follows you with bad intention
He who wishes to do evil to you in this Christmas time
The wind is blowing but some of it is good air
Some of it is bad air
The wind blowing is made up of good and bad
Some people have bad intentions
And some people have good intentions
As for any with good intentions
May God bless them, otherwise
He who is thinking evil, will end up in evil
At certain times, they decide to go to Pepease
They decide to go to Abetifi
They are going here, Kumase
Someone will be jealous that they are roaming about like that
He may wish that they are disgraced
As for that, you the mighty one
No-one wishes blessing for his enemy
On that, whatever you like
You may do such a person
For him or her to feel the pinch
So that we will know those who do not wish
The good of this town
May we drink at the funeral of those
Who do not wish the progress of the town
Blessing to all who are gathered here
Blessing to our souls
Blessing to our *abosom* (gods)[4]

We expressed our gratitude for the libation with the customary *"monni kasa!"* (well spoken!). The schnapps was passed around for a farewell drink. Then, although we had formally closed our gathering, the conversation continued.

Glossary

ababawa (pl. *mmabawa*)   young woman (after puberty before giving birth)

aberantee (pl. *mmerantee*)   adolescent, young man (after puberty)

aberewa   old woman; female elder

abofra (pl. *mmofra*)   child, boy, girl; servant, attendant; person inferior in rank

abusua (pl. *mmusua*)   matrilineage

abusuapanyin   lineage head

aduru (pl. *nnuru*)   medicine

adwuma   work, labor (especially agricultural work); employment of any kind; trade, profession

afoofi   leisure

agoro   play, game; performance (ritual), singing and dancing

agya   father; master

ahenfie   chief's palace

ahenkwaa (pl. *nhenkwaa*)   palace attendant, servant of a chief

akɔm   divination

akwadaa   child; very old man

akwakoraa (pl. *nkwakoraa*)   very old man

akwankwaa (pl. *nkwankwaa*)   young man, commoner with no office

akwantufoɔ   travelers, migrants

anansesεm   stories about the spider Kwaku Ananse; stories

aware   marriage, the state of being married

borɔn (pl. *mmorɔn*)   ward of a town

ekuo   hunters association

ena   mother

εsono   elephant

kora (pl. *akorafoɔ*)   co-wife

krakye (pl. *akrakyefoɔ*)   clerk, scholar

mogya   blood, shared within the matrilineage

mpena   girlfriend, concubine

nsumankwaahene   leader of those responsible for royal charms and amulets

ntɔrɔ (or *ntɔn*)   totemic spirit, inherited patrilineally

ɔbaa (pl. *mmaa*)   woman

ɔbarima (pl. *mmarima*)   man; valiant man, hero

ɔbarima pa   a good, real, valiant man

ɔbirɛmpɔn (pl. *abirɛmpɔn*)   big man; Asante title

ɔbɔfo (pl. *abɔfoɔ*)   senior hunter

ɔbɔmmɔfo (pl. *abɔmmɔfoɔ*)   junior hunter

ɔbosom (pl. *abosom*)   lesser gods (compared to the supreme god, Ɔnyame); *abosom* live in rocks, rivers, etc.

ɔbosomfo (pl. *abosomfoɔ*)   priest (used for Tegare priests)

ɔdehyeɛ (pl. *adehyeɛ*)   free-born person; noble man/woman; (matrilineally descended) royal of a stool or office

ɔdekuro   headman, village chief

odunsini   herbalist

ɔhemaa (pl. *ahemaa*)   queenmother

ɔhene (pl. *ahene*)   divisional chief

ɔheneba (pl. *ɔhenemma*)   child of a chief

ɔkatakyie   hero; a brave, valiant, bold, undaunted, courageous, powerful, mighty man; giant

ɔkɔmfo (pl. *akɔmfoɔ*)   male or female diviner (of an *ɔbosom*)

ɔkrawa   barren, childless man; impotent man

ɔkyeame (pl. *akyeame*)   spokesperson, linguist

ɔman   town; inhabitants of a town as a political body; state, nation

ɔmanhene   paramount chief

ɔpanyin (pl. *mpanyinfoɔ*)   elder

osigyafo (pl. *asigyafoɔ*)   unmarried man or woman

ɔwura   mister, gentleman

pato   three-walled room; sitting area with an open front

suban   character

tiri nsa   head-drink

tiri sika   head-money

ware   to marry, to take in marriage

wɔfa (pl. *wɔfanom*)   maternal uncle, often head of the matrilineage

wɔfase   nephew, niece (of the same matrilineage)

yere   wife

Notes

Prologue and Personae

1. The archival sources I consulted are listed in the bibliography.

2. Elizabeth Tonkin, *Narrating Our Pasts: The Social Construction of Oral History* (Cambridge: Cambridge University Press, 1992), 58. Tonkin distinguishes between written and oral genres, defined as "patterned expectancy," labeling an agreement between speaker and listener. In oral genres, "the occasion of performance is clearly important and may be definite to the audience's expectations" (51).

3. For proverbs and the intersection of masculinities and language, see Kwesi Yankah, *The Proverb in the Context of Akan Rhetoric: A Theory of Proverb Praxis* (Bern: Peter Lang, 1989); and Chenjerai Shire, "Men Don't Go to the Moon: Language, Space and Masculinities in Zimbabwe," in *Dislocating Masculinity*, ed. A. Cornwall and N. Lindisfarne, 147–58 (London: Routledge, 1994).

4. For feminist self-positioning, see Susan Geiger, *TANU Women: Gender and Culture in the Making of Tanganyikan Nationalism, 1955–1965* (Portsmouth, N.H.: Heinemann, 1997); Belinda Bozzoli, with Mmantho Nkotsoe, *Women of Phokeng: Consciousness, Life Strategy, and Migrancy in South Africa, 1900–1983* (Portsmouth, N.H.: Heinemann, 1991); Sarah Mirza and Margaret Strobel, eds., *Three Swahili Women: Life Histories from Mombasa, Kenya* (Bloomington: Indiana University Press, 1989); Marjorie Shostak, *Nisa: The Life and Words of a !Kung Woman* (Cambridge, Mass.: Harvard University Press, 1981); Shula Marks, ed., *Not Either an Experimental Doll: The Separate Worlds of Three South African Women* (Bloomington: Indiana University Press, 1987); Berida Ndambuki and Claire Robertson, *"We Only Come Here to Struggle": Stories from Berida's Life* (Bloomington: Indiana University Press, 2000); and particularly Ruth Behar, *Translated Woman: Crossing the Border with Esperanza's Story* (Boston: Beacon, 1993). For postmodern critiques of Westerners doing research in non-Western settings, see Sherna Berger Gluck and Daphne Patai, eds., *Women's Words: The Feminist Practice of Oral History* (New York: Routledge, 1992); and the debate between Kirk Hoppe and Heidi Gengenbach in, respectively, "Whose Life Is It, Anyway? Issues of Representation in Life Narrative Texts of African Women," *International Journal of African Historical Studies* (*IJAHS*) 26, no. 3 (1993): 623–36; and, "Truth-Telling and the Politics of Women's Life History Research in Africa: A Reply to Kirk Hoppe," *IJAHS* 27, no. 3 (1994): 619–27.

5. Emmanuel Akyeampong, *Drink, Power, and Cultural Change: A Social History of Alcohol in Ghana, c. 1800 to Recent Times* (Portsmouth, N.H.: Heinemann, 1996), 161.

6. Geiger, *TANU Women*, xvi.

7. Behar, *Translated Woman*, 272.

8. For libations, see Kwesi Yankah, *Speaking for the Chief: Okyeame and the Politics of Akan Royal Oratory* (Bloomington: Indiana University Press, 1995), 172–80. Many Christian churches frown upon the practice; see S. G. Williamson, *Akan Religion and Christian Faith* (Accra: Ghana Universities Press, 1965), 132. Some of my academic predecessors took a different route by not disclosing the research location and informants' names. Wolf Bleek called the town of Kwawu-Tafo "Ayere" ("it has become tough") to protect his informants; he also published under a pseudonym. Returning twenty years later, Bleek found that his friends in Kwawu-Tafo were disappointed about not being mentioned; see his *Marriage, Inheritance and Witchcraft: A Case Study of a Rural Ghanaian Family* (Leiden: Afrika-Studiecentrum, 1975), 32. I am grateful to Sjaak van der Geest for sharing his research experience (Kwawu-Tafo, October 1994). Bleek's case is not isolated. Clifford Geertz recalled that he and Hildred Geertz had referred to the Indonesian town Pare, the location of their 1950s research, as Modjokuto in their published work. Now Geertz uses the name Pare. He noted, "The last time I was there, in 1986, one of my old informants had gone through the Indonesian translation of the social history of the town that I wrote. I had changed the names of the people as well as the town, but he wrote all the right names in and photocopied it and sent it around to everybody" (Richard Handler, "An Interview with Clifford Geertz," *Current Anthropology* 32, no. 5 [1991]: 605).

1. "To Be a Man Is Hard"

1. For a periodization and overview of this scholarship, see Nancy Hunt, introduction to "Gendered Colonialism in African History," *Gender and History* (special issue) 8, no. 3 (1996): 323–37; and idem, "Placing African Women's History and Locating Gender," *Social History* 14, no. 3 (1989): 359–79. Recent collections include Ayesha Imam, Amina Mama, and Fatou Sow, eds., *Engendering African Social Sciences* (Dakar: CODESRIA, 1997); Dorothy Hodgson and Sheryl McCurdy, eds., *"Wicked" Women and the Reconfiguration of Gender in Africa* (Portsmouth, N.H.: Heinemann, 2001); and Jean Allman, Susan Geiger, and Nakanyike Musisi, eds., *Women in African Colonial Histories* (Bloomington: Indiana University Press, 2002).

2. Luise White, "Separating the Men from the Boys: Constructions of Gender, Sexuality, and Terrorism in Central Kenya, 1939–1959," *IJAHS* 23, no. 1 (1990): 3.

3. Laura Fair, *Pastimes and Politics: Culture, Community, and Identity in Post-Abolition Urban Zanzibar, 1890–1945* (Athens: Ohio University Press, 2001), 228; Frederick Cooper, "Industrial Man Goes to Africa," in *Men and Masculinities in Modern Africa*, ed. L. A. Lindsay and S. F. Miescher (Portsmouth, N.H.: Heinemann, 2003), 128–37; and David William Cohen and E. S. Atieno Odhiambo, *Burying SM: The Politics of Knowledge and the Sociology of Power in Africa* (Portsmouth, N.H.: Heinemann, 1992), an analysis of the legal struggle over the corpse of a prominent lawyer in postcolonial Kenya. Other works include Lisa A. Lindsay and Stephan F. Miescher, eds., *Men and Masculinities in Modern Africa* (Portsmouth, N.H.: Heinemann, 2003); Robert Morrell, ed., *Changing Men in Southern Africa* (London: Zed, 2001); idem, "Masculinities in Southern Africa," *Journal of Southern African Studies* (*JSAS*) (special issue) 24, no. 4 (1998): and Lahoucine Ouzgane, ed., "African Masculinities," *Journal for Men's Studies* (special issue) 10, no. 3 (2002). A few anthropological studies explore male genders and constructions of masculinity and yet are not concerned with historical change: T. O. Beidelman, *The Cool Knife: Imagery of Gender, Sexuality, and Moral Education in Kaguru*

Initiation Ritual (Washington, D.C.: Smithsonian, 1997); John Wood, *When Men Are Women: Manhood among Gabra Nomads in East Africa* (Madison: University of Wisconsin Press, 1999); and Rudi Gaudio, "Male Lesbians and Other Queer Notions in Hausa," in *Boy-Wives and Female Husbands,* ed. S. O. Murray and W. Roscoe (New York: St. Martin's, 1998), 115–28.

4. R. W. Connell, *Masculinities* (Berkeley: University of California Press, 1995), 84.

5. Ibid., 76–81. For a critique of Connell, see Andrea Cornwall and Nancy Lindisfarne, "Dislocating Masculinity: Gender, Power, and Anthropology," in *Dislocating Masculinity,* ed. A. Cornwall and N. Lindisfarne (London: Routledge, 1994), 20; cf. Robert Morrell, "Of Boys and Men: Masculinity and Gender in Southern African Studies," *JSAS* 24, no. 4 (1998): 605–30. For the literature on masculinity outside Africa, see the review by Judith Allen, "Men Interminably in Crisis? Historians on Masculinity, Sexual Boundaries, and Manhood," *Radical History Review* 82 (2002): 191–207. Imperial masculinities are explored by Mrinalini Sinha, *Colonial Masculinity: The "Manly Englishman" and the "Effeminate Bengali" in the Late Nineteenth Century* (Manchester: Manchester University Press, 1995). A good introduction is provided by Rachel Adams and David Savran, eds., *The Masculinity Studies Reader* (Malden, Mass.: Blackwell, 2002).

6. Lisa Lindsay and I suggested three methodological perspectives for exploring historical constructions of masculinity in modern Africa: a focus on discourse, on practice, and on formations of identities and subjectivity. See Stephan Miescher and Lisa Lindsay, "Introduction: Men and Masculinities in Modern African History," in Lindsay and Miescher, eds., *Men and Masculinities in Modern Africa,* 7–8.

7. For "middle figures," see Nancy Hunt, *A Colonial Lexicon of Birth Ritual, Medicalization, and Mobility in the Congo* (Durham, N.C.: Duke University Press, 1999). I am inspired by two impressive African microhistories: T. C. McCaskie, *Asante Identities: History and Modernity in an African Village, 1850–1950* (Edinburgh: Edinburgh University Press, 2000); and Landeg White, *Magomero: Portrait of an African Village* (Cambridge: Cambridge University Press, 1987). For a genealogy of "micro-history," see Carlo Ginzburg, "Mikro-Historie: Zwei oder drei Dinge, die ich von ihr weiss," *Historische Anthropologie* 1, no. 2 (1993): 169–92.

8. According to the 1984 census, Nkawkaw had 34,068 inhabitants; Abetifi, 7,373; Pepease, 2,838; Obo, 5,279; and Mpraeso, 6,678. The numbers fluctuate because of Kwawu migration; over a funeral weekend the population of the ridge towns can easily triple (Kofi Nkansa-Kyeremateng, *The Story of Kwawu* [Accra: Presbyterian Press, 1990], 2). The few anthropological studies about Kwawu include Philip Bartle, "Urban Migration and Rural Identity: An Ethnography of a Kwawu Community, Obo, Ghana" (Ph.D. dissertation, University of Ghana, 1978); idem, *Cyclical Migration and the Extended Community: A West African Example* (Leiden: Afrika Studiecentrum, 1980); Wolf Bleek, *Marriage, Inheritance and Witchcraft: A Case Study of a Rural Ghanaian Family* (Leiden: Afrika-Studiecentrum, 1975), 32; and idem, "Sexual Relationships and Birthcontrol in Ghana: A Case Study of a Rural Town" (Ph.D. dissertation, University of Amsterdam, 1976). Following practice by the Institute of African Studies, University of Ghana, Legon, I use the spelling *Kwawu* and not the colonial orthography *Kwahu;* in all citations the original spelling is left intact.

9. For Basel Mission beginnings in Kwawu, see annual reports, Eugen Werner, Abetifi, January 10, 1877, Basel Mission Archive (BMA), D-1.28, 259; Eugen Werner, Abetifi, February 27, 1878, BMA, D-1.29, 266; and Friedrich Ramseyer, Abetifi, January

29, 1879, BMA, D-1.30, 258, partially printed in *Jahresbericht der Evangelischen Missions-Gesellschaft zu Basel (JB)* 62 (1877): 98–100; *JB* 63 (1878): 87–90; and *JB* 64 (1879): 71–73; for the *Salem* purchase, see "Landkäufe," Abetifi Presbyterian Church (APC); cf. Peter Haenger, "Die Basler Mission im Spannungsbereich afrikanischer Integrationsversuche und europäischer Kolonialpolitik. Vorbereitung und Anfangszeit der 'Asante Mission' in Abetifi, Kwawu" (Master's thesis, University of Basel, 1989). For missionary rules, see *Ordnung für die evangelischen Gemeinden der Basler Mission in Ostindien und Westafrika*, 1865, BMA, D-9.1c, 11a; and *Ordnung für die evangelischen Gemeinden der Basler Mission auf der Goldküste*, revised 1902, BMA, D-9.1c, 13b. For other Basel Mission settlements, see David Brokensha, *Social Change at Larteh, Ghana* (Oxford: Clarendon, 1966), 19; John Middleton, "One Hundred and Fifty Years of Christianity in a Ghanaian Town," *Africa* 53, no. 3 (1983): 3–19; and Sonia Abun-Nasr, *Afrikaner und Missionar: Die Lebensgeschichte von David Asante* (Basel: Schlettwein, 2003); cf. Paul Jenkins, "The Basel Mission in West Africa and the Idea of the Christian Village Community," in *Wholeness in Christ: The Legacy of the Basel Mission in India*, ed. G. Shir (Balmatta, Mangalore: Karnataka Theological Research Institute, 1985), 18–20. For the Basel Mission's bureaucratic and rule-bound organization, see Jon Miller, *The Social Control of Religious Zeal* (New Brunswick, N.J.: Rutgers University Press, 1994). For missionary ideas about femininity, see Simone Prodolliet, *Wider die Schamlosigkeit und das Elend der heidnischen Weiber. Der Export des europäischen Frauenideals in die Kolonien durch die Basler Frauenmission* (Zurich: Limmat Verlag, 1987); cf. Jean Allman and Victoria Tashjian, *"I Will Not Eat Stone": A Women's History of Colonial Asante* (Portsmouth, N.H.: Heinemann, 2000), 183–208. For missionary work elsewhere, see T. O. Beidelman, *Colonial Evangelism: A Socio-historical Study of an East African Mission at the Grassroots* (Bloomington: Indiana University Press, 1982); and Jean Comaroff and John Comaroff, *Of Revelation and Revolution: Christianity, Colonialism, and Consciousness in South Africa*, vol. 1 (Chicago: University of Chicago Press, 1991); and idem, *Of Revelation and Revolution: The Dialectics of Modernity on a South African Frontier*, vol. 2 (Chicago: University of Chicago Press, 1997). For a different interpretation, foregrounding African agency, see Paul Landau, *The Realm of the Word: Language, Gender, and Christianity in a Southern African Kingdom* (Portsmouth, N.H.: Heinemann, 1995); and Meredith McKittrick, *To Dwell Secure: Generation, Christianity, Colonialism in Ovamboland* (Portsmouth, N.H.: Heinemann, 2002); cf. Elizabeth Elbourne, "Word Made Flesh: Christianity, Modernity, and Cultural Colonialism in the Work of Jean and John Comaroff," *American Historical Review (AHR)*, 108, no. 2 (2003): 435–59.

10. Kwame Arhin, "The Role of the Presbyterian Church in the Economic Development of Ghana," *Research Review* (New Series) 1, no. 2 (1985): 153, 160. See reports by Eugen Werner, Abetifi, April 13, 1876; and Jakob Weimer, August 3, 1876, BMA, D-1.28, 247 and 253, published in *Evangelischer Heidenbote (HB)* 49, no. 11 (1876): 85–86; his wife, Mrs. R. Werner-Niehans, Abetifi, June 16, 1878, BMA, D-1.30, 254, later published in *HB* 51, no. 10 (1878): 75–76; E. Werner, June 18, 1878, BMA, D-1.30, 244; and Friedrich Ramseyer, annual report, Abetifi, February 6, 1891, BMA, D-1.53, 126. Kofi Nkansa-Kyeremateng, *One Hundred Years of the Presbyterian Church in Kwahu* (Accra: Presbyterian Press, 1976), 14, lists figures of the Basel Mission congregation in Kwawu: 41 members in 1880, 273 in 1890, 1,652 in 1900, and 2,741 in 1910.

11. Kwamina Dickinson, *A Historical Geography of Ghana* (Cambridge: Cambridge University Press, 1969), 290–91. Expelled in 1917–18 because of their close connection to Germany, Basel missionaries returned in 1926; see Hermann Witschi, *Geschichte der*

Basler Mission, 1914–1919, vol. 4 (Basel: Basileia Verlag, 1965), 162–95; and idem, *Geschichte der Basler Mission, 1920–1940,* vol. 5 (Basel: Basileia Verlag, 1970), 304–305; cf. Noel Smith, *The Presbyterian Church of Ghana, 1835–1960* (Accra: Ghana Universities Press, 1966), 148–54, 160–64.

12. Sophy Osafo, "How Children Are Brought Up in Kwahu" (Thesis, Institute of Education, University College, Achimota, 1950–51), 36. In the 1940s Kwawu had one government school (Obo). All government-assisted schools were Presbyterian (a junior/senior school in Abetifi and junior schools in Mpraeso and Nkwatia); three of the four approved (but nonassisted) senior schools were Presbyterian (Mpraeso, Nkwatia, and Nkawkaw). Among approximately sixty nonassisted junior/infant schools, twenty-three were Presbyterian; twelve, Roman Catholic; seven, Methodist; four, English Church Mission; four, African Universal; two, Salvation Army; and one each, Seventh Day Adventist, Orthodox Mission, and First Century Gospel. Two were jointly run by the Presbyterian and Methodist Churches. See Education Department, "Survey of Facilities for Education in the Kwahu District," October 10, 1944, National Archives of Ghana (NAG), RG 3/1/249.

13. Kwasi Mawu established himself in Pepease in the early 1940s. Other important Tegare priests were Kwasi Fofie of Nkwantanan and Yaw Tawiah of Abetifi; see confidential police reports, "Tigare alias Gare Fetish," Nkawkaw, June 11, 1944; and "Tigare Fetish at Abetifi," Mpraeso, December 15, 1944, NAG-K, ADM/KD 29/6/69. Meyer Fortes, "Ashanti Social Survey: A Preliminary Report," *Rhodes-Livingstone Journal* 6 (1948): 6, coined the term "witch-finding cults." See also T. C. McCaskie, "Anti-Witchcraft Cults in Asante: An Essay in the Social History of an African People," *History in Africa (HA)* 8 (1981): 125–54; and Hans Debrunner, *Witchcraft in Ghana: A Study on the Belief in Destructive Witches and Its Effects on the Akan Tribes* (Accra: Presbyterian Book Depot, 1959), 106–108.

14. Natasha Gray, "Witches, Oracles, and Colonial Law: Evolving Anti-Witchcraft Practices in Ghana, 1927–1932," *IJAHS* 34, no. 2 (2001): 339–41.

15. M. J. Field, *Search for Security: An Ethno-Psychiatric Study of Rural Ghana* (London: Faber and Faber, 1960). Barbara Ward suggested that these cults were an expression of "emotional malaise" as a result of structural changes; see "Some Observations on Religious Cults in Ashanti," *Africa* 26, no. 1 (1956): 47–61; this interpretation is refuted by Jack Goody noting the long history of shrine import and innovation, in his "Anomie in Ashanti?" *Africa* 27, no. 4 (1957): 356–63. See Gray's discussion of different interpretations in "Witches, Oracles, and Colonial Law," 361–62.

16. For an official assessment, see J. A. Cowley, "The Tegare Fetish" (1949), Rhodes House (RH), MSS. Afr. s. 1051; for a missionary view, see Otto Rytz, annual report, Kumase, March 31, 1944, BMA, D-11, 11. The Gold Coast's Christian Council expressed a similar sentiment in a pamphlet, "Tigare or Christ" (Accra: Achimota College Press, 1947), BMA D-4-3, 5.

17. For the beginnings of Akan societies, see Ivor Wilks, *Forest of Gold: Essays on the Akan and Kingdom of Asante* (Athens: Ohio University Press, 1993), chaps. 1–2; and Ray Kea, *Settlements, Trade, and Polities in the Seventeenth-Century Gold Coast* (Baltimore, Md.: Johns Hopkins University Press, 1982). There is an extensive, state-centric scholarship on Asante, including Ivor Wilks, *Asante in the Nineteenth Century: The Structure and Evolution of a Political Order* (Cambridge: Cambridge University Press, 1975); Larry Yarak, *Asante and the Dutch, 1744–1873* (Oxford: Clarendon, 1990); and T. C. McCaskie, *State and Society in Pre-Colonial Asante* (Cambridge: Cambridge University Press, 1995);

cf. Kwame Arhin, *West African Traders in Ghana in the Nineteenth and Twentieth Centuries* (London: Longman, 1979). The 1960 census recorded 2,964,580 Akan people, 44.1 percent of Ghana's population (Stefan von Gnielinski, *Ghana: Tropisches Entwicklungsland an der Oberguineaküste* [Darmstadt: Wissenschaftliche Buchgesellschaft, 1986], 100).

18. There are only a few historical studies on Kwawu, among them Kwabena Ameyaw-Gyamfi, "Kwahu: An Early Forest State," in *Ghana Notes and Queries* 9 (1966): 39–45, based on an earlier account by Edmond Perregaux, "A Few Notes on Kwahu," *Journal of the African Society* 2, no. 8 (1903): 444–50; cf. Nkansa-Kyeremateng, *Story of Kwawu*. For Kwawu's breakaway, see Thomas Lewin, *Asante before the British: The Prempean Years, 1875–1900* (Lawrence: Regents Press of Kansas, 1978), 103–104; for "Greater Asante," conceived as a "cultural and contiguous group—the Akans," see Kwame Arhin, "The Structure of Greater Ashanti (1700–1824)," *Journal of African History (JAH)* 8, no. 1 (1967): 65–84.

19. McCaskie, *State and Society*, 85–99. Emmanuel Akyeampong, "Sexuality and Prostitution among the Akan of the Gold Coast, c. 1650–1950," *Past and Present* 156 (1997): 144–73, provides evidence of "public women" who satisfied bachelors' sexual needs in precolonial Akan societies. Women were considered jural minors; adultery, understood as theft, "located women as a convertible economic good," and adultery compensation was determined by the offended husband's rank; see T. C. McCaskie, "State and Society, Marriage and Adultery: Some Considerations towards a Social History of Precolonial Asante," *JAH* 22, no. 4 (1981): 489. For gendered production practices among commoners, see Allman and Tashjian, "*I Will Not Eat Stone*," 6–7; cf. Gareth Austin, " 'No Elders Were Present': Commoners and Private Ownership in Asante, 1807–96," *JAH* 37, no. 1 (1996): 1–30.

20. McCaskie, *State and Society*, 85.

21. Kwame Arhin, "Asante Military Institutions," *Journal of African Studies (JAS)* 7, no. 1 (1980): 24–25. About five hundred to one thousand men were organized in bands, so-called *Asafo* companies, under the leadership of an *Asafohene* (captain); see C. C. Reindorf, *History of the Gold Coast and Asante* (Basel: Missionsbuchhandlung, 1895), 119–23.

22. See the suggestive essay by Emmanuel Akyeampong and Pashington Obeng, "Spirituality, Gender, and Power in Asante History," *IJAHS* 28, no. 3 (1995): 481–508. Cf. Kwame Arhin, "The Political and Military Roles of Akan Women," in *Female and Male in West Africa*, ed. C. Oppong (London: Allen and Unwin, 1983), 91–98; Agnes Akosua Aidoo, "Asante Queen Mothers in Government and Politics in the Nineteenth Century," in *Black Women Cross-Culturally*, ed. F. C. Steady (Cambridge, Mass.: Schenkman, 1985), 65–77; and Wilks, *Forests of Gold*, chap. 10. For the *mmobomme* ritual, see Adam Jones, " 'My Arse for Akou': A Wartime Ritual of Women on the Nineteenth-Century Gold Coast," *Cahiers d'Études africaines* 132, nos. 33–34 (1993): 548; and A. J. Walker, "Kwahu," *Gold Coast Review* 1, no. 1 (1925): 20. For praise poetry, see Kwame Arhin, "The Asante Praise Poems: The Ideology of Patrimonialism," *Paideuma* 32 (1986): 163–97; and Kwesi Yankah, "To Praise or Not to Praise the King: The Akan *Apaee* in the Context of Referential Poetry," *Research in African Literatures* 14, no. 3 (1983): 381–400.

23. Emmanuel Akyeampong, " 'Wo pe tam won pe ba' ('You like cloth but you don't want children'): Urbanization, Individualism and Gender Relations in Colonial Ghana, c. 1900–39," in *Africa's Urban Past*, ed. D. M. Anderson and R. Rathbone (Oxford: James Currey, 2000), 233. For the blurring of gender in old age, see Akyeampong

and Obeng, "Spirituality, Gender, and Power," 492. Cf. Sjaak van der Geest, "Ɔpanyin: The Ideal of Elder in the Akan Culture of Ghana," *Canadian Journal of African Studies (CJAS)* 32, no. 3 (1998): 449–93. Ideas of adult masculinity and fatherhood are discussed in Eugene Addow, "Notes on Kwahu" (ca. 1927), in R. S. Rattray Papers, ms. 102: 1, Royal Anthropological Institute, London; and Jean Allman, "Fathering, Mothering and Making Sense of *Ntamoba:* Reflections on the Economy of Child-Rearing in Colonial Asante," *Africa* 67, no. 2 (1997): 296–321. Elsewhere in Africa, male (and female) elders also mediated junior men's access to adult masculinity; see McKittrick, *To Dwell Secure,* 79–81; and Elias Mandala, *Work and Control in a Peasant Economy: A History of the Lower Tchiri Valley in Malawi, 1859–1960* (Madison: University of Wisconsin Press, 1990), 26–32. For similar masculinity ideals in Yoruba society, see Lisa Lindsay, "Money, Marriage, and Masculinity on the Colonial Nigerian Railway," in Lindsay and Miescher, eds., *Men and Masculinities in Modern Africa,* 138–55.

24. For the *ɔbirεmpɔn,* see Kea, *Settlements, Trade, and Politics,* 90–93; McCaskie, *State and Society,* 42–49; Wilks, *Forest of Gold,* 136–44; and Kwame Arhin, "Rank and Class among the Asante and Fante in the Nineteenth Century," *Africa* 53, no. 1 (1983): 2–22.

25. The Gold Coast Constabulary was first called the Hausa Armed Police. In 1894 it was divided into a civil (Fante) and larger (Hausa) paramilitary force, the latter becoming, in 1901, the Gold Coast Regiment. See David Killingray, "Imagined Martial Communities: Recruiting for the Military and Police in Colonial Ghana, 1860–1960," in *Ethnicity in Ghana,* ed. C. Lentz and P. Nugent, 119–36 (London: Macmillan, 2000); cf. Anthony Clayton and David Killingray, *Khaki and Blue: Military and Police in British Colonial Africa* (Athens: Ohio University Center for International Studies, 1989), 145–95.

26. Francis Crowther, "Notes on a District of the Gold Coast," *Quarterly Journal of the Institute of Commercial Research in the Tropics* (Liverpool University) 3 (1906): 178. For missionaries praising Kwawu "industriousness," see E. Werner, Kyebi, May 6, 1875, BMA, D-1.27, 257.

27. On hunting and fishing, see the report by H. N. Thompson, conservator of forests, December 1908, and District Commissioner (DC) Hobbs's inquiry about Kwawu-Kumawu land dispute with testimonies by fishermen, April 15–16, 1912, NAG, ADM 11/1/242. For the northern markets, see Arhin, *West African Traders,* chaps. 3 and 4; and Marion Johnson, "The Slaves of Salaga," *JAH* 27, no. 2 (1986): 341–62. Cf. Peter Garlick, "The Development of Kwahu Business Enterprise in Ghana: An Essay in Recent Oral Tradition," *JAH* 8, no. 3 (1969): 463–80; and idem, *African Traders and Economic Development in Ghana* (Oxford: Clarendon, 1971), 57–58.

28. See Philip Foster, *Education and Social Change in Ghana* (Chicago: University of Chicago Press, 1965), 50–51, 78–91.

29. The stigma of slave origin was preserved but not mentioned, reflected in the maxim, "*Obi nkyere obi ase*" (No one must disclose the origin of another) (R. S. Rattray, *Ashanti Law and Constitution* [Oxford: Clarendon, 1929], 40). In 1876, when the Basel Mission's labor force went on strike over wages in Begoro, the strikers challenged the social obligations of the missionaries, perceived as new *abirεmpɔn* (big men); see Peter Haenger, *Slaves and Slave Holders on the Gold Coast: Towards an Understanding of Social Bondage in West Africa,* trans. C. Handford (Basel: Schlettwein, 2000 [1997]), 141–42. Women and children were more likely to remain enslaved; cf. Claire Robertson, "Post-

Proclamation Slavery in Accra: A Female Affair," in *Women and Slavery in Africa,* ed. C. Robertson and M. Klein (Madison: University of Wisconsin Press, 1983), 220–45; and Raymond Dumett and Marion Johnson, "Britain and the Suppression of Slavery in the Gold Coast Colony," in *The End of Slavery in Africa,* ed. S. Miers and R. Roberts (Madison: University of Wisconsin Press, 1988), 71–116.

30. Akyeampong, " 'Wo pe tam,' " 224, 230. For urbanization, see Margaret Peil, *The Ghanaian Factory Worker: Industrial Man in Africa* (Cambridge: Cambridge University Press, 1972), 4–12; and John Parker, *Making the Town: Ga State and Society in Early Colonial Accra* (Portsmouth, N.H.: Heinemann, 2000), 200. For migration to mines, see Jeff Crisp, *The Story of an African Working Class: Ghanaian Miners' Struggle, 1870–1980* (London: Zed, 1984), 19–20; and Raymond Dumett, *El Dorado in West Africa: The Gold Mining Frontier, African Labor, and Colonial Capitalism in the Gold Coast, 1875–1900* (Athens: Ohio University Press, 1998), 49–50, 176–77.

31. Emmanuel Akyeampong addresses gendered generational struggles in *Drink, Power, and Cultural Change: A Social History of Alcohol in Ghana, c. 1800 to Recent Times* (Portsmouth, N.H.: Heinemann, 1996), 47–69. For such struggles elsewhere in Africa, cf. McKittrick, *To Dwell Secure;* and Patrick Harries, *Work, Culture, and Identity: Migrant Laborers in Mozambique and South Africa c. 1860–1910* (Portsmouth, N.H.: Heinemann, 1994). From an extensive literature on cocoa and gender, see Gwendolyn Mikell, *Cocoa and Chaos in Ghana* (New York: Paragon, 1989); and Allman and Tashjian, *"I Will Not Eat Stone."* For the feminization of pawning, see Gareth Austin, "Human Pawning in Asante, 1800–1950: Markets, Coercion, Gender and Cocoa," in *Pawnship in Africa,* ed. T. Falola and P. E. Lovejoy (Boulder: Westview, 1994), 119–59. For the feminization of the market, see Gracia Clark, *Onions Are My Husband: Survival and Accumulation by West African Market Women* (Chicago: Chicago University Press, 1994). For scouting as a training site forging young men into leaders of tomorrow, see the governor's speech published in the *Times of West Africa* (*TWA*), December 20, 1932, and subsequently endorsed by readers, *TWA,* December 21, 1932. Thanks to John Campbell for this reference.

32. Jean Allman, "Rounding Up Spinsters: Gender Chaos and Unmarried Women in Colonial Asante," *JAH* 37, no. 2 (1996): 195–214; and Penelope Roberts, "The State and the Regulation of Marriage in Sefwi Wiaso (Ghana), 1900–1940," in *Women, State and Ideology,* ed. H. Afshar (London: Macmillan), 48–69.

33. For challenges by commoners, see Jarle Simensen, "The Asafo Movement of Kwahu, Ghana: A Mass Movement for Local Reform under Colonial Rule," *IJAHS* 8, no. 3 (1975): 383–406. Nation building did not lead to gender equality. While the CPP government expanded educational opportunities for boys *and* girls, most women remained in subordinate positions. See Claire Robertson, *Sharing the Same Bowl: A Socioeconomic History of Women and Class in Accra, Ghana* (Bloomington: Indiana University Press, 1984), 241; E. A. Haizel, "Education in Ghana, 1951–1966," and Takyiwaa Manuh, "Women and Their Organizations during the Convention People's Party Period," both in *The Life and Work of Kwame Nkrumah,* ed. K. Arhin (Trenton, N.J.: Africa World Press, 1993), 53–81 and 101–27, respectively. For the NLM, cf. Pashington Obeng, "Gendered Nationalism: Forms of Masculinity in Modern Asante of Ghana," in Lindsay and Miescher, eds., *Men and Masculinities in Modern Africa,* 192–208.

34. Records of Presbyterian congregations provide evidence about gendered conflicts, particularly about competing ideas of masculinity, for example, "Nkawkaw Chronicle 1938–1958," Presbyterian Church Archive (PCA) 6/9, passim; cf. Stephan F.

Miescher, " 'Called to work for the Kingdom of God': The Challenges of Presbyterian Masculinity in Colonial Ghana," in *Readings in Gender in Africa*, ed. A. Cornwall (Bloomington: Indiana University Press, 2005), 187–95. More work is needed to explore employers' and governments' gendered discourse and workers' practices, but see Richard Jeffries, *Class, Power, and Ideology in Ghana: The Railwaymen of Sekondi* (Cambridge: Cambridge University Press, 1978); Christine Oppong, *Middle African Marriage: A Family Study of Ghanaian Senior Civil Servants* (London: Allen and Unwin, 1981); also see policing studies by Clayton and Killingray, *Khaki and Blue*, 12–26; and David Killingray, "Guarding the Extending Frontier: Policing the Gold Coast, 1865–1913," in *Policing the Empire*, ed. D. M. Anderson and D. Killingray (Manchester: Manchester University Press, 1991), 106–25. For elsewhere in West Africa, see railway men developing a self-conception as breadwinner in Lisa Lindsay, *Working with Gender: Wage Labor and Social Change in Southwestern Nigeria* (Portsmouth, N.H.: Heinemann, 2003); and colonial officials and employers who tended to feminize and infantilize African miners in Carolyn Brown, "A 'Man' in the Village Is a 'Boy' in the Workplace: Colonial Racism, Worker, Militance, and Igbo Notions of Masculinity in the Nigerian Coal Industry," in Lindsay and Miescher, eds., *Men and Masculinities in Modern Africa*, 156–74.

35. See Connell, *Masculinities*, 89, who worked with a life history method to explore the dynamics of masculinity among groups of Australian men. Cf. the extensive review by Paul Riesman, "The Person and the Life Cycle in African Social Life and Thought," *African Studies Review (ASR)* 29, no. 2 (1986): 71–138.

36. For a presentation of unmediated voices, see Marjorie Shostak, *Nisa: The Life and Words of a !Kung Woman* (Cambridge, Mass.: Harvard University Press, 1981); Sarah Mirza and Margaret Strobel, eds., *Three Swahili Women: Life Histories from Mombasa, Kenya* (Bloomington: Indiana University Press, 1989); Jean Davison and the Women of Mutira, *Voices from Mutira: Changes in the Lives of Rural Gikuyu Women, 1910–1995* (Boulder: Lynne Rienner, 1996); Mpho 'M'atsepo Nthunya, *Singing Away the Hunger: Stories of Life in Lesotho* (Pietermaritzburg: University of Natal Press, 1996); and Berida Ndambuki and Claire Robertson, *"We Only Come Here to Struggle": Stories from Berida's Life* (Bloomington: Indiana University Press, 2000). For life histories of men, see Tim Keegan, *Facing the Storm: Portraits of Black Lives in Rural South Africa* (London: Zed, 1988); and Pat Caplan, *African Voices, African Lives: Personal Narratives from a Swahili Village* (London: Routledge, 1997). For the other approach, see Belinda Bozzoli, with M. Nkotsoe, *Women of Phokeng: Consciousness, Life Strategy, and Migrancy in South Africa, 1900–1983* (Portsmouth, N.H.: Heinemann, 1991); Charles van Onselen, *The Seed Is Mine: The Life of Kas Maine, a South African Sharecropper, 1894–1985* (New York: Hill and Wang, 1996); and Susan Geiger, *TANU Women: Gender and Culture in the Making of Tanganyikan Nationalism, 1955–1965* (Portsmouth, N.H.: Heinemann, 1997); cf. Luise White, *The Comforts of Home: Prostitution in Colonial Nairobi* (Chicago: University of Chicago Press, 1990). For a discussion of the methodology, see Susan Geiger, "Women's Life Histories: Method and Content," *Signs* 11, no. 2 (1986): 334–51; Personal Narratives Group, *Interpreting Women's Lives: Feminist Theory and Personal Narratives* (Bloomington: Indiana University Press, 1989); Charles van Onselen, "The Reconstruction of a Rural Life from Oral Testimony: Critical Notes on the Methodology Employed in the Study of a Black South African Sharecropper," *Journal of Peasant Studies* 20, no. 3 (1993): 494–514. Anthropologists were the first to develop the life history methodology; see Corinne Kratz, "Conversations and Lives," in *African Words, African Voices*, ed. L. White, S. F. Miescher, and D. W. Cohen (Bloomington: Indiana University Press, 2001), 127–61. An

early, yet later an influential African life history is M. F. Smith, *Baba of Karo: A Woman of the Muslim Hausa* (London: Faber and Faber, 1954).

37. James Peacock and Dorothy Holland, "The Narrated Self: Life Story in Process," *Ethos* 21, no. 4 (1993): 372, 376. Geiger presents collective biographies by telling "women's narratives or 'political' life histories"; see *TANU Women,* 66, 202; and Richard Werbner, *Tears of the Dead: The Social Biography of an African Family* (Washington, D.C.: Smithsonian Institution, 1992).

38. Alessandro Portelli, *The Death of Luigi and Other Stories: Form and Meaning in Oral History* (Albany: State University of New York Press, 1991), 54; cf. Elizabeth Tonkin's formulation, "oral history as an interactive process," in *Narrating Our Pasts: The Social Construction of Oral History* (Cambridge: Cambridge University Press, 1992), 134.

39. For a discussion of this development in African oral historiography, see David William Cohen, Stephan Miescher, and Luise White, "Introduction: Voices, Words, and African History," in White, Miescher, and Cohen, eds., *African Words, African Voices,* 1–27. In her recent book Luise White offers a thorough "meditation on the uses of oral history," suggesting "to treat oral and written material as being equal but distinct forms of recording the past" (*Speaking with Vampires: Rumor and History in Colonial Africa* [Berkeley: University of California Press, 2000], 51–52, passim). Paul Thompson provides an overview of European oral historiography, *The Voice of the Past: Oral History,* 3rd ed. (Oxford: Oxford University Press, 2000), 116–72.

40. Amina Mama, *Beyond the Masks: Race, Gender, and Subjectivity* (London: Routledge, 1995), 99.

41. Jerrold Seigel, "Problematizing the Self," in *Beyond the Cultural Turn,* ed. V. E. Bonnell and L. Hunt (Berkeley: University of California Press, 1999), 297. Seigel offers the notion of " 'concrete' selfhood"—that is, selfhood understood as "heterogeneous combinations" of the bodily, the relational, and the reflexive, and not as constructed purely out of any one (299). For the shortcomings of the cultural turn concerning subjectivity, cf. Victoria Bonnell and Lynn Hunt, introduction to *Beyond the Cultural Turn: New Directions in the Study of Society and Culture,* ed. idem (Berkeley: University of California Press, 1999), 22. For example, Megan Vaughan has much to say about the working of biomedical discourse in the making of colonial subjects in Africa but remains on less secure ground to examine the lived experiences of those subjected to these discourses; see her *Curing Their Ills: Colonial Power and African Illness* (Stanford, Calif.: Stanford University Press, 1991).

42. Seigel, in "Problematizing the Self," offers a concise intellectual history of the Western self. For a different, African trajectory, see Karin Barber, *The Generation of Plays: Yoruba Popular Life in Theater* (Bloomington: Indiana University Press, 2000), 358.

43. Meyer Fortes, "The Concept of the Person among the Tallensi," in *La notion de personne in Afrique noire,* ed. G. Dieterlen (Paris: Éditions du Centre Nationale de la Recherche Scientifique, 1973), 287. Fortes noted that the subjective side of personhood is "difficult to deal with" and "in many aspects outside the range of an ethnographic account" (311). For other anthropological and philosophical studies, see *The Category of the Person: Anthropology, Philosophy, History,* ed. Michael Carrithers, Steven Collins, and Steven Lukes (Cambridge: Cambridge University Press, 1985); Riesman, "Person and Life Cycle"; Grace Gredys Harris, "Concepts of Individual, Self, and Person in Description and Analysis," *American Anthropologist* 91 (1989): 599–612; *Personhood and Agency: The Experiences of Self and Other in African Cultures,* ed. Michael Jackson and Ivan Karp

(Washington, D.C.: Smithsonian Institution, 1990); and *African Philosophy as Cultural Inquiry*, ed. Ivan Karp and D. A. Masolo (Bloomington: Indiana University Press, 2000).

44. Kwame Gyekye, *Tradition and Modernity: Philosophical Reflections on the African Experience* (New York: Oxford University Press, 1997), 51; cf. Gyekye's discussion of objective components of personhood in Akan societies in *An Essay on African Philosophical Thought: The Akan Conceptual Scheme* (Cambridge: Cambridge University Press, 1987), 85–103.

45. Riesman, "Person and Life Cycle," 103, 112.

46. Jackson and Karp, introduction to Jackson and Karp, eds., *Personhood and Agency*, 27.

47. Gyekye, *Tradition and Modernity*, 59. For a rejection of an individual notion of the self, see John Mbiti, *African Religions and Philosophy*, 2nd ed. (Portsmouth, N.H.: Heinemann, 1990); and Ifeanyi Menkiti, "Person and Community in African Traditional Thought," in *African Philosophy: An Introduction*, 2nd ed., ed. R. A. Wright (Washington, D.C.: University Press of America, 1979), 157–68. Critical of Mbiti are Karp and Masolo, *African Philosophy as Cultural Inquiry*, particularly the contributions by Didier Kaphagawani, "Some African Conceptions of the Person," 66–79; and Rosalind Shaw, " 'Tok A, Lef Af': A Political Economy of Temne Techniques of Secrecy and Self," 25–49. Shaw shows how concepts of personhood and selves are subject to change, agents of ever-changing economic and social histories.

48. Richard Werbner suggests the need to study the "intertwined pair" of the "subjective" and the "intersubjective," particularly to historicize intersubjectivity, largely neglected in postcolonial studies, "Introduction: Postcolonial Subjectivities," in *Postcolonial Subjectivities in Africa*, ed. R. Werbner (London: Zed, 2002), 1–2; but see Michael Jackson, *Minima Ethnographica: Intersubjectivity and the Anthropological Project* (Chicago: University of Chicago Press, 1998).

49. Frantz Fanon, in *Black Skin, White Masks*, trans. C. L. Markmann (New York: Grove, 1967 [1952]), argued most prominently for a fractured self.

2. CHILDREN AND CHILDHOOD

1. *Mmofraase* is defined as "the time of birth or infancy to puberty"; see J. G. Christaller, *Dictionary of the Asante and Fante Language*, 2nd ed., rev. and enl. (Basel: Basel Evangelical Missionary Society, 1933), 318. The term *abofra* (child) is not gendered, but the adjectives *barima* (male) and *baa* (female) may be added to distinguish between boys and girls.

2. Anthropologists have written about children's relations and play, about rituals marking the end of childhood; see Paul Riesman, "The Person and the Life Cycle in African Social Life and Thought," *ASR* 29, no. 2 (1986): 82–85. Feminist scholars have addressed child rearing as women's work, particularly mothers' increased obligations because of absent fathers in colonial economies, and children's work; see *Growing Up in a Divided Society: The Contexts of Childhood in South Africa*, ed. Sandra Burman and Pamela Reynolds (Johannesburg: Ravan, 1986); Pamela Reynolds, *Dance Civet Cat: Child Labor in the Zambezi Valley* (Athens: Ohio University Press, 1991); Elizabeth Schmidt, *Peasants, Traders, and Wives: Shona Women in the History of Zimbabwe, 1870–1939* (Portsmouth, N.H.: Heinemann, 1992); and Anne Mager, *Gender and the Making of a South African Bantustan: A Social History of the Ciskei, 1945–1959* (Portsmouth, N.H.: Heinemann, 1999); for urban youth, see Clive Glaser, *Bo-Tsotsi: The Youth Gangs of Soweto* (Ports-

mouth, N.H.: Heinemann, 2000); and Andrew Burton, "Urchins, Loafers and the Cult of the Cowboy: Urbanization and Delinquency in Dar es Salaam, 1919–61," *JAH* 42, no. 2 (2001): 199–216. Most life histories include sections on childhood; see Charles van Onselen, *The Seed Is Mine: The Life of Kas Maine, a South African Sharecropper, 1894–1985* (New York: Hill and Wang, 1996), 15–49; and Belinda Bozzoli, with Mmantho Nkotsoe, *Women of Phokeng: Consciousness, Life Strategy, and Migrancy in South Africa, 1900–1983* (Portsmouth, N.H.: Heinemann, 1991), 39–56. They also include brief portraits of women reporting about work experiences as children; see Claire Robertson, *Sharing the Same Bowl: A Socioeconomic History of Women and Class in Accra, Ghana* (Bloomington: Indiana University Press, 1984), 69–70, 124–25, 165–67, 227–29. Outside Africa there is an extensive historiography on childhood and youth; cf. Kathleen Alaimo, "Childhood and Adolescence in Modern European History," *Journal of Social History* 34, no. 3 (1991): 591–602.

3. Barrington Kaye paid little attention to historical contexts, gender, and class; nor did he acknowledge that attitudes toward children might be contested (*Bringing Up Children in Ghana: An Impressionistic Survey* [London: Allen and Unwin, 1962]). Thirty-seven Ghanaian students conducted Kaye's research; among them was Sophy L. A. Osafo, "How Children Are Brought Up in Kwahu" (Thesis, Institute of Education, University College, Achimota, 1950–51). Early studies by social scientists include F. W. Grant, *The Nutrition and Health of Children in the Gold Coast* (Chicago: University of Chicago Press, 1955).

4. "The literate African, who is the highly educated product of one of our Universities, has had to pay a certain penalty for the acquisition of his Western learning, for he has of necessity been cut off in great measure from his own country, customs, and beliefs" (R. S. Rattray, *Ashanti Law and Constitution* [Oxford: Clarendon, 1929], vii). Writing about Kwawu, Rattray noted: "I wonder what it is that seems so often to enable these Africans of the past generation, and gives to them that indefinable something which their Europeanised fellow-countrymen so often seem to lack" ("The Mausoleum of 'Ampon Agyei," *Blackwood's Magazine* 223 (1928): 844; cf. idem, *Ashanti* (Oxford: Clarendon, 1923), and *Religion and Art in Ashanti* (Oxford: Clarendon, 1927). On Rattray's career and ambiguous position as government anthropologist gathering information to facilitate the introduction of indirect rule, and as a folklorist romanticizing precolonial Asante, see Theodore von Laue, "Anthropology and Power: R. S. Rattray among the Ashanti," *African Affairs* 75, no. 298 (1976): 33–54; and T. C. McCaskie, "R. S. Rattray and the Construction of Asante History: An Appraisal," *HA* 10 (1983): 187–206.

5. Rattray, *Ashanti Law*, 19, 47–55; and idem, *Ashanti*, 45–74. For the *ntɔrɔ*, see T. C. McCaskie, *State and Society in Pre-Colonial Asante* (Cambridge: Cambridge University Press, 1995), 168–75; and my discussions with interview partners Kwaku Marfo (Pepease, September 19, 1994, with the assistance of Douglas Asomani), J. A. Wahyee and Kwadwo Donkor (Abetifi, November 11, 1994, with the assistance of Joseph Kwakye), and Ɔkyeame Kwabena Asante (Pepease, November 27, 1994, with the assistance of Kwame Fosu). For similar findings, see Jean Allman and Victoria Tashjian, *"I Will Not Eat Stone": A Women's History of Colonial Asante* (Portsmouth, N.H.: Heinemann, 2000), 104.

6. Rattray, *Ashanti Law*, 11–13.

7. Meyer Fortes, "Kinship and Marriage among the Ashanti," in *African Systems of Kinship and Marriage*, ed. A. Radcliffe-Brown and D. Forde (London: Oxford University Press, 1950), 253, 283; and "The Ashanti Social Survey: A Preliminary Report,"

The Rhodes-Livingstone Journal 6 (1948): 1–37. For his theoretical exposition, see "Time and Social Structure: An Ashanti Case Study," in *Social Structure*, ed. M. Fortes (Oxford: Clarendon, 1949), 1–32; cf. Sally Falk Moore, *Anthropology and Africa: Changing Perspectives on a Changing Scene* (Charlottesville: University Press of Virginia, 1994), 32–36.

8. Allman and Tashjian, *"I Will Not Eat Stone,"* 87–89, 105.

9. Francis Crowther, "Notes on a District of the Gold Coast," *Quarterly Journal of the Institute of Commercial Research in the Tropics* (Liverpool University) 3 (1906): 177. For the cocoa revolution, cf. Polly Hill, *The Migrant Cocoa-Farmers of Southern Ghana: A Study in Rural Capitalism* (Cambridge: Cambridge University Press, 1963); and Gwendolyn Mikell, *Cocoa and Chaos in Ghana* (New York: Paragon, 1989).

10. For new roads, see DC H. J. Hobbs to Commissioner, Eastern Province (CEP), October 10, 1911; and July 14, 1913, NAG, ADM 11/1/298. For the construction of the railway line Accra–Nsawam–Mangoase–Koforidua–Tafo–Nkawkaw–Kumase, see *The Gold Coast Handbook, 1928*, 3rd ed., ed. John Maxwell (London: Crown Agent of the Colonies, 1928), 123; and Peter Gould, *The Development of the Transportation Pattern in Ghana* (Evanston, Ill.: Department of Geography, Northwestern University, 1960), 32–37, 51. For political turmoil, see Jarle Simensen, "The Asafo of Kwawu, Ghana: A Mass Movement for Local Reform under Colonial Rule," *IJAHS* 8, no. 3 (1975): 383–406; and E.A.E. Asiama, *The Mass Factor in Rural Politics: The Case of the Asafo Revolution in Kwahu Political History* (Accra: Ghana Universities Press, 2000).

11. Emmanuel Akyeampong, *Drink, Power, and Cultural Change: A Social History of Alcohol in Ghana, c. 1800 to Recent Times* (Portsmouth, N.H.: Heinemann, 1996), 13–14. According to Akan worldview, the spiritual world consists of Ɔnyame (Supreme Being), *abosom* (lesser gods), and *nsamanfoɔ* (ancestors). It was the elder's prerequisites to communicate with the ancestors and gods through libation, a prayer during which *nsa* (alcoholic drink) is poured to the ground (ibid., 5). Cf. Eugenia Herbert, *Iron, Gender, and Power: Rituals of Transformation in African Societies* (Bloomington: Indiana University Press, 1993).

12. "How Children Are Brought Up," 24. For an early elaboration of this colonial trope, see Gold Coast, *Report on the Census of the Gold Coast Colony for the Year 1891* (London: Waterlow, 1891), 14; and for the missionary view, see Edmond Perregaux, "Chez les Achanti," *Bulletin de la Société neuchâteloise de Géographie* 17 (1906): 179. Others provided a more positive account about the "industrious people" of Kwawu: Crowther, "Notes on a District," 178; and Decima Moore and Major F. G. Guggisberg (later Gold Coast governor) who spent "four delightful weeks in Abetifi" during February 1906 and commented about the "willing nature of the native as a worker" (*We Two in West Africa* [London: Heinemann, 1909], 305).

13. According to Christaller, *Dictionary*, 110, *adwuma* refers to "work, labour, espec. agricultural work, manual work; employment of any kind." For a similar pattern of gendered work in nineteenth-century France, see Colin Heywood, *Childhood in Nineteenth-Century France: Work, Health, and Education among the "Classes Populaires"* (Cambridge: Cambridge University Press, 1988), 48.

14. Phil Bartle, "Urban Migration and Rural Identity: An Ethnography of a Kwawu Community, Obo, Ghana" (Ph.D. dissertation, University of Ghana, 1978), 101. By the 1950s this former "hunting desert" was dominated by cocoa and food farming, J. R. Wallis, "The Kwahus: Their Connection with the Afram Plain," *Transactions of the Gold Coast and Togoland Historical Society* 1, no. 3 (1953): 24.

15. J. A. Wahyee, Abetifi, August 25, 1993; and Wahyee and Yaw Apea, September

18, 1994, with the assistance of Joseph Kwakye. See the detailed description by A. G. Fraser, "The Cult of the Kwahu Hunter on the Question of the Sasa Animals, Especially the Elephant," *Gold Coast Review* 4, no. 2 (1928): 155–71. Cf. Rattray, *Religion and Art,* 184–85; and T. C. McCaskie, "People and Animals: Constru(ct)ing the Asante Experience," *Africa* 62, no. 2 (1992): 221–47; for hunters, see 235–37; for elephants, see idem, *State and Society,* 43–44, 311.

16. H. N. Thompson, December 1908, NAG, ADM 11/1/242. Thompson was influential in creating the Gold Coast Forestry Department in 1909; cf. Emmanuel Akyeampong, *Between the Sea and the Lagoon: An Eco-social History of the Anlo of Southeastern Ghana, c. 1850 to Recent Times* (Athens: Ohio University Press, 2001), 19. About hunting in the Afram Plains sixteen years earlier, see Friedrich Ramseyer, Abetifi, February 4, 1892, BMA, D-1.55, 113.

17. Moore and Guggisberg, *We Two in West Africa,* 288; and Wahyee, August 25, 1993; these "Germans" were most likely agents of the Basel Mission Trading Company.

18. Wahyee and Apea, September 18, 1994.

19. The song is quoted by Fraser, "Kwahu Hunter," 167. Cf. J. H. Nketia, who recorded hunters' songs in Abetifi during the 1950s and described their associations and celebrations (*Drumming in Akan Communities of Ghana* [Accra: University of Ghana Press, 1963], 75–89). T. E. Kyei distinguishes three grades of hunters, the third an "amateur" who did not kill to sell, and the two other grades similar to Fraser and Wahyee, but with different names (*Our Days Dwindle: Memories of My Childhood Days in Asante* [Portsmouth, N.H.: Heinemann, 2001], 34).

20. Kyei, *Our Days Dwindle,* 37.

21. J. A. Wahyee, Kwadwo Donkor, and E. V. Osei, Abetifi, October 31, 1994, with the assistance of Joseph Kwakye. Baptismal classes were crucial in the Basel Mission's conversion efforts; see *Ordnung für die Evangelischen Gemeinden der Basler Mission auf der Goldküste,* rev. (1902) (hereafter, *Gemeindeordnung*), 15–16, BMA, D-9.1c, 13b; and Rev. D. E. Akwa's report about proselytizing strategies like baptismal classes, street preaching, and Sunday school (Abetifi, February 22, 1917, BMA, D-3.7).

22. Kwaku Marfo, Pepease, September 8, 1993; and September 19, 1994, with the assistance of Douglas Asomani.

23. *Asuman* could be "composed of virtually anything that 'held' an efficacious aspect of power(s) (e.g., hair, beads, teeth, feathers, leather, scraps of paper with Koranic writing/ Islamic cabalistic formulae, etc.)" (McCaskie, *State and Society,* 312, 111). As a diviner, an ɔkɔmfo gets possessed by *abosom* (lesser gods), characterized by McCaskie as "powers of supernatural origin, anthropomorphized as the 'children' or as the 'servants' of *onyame* [the supreme god]" (ibid., 276), Cf. Rattray, *Religion and Art,* 39; and Bartle's discussion of Kwawu cosmology ("Urban Migration," 304–72). For recollections of Kwasi Nyame, see E. F. Opusuo, Pepease, November 24, 1993.

24. Kwaku Marfo, Pepease, September 8, 1993; and September 15, 1993, with the assistance of Douglas Asomani.

25. Marfo, September 8, 1993; cf. Sjaak van der Geest, "Money and Respect: The Changing Value of Old Age in Rural Ghana," *Africa* 67, no. 4 (1997): 434–59. The proverb is listed as No. 159 in J. G. Christaller, *Twi Mmebusɛm: Mpensa-Ahansia Mmoaano—A Collection of Three Thousand and Six Hundred Tshi Proverbs* (Basel: Evangelical Missionary Society, 1879); and idem, compiler, *Three Thousand Six Hundred Ghanaian Proverbs,* ed. and trans. Kofi R. Lange (Lewiston, N.Y.: Edwin Mellen, 1990).

26. Peter K. Sarpong, *Ghana in Retrospect: Some Aspects of Ghanaian Culture* (Accra: Ghana Publishing Corporation, 1974), 94; cf. Rattray, *Religion and Art,* 13.

27. In Akan speech a proverb puts matters short: *"ɔtwa asɛm tiaa"* (It abbreviates the speech); see Kwesi Yankah, "Proverbs: The Aesthetics of Traditional Communication," *Research in African Literatures* 20, no. 3 (1989): 328. Discussing the same proverb with J. A. Wahyee and E. V. Osei Addo, Kwadwo Donkor summarized their interpretations: "In anything you say, whether concerning your father or your *abusua,* speak well. Mentioning the family home, or something, if you say bad things, you have disgraced the whole family" (Abetifi, October 31, 1994, with the assistance of Joseph Kwakye). In a different explanation, Ɔkyeame Kwabena Asante emphasized loyalty owed to one's father: "Whether he is good or not, he is still your father. . . . Excuse me to say, maybe your father is mad, roaming about in the street. When he is seen, and people say, he is your father, you go away. It means that you have pointed to your father's village with your left hand. Because . . . you deny him by saying, he is not my father, you have pointed your left hand to him." He concluded: "You should say, yes, there is my father. Whether your father is good or not, he is your father" (Pepease, October 29, 1994, with the assistance of Kwame Fosu). For the power of silences in the production of history, see David William Cohen, *The Combing of History* (Chicago: University of Chicago Press, 1993).

28. E. K. Addo, Abetifi, September 28 and November 24, 1994, with the assistance of Kwame Fosu. Cf. Kwame Arhin, *West African Traders in the Nineteenth and Twentieth Centuries* (London: Longman, 1979), 51–65. Atebubu and Salaga were important slave markets—not mentioned by Addo, but see Wahyee and Apea, September 18, 1994; and Marion Johnson, "The Slaves of Salaga," *JAH* 27, no. 2 (1986): 341–62.

29. Upon his death in 1980, Sampong was eulogized as the first Kwawu trader to arrive in Accra in 1916; see the biographical portrait by his son, H. A. Osafo-Sampong, in "Burial Service Programme for the late Opanyin Joseph Edward Sampong, 1876–1980," Presbyterian Church, Abetifi, May 3, 1980, E. K. Addo's Papers (AP). Cf. Peter Garlick, "The Development of Kwahu Business Enterprise in Ghana since 1874: An Essay in Recent Oral Tradition," *JAH* 8, no. 3 (1967): 468–73; and *African Traders and Economic Development in Ghana* (Oxford: Clarendon, 1971). One of Garlick's main informants was J. E. Sampong.

30. Addo, November 24, 1994. Cf. *Gold Coast Leader,* November 30, 1918, cited in David Patterson, "The Influenza Epidemic of 1918–19 in the Gold Coast," *JAH* 24, no. 3 (1983): 494; for the demographic impact, see 497.

31. Addo, September 28, 1994. Cf. J. E. Sampong's biographical portrait in "Burial Service Programme."

32. Ɔkyeame Asante, October 29, 1994.

33. E. F. Opusuo, Pepease, December 21, 1992, and August 22, 1993. His paternal grand-uncle, Kwaku Opusuo Frempong, occupied as Kwaku Akuamoa VI the Odiawuo (paramount) stool from 1916 until his death, 1925; cf. DC H. J. Hobbs, March 20, 1916, commenting on Kwaku Opusuo's enstoolment, NAG, ADM 11/1/598, and Kofi Nkansa-Kyeremateng, *The Story of Kwawu* (Accra: Presbyterian Press, 1990), 35. Cocoa prices peaked in 1920 and then dropped sharply the following year. Still, the export volume during the 1920s steadily increased from 124,800 tons (1920) to 238,100 tons (1929); see G. B. Kay, *The Political Economy of Colonialism in Ghana* (Cambridge: Cambridge University Press, 1972), 336–39. Kwaku Adu's example, emphasizing close ties and in-

vestment in home communities, challenges Jeff Crisp's argument of miners' full prole-tarianization, *The Story of an African Working Class: Ghanaian Miners' Struggles, 1870–1980* (London: Zed, 1984). For a similar critique, cf. Carola Lenz and Veit Erlmann, "A Working Class in Formation?" *Cahiers d'Études africaines* 113, nos. 29–30 (1989): 69–111.

34. E. F. Opusuo, Pepease, December 21, 1992, and April 4, 1993. Opusuo's pa-ternal grandfather Kwasi Diawuo II was the Ɔmanhene of Kwawu from 1909 until de-stooled in 1915; see the correspondence about his tenure as ɔmanhene, especially the report by Secretary of Native Affairs (SNA) Francis Crowther, November 9, 1909; the inquiry by DC H. J. Hobbs about Kwasi Diawuo's destoolment, July 15, 1915; and Diawuo's petition to the governor, March 21, 1916, NAG, ADM 11/1/598.

35. For a similar argument, see Allman and Tashjian, *"I Will Not Eat Stone,"* 88.

36. For restrictions placed on Kwawu traders in Akyem Abuakwa, see NAG, ADM 11/1/1639; owing to pressure by the colonial administration insisting on "free trade," Ofori Atta I and his council were forced to withdraw the order; cf. Jarle Simensen, "Commoners, Chiefs and Colonial Government" (Ph.D. dissertation, University of Trondheim, 1975), 108–109; and Richard Rathbone, *Murder and Politics in Colonial Ghana* (New Haven: Yale University Press, 1993), 58. By 1910 Ghana was the world's largest exporter of cocoa, and over the next sixteen years exports rose tenfold; see Sara Berry, *No Condition Is Permanent* (Madison: University of Wisconsin Press, 1993), 71.

37. A. K. Boakye Yiadom, Abetifi, August 26, 1993, August 24, 1994, and No-vember 15, 1994. Cf. "My Life History: The Autobiography of Akasease Kofi Boakye Yiadom," A. K. Boakye Yiadom's Papers (BYP). Thanks to Kwame Fosu for assistance in translating this text from Twi into English. Garlick pointed out the "notable" number of Kwawu traders in Accra who started as tailors to acquire capital (*African Traders*, 35). The railway line Accra–Kumase was completed in 1923 when the final stretch between Juaso and Nkawkaw, including a station at Akwasihu, was opened (*Gold Coast Handbook*, 123).

38. His mother died in 1982; Rev. E.K.O. Asante, Abetifi, January 19, 1993, Feb-ruary 2, 1993, August 17, 1993, and September 30, 1994. For bead traders, see Robert-son, *Sharing the Same Bowl*, 103–106.

39. Reverend Asante, August 17, 1993.

40. J.W.A. Amoo, "The Effect of Western Influence on Akan Marriage," *Africa* 16, no. 2 (1946): 229.

41. Reverend Asante, August 17, 1993; and Nana Atta Daaku, Abetifi, August 10, 1993. While eating with elders in Abetifi, I was told the proverb, *"Ɔpanyin didi adibɔne a, oyi n'asanka"* (If an elder eats greedily [not leaving any food behind], he has to remove [wash] his own dish) (Ɔpanyin Yao Annor, November 16, 1994); the proverb is listed by Christaller, *Twi Mmebusɛm*, as No. 2600. For children's eating habits, cf. Bartle, "Urban Migration," 200.

42. Garlick, *African Traders*, 58. His study is based on fieldwork among traders in Accra (of whom 77.6 percent were from Kwawu) from 1959 to 1962.

43. Reverend Asante, February 2, 1993, and September 30, 1994. On November 23, 1994, Asante and I visited his old family house. For Kwabena Adofo's influence as Akwamuhene, see the case Ɔkyeame Kwame Ansong v. Kwaku Ansong, Native Tribunal of the Adɔntenhene, Abetifi, June 14, 1943, Kwawu Traditional Council (KTC), 4:190–210; discussed in Stephan Miescher, "Of Documents and Litigants: Disputes on Inher-

itance in Abetifi—a Town of Colonial Ghana," *Journal of Legal Pluralism and Unofficial Law* 39 (1997): 81–119.

44. Rev. E.K.O. Asante, January 19, 1993, February 2, 1993, June 7, 1993, and September 7, 1994. The *Akwamuhene* is third in command in Abetifi after the divisional chief (*Ɔhene* of Abetifi and *Adɔntenhene* of Kwawu) and his replacement, *Kurontehene* of Abetifi. The Adako *abusua* received the Akwamu stool during the "Krepi war" when Kwawu was fighting with its Asante overlord against the Ewe in 1869; see Rev. E.K.O. Asante, May 18, 1993. For Adaakwa's eloquence in judicial matters, see his intervention as a member of the *Adɔntenhene's* court settling an inheritance dispute, *Yao Asamoah v. Kwaku Dankyi,* Native Tribunal of Abetifi, October 20, 1932, KTC, 1:372–81. From 1918 to 1965 no *afahye* festival was celebrated because of ongoing chieftaincy disputes throughout Kwawu; despite futile attempts "it was unanimously decided that the annual celebration of Yam Custom locally known as 'Afahye' the observance which has been neglected for considerable numbers of years should be resuscitated" (Minutes of the Kwahu State Council Meeting, Nkwatia, February 22–29, 1940, KTC, 43:32–46). For the *odwira's* meaning in precolonial Asante, see McCaskie, *State and Society,* 144–242.

45. In the early 1980s the forest around Abene burned down during a devastating fire. The Ampon Agyei mountain is now totally exposed with only one old tree visible from far away. Rattray, who climbed the Ampon Agyei during his Kwawu stay in 1927, reported about the veneration of Ampon Agyei ("Mausoleum," 346). For other versions of the legend, see Edmond Perregaux, "A Few Notes on Kwahu," *Journal of the African Society* 2, no. 8 (1906): 446; Kwabena Ameyaw-Gyamfi, "Kwahu: An Early Forest State," *Ghana Notes and Queries* 9 (1966): 42; and Nkansa-Kyeremateng, *Story of Kwawu,* 19. I heard versions from G. F. Debra, Abetifi, April 13, 1993, Nana Adamu Nyanko, Bepong, June 27, 1993, and Ɔkɔmfo Ama Yeboaa, Nkwantanan, September 20, 1993.

46. Moore and Guggisberg, *We Two in West Africa,* 282. Ten years earlier Sheriff J. R. Philips reported "Obo as the largest [town that] contains probably five thousands inhabitants" (Kyebi, Akim, December 18, 1893, to Colonial Secretary (CS), NAG, ADM 11/1/1445). For Obo's resistance to the Basel Mission, see Ramseyer's letter to the governor complaining about the Obo chief's reluctance allowing one of his subjects to join the Basel Mission congregation in Mpraeso, Abetifi, April 18, 1888, NAG, ADM 11/1/1445. Cf. Bartle, "Urban Migration," 80–82.

47. She died in 1982. See Kofi Ankoma, Obo, April 30, 1993, and April 29, 1993. Fieda Fofie is a *dabɔne,* a bad, unlucky day, that is, a sacred and ritually important day in the Akan calendar that is celebrated every six weeks on a Friday. For the Akan calendar, see Philip Bartle, "Forty Days: The Akan Calendar," *Africa* 48, no. 1 (1978): 80–84; and McCaskie, *State and Society,* 151–55.

48. Emmanuel Akyeampong and Pashington Obeng, "Spirituality, Gender and Power in Asante History," *IJAHS* 28, no. 3 (1995): 491. For the limits of female masculinity, a social position usually regarded the preserve of men, see Nwando Achebe, "'And She Became a Man': King Ahebi Ugbabe in the History of Enugu-Ezike, Northern Igboland, 1880–1948," in *Men and Masculinities in Modern Africa,* ed. L. A. Lindsay and S. F. Miescher (Portsmouth, N.H.: Heinemann, 2003), 52–68.

49. Kofi Ankoma, Obo, March 25, 1993, April 29, 1930, April 30, 1993, June 1, 1993, and September 9, 1994.

50. Christaller, *Dictionary,* 131, 59; Emmanuel Akyeampong and Charles Ambler argue that "the opposition between work time and leisure is central to the Akan definition

of *afuofi* [*afoofi*]" ("Leisure in African History: An Introduction," *IJAHS* 35, no. 1 [2002]: 7). For the Akan calendar, see Bartle, "Forty Days," 81; and McCaskie, *State and Society,* 155. See the discussion on time in Phyllis Martin, *Leisure and Society in Colonial Braz-zaville* (Cambridge: Cambridge University Press), 4–5; see also examples of African rural time in E. E. Evans-Pritchard, "Nuer Time Reckoning," *Africa* 12, no. 2 (1939): 189–216; and Jan Vansina, *The Tio Kingdom of the Middle Congo, 1880–1892* (London: Oxford University Press, 1973), 159, 163–68. Thanks to Emmanuel Akyeampong for clarification concerning the term *afoofi.*

51. Martin, *Leisure and Society,* 8, 10. See Akyeampong and Ambler, "Leisure in African History," and other contributions in their special issue of *IJAHS.* Cf. Anthony Giddens, "Notes on the Concepts of Play and Leisure," *Sociological Review* 12, no. 1 (1964): 73–89.

52. Johan Huizinga, *Homo Ludens: A Study of the Play Element in Culture* (New York: Harper and Row, 1970), 26–32.

53. Reverend Asante, January 16, 1993. For hide-and-seek and draught, see Opu-suo, April 4, 1993; and Marfo, September 19, 1994. Cf. Ɔkyeame Asante, October 29, 1994.

54. J. B. Danquah, *Gold Coast: Akan Laws and Customs and the Akim Abuakwa Constitution* (London: Routledge, 1928), 229; cf. Kaye, *Bringing Up Children in Ghana,* 192, and, more generally, Sigrid Paul, "The Wrestling Tradition and Its Social Functions," in *Sport in Africa,* ed. J. Baker and J. Mangan (New York: Africana, 1987), 23–46.

55. See the following Abetifi interviews: Adelaide Opong, April 14, 1993, with the assistance of Joseph Kwakye, as well as Felicia Asante, August 22, 2000; Agnes Sampong, August 22, 2000; Alice Ofosuhemaa, August 22, 2000; Paulina Ago Acheampong, Sep-tember 1, 2001, all with the assistance of Pearl Ofosu. Cf. Opusuo, April 4, 1993. For *asɔ,* see Akua Nimako, Abetifi, July 14, 1993, with the assistance of Joseph Kwakye; Wahyee, Donkor, Addo, October 31, 1994; Osafo, "How Children Are Brought Up," 20; and Kaye, *Bringing Up Children in Ghana,* 190–91. Perregaux reported about young girls carrying around small dolls on their backs ("Chez les Achanti," 179). Cf. the fine description of girls' play by Christiane Cartry, "Jeux d'enfants Gourmantché," in *Systèmes de signes* (Paris: Hermann, 1978), 73–78; and Berida Ndabuki and Claire Robertson, *"We Only Come Here to Struggle": Stories from Berida's Life* (Bloomington: Indiana University Press, 2000), 5.

56. Perregaux, "Chez les Achanti," 179. His title is misleading since the majority of the evidence was gathered in Kwawu. Cf. Kyei's detailed account of *amantoɔ* (rubber trap laying) to catch birds, in *Our Days Dwindle,* 181–85.

57. Boakye Yiadom, June 27, 1993; Reverend Asante, January 26, 1993.

58. Wahyee and Apea, September 18, 1994. This game was played in other Kwawu towns; for Pepease, see Marfo, September 19, 1994, and Ɔkyeame Asante, October 29, 1994; for Obo, see Ankoma, September 30, 1994.

59. Boakye Yiadom, June 27, 1993; and Wahyee and Apea, September 18, 1994. Abetifi's old town, Manem, has four *mmorɔn* (wards): *Dome, Dweneaso, Ɔkyɛmase,* and *Kubase. Aberem,* the separate "Christian Quarters," established by the Basel Mission, is also called *Baselmu, Salem,* or *Sukuumu.*

60. Kyei, *Our Days Dwindle,* 180, 47.

61. The competitiveness resembles boys' societies among the Afikpo in southeastern Nigeria, "designed to show and to test physical skills and superiority" and independent

from parental authority, "while being emulative of male adult activities and values" (Simon Ottenberg, "Boys' Secret Societies at Afikpo," in *African Religious Groups and Beliefs*, ed. S. Ottenberg (Cupertino, Calif.: Folklore Institute, 1982), 178.

62. Mager, *Gender and the Making of a South African Bantustan*, 131.

63. For military officials, northerners had distinct "martial virtues," while southerners were "softened by Christian mission education and close contact with European 'Civilization' "; see Anthony Clayton and David Killingray, *Khaki and Blue: Military and Police in British Colonial Africa* (Athens: Ohio University Center for International Studies, 1989), 175. For the organization of the Gold Coast Regiment, cf. *Gold Coast Handbook*, 184–85. Muhammad Abbas recalled his grandfather Kwasi Da Tano who, as a Kwawu man, disguised himself as a "Northerner to join the Gold Coast Regiment during World War I" (Abetifi, April 10, 1993).

64. For Asafo challenges to established hierarchies in Kwawu since 1905, see the extensive report by A.F.E. Fieldgate, "Inquiry into Kwahu Affairs," August 17, 1932, NAG, CSO 21/22/11; and other files on Asafo activities, NAG, ADM 11/1/598, 11/1/738, and 11/1/1445; cf. Simensen, "The Asafo of Kwawu." In Accra, after the end of Asafo feuds, a new leisure activity, *Asafo atwele* (group fighting), emerged during the 1920s; cf. Emmanuel Akyeampong, "Bukom and the Social History of Boxing in Accra: Warfare and Citizenship in Precolonial Ga Society," *IJAHS* 35, no. 1 (2002): 39–60.

65. Okyeame Asante, October 29, 1994.

66. Opusuo, March 24, 1993, and August 27, 1994, repeating the same story; Boakye Yiadom, June 27, 1993; and Kaye, *Bringing Up Children in Ghana*, 191.

67. Wahyee, Donkor, and Addo, October 31, 1994. For other games played by boys and girls, see Boakye Yiadom, August 28, 1994, who recalled one game in which a player placed a stone in front of a person who passed it onto the next while singing a song; F. Asante, August 22, 2000, and Ofosuhemaa, August 22, 2000, mentioned the word game *kasa agum* and the ball game *asoba*.

68. Kyei, *Our Days Dwindle*, 180. See also Kyei's study, "Some Notes on Marriage and Divorce among the Ashantis," 4, NAG, RG 3/1/304, now published with slight editorial changes as *Marriage and Divorce among the Asante: A Study Undertaken in the Course of the Ashanti Social Survey (1945)*, Cambridge African Monographs 14 (Cambridge: African Studies Center, 1992), 14. For Kwawu marriage norms, cf. Eugene Addow, "Notes on Kwahu" (ca. 1927), in R. S. Rattray Papers, ms. 102: 1, Royal Anthropological Institute, London.

69. Wahyee, Donkor, and Addo, October 31, 1994.

70. See Hans Medick, "Village Spinning Bees: Sexual Culture and Free Time among Rural Youth in Early Modern Germany," in *Interest and Emotion*, ed. H. Medick and D. W. Sabean (Cambridge: Cambridge University Press, 1984), 317–39.

71. For this shift, see Victoria B. Tashjian, " 'It's mine' and 'It's ours' Are Not the Same Thing: Changing Economic Relations between Spouses in Asante," in *The Cloth of Many Colored Silks*, ed. J. Hunwick and N. Lawler (Evanston, Ill.: Northwestern University Press, 1996), 205–22; and Allman and Tashjian, *"I Will Not Eat Stone,"* 61.

72. Rattray, *Ashanti Law*, 13; see his collection *Ashanti Folktales* (Oxford: Clarendon, 1930).

73. For a gendered reading of *anansesɛm*, see Mercy Oduyoye, *Daughters of Anowa: African Women and Patriarchy* (Maryknoll, N.Y.: Orbis, 1995), 36–54; cf. Kwesi Yankah, *The Akan Trickster Cycle: Myth or Folklore?* (Bloomington: Indiana University African Studies Program, 1983), 8. Ifi Amadiume noted the gendered nature of stories told by

women and men among the Nnobi (Igbo) of southeastern Nigeria (*Male Daughters, Female Husbands: Gender and Sex in an African Society* [London: Zed, 1987], 84–85).

74. Opusuo, March 24, 1993, and Ɔkyeame Kwabena Asante, Pepease, August 27, 1993, with the assistance of Joseph Kwakye; cf. Addo, November 24, 1994. See Kyei's vivid account of entering the world of *anansesɛm* when, as a small child, he walked with his parents through the forest, in *Our Days Dwindle*, 3–6. For precolonial Shona society, where "evening folktales (*ngango*) [were] told by old women to gatherings of children," see Schmidt, *Peasants, Traders, and Wives*, 23.

75. Opusuo, March 24, 1993. The same story appears in Rattray, *Folktales*, 4–7; a variant is presented by Yankah, *Akan Trickster*, 3. See also Reverend Asante, January 26, 1993; Ɔkyeame Asante, October 29, 1994; and Kaye, *Bringing Up Children in Ghana*, 192–93.

76. Opusuo, March 24, 1993. Cf. Reverend Asante, February 2, 1993.

77. In Asante middle schools in the 1950s, *anansesɛm* were regarded as "childish" (Kaye, *Bringing Up Children in Ghana*, 193). Cf. Isabel Hofmeyr, *"We Spend Our Years as a Tale That Is Told": Oral Historical Narrative in a South African Chiefdom* (Portsmouth, N.H.: Heinemann, 1994), 54; and Felix Karlinger, *Grundzüge einer Geschichte des Märchens im deutschen Sprachraum* (Darmstadt: Wissenschaftliche Buchgesellschaft, 1983), 50.

78. Ɔkyeame Asante, October 29, 1994.

79. For the performative context of *anansesɛm*, see Yankah, *Akan Trickster*, 11–12. I witnessed an afternoon of storytelling among the *mpanyinfoɔ* (elders) of the Ɔmanhene (paramount chief) of Kwawu at Abene, June 15, 1993. The male elders, together with the *ɔhemaa* (queenmother), were sitting in the *pato* of the house of Nana E. K. Ofosu, *Adehyeɛhene* (head of the "royal" family) of Abene. Each man on the *pato* shared one story and then the women who had come to listen joined the circle, contributing additional *anansesɛm*. Frequently the narrator was interrupted by the audience. Each tale was followed by a song that led into the next story. For Valtyn, South Africa, Hofmeyr observed a rigid gender division with two distinct spheres that encompassed the content and loci of storytelling: female storytelling, mainly fictional tales, was associated with the hut, while male storytelling, historical narratives, found its place in courtyards (*We Spend Our Years*, 9, 25, passim).

80. Kwame Gyekye, *An Essay on African Philosophical Thought: The Akan Conceptual Scheme* (Cambridge: Cambridge University Press, 1987), 150; J. A. Wahyee and Kwadwo Donkor, Abetifi, November 28, 1994, with the assistance of Joseph Kwakye.

81. A. J. Walker, "The Kwahus," *Gold Coast Review* 1, no. 1 (1925): 21.

82. Christaller, *Dictionary*, 558. For a description of *ɔware* rules, see Rattray, *Religion and Art*, 382–90. For an overview, see Thomas Reefe, "The Biggest Game of All: Gambling in Traditional Africa," in *Sport in Africa*, ed. W. J. Baker and J. Mangan (New York: Africana, 1987), 47–78.

83. Wahyee and Apea, September 18, 1994. Christaller provided a similar description: "*The seed of a climbing plant*... smaller and flatter than a horse-chestnut, used in a certain game (reminding of billiards) in which it is forcibly jerked by the fingers upon an elevated mat against one or more seeds of the same kind thrown by others; ... the victor is to strike his antagonists with the hand, or to receive ground-nuts, cowries &c. from them" (*Dictionary*, 508). Recalling his own childhood, Emmanuel Akyeampong suggested that "unfairness actually resulted from weighting the marble with substances. Such marbles "were disqualified" (written communication, October 19, 2003). Cf. Kyei, *Our Days Dwindle*, 180.

84. Wahyee and Donkor, November 28, 1994; cf. Wahyee and Apea, September 18, 1994.

85. See *Gemeindeordnung*, 45, 48–49, and Presbyterian Church of the Gold Coast, *Regulations, Practice and Procedures*, rev. (1929) (hereafter, *Regulations*), 27–29, BMA, D-9.1c, 13d.

86. Marfo, September 19, 1994.

87. Reefe, "Biggest Game," 65; and Perregaux, "Chez les Achanti," 180–81. Cf. Beverly Grier, "Pawns, Porters, and Petty Traders: Women in the Transition to Cash Crop Agriculture in Colonial Ghana," *Signs* 17, no. 2 (1992): 304–28; and Gareth Austin, "Human Pawning in Asante, 1800–1950: Markets, Coercion, Gender and Cocoa," in *Pawnship in Africa*, ed. T. Falola and P. E. Lovejoy (Boulder: Westview, 1994), 119–59.

88. Ago Acheampong, September 1, 2001; cf. F. Asante, August 22, 2000, and Sampong, August 22, 2000.

89. Clifford Geertz, "Deep Play: Notes on a Balinese Cockfight," *Daedalus* 101 (1972): 1–37; see the critique by Cohen, *Combing of History*, 20–22, 126 n., and others cited there. For a contestation of elders, cf. Akyeampong, *Drink, Power, and Cultural Change*, 14, 141.

90. Wahyee, Donkor, and Addo, October 31, 1994; and Wahyee and Apea, September 18, 1994. For the meaning of *agorɔ*, see Christaller, *Dictionary*, 144. During a religious performance, an *ɔkɔmfo* divines by dancing to the sound of drums and singing, also referred to as *agorɔ* (the activity *di agorɔ*) or by the term *akɔm*; see McCaskie, *State and Society*, 290, 113.

91. David Coplan, "Go to My Town, Cape Coast! The Social History of Ghanaian Highlife," in *Eight Urban Musical Cultures*, ed. B. Nettl (Urbana: University of Illinois Press, 1978), 103. According to John Collins's informant, highlife musician Kwaa Mensa, *ahyiko* was played with a "concertina or accordion, clips, and carpenter's saw where the saw is bent and an iron is used to rattle its face" (*West African Pop Roots* [Philadelphia: Temple University Press, 1992], 35–36). Cf. Catherine Cole, *Ghana's Concert Party Theatre* (Bloomington: Indiana University Press, 2001), 142.

92. Wahyee, Donkor, and Addo, October 31, 1994; and Wahyee and Donkor, November 28, 1994. For the *ɔkɔba*, also referred to as *bagyina ba* (a child "propped to stand," i.e., to survive), frequently given an uncomplimentary name with derogatory connotation like Donkor (from *dɔnkɔ*, slave), see Kyei, *Marriage and Divorce*, 139; Kaye, *Bringing Up Children in Ghana*, 60; and Rattray, *Religion and Art*, 65.

93. Wahyee, Donkor, and Addo, October 31, 1994. Cf. Addo, November 24, 1994.

94. Wahyee and Donkor, November 28, 1994. Danquah listed a series of dance companies and bands that were popular in the first three decades of the twentieth century: "Asiko, Ankedam, Franapo (Fernado Po), Ahima, Siti, and the more modern craze of brass bands. Dances and bands like these go to make the life pleasure of an Akan boy or girl" (*Gold Coast*, 229).

95. Akyeampong, *Drink, Power, and Cultural Change*, 58–62; and cf. John Parker, *Making the Town: Ga State and Society in Early Colonial Accra* (Portsmouth, N.H.: Heinemann, 2000), 203–205. For different colonial contexts, see Martin, *Leisure and Society*, 129–33, 151–52; and Terence Ranger, *Dance and Society in Eastern Africa, 1890–1970: The Beni Ngoma* (London: Heinemann, 1975). For the idea of "gender performativity," see Judith Butler, *Gender Trouble: Feminism and the Subversion of Identity* (New York: Routledge, 1990), 139–41.

96. This fascination is well captured by Kyei who commented on "children-

spectators" following the Agogo brass band, "unmindful of gutters or of any obstacles," stumbling and bruising themselves in excitement. He also observed how big men could be spotted observing the *ositi* dance competition in Agogo during the 1920s (*Our Days Dwindle*, 139–42). For the *ɔbirɛmpɔn*, see McCaskie, *State and Society*, 42–49.

97. *Gemeindeordnung*, 33–35; and cf. *Regulations*, 20–21. For the creation of a bourgeois notion of childhood in Germany, the home country of most Basel missionaries, see Heidi Rosenbaum, *Formen der Familie: Untersuchungen zum Zusammenhang von Familienverhältnissen, Sozialstruktur und sozialem Wandel in der deutschen Gesellschaft des 19. Jahrhunderts* (Frankfurt am Main.: Suhrkamp, 1982), 267–71.

98. In premodern Europe children formed their own roaming bands, and boys engaged in "Knabenkrieg," with different village sections fighting one another. See *Kinderstuben: Wie Kinder zu Bauern, Bürgern, Aristokraten wurden, 1700–1850*, ed. Jürgen Schlumbohm (München: Deutscher Taschenbuch Verlag, 1983), 72.

99. See Lisa Lindsay, *Working with Gender: Wage Labor and Social Change in Southwestern Nigeria* (Portsmouth, N.H.: Heinemann, 2003).

3. Forms of Education

1. In most scholarship on Africa, "formal education" refers to "Western" (missionary or government) schools organized after a European model, whereas "informal education" reflects local, indigenous ways of training; see Philip Foster, *Education and Social Change in Ghana* (Chicago: University of Chicago Press, 1965), 1. In 1931, of the 336 government-assisted schools, 111 belonged to the Presbyterian Church (former Basel Mission), 68 to the Ewe (Trans Volta) Presbyterian Mission (former Bremen Mission), 57 to the Wesleyan Methodist, and 48 to the Roman Catholic Church; only 24 were "government schools," remaining outside direct missionary influence. See A. W. Cardinall, *The Gold Coast, 1931* (Accra: Government Printer, 1932), 192.

2. Richard Morrell, "Boys, Gangs, and the Making of Masculinity in the White Secondary Schools of Natal, 1880–1930," *Masculinities* 2, no. 2 (1994): 56.

3. Deborah Gaitskell, "Devout Domesticity? A Century of African Women's Christianity in South Africa," in *Women and Gender in Southern Africa to 1945*, ed. C. Walker (Cape Town: David Philip, 1990), 251–71; Elisabeth Schmidt, *Peasants, Traders, and Wives: Shona Women in the History of Zimbabwe, 1870–1939* (Portsmouth, N.H.: Heinemann, 1992), chap. 5; Diana Jeater, *Marriage, Perversion, and Power: The Construction of Moral Consciousness in Southern Rhodesia, 1894–1930* (Oxford: Oxford University Press, 1993), 236–37; and Jean Allman, "Making Mothers: Missionaries, Medical Officers and Women's Work in Colonial Asante, 1924–1945," *History Workshop Journal* 38 (1994): 23–47. Jean Comaroff and John Comaroff's first volume of *Of Revelation and Revolution: Christianity, Colonialism, and Consciousness in South Africa* (Chicago: University of Chicago Press, 1991) ignores the importance of African mediators; their second volume, *Of Revelation and Revolution: The Dialectics of Modernity on a South African Frontier* (Chicago: University of Chicago Press, 1997), 65, 78–93, is more attentive to "native agency." For other studies focusing on African Christian agents, see Paul Landau, *The Realm of the World: Language, Gender, and Christianity in a Southern African Kingdom* (Portsmouth, N.H.: Heinemann, 1995), 132–59; and Carol Summers, *Colonial Lessons: Africans' Education in Southern Rhodesia, 1918–1940* (Portsmouth, N.H.: Heinemann, 2002). Cf. Terence Ranger, *Are We Not Also Men? The Samkange Family and African Politics in Zimbabwe, 1920–1964* (Portsmouth, N.H.: Heinemann, 1995); and

Nancy Hunt, *A Colonial Lexicon of Birth Ritual, Medicalization, and Mobility in the Congo* (Durham, N.C.: Duke University Press, 1999).

4. But see David Owusu-Ansah, "History of Islamic Education in Ghana: An Overview," *Ghana Studies* 5 (2002): 61–81.

5. Claire Robertson, *Sharing the Same Bowl: A Socioeconomic History of Women and Class in Accra, Ghana* (Bloomington: Indiana University Press, 1984), 134–37, 104. For "assistants" or "apprentices" among female traders in Asante, see Gracia Clark, *Onions Are My Husband: Survival and Accumulation by West African Market Women* (Chicago: University of Chicago Press, 1994), 191–92. Paulina Ago Acheampong recalled her apprenticeship in sewing at the Basel Mission Girls School in Agogo, Abetifi, September 1, 2001, with the assistance of Pearl Ofosu.

6. For gendered crafts, see R. S. Rattray, *Religion and Art in Ashanti* (Oxford: Clarendon, 1927), 221, 233, 271, 301; and idem, *Ashanti* (Oxford: Clarendon, 1923), 301. For the organization of offices at the Asantehene's court in precolonial Kumase, see Ivor Wilks, *Asante in the Nineteenth Century: The Structure and Evolution of a Political Order* (Cambridge: Cambridge University Press, 1975), chap. 11; Wilks argued that the *Gyaasewa* stool (treasury) provided the "model" for service stools following the rule "that no 'sons' should succeed until the 'brothers' had been exhausted, and no 'grandsons' until the 'sons' had been exhausted." These service stools were not "patrilineally" inherited, although sons might succeed (noting a trend of "patrifiliation"), but "having the requisite skills for a specific office was heavily weighted" (ibid., 463–64).

7. R. S. Rattray, *Ashanti Law and Constitution* (Oxford: Clarendon, 1929), 9–10. For the training of drummers, see J. H. Nketia, *Drumming in Akan Communities of Ghana* (London: Thomas Nelson, 1963), 155–57. Nketia distinguished between "state drummers," offices passed down patrilineally, and "popular drumming or drumming by association," chosen by a person's own initiative.

8. Jean Allman and Victoria Tashjian, *"I Will Not Eat Stone": A Women's History of Colonial Asante* (Portsmouth, N.H.: Heinemann, 2000), 88–89. For the southern town of Larteh, David W. Brokensha dated new occupations in the decades after 1870 (*Social Change at Larteh, Ghana* [Oxford: Clarendon, 1966], 53). Cf. Margaret Peil's research about changes in male apprenticeships in "The Apprenticeship System in Accra," *Africa* 60, no. 2 (1970): 137–50, in which she notes the introduction of new occupations for literate young men like printmaking and, since the 1950s, radio repair.

9. Sara Berry, *Fathers Work for Their Sons* (Berkeley: University of California Press, 1985), 135, 141–44.

10. Sophy Osafo, "How Children Are Brought Up in Kwahu" (Thesis, Institute of Education, University College, Achimota, 1950–51), 24. Cf. Esther Goody's discussion of "modern apprenticeships," especially for Ghana and Nigeria, in *Parenthood and Social Reproduction: Fostering and Occupational Roles in West Africa* (Cambridge: Cambridge University Press, 1982), 188–205.

11. J. A. Wahyee, Abetifi, November 28, 1994, with the assistance of Joseph Kwakye. For the importance of migration within the life cycle, see Philip Bartle, "Urban Migration and Rural Identity: An Ethnography of a Kwawu Community, Obo, Ghana" (Ph.D. dissertation, University of Ghana, 1978). Others talked about the relation between apprenticeship and migration: the former sandal maker and trader Nana Okyere Ampadu II, *Kyidomhene* of Kwawu (born 1913), Pepease, September 12, 1994, with the assistance of E. F. Opusuo and Kwame Fosu; the former driver Yaw Emmanuel Anim (born ca. 1917), Abetifi, June 29, 1993, with the assistance of Douglas Asomani; and the former

shoemaker and cocoa farmer Yaw Mensa (born ca. 1918), Nkwantanan, July 27, 1993, with the assistance of Pearl Ofosu.

12. Kwawu towns had a "specialization of trading activities"; in addition to the bead trade, the rubber trade was in the hands of Obo traders, while trading in cloth was dominated by people from Obomeng. See Peter Garlick, "The Development of Kwahu Business Enterprise in Ghana since 1874: An Essay in Recent Oral Tradition," *JAH* 8, no. 3 (1967): 476.

13. J. A. Wahyee, Abetifi, September 18, 1994; and J. A. Wahyee and Kwadwo Donkor, Abetifi, August 25, 1993, both with the assistance of Joseph Kwakye; and Robertson, *Sharing the Same Bowl*, 104–105, 234–35. Bead names are listed by J. G. Christaller, *A Dictionary of the Asante and Fante Language, Called Tschi (Twi)*, 2nd ed., rev. and enl. (Basel: Basel Evangelical Missionary Society, 1933), 171; see the description of beads at the Abetifi market by Decima Moore and F. G. Guggisberg, *We Two in Africa* (London: Heinemann, 1909), 299–301.

14. Ɔpanyin Kwaku Marfo, Pepease, September 8, 1993, with the assistance of Douglas Asomani.

15. For the spiritual powers of the *nsumankwaahene*, see Emmanuel Akyeampong and Pashington Obeng, "Spirituality, Gender, and Power in Asante History," *IJAHS* 28, no. 3 (1995): 503.

16. Ɔkyeame Kwabena Asante, Pepease, August 27, 1993, with the assistance of Joseph Kwakye; and November 27, 1994, with the assistance of Kwame Fosu. Cf. the discussion about agreements between master and the apprentice's father or guardian, based on research in the early 1960s, in Brokensha, *Social Change at Larteh*, 258–60.

17. Ɔkyeame Asante, Pepease, August 27, 1993, and November 27, 1994; see Ɔkyeame Kwabena Asante, Pepease, October 29, 1994, with the assistance of Kwame Fosu. For a classification of Akan healers—herbalist, diviner, birth attendant, bone setter, and exorcist—see Kofi Appiah-Kubi, *Man Cures, God Heals: Religion and Medical Practice among the Akans of Ghana* (Totowa, N.J.: Allanheld, Osmun, 1981), 35–36.

18. Ɔkyeame Asante, October 29, 1994, and November 27, 1994.

19. Ɔkyeame Asante, August 27, 1993.

20. Appiah-Kubi, *Man Cures, God Heals*, 81.

21. Ɔkyeame Asante, October 29, 1994. Clark noted that an Asante trader's apprentice is referred to as *akwadaa* (child) with the "connotation of inexperience and lack of knowledge, but also the positive qualities of confidence and energy associated with youth" (*Onions Are My Husband*, 197).

22. E. K. Addo, Abetifi, September 24, 1994, with the assistance of Kwame Fosu.

23. The railway line Accra–Nsawam was opened in 1910, extended to Mangoase in 1913, to Koforidua in 1915, and to Tafo in 1917; work for the final piece was started from Tafo and Kumase simultaneously, reaching Nkawkaw (Kwawu) and Juaso (Asante Akyem) in 1922; the two portions were connected in 1923 (*The Gold Coast Handbook*, ed. John Maxwell, 3rd ed. [London: Crown Agents for the Colonies, 1928], 123).

24. Addo, September 24 and 28, 1994, as well as E. K. Addo, Abetifi, November 24, 1994. For a list of Presbyterian moderators, see Noel Smith, *The Presbyterian Church of Ghana, 1835–1960* (Accra: Ghana Universities Press, 1966), 294. For Sampong's conversion, cf. the biographical portrait by his son H. A. Osafo-Sampong, "Burial Service Programme for the Late Opanyin Joseph Edward Sampong, 1876–1980," Presbyterian Church, Abetifi, May 3, 1980, AP.

25. Foster, *Education and Social Change*, 6. For a study on child development and

socialization focusing on consensual aspects of education, see Barrington Kaye, *Bringing Up Children in Ghana: An Impressionistic Survey* (London: Allen and Unwin, 1962). More attentive to differentiation is the comparative study by Goody, *Parenthood and Social Reproduction*.

26. Smith, *Presbyterian Church*, 165–89; and Wilhelm Schlatter, *Geschichte der Basler Mission, 1815–1915*, vol. 3 (Basel: Missionsbuchhandlung, 1916), 91–99.

27. Gold Coast, *Education Ordinance 1882* (Nos. 4 and 9 of 1882); and *Education Ordinance 1887* (No. 14 of 1887), NAG, ADM 4/1. After introducing new policies in 1909, the government only developed a comprehensive educational policy in the 1920s; see Cardinall, *Gold Coast*, 184–85; Foster, *Education and Social Change*, 81–89; and Schlatter, *Geschichte der Basler Mission*, 3:185–86. For the expulsion, cf. Hermann Witschi, *Geschichte der Basler Mission, 1914–1919*, vol. 4 (Basel: Basileia Verlag, 1965), 162–95. Basel Mission schools were praised by Governor Guggisberg, *The Gold Coast: A Review of the Events of 1920–1926 and the Prospects of 1927–1928* (Accra: Government Printing Works, 1927), 201; and by the Phelps-Stokes Commission, T. J. Jones, *Education in Africa: A Study of West, South and Equatorial Africa by the African Education Commission* (New York: Phelps-Stokes Fund, 1922), 133–37.

28. Eugen Werner, Abetifi, September 5, 1877, BMA, D-1.29, 261. For the development of Basel Mission "outstations," see Philip Kwabi's report, Mpraeso, May 21, 1883, BMA, D-1.37, 88, and the overview by Kofi Nkansa-Kyeremateng, *One Hundred Years of the Presbyterian Church in Kwahu* (Accra: Presbyterian Press, 1976), 33–54. For the practice of fostering, particularly its continuous popularity across West Africa in the twentieth century, see Goody, *Parenthood and Social Reproduction;* for Kwawu, cf. Osafo, "How Children Are Brought Up," 31–32.

29. Friedrich Ramseyer, annual report, Abetifi, February 1890, BMA, D-1.51, 86. Ramseyer did not mention that some members of Basel Mission congregations pawned their children and more often accepted pawns for debts; see the report by Deacon Anteson of April 1894, as well as the extensive discussion by Peter Haenger, *Slaves and Slave Holders on the Gold Coast: Towards an Understanding of Social Bondage in West Africa,* trans. C. Handford (Basel: Schlettwein, 2000 [1999]), 180–81, passim. On pawning in Asante, see R. S. Rattray, *Ashanti Law and Constitution* (Oxford: Clarendon, 1929), 47–55; and T. C. McCaskie, *State and Society in Pre-Colonial Asante* (Cambridge: Cambridge University Press, 1995), 40–41.

30. Gottlieb Dilger, annual report, Abetifi, January 17, 1884, BMA, D-1.37, 96.

31. Friedrich Ramseyer, February 1890, and Johannes Tschopp, annual school report, Abetifi, February 9, 1886, BMA, D-1.43, 137.

32. Friedrich Ramseyer, Abetifi, May 5, 1888, and October 1889, BMA, D-1.49, 85, D-1.51, 85; see Ramseyer's frequent letters to colonial officials in "Kwahu District, Native Affairs," NAG, ADM 11/1/1445. Cf. Kwame Arhin, "The Missionary Role on the Gold Coast and in Ashanti: Reverend F. A. Ramseyer and the British Take-over of Ashanti, 1869–1894," *Research Review* 4, no. 2 (1968): 1–15. For Kwawu's protectorate treaty, see Peter Haenger, "Die Basler Mission im Spannungsbereich afrikanischer Integrationsversuche und europäischer Kolonialpolitik. Vorbereitung und Anfangszeit der 'Asante Mission' in Abetifi, Kwawu" (Master's thesis, University of Basel, 1989), 68–73; the treaty's text is reprinted in Kofi Nkansa-Kyeremateng, *The Story of Kwawu* (Accra: Presbyterian Press, 1990), 40–41.

33. Friedrich Ramseyer noted a father's exclusion because he was pressed by his children's *abusua* not to send them to school (annual report, Abetifi, March 16, 1893,

BMA, D-1.57, 125). Jakob Haasis noted that Kwaku Mensa, son of a Christian father, was prevented from attending school because his *abusua* had already agreed to pawn him (annual report, Abetifi, January 24, 1883, BMA, D-1.57, 126). For school enrollment figures, see Nkansa-Kyeremateng, *One Hundred Years*, 14.

34. Nancy Rose Hunt, "The Colonial Fairy Tales and Knife and Fork Doctrine in the Heart of Africa," in *African Encounters with Domesticity*, ed. K. T. Hansen (New Brunswick, N.J.: Rutgers University Press, 1992), 151.

35. Smith, *Presbyterian Church*, 56, 181 n.; cf. Schlatter, *Geschichte der Basler Mission*, 3:92–93. With its interest in girls' education, the Basel Mission distinguished itself from other mission schools and the colonial government. For a similar institution in South Africa, see Heather Hughes, " 'A lighthouse of African womanhood': Inanda Seminary, 1869–1945," in *Women and Gender in Southern Africa to 1945*, ed. C. Walker (Cape Town: David Philip, 1990), 197–220. For Basel Mission female gender ideals, cf. Simone Prodolliet, *Wider die Schamlosigkeit und das Elend der heidnischen Weiber. Der Export des europäischen Frauenideals in die Kolonien durch die Basler Frauenmission* (Zurich: Limmat Verlag, 1987).

36. An industrial school at Christiansborg, founded in 1877, offered three years of apprenticeships in carpentry and metalwork, shaping young men into skilled craftsmen; see Karl Rennstich, *Handwerks-Theologen und Industrie Brüder als Botschafter des Friedens: Entwicklungshilfe der Basler Mission im 19. Jahrhundert* (Stuttgart: Missionsverlag, 1985). Some craftsmen found employment across West and Central Africa, particularly in the Congo Free State in the 1880s; this exodus caused concern in the colonial administration (Polly Hill, *The Migrant Cocoa-Farmers of Southern Ghana: A Study in Rural Capitalism* [Cambridge: Cambridge University Press, 1963], 166 n.).

37. Friedrich Ramseyer, Abetifi, April 26, 1891, BMA, D-1.53, 127.

38. Friedrich Jost, Abetifi, July 21, 1897, BMA, D-1.67, 133.

39. Gottlieb Dilger, January 17, 1884.

40. Jakob Haasis, annual report, Abetifi, February 18, 1896, BMA, D-1.63, 126; cf. idem, Abetifi, November 4, 1895, BMA, D-1.63, 121.

41. Herrmann Henking, annual reports, Abetifi, March 20, 1917, and June 10, 1918, BMA, D-3.7, D-3.8. Bartle, "Urban Migration," 203, noted that the ruling *abusua* of Obo was not very accommodating of the Basel Mission and the colonial administration, but the *abusua* led by the *Ankobeahene* welcomed the government's educational efforts and provided land.

42. Arthur Jehle's comments in the margins of Gottlieb Stern, annual report, Abetifi, February 2, 1917, BMA, D-3.7. For the beginnings of cocoa, see Hill, *Migrant Cocoa-Farmers;* and Francis Crowther, "Notes on a District of the Gold Coast," *Quarterly Journal of the Institute of Commercial Research in the Tropics* (Liverpool University) 3 (1906): 178.

43. *JB* 97 (1912): 55. For cocoa farmers' investments, cf. Foster, *Education and Social Change*, 126–27; and Meyer Fortes, "The Ashanti Social Survey: A Preliminary Report," *Rhodes-Livingstone Journal* 6 (1948): 9, 32–33. Hill compared "ostentatious educational expenditure" of Akuapem cocoa farmers to "building a colossal house" (*Migrant Cocoa-Farmers*, 191). For similar patterns in Nigeria, see Berry, *Fathers*, 76–78, 103–107.

44. Rev. D. E. Akwa, annual report, Abetifi, February 22, 1917, BMA, D-3.7; and Herrmann Henking, June 10, 1918. During World War I the export volume of cocoa stagnated, falling in 1918. Only cocoa producers with low transportation costs had a market; see G. B. Kay, *The Political Economy of Colonialism in Ghana* (Cambridge: Cam-

bridge University Press, 1972), 336; and Sara Berry, *No Condition Is Permanent: The Social Dynamics of Agrarian Change in Sub-Saharan Africa* (Madison: University of Wisconsin Press, 1993), 71–72.

45. "District Record Book, Mpraeso," 152, April 24, 1923, NAG, ADM 34/5/2.

46. Explaining the category "education," the 1921 census officer defined literacy as Standard VII; in 1931 the census category referred to "Education in or over Standard IV"; and in 1948 the census distinguished between "Standard III–IV" and "Standard VII or higher" (Gold Coast, *Census Report 1921* [Accra: Government Press, 1923], 46, App. K, 18; *The Gold Coast, 1931, Appendices, Containing Comparative Returns and General Statistics of the 1931 Census* [Accra: Government Printer, 1932], 105; and *Census of Population, 1948* [London: Crown Agents, 1950], 124). Bartle rightfully observed that the 1948 census figures of Kwawu literacy were too low, since they ignored the migrancy of literate people residing in Accra and other commercial centers ("Urban Migration," 205).

47. Rev. E.K.O. Asante, Abetifi, February 2, 1993, and September 30, 1994.

48. Kofi Boakye Yiadom, Abetifi, August 28, 1994. See the descriptions of street preaching by Rev. D. E. Akwa, annual report, Abetifi, February 15, 1916; and Rev. Charles Martinson, annual report, Bompata, February 11, 1916, both in BMA, D-3.6.

49. A. K. Boakye Yiadom, Abetifi, June 27, 1993, and August 28, 1994, as well as his "Autobiography: My Own Life" (hereafter, "MOL"), 2 vols. (1946–1981), 1:1–2, BYP.

50. E. F. Opusuo, Pepease, December 21, 1992. Nana Kwabena Owusu Mensa II occupied the Pepease stool from 1931 to 1950; settling a long-standing dispute with Abetifi, he succeeded in gaining recognition as *Kyidomhene* of Kwawu; see G. P. Johnson, Secretary Kwahu State Council to Acting DC, Mpraeso, August 1, 1940, NAG, ADM 32/1/127. After the Abetifi seminary was relocated to Akropong in 1924, the government established a survey school in the empty buildings. Although in Abetifi for only a few years, the school left a legacy behind: elders recalled working as stewards for the European teachers. The school literally altered the Kwawu landscape, because students laid out and constructed the motor road from the Abetifi Christian Quarters over the next ridge to the neighboring town of Pepease. Cf. G. F. Debra, April 13, 1993, who stayed as houseboy with headmaster A. G. Fraser Jr. (son of Reverend Fraser); and Reverend Asante, Abetifi, October 18, 1994, and January 26, 1993.

51. Revised as *Regulations, Practice and Procedure of the Presbyterian Church of the Gold Coast* (1929), BMA, D-9.1c.13d. In 1918 Abetifi had 779 communicants; in 1938, 886; in 1918 the whole Ghanaian Presbyterian Church had 14,292 communicants; and in 1938, 26,574 (Smith, *Presbyterian Church*, 217, 292). Karl Hartenstein addressed the changes in the "new era" (*Anibue: Die "Neue Zeit" auf der Goldküste und unsere Missionsaufgabe* [Stuttgart: Evangelischer Missionsverlag, 1932], 53–62, 99). See the case of Native Tribunal of Abetifi, *Adjoa Adobea* vs. *Kojo Diawuo*, November 2, 1931, in which the Christian plaintiff was reminded to take the dispute with her husband to the presbyters (KTC, 7:126–35).

52. Opusuo, Pepease, December 21, 1992, and April 4, 1993. For those outside schools, see Wahyee and Donkor, August 25, 1993; for dress, see Rev. E.K.O. Asante, Abetifi, August 17, 1993; and Boakye Yiadom, August 28, 1994. Cf. Osafo, "How Children Are Brought Up," 33, who reported about "jealousy" among siblings since those attending school required "better clothing, do less work at home, and have various privileges."

53. E. F. Opusuo, Pepease, August 22, 1993.

54. Rev. E.K.O. Asante, Abetifi, January 26, 1993; and Boakye Yiadom, November 15, 1994. For the veneration of Tano, see Rattray, *Ashanti*, 172–202. Cf. Isabel Hofmeyr's comments of how missionary texts like *The Pilgrim's Progress*, published in Twi translation by the Basel Mission, traveled across the imperial world, being read and being listened to (Isabel Hofmeyr, "John Bunyan, His Chair, and a Few Other Relics: Orality, Literacy, and the Limits of Area Studies," in *African Words, African Voices*, ed. L. White, S. F. Miescher, and D. W. Cohen [Bloomington: Indiana University Press, 2001], 78–90).

55. Elizabeth Ntim, Abetifi, August 26, 1993, with the assistance of Pearl Ofosu. Yaa Annoah (born ca. 1922) completed only three years of school, paid by her father's younger brother, Master Ntim (Elizabeth Ntim's late husband), and then she was assigned to take of her younger siblings; Abetifi, April 17, 1993, with the assistance of Douglas Asomani. Alice Ofosuhemaa (born 1928) reached Standard II before quitting school (Abetifi, August 22, 2000, with the assistance of Pearl Ofosu).

56. Adelaide Opong, Abetifi, April 14, 1993, with the assistance of Joseph Kwakye. Reverend Jehle's wife arrived in Abetifi in 1908. Her letters contain vivid descriptions of teaching "house girls" the preparation of European food. Thanks to Rev. U. Jehle for access to his grandparents' correspondence. For missionary training of house servants, see Allman, "Making Mothers," 41; Gaitskell, "Devout Domesticity," 254–56; and especially Hunt, "Colonial Fairy Tales."

57. Paulina Addo, Abetifi, April 18, 1993, with the assistance of Douglas Asomani. Cf. accounts by Felicia Asante, Abetifi, August 22, 2000, and Agnes Sampong, Abetifi, August 22, 2000, both with the assistance of Pearl Ofosu.

58. "District Record Book," 152, April 24, 1923, and June 2, 1926.

59. Kofi Ankoma, Obo, March 25, April 29, and April 30, 1993.

60. Boakye Yiadom, "MOL," 1:6.

61. "District Record Book," 153–54, January 24, 1923, and November 11, 1926. The Phelps-Stokes Commission noted that "arrangement for the pupils' sleeping and eating were formerly very crude" but "fortunately . . . being corrected under the direction of the Scottish Mission" (Jones, *Education in Africa*, 136). Cf. Fred Agyemang, *A Century with Boys: The Story of the Middle Boarding School in Ghana, 1867–1967* (Accra: Waterville, 1967); Smith, *Presbyterian Church*, 167–70; and Nkansa-Kyerementeng, *Story of Kwawu*, 71.

62. Agyemang, *Century with Boys*, 49.

63. Inspector of Schools, J. Spio-Garbah to Director of Education, c. 1932, NAG, RG 3/1/144. By 1931 there were seven Presbyterian boys' and three girls' middle boarding schools.

64. See Michel Foucault, *Discipline and Punish: The Birth of the Prison*, trans. A. Sheridan (New York: Vintage, 1977 [1975]).

65. E. F. Opusuo, Pepease, August 27, 1994; and *Verordnung für die Basler Missionsstationen: VI. Schulordnung* (1869), 41, BMA, Q-9.22.

66. Historians have identified processes of reorganizing time and work to "make" industrial workers and their responses; for Africa, see Frederick Cooper, "Colonizing Time: Work Rhythms and Labor Conflicts in Colonial Mombasa," in *Colonialism and Culture*, ed. N. Dirks (Ann Arbor: University of Michigan Press, 1992), 209–45; and, for a more comparative view, see idem, "Urban Space, Industrial Time, and Wage Labor in Africa," in *Struggle for the City*, ed. F. Cooper (Beverly Hills: Sage, 1983), 7–50; also

cf. Kaletso Atkins, *The Moon Is Dead! Give Us Our Money! The Cultural Origins of an African Work Ethic, Natal, South Africa, 1843–1900* (Portsmouth, N.H.: Heinemann, 1993), 78–99. For Britain, see E. P. Thompson, "Time, Work-discipline and Industrial Capitalism," *Past and Present* 38 (1967): 56–97.

67. Agyemang, *Century with Boys*, 34.

68. Rev. E.K.O. Asante, Abetifi, May 18, 1993. The acronym ASOBA stands for Rev. E. M. *A*siedu (who was stationed in Abetifi from 1927 to 1933), and the four teachers, I. O. *S*ampong, W. D. *O*pare, E. D Amponsa *B*udu, and A. E. Sakyima *A*moako. I visited the school grounds with Reverend Asante on November 23, 1994, and with Boakye Yiadom on December 5, 1994.

69. E. K. Addo's testimony about his late brother Isaiah Osafo Sampong (1900–1943) in "The Memorable Tribute to Mr. & Mrs. I. O. Sampong," n.d. (ca. 1985), Rev. E.K.O. Asante's Papers (ASP).

70. Reverend Asante, January 26, 1993, was in house 2 (red); Opusuo, August 27, 1994, house 3 (green); Boakye Yiadom, December 5, 1994, two years in house 3 and then switched to house 4 (yellow). Agyemang, who enrolled at the Abetifi Boarding School in 1930, recalled his initiation of having to fetch water for seniors at 3 A.M.; in Akropong, the initiation involved the telling of the school's history combined with physical beatings (*Century with Boys*, 51–54, 62); cf. B. E. Ofori, Akropong, January 5, 1993. For the British public school system, see J. R. de S. Honey, *Tom Brown's Universe: The Development of the Victorian Public School* (London: Millington, 1977).

71. Reverend Asante, August 17, 1993; Agyemang, *Century with Boys*, 42, lists the prospectus items. For the creation of new needs for consumer products like soap as part colonialism and part global capitalism, see Timothy Burke, *Lifebuoy Men, Lux Women: Commodification, Consumption and Cleanliness in Modern Zimbabwe* (Durham, N.C.: Duke University Press, 1996).

72. Agyemang, *Century with Boys*, 75.

73. E. F. Opusuo, Pepease, August 22, 1993.

74. Comaroff and Comaroff, *Of Revelation and Revolution*, 1:233.

75. Arthur Wilkie, "An Attempt to Conserve the Work of the Basel Mission to the Gold Coast," *International Review of Missions* 9 (1920): 88, 91. Yao Boateng, a 1950s graduate, noted the "harsh discipline and strong religious indoctrination" of the Abetifi Boarding School ("The Catechism and the Rod: Presbyterian Education in Ghana," in *African Reactions to Missionary Education*, ed. E. H. Berman [New York: Teachers' College Press, Columbia University], 83).

76. Reverend Asante, February 2, 1993.

77. *Worship in School* (Accra: Scottish Mission Book Depot, 1933), 17–18, BMA, Sch. 6473, 21.

78. Reverend Asante, February 2, 1993; during Asante's burial service on August 2, 1997, the congregation sang this hymn, based on Psalm 37, 5 (Twi Hymn 265).

79. Reverend Asante, August 17, 1993. Edmond Perregaux (1868–1905), the nephew of F. Ramseyer, served in Abetifi from 1891 to 1901; he died in Kumase. Cf. Agyemang, *Century with Boys*, 86–90; and Comaroff and Comaroff, *Of Revelation and Revolution*, 1:219.

80. "My Life History: The Autobiography of Akasease Kofi Boakye Yiadom" (hereafter, "Autobiography"), 2, BYP, and Opusuo, August 22, 1993.

81. Opusuo, December 21, 1992. Akuamoa Akyeampong was *Ɔmanhene* of

Kwawu from 1932 to 1952 and from 1962 to 1971; cf. his daughter's recollections, Paulina Ago Acheampong, September 1, 2001; and Nkansa-Kyeremateng, *Story of Kwawu*, 37.

82. Meyer Fortes, "Kinship and Marriage among the Ashanti," in *African Systems of Kinship and Marriage*, ed. A. Radcliffe-Brown and D. Forde (London: Oxford University Press, 1950), 268. According to his statistical data, half the children (n = 700) were supported by their fathers, only 25 percent by maternal uncles, and between 10 and 15 percent by mothers.

83. Osafo, "How Children Are Brought Up," 35.

84. Allman and Tashjian, *"I Will Not Eat Stone,"* 91.

85. "Prospectus Presbyterian Girls Middle School, Agogo," dated July 11, 1953, ASP. In 1930 the Basel Mission also opened a hospital in Agogo; cf. Hermann Witschi, *Geschichte der Basler Mission, 1920–1940*, vol. 5 (Basel: Basileia Verlag, 1970), 315, 341–43.

86. Hartenstein, *Anibue*, 107; cf. Gertrud Goetz, annual report, January 23, 1933, BMA, D-11, 3.

87. Felicia Asante, August 22, 2000. For an account of how European women had to carve out their space within the patriarchal structure of the Basel Mission, see Waltraud Haas, *Erlitten und erstritten: Der Befreiungsweg von Frauen in der Basler Mission, 1816–1966* (Basel: Basileia Verlag, 1994), which includes a brief portrait of Gertrud Goetz, 95–101. Rosmarie Tschudin-Gehr further elaborated on women's position in the Basel Mission, Gelterkinden, September 17, 2001.

88. Adelaide Opong, April 14, 1993. Christaller translates *basabasa* as "confused, perplexed, disordered, disorderly" (*Dictionary*, 9).

89. Adelaide Opong, April 14, 1993.

90. Annual Address, *Legislative Council Debates, 1925–26*, cited after Kay, *Political Economy*, 293; cf. 32–33.

91. Foster, *Education and Social Change*, 166–70. In 1927, when the 1925 Education Ordinance came into effect, grants to assisted schools in the Colony, Ashanti, and Togoland totaled almost £70,000, more than twice the amount of the previous year (David Kimble, *A Political History of Ghana: The Rise of Gold Coast Nationalism, 1850–1928* [Oxford: Clarendon, 1963], 119). Increased state intervention in mission schools was not unique to the Gold Coast in the 1920s; for colonial Zimbabwe, see Summers, *Colonial Lessons*, chap. 1.

92. Jones, *Education in Africa*, 11; cf. T. O. Beidelman, *Colonial Evangelism: A Socio-historical Study of an East African Mission at the Grassroots* (Bloomington: Indiana University Press, 1982), 120. Booker T. Washington was the long-term principal of the Tuskegee Institute in Alabama. His truce with white Southerners, the "Atlanta Compromise," was held responsible for cementing a system of racial segregation and political disenfranchisement of African Americans, instead of insisting on racial parity and equal opportunities in education; cf. W.E.B. Du Bois, *The Souls of Black Folk* (Chicago: McClurg, 1903), chap. 3.

93. Jones, *Education in Africa*, 18–21, 25, 27.

94. W.E.B. Du Bois, "Education in Africa: A Review of the Recommendations of the African Educational Committee," *The Crisis* (June 1926): 86–89. The conference of African missionaries at High Leigh, attended by most British mission societies, "unanimously endorsed Dr. Jones's educational programme" (J. H. Oldham, "Christian Education in Africa," *Church Missionary Review* 75 [June 1925]: 12).

95. *Gold Coast Leader*, July 10 and 24, 1926. Cf. Kimble, *Political History*, 114; and Foster, *Education and Social Change*, 155–66.

96. Great Britain, Colonial Office, *Memorandum on Education Policy in British Tropical Africa* (London: His Majesty's Stationery Office, 1925), 5 (emphasis added); and idem, *Memorandum on the Education of African Communities* (London: His Majesty's Stationery Office, 1935).

97. James Mangan, *The Games Ethic and Imperialism: Aspects of the Diffusion of an Ideal* (New York: Viking, 1986), 18. For a nuanced study on manliness and race, see Gail Bederman, *Manliness and Civilization: A Cultural History of Gender and Race in the United States, 1880–1917* (Chicago: University of Chicago Press, 1995).

98. Reverend Asante, January 26, 1993; for "traditional games," see chapter two.

99. Football, along with cricket and field hockey, arrived first in the towns of British colonial Africa in the late nineteenth, early twentieth centuries; competitive sports were slower to arrive in Francophone Africa; see Laura Fair, "Kickin' It: Leisure, Politics and Football in Colonial Zanzibar, 1900s–1950s," *Africa* 67, no. 2 (1997): 225, 246 n.; Phyllis Martin, *Leisure and Society in Colonial Brazzaville* (Cambridge: Cambridge University Press, 1995), chap. 4; and Peter Alegi, "Playing to the Gallery? Sport, Cultural Performance, and Social Identity in South Africa, 1920s–1945," *IJAHS* 35, no. 1 (2002): 17–38.

100. Reverend Asante, January 26, 1993.

101. Opusuo, August 27, 1994. Football's popularity among boys not attending school in 1950 Kwawu was noted by Osafo ("How Children Are Brought Up," 26). For a "vernacularization" of football styles in urban South Africa, see Alegi, "Playing to the Gallery?"

102. Martin, *Leisure and Society*, 101.

103. Reverend Asante, January 26, 1993, and Opusuo, August 27, 1994.

104. James Mangan, "Ethics and Ethnocentricity: Imperial Education in British Tropical Africa," in *Sport in Africa*, ed. W. J. Baker and J. A. Mangan (New York: Africana, 1987), 146. For the importance of "games," particularly football, cricket, hockey, and running sports, at Achimota College, see Gold Coast, *Achimota College* (London: Crown Agent for the Colonies, 1932), 18, 40–41.

105. Martin, *Leisure and Society*, 108.

106. Boakye Yiadom, June 27, 1993; in "Autobiography," 2, he noted being "the senior goal keeper from Standard IV till Standard VII." For nicknames, see Alegi, "Playing to the Gallery?" 32.

107. Testimony by C.G.J. Amanin, Abetifi, December 7, 1939, BYP.

108. R. W. Connell, *Masculinities* (Berkeley: University of California Press, 1995), 30.

109. Fair, "Kickin' It," 227.

110. See Agyemang's discussion of the Empire Day celebration at the Osu Basel Mission middle school in 1909: the afternoon "devoted to athletics and games by school children," in the evening "entertainment night with songs, recitations, short plays, stories and organ recitals by the boys" (*Century with Boys*, 68). For the transformation of school plays, produced for Empire Day festivities, into successful commercial enterprises, cf. Catherine Cole, *Ghana's Concert Party Theatre* (Bloomington: Indiana University Press, 2001), 24–25, 78–79.

111. Report on Baden-Powell's lecture (delivered more than fifty times between 1907 and 1908), *Hereford Times*, November 16, 1907; reprinted in Robert MacDonald,

Sons of the Empire: The Frontier and the Boy Scout Movement, 1890–1918 (Toronto: University of Toronto Press, 1993), 243–47. For scouting's "masculinist ideology," see ibid., 17, passim. Cf. John Springhall, *Youth, Empire and Society: British Youth Movements, 1883–1942* (London: Croom Helm, 1977); and Michael Rosenthal, *The Character Factory: Baden-Powell and the Origins of the Boy Scout Movement* (New York: Pantheon, 1986).

112. *Gold Coast Handbook,* 163–64; according to the 1931 Census, there were 2,000 scouts (including 18 European scout commissioners), the vast majority boys; in the county of Koforidua (Eastern Province), there were 169 scouts, 91 cubs, and 31 officers; see Cardinall, *Gold Coast, 1931,* 200. By 1946 the number of scouts had swelled to 12,421 (Chief Scout Commissioner H. Gibb to Executive Committee, Accra, March 25, 1946, Rhodes House (RH), Henry Venom Cusack papers, MSS Afr. s. 318. So far scouting in colonial Africa has attracted little attention by historians, but see Lisa Lindsay, "Putting the Family on Track: Gender and Domestic Life on the Colonial Nigerian Railway" (Ph.D. dissertation, University of Michigan, 1996), 324–33; and Timothy Parsons, *Race, Resistance, and the Boy Scout Movement in British Colonial Africa* (Athens: Ohio University Press, 2004).

113. W. H. Donald, "The Boy Scout Movement in the Gold Coast," *Gold Coast Teacher's Journal* (*GCTJ*) 4, no. 1 (1932): 24–25. This journal was published by the Education Department and distributed free of charge among teachers. See also the file "Boy Scouts," NAG, CSO 25/1/84, passim.

114. *Gold Coast Handbook,* 163.

115. Donald, "Boy Scout Movement," 27–28. Cf. Allen Warren, "Popular Manliness: Baden-Powell, Scouting and the Development of Manly Character," in *Manliness and Morality,* ed. J. A. Mangan and J. Walvin (Manchester: Manchester University Press, 1987), 199–219; and Jeffrey Hantover, "The Boy Scouts and the Validation of Masculinity," *Journal of Social Issues* 34, no. 1 (1978): 184–95.

116. Opusuo, August 27, 1994.

117. Boakye Yiadom, August 28, 1994, and November 15, 1994. E.V.C. Darko is remembered as a model teacher; see Adelaide Opong, April 23, 1993, his niece who lived with him when he was the Abetifi Boarding School headmaster.

118. In 1930, 601 students were enrolled in secondary schools—571 men and 30 women (84 men at government technical schools, 68 at Achimota, 376 at assisted schools, and 43 at nonassisted schools; 10 women at Achimota and 20 in nonassisted schools). By 1940 the secondary school enrollment had increased to 2,635—2,327 were men and 308 women (98 men at government technical schools, 218 at Achimota, 798 at assisted schools, and 1,213 at nonassisted schools; 85 women at Achimota and 223 at nonassisted schools); noteworthy is the sharp increase in the number of nonassisted secondary schools. With regard to training colleges, 555 students were enrolled in 1930—509 men and 46 women (146 men at Achimota and 363 at mission institutions; 15 women at Achimota and 31 at mission institutions). By 1940 training college enrollment had only slightly increased to 582, 384 men and 198 women (110 men at Achimota and 274 at mission institutions; 79 women at Achimota and 119 at mission institutions); see Gold Coast, *Report of the Education Committee, 1937–1941* (Accra: Government Printer, 1942), 31.

119. Rev. E.K.O. Asante, Abetifi, September 5, 1994, who had hoped to attend Achimota. Unlike the Methodist Mission which opened its first boys' secondary school at Cape Coast already in 1876 (called Mfantsipim since 1909), the first Presbyterian boys' secondary school was established at Odumase-Krobo only in 1938; cf. Foster, *Education*

and Social Change, 102; and Smith, *Presbyterian Church,* 176–77. In 1930 the fees of secondary schools varied from approximately £18 (Mfantsipim) to £50 (Achimota) per annum (Cardinall, *Gold Coast,* 191–92). The government guarded its bond obligations and privileges closely; see the controversy when the Ashanti Confederacy Council tried to issue a second bond for two Presbyterian Training College students, forcing them to teach in its schools (Director of Education to Provincial Education Officer, Ashanti, October 6, 1947, NAG, RG 3/1/333).

120. Opusuo, December 21, 1992; cf. Foster, *Education and Social Change,* 190–99.

121. The Basel Mission founded Ghana's oldest seminary for training teachers and catechists at Akropong in 1848, and the Abetifi seminary followed in 1898; they merged in 1924 with the location in Akropong. For reactions to reforms, see *JB* 114 (1929): 33–37; and Wilhelm Stamm's report, Akropong, July 1929, BMA, D-4-3, 1. Since 1927 the Basel Mission was again represented on the College staff with one missionary responsible for the catechist course (cf. Witschi, *Geschichte der Basler Mission,* 5:319).

122. The Basel Mission structure had consisted of two years of teachers' training followed by a two-year catechist course; cf. *JB* 97 (1912): 59–60. In 1922 teachers' training was expanded at the expense of the catechist course. Cf. Smith, *Presbyterian Church,* 178–80, 192; J. Yeboa-Dankwa, *Presbyterian Training College, Akropong-Akwapim (Founded 1948) 125th Anniversary Celebrations* (Accra: Waterville, 1973), 46–49; and Kimble, *Political History,* 119. In 1928 the opening of new buildings coincided with the centenary of the Basel Mission's arrival; Stamm provides a description of the physical improvements; see Wilhelm Stamm, July 1929.

123. Yeboa-Dankwa, *Presbyterian Training College,* 55, and Reverend Asante, August 17, 1993. The overdressing of students was an ongoing grievance. Arthur Jehle described students coming to class "in *full-dress*" with "collar," presenting themselves more as "young gentlemen" than as humble Christians (*JB* 98 (1913): 101); cf. Randall Packard, "The 'Healthy Reserve' and the 'Dressed Native': Discourses on Black Health and the Language of Legitimation in South Africa," *American Ethnologist* 16, no. 4 (1989): 686–703.

124. Opusuo, August 27, 1993. Cf. Agyemang's account about maintaining latrines at Presbyterian boys' boarding schools (*Century with Boys,* 57–58); latrines were filled every six months and then emptied after some time of composting. Digging out, pupils with the least seniority performed the most arduous task.

125. Opusuo, December 21, 1992.

126. Wilhelm Stamm, Akropong, August 1, 1929, BMA, D-4-3, 1. Pupils at middle boarding schools also relied on outside caterers; see Agyemang, *Century with Boys,* 46.

127. *Gold Coast Independent,* May 25, 1929.

128. Reverend Asante, August 17, 1993. Cf. Ofori, January 5, 1993; and L. M. Date-Ba, Mamfe, January 20, 1993.

129. Wilhelm Stamm, August 1, 1929.

130. Reverend Asante, August 17, 1993. For similar recollections about cassava, see T. E. Kyei, *Our Days Dwindle: Memories of My Childhood Days in Asante* (Portsmouth, N.H.: Heinemann, 2001), 126. These days, food habits have changed considerably among Akan people. Owing to the high prices of plantains, much cassava is planted and consumed in Kwawu.

131. Reverend Asante, August 17, 1993. Often teachers' wives supplied bread for Presbyterian schools; see Adelaide Opong, April 14, 1993; and Felicia Asante, August

22, 2000. Opposition to Kru men as cooks was not an isolated case. At Achimota in 1927, Vice Principal J.E.K. Aggrey heard a complaint from a student's father about Kru cooks, considered to be "thieves and rascals," preparing food; see Edwin Smith, *Aggrey of Africa: A Study in Black and White* (London: Student Christian Movement, 1929), 263–64.

132. *Gold Coast Independent*, May 25, 1929.

133. Wilhelm Stamm, August 1, 1929; for the missing religious focus, see Stamm's earlier report of July 1929.

134. Inspector D. W. Oettli to Wilhelm Stamm, Basel, October 16, 1929, BMA, D-4-4, 3. Yet, in a later report, Stamm acknowledged that there were reasons for the strike since the quality of the food was not always "satisfactory" (Akropong, January 1, 1936, BMA, D-11, 8).

135. Cf. Yeboa-Dankwa, *Presbyterian Training College*. Inspector Oettli assured Stamm that his "two reports will not be published, of course," October 16, 1929; Stamm noted the frequency of strikes (August 1, 1929). For food protests elsewhere, see the strike about insufficient food and harsh punishment at the Basel Mission Girls School; Helene Schlatter (Agogo, September 13, 1932), who considered such "revolts" as "fashionable" at boarding schools, requested *not* to disseminate her account among missionary supporters in Europe (BMA, D-11, 8). Another food strike occurred at the Assuanysi middle boarding school, Central Province, in 1941; cf. correspondence in NAG, CSO 18/5/17. Nelson Mandela wrote that a student election boycott, the result of an "unsatisfactory" diet at Fort Hare in the early 1940s, "change[d] the course of my life" (*Long Walk to Freedom: The Autobiography of Nelson Mandela* [Boston: Little, Brown, 1994], 51).

136. Stamm wrote with misgivings that the college leadership had become too concerned about responding to students' dietary complaints to prevent another strike; such "blunders" by his Scottish colleagues might be the reasons for an increased "spirit of resistance" among students (January 20, 1936).

137. E. F. Opusuo, Pepease, April 2, 1993, December 21, 1993, March 24, 1993, and August 22, 1993; cf. Reverend Ako-Addo, Akropong, January 21, 1993; Date-Ba, January 20, 1993; Ofori Anyinam, Pepease, May 5, 1993; B. E. Ofori, Akropong, October 13, 1993; Rev. T. A. Osei, Akropong, January 5, 1993; G. O. Reynolds, Mamfe, January 6, 1993; Ofori, January 5, 1993; and L. M. Date-Ba, Mamfe, September 19, 1993. See the prominence of (a German) discipline in oral histories recorded by Dennis Laumann, "Remembering and Forgetting the German Occupation of the Central Volta Region of Ghana" (Ph.D. dissertation, University of California, Los Angeles, 1999), 166–68, 275–78.

4. The Employment of Men

1. K. A. Busia, *The Position of the Chief in the Modern Political System of Ashanti* (Oxford: Oxford University Press, 1951), 132. Emmanuel Akyeampong refers to *akrakyefoɔ* as gentlemen, in "What's in a Drink? Class Struggle, Popular Culture and the Politics of *Akpeteshie* (Local Gin) in Ghana, 1930–67," *JAH* 37, no. 2 (1996): 233. Jean Allman has suggested a historicized definition for school leavers in Asante, evoking continuity with the precolonial social group of *nkwankwaa* (commoners) or "youngmen," deprived of access to chiefly office and wealth; see Allman, *The Quills of the Porcupine: Asante Nationalism in an Emergent Ghana* (Madison: University of Wisconsin Press,

1993), 28–36. Here the focus is on the impact of colonial education like in Kwame Arhin's discussion of the nineteenth-century Fante coast; see Arhin, "Rank and Class among the Asante and Fante in the Nineteenth Century," *Africa* 53, no. 1 (1983): 17.

2. Pierre Bourdieu, *Outline of a Theory of Practice*, trans. R. Price (Cambridge: Cambridge University Press, 1977 [1972]), 214 n. Yet see Elizabeth Tonkin's expanded notion of habitus with more attention to subjectivity, in *Narrating Our Pasts: The Social Construction of Oral History* (Cambridge: Cambridge University Press, 1992), 107.

3. For an earlier period, David Kimble refers to *akrakyefoɔ* and self-employed professionals and businessman as "new *élite*"; see Kimble, *Political History of Ghana: The Rise of Gold Coast Nationalism, 1850–1928* (Oxford: Clarendon, 1963), 135–41. For *akrakyefoɔ*'s aspirations, see Busia, *The Position of the Chief*, 132–33; and Stephanie Newell, *Literary Culture in Colonial Ghana: "How to play the game of life"* (Bloomington: Indiana University Press, 2002), 27–52.

4. T. O. Beidelman, *Colonial Evangelism: A Socio-historical Study of an East African Mission of the Grassroots* (Bloomington: Indiana University Press, 1982), 212.

5. Nancy Hunt, *A Colonial Lexicon of Birth Ritual, Medicalization, and Mobility in the Congo* (Durham, N.C.: Duke University Press, 1999), 12. An extensive literature on cultural brokers in Africa was initiated by Max Gluckman's work on chiefs and headmen. See Gluckman, "Analysis of a Social Situation in Modern Zululand," *Bantu Studies* 14 (1940): 1–30, 147–74; and idem, J. C. Mitchell, and J. A. Barnes, "The Village Headman in British Central Africa," *Africa* 19, no. 2 (1949): 89–101. Cf. Norman Long, *Social Change and the Individual: A Study of the Social and Religious Responses to Innovation in a Zambiam Rural Community* (Manchester: Manchester University Press, 1968); and E. S. Atieno-Odhiambo, "Luo Perspectives on Knowledge and Development: Samuel G. Ayani and Paul Mbuya," in *African Philosophy as Cultural Inquiry*, ed. I. Karp and D. A. Masalo (Bloomington: Indiana University Press, 2000), 244–58.

6. For early West African middle figures, see Paul Jenkins, ed., *The Recovery of the West African Past: African Pastors and African History in the Nineteenth Century, C. C. Reindorf and Samuel Johnson* (Basel: Basler Afrika Bibliographien, 1998); Sonia Abun-Nasr, *Afrikaner und Missionar: Die Lebensgeschichte von David Asante* (Basel: Schlettwein, 2003); and Joseph Boston May's life history by Leo Spitzer, *Lives in Between: Assimilation and Marginality in Austria, Brazil, West Africa, 1780–1945* (Cambridge: Cambridge University Press, 1989), 40–72; cf. idem, *The Creoles of Sierra Leone: Responses to Colonialism, 1870–1945* (Madison: University of Wisconsin Press, 1974).

7. C. C. Reindorf, *The History of the Gold Coast* (Basel: Missionsbuchhandlung, 1895), 229.

8. Andreas Bauer, "Der Fetisch Aberewa, ein neues Missionshindernis," *JB* 93 (1908): 91–95; and reports in *JB* 97 (1912): 55–59; 92 (1907): 35–37. For the *aberewa* shrine, see T. C. McCaskie, "Anti-Witchcraft Cults in Asante: An Essay in the Social History of an African People," *HA* 8 (1981): 138–41.

9. Emil Nothwang, *Akropong Middle School, Jubilee Handbook, 1867–1917*, cited after *JB* (1918): 32.

10. Governor Guggisberg, Legislative Council Debates, cited after G. B. Kay, *The Political Economy of Colonialism in Ghana* (Cambridge: Cambridge University Press, 1972), 279.

11. Great Britain, Colonial Office, *Report of the Commission of Enquiry into the Disturbances in the Gold Coast, 1948* (London: His Majesty's Stationery Office, 1948) [Watson Commission], 30–31, 64–67. Cf. Philip Foster, *Education and Social Change in*

Ghana (Chicago: University of Chicago Press, 1965), 190–99; and Dennis Austin, *Politics in Ghana* (London: Oxford University Press, 1964), 16.

12. Fred Agyemang, *Century with Boys: The Story of Middle Boarding Schools in Ghana, 1867–1967* (Accra: Waterville, 1967), 92. In 1930, 1,064 boys and 63 girls sat for the Standard VII certificate exam; only 278 boys (26.1 percent) and 16 girls (25.4 percent) passed. In 1933, 1,905 boys and 216 girls sat; 834 boys (43.8 percent) and 99 girls (45.8 percent) passed (figures in A. W. Cardinall, *The Gold Coast, 1931* [Accra: Government Printer, 1932], 190; and in *GCTJ* 6, no. 2 [1934]: 179).

13. Cf. the announcement for hiring sanitation officers, "candidates who have passed the 7th Standard, who are not more than 24 years of age and not less than 5 feet 7 inches in height need apply. All candidates must produce two testimonials as to character and will be medically examined before appointment," *Gold Coast Independent,* January 27, 1934. Thanks to Megan Bagdonas for this reference.

14. Claire Robertson, *Sharing the Same Bowl: A Socioeconomic History of Women and Class in Accra, Ghana* (Bloomington: Indiana University Press, 1984), 163. Following the Standard VII examination, girls could receive "Domestic Science Certificates" even if they had failed in arithmetic, composition, or reading (*GCTJ* 6, no. 2 [1934]: 179 n.).

15. Editorial, *Gold Coast Independent,* June 29, 1929.

16. "Marjorie Mensah," *TWA,* November 6, 1931; thanks to Robin Steele for this reference. For Mabel Dove, see La Ray Denzer, "Gender and Decolonization: A Study of Three Women in West African Public Life," in *People and Empires in African History,* ed. J. F. Ade Ajayi and J.D.Y. Peel (London: Longman, 1992), 217–36.

17. But see Karin Barber, ed., *Africa's Hidden Histories: Person, Text, and the Colonial State* (Bloomington: Indiana University Press, 2006).

18. *Gold Coast Times,* June 1, 1935; originally published in *West Africa,* April 20, 1935.

19. A. K. Boakye Yiadom, "Autobiography: My Own Life" (hereafter, "MOL"), 1:10, written like a diary, BYP; and W. K. Hancock, *Survey of British Commonwealth Affairs 1918–1939,* cited after D. K. Fieldhouse, *Merchant Capital and Economic Decolonization: The United Africa Company, 1929–1987* (Oxford: Clarendon, 1994), x; UAC, a subsidiary of Unilever, was formed in 1929 by the amalgamation of Niger Company and African & Eastern Trade Company (formerly Miller Bros. and F. & A. Swanzy).

20. A. K. Boakye Yiadom, "My Life History: The Autobiography of Akasease Kofi Boakye Yiadom" (hereafter, "Autobiography"), 3, BYP; and "MOL," 1:10–11. In 1933 nine Abetifi Boarding School students sat for the Standard VII certificate exam; all passed. Yet across the Gold Coast Colony, only 43.8 percent passed (*GCTJ* 6, no. 2 [1934]: 178). Cf. Nana Atta Boateng Daaku, born 1927, who worked as a cocoa broker upon receiving his Standard VII certificate in the late 1940s (Abetifi, December 30, 1992, and August 12, 1993).

21. Boakye Yiadom, "MOL," 1:11; cf. "The Plight of the African Mercantile Clerk," *Gold Coast Times,* June 1, 1935; and Timothy Burke, *Lifebuoy Men, Lux Women: Commodification, Consumption and Cleanliness in Modern Zimbabwe* (Durham, N.C.: Duke University Press, 1996).

22. Kofi Boakye Yiadom, Abetifi, August 28, 1994. The back of the card reads: "From Yiadom Boakye Catechist in Charge of the Presbyterian Church Konongo, Ash. Akim, 22.12.38—To His Beloved Younger Father, Mr. D. B. Bruce Preko, 'Kingsway Street', Abetifi, Kwahu." Then, in a different handwriting, "Received on Thu. 24.12.38, D. Y. Preko Bruce." The recipient lived in an impressive storied building erected by his

father, Yaw Bruce Preko, a trader. In Akan aesthetic, a head-to-shoulder portrait is not the preferred photograph; my interview partners usually selected full-body photographs, showing them from head to feet.

23. Micaela di Leonardo, "The Female World of Cards and Holidays: Women, Families, and the Work of Kinship," *Signs* 12, no. 3 (1984): 440–53. Decorating living spaces with flowers was not practiced in Kwawu towns or in other Akan settlements, with the exception of mission stations, colonial buildings, and homes of the educated elite; about the "absence" of flowers in Africa, see Jack Goody, *The Culture of Flowers* (Cambridge: Cambridge University Press, 1993), 11.

24. In a letter dated March 1, 1995, A. K. Boakye Yiadom recalled five names of diary-writing classmates. As elsewhere, the Gold Coast Press regularly published letters by its readers; cf. Nancy Hunt, "Letter-Writing, Nursing Men and Bicycles in the Belgian Congo: Notes toward the Social Identity of a Colonial Category," in *The Paths towards the Past*, ed. R. W. Harms et al. (Atlanta: African Studies Press, 1994), 187–210.

25. E. K. Addo, Abetifi, September 28, 1994. Although J.E.K. Aggrey (1875–1927), the first African assistant vice chancellor of Achimota College, died less than six months after its opening, he became a model figure for *akrakyefoɔ*, frequently evoked in conversation. Yet there is a paradox in Aggrey's legacy. While appropriated by colonial officials as the "prototype of the new industrially educated African," he symbolized for many Africans the achievements of higher education and "epitomized a wider African, even Pan-African, world." See Thomas Howard, "West Africa and the American South: Notes on James E. K. Aggrey and the Idea of a University for West Africa," *JAS*, 2, no. 4 (1975): 445–65; cf. Edwin Smith, *Aggrey of Africa: A Study in Black and White* (London: Student Christian Movement, 1929).

26. Both are titled "Book II," starting with June 23, 1932, day number 426; Addo must have begun Book I in early 1931. The following is based on the revised version, cited as Addo-Diaries. I am grateful to Kwabena Ofori Atta Addo for providing me access to his father's papers (AP). For the Pietist origins of the Presbyterian practice of diary writing, introduced by the Basel Mission, see Stephan Miescher, " 'My Own Life': A. K. Boakye Yiadom's Autobiography—Writing and Subjectivity of a Ghanaian Teacher-Catechist," in *Africa's Hidden Histories: Person, Text, and the Colonial State*, ed. K. Barber (Bloomington: Indiana University Press, 2006); for an example of a station diary by a teacher-catechist, see the one for Tafo, 1931–33, PCA, 10/4.

27. Addo-Diaries, November 8, 1934, September 6, 1932, and October 1, 1933.

28. Ibid., November 14, 1932, and December 23, 1933; cf. Kay, *Political Economy*, 338–39.

29. Addo recorded instructions, which he and another relative, Yaw Preko, received from Kwakye, "that we may act as servants or who [are] under authority. We accept it" (Addo-Diaries, May 8, 1934, and February 7 and 28, 1934). Providing capital and goods to female traders, shopkeepers were an important link in the "feminization of the marketplace." See Gracia Clark, *Onions Are My Husband: Survival and Accumulation by West African Market Women* (Chicago: University of Chicago Press, 1994), 318; cf. Jean Allman and Victoria Tashjian, *"I Will Not Eat Stone": A Women's History of Colonial Asante* (Portsmouth, N.H.: Heinemann, 2000), 13–18.

30. Addo-Diaries, November 10, 1934, and May 5, 1934.

31. E. K. Addo, Abetifi, November 24, 1994. A. J. Ocansey, who had founded the Palladium Cinema, Accra, opened the Mikado, Nsawam. The *Gold Coast Spectator,* January 23, 1932, reported: "The large audience which was composed of Europeans and

Africans was a select one. Dancing which followed the pictures until about 2 o'clock in the morning. 'Cpn' Kidd' the famous serial picture and a 'talkie' were the films shown on the occasion. Music was provided by Lamptey and his Orchestra." For Ocansey, see Catherine Cole, *Ghana Concert Theatre* (Bloomington: Indiana University Press, 2001), 72–74; for the emergence of boxing as a spectator sport, see Emmanuel Akyeampong, "Bukom and the Social History of Boxing in Accra: Warfare and Citizenship in Pre-colonial Ga Society," *IJAHS* 35, no. 1 (2002): 39–60.

32. Addo-Diaries, September 11, 1932, and February 19, 1933, as well as March 30–31, and April 8, 1934. For Mmofraturo, see Allman and Tashjian, *"I Will Not Eat Stone,"* 196–200.

33. Addo-Diaries, July 30, 1932, and July 3, 1932.

34. In Nsawam, Addo hosted the Abetifi teachers, Mr. Ntim and cousin I. O. Sampong (ibid., January 15, 1933, and October 26, 1934). For the Agogo visit, see ibid., April 6–7, 1933; cf. reports about "filthy drains" in Suhum or stray animals in Pepease, *Gold Cost Independent,* March 30 and May 19, 1935. For the Agogo hospital and girls' school, cf. Hermann Witschi, *Geschichte der Basler Mission, 1920–1940,* vol. 5 (Basel: Basileia Verlag, 1970), 315, 318.

35. Dated January 1, 1944, AP.

36. David Killingray, "Military and Labour Recruitment in the Gold Coast during the Second World War," *JAH* 23, no. 1 (1982): 84–85. Early in the twentieth century the army had assisted civilian authorities to uphold internal peace; with the increase of a police force, such military support became less urgent. Cf. Nancy Lawler, *Soldiers, Airmen, Spies, and Whisperers: The Gold Coast in World War II* (Athens: Ohio University Press, 2002), 25–38; and F. M. Bourret, *The Gold Coast: A Survey of the Gold Coast and British Togoland, 1919–1945* (Stanford, Calif.: Stanford University Press, 1949), 152–64.

37. Wendell Hollbrook, "Oral History and the Nascent Historiography for West Africa and World War II: A Focus on Ghana," *International Journal of Oral History* 3 (1982): 157. See Hollbrook's account of resistance against forced conscription in Konongo in late 1942 in "The Impact of the Second World War on the Gold Coast, 1939–1945" (Ph.D. dissertation, Princeton University, 1978), 205. Cf. Killingray, "Military and Labour Recruitment," 92–93.

38. Ɔkyeame Kwabena Asante, Pepease, November 27, 1994.

39. Ɔkyeame Asante, Pepease, August 27, 1993, October 29, 1994, and November 27, 1994. Cf. the recollections of other ex-servicemen who fought in the Far East (Nana Adamu Nyanko, Bepong, June 27, 1993, and Emmanuel Anim, Abetifi, June 29, 1993).

40. Boakye Yiadom, November 15, 1994, and August 28, 1994. Phyllis Martin reported about the "attraction" of uniforms, especially those of boy scouts ("Contesting Clothes in Colonial Brazzaville," *JAH* 35, no. 3 [1994]: 410).

41. Boakye Yiadom, November 15, 1994; and "MOL," 1:11. Killingray noted recruitment efforts that used modern media of mobile cinema showing newsreels and aircrafts dropping flyers ("Military and Labour Recruitment," 91); cf. Lawler, *Soldiers, Airmen, Spies, and Whisperers,* 56–65.

42. For the interrelations between literacy and orality, see Isabel Hofmeyr, *"We Spend Our Years as a Tale That Is Told": Oral Historical Narrative in a South African Chiefdom* (Portsmouth, N.H.: Heinemann, 1994); cf. Karin Barber, "Literacy, Improvisation, and the Public in Yoruba Popular Theatre," in *The Pressures of the Text,* ed. S. Brown (Birmingham, Centre of West African Studies, University of Birmingham, 1995),

6–27; and *The Generation of Plays: Yoruba Popular Life in Theater* (Bloomington: Indiana University Press, 2000), 310–11, 317–21.

43. Boakye Yiadom, November 15, 1994.

44. Basic training was extended from three to six months during wartime; see Anthony Clayton and David Killingray, *Khaki and Blue: Military and Police in British Colonial Africa* (Athens: Ohio University Center for International Studies, 1989), 179.

45. Boakye Yiadom, "Autobiography," 6; and "MOL," 1:12. According to Killingray, "there was a high rejection rate on medical grounds but when the army urgently required men it lowered the standard of health and height" ("Military and Labour Recruitment," 88). In the Eastern and Central Province, the rejection rate for recruits up to March–April 1941 was over 40 percent. Holbrook mentioned a rejection rate of 45 percent, and as high as 75 percent in some districts of the Eastern Province in 1941 ("Oral History," 159–60).

46. Gregory Mann, "Old Soldiers, Young Men: Masculinity, Islam, and Military Veterans in Late 1950s Soudan Français (Mali)," in *Men and Masculinities in Modern Africa*, ed. L. A. Lindsay and S. F. Miescher (Portsmouth, N.H.: Heinemann, 2003), 74.

47. Gold Coast, *Scheme for the Employment of Two Hundred Selected Ex-Servicemen as Teachers and for Their Subsequent Training in Teacher-Training Colleges (Colony and Ashanti)* (Accra: Government Printing Department, 1945); ex-servicemen who were not over twenty-six years of age and had a Standard VII certificate or a Cambridge School Certificate Examination were eligible to apply. In March 1948 Boakye Yiadom submitted his application; on May 21, 1948, the Education Department informed him that the resettlement scheme was closed, both in BYP.

48. Presbyterian Church of the Gold Coast to Boakye Yiadom, April 20, 1953; and Boakye Yiadom to Synod Clerk, Presbyterian Church, Abetifi, August 26, 2000, both in BYP.

49. Ankoma, April 27–28, 1993. The Gold Coast Police was established by the Police Ordinance of 1894, replacing the Gold Coast Constabulary. See W. H. Gillespie, *A History of the Gold Coast Police, 1844–1955* (Accra: Government Printer, 1955), 32; *The Gold Coast Handbook*, ed. John Maxwell (London: Crown Agents for the Colony, 1928), 154–56; and David Killingray, "Imagined Martial Communities: Recruiting for the Military and Police in Colonial Ghana, 1860–1960," in *Ethnicity in Ghana*, ed. C. Lentz and P. Nugent (London: Macmillan, 2000), 119–36.

50. Gillespie, *Gold Coast Police*, 62; cf. Ioné Acquah, *Accra Survey* (London: University of London Press, 1958), appendix.

51. Clayton and Killingray, *Khaki and Blue*, 15.

52. Ankoma, March 25, April 29, and April 30, 1993. Kwame Asiama died in 1992, at the age of one hundred; his funeral program is among Ankoma's papers. Cf. Clayton and Killingray, *Khaki and Blue*, 16.

53. Ankoma, April 29, 1993. The escort police was formed in 1902; the distinction between *literate* general police and *illiterate* escort police was suggested in 1919 and was fully implemented in the 1930s after gradually retiring all illiterate members of the general police (Gillespie, *Gold Coast Police*, 54, 61).

54. Maxwell, *Gold Coast Handbook*, 155.

55. Clayton and Killingray, *Khaki and Blue*, 15. Gillespie noted that the escort police division "quickly obtained the reputation it has never lost, being 'more attractive to the up-country native and has proved most reliable' " (*Gold Coast Police*, 35).

56. Ankoma, April 27–28, 1993.

57. For the legacy of Yaa Asantewaa, see A. Adu Boahen, *Yaa Asantewaa and the Asante-British War of 1900–1* (Accra: Sub-Saharan Publishers, 2003); and the special issue of *Ghana Studies* 3 (2000). Cf. Pashington Obeng, "Gendered Nationalism: Forms of Masculinity in Modern Asante of Ghana," in Lindsay and Miescher, eds., *Men and Masculinities in Modern Ghana,* 192–208.

58. Ankoma, April 27–28, 1993. Cf. the debate about opening the South African police force to women in Keith Shear, " 'Not Welfare or Uplift Work': White Women, Masculinity and Policing in South Africa," *Gender and History* 8, no. 3 (1996): 393–415.

59. During the peak years of 1942 and early 1943, as many as two hundred to three hundred planes of the U.S. Air Force stopped daily at Accra airport alone for checking and refueling on their way north and east; see Bourret, *Gold Coast,* 156. William Adamson, a former U.S. communication officer, provided a vivid account of his stay in Accra in the early 1940s (Newark, Delaware, December 26, 1995).

60. Ankoma, April 27–28, and April 29, 1993. In 1948 there were 120 European and 2 African gazetted officers; by 1960, these proportions were almost reversed (Clayton and Killingray, *Khaki and Blue,* 25).

61. Nana Ofori Atta declared in the Akyem Abuakwa State Council that *akrakyefoɔ* subscribed to newspapers and "distorted the news to their illiterate brethren to the detriment of the peace of the state"; see Jarle Simensen, "Rural Mass Action in the Context of Anti-Colonial Protest: The Asafo Movement of Akim Abuakwa, Ghana," *CJAS* 8, no. 1 (1974): 36. For Nana Ofori Atta, cf. Richard Rathbone, *Murder and Politics in Colonial Ghana* (New Haven, Conn.: Yale University Press, 1993).

62. Jarle Simensen, "Asafo Movement of Kwahu, Ghana: A Mass Movement for Local Reform under Colonial Rule," *IJAHS* 8, no. 3 (1975): 399–406; also see "Inquiry into Kwahu Native Affairs" by A.F.E. Fieldgate [Fieldgate Inquiry], August 17, 1932, NAG, CSO 21/22/11, particularly E. R. Addow (Kwame Mossi), "History of the Kwahu Asafo," appendix E. Cf. Addow's articles on Akan drumming, *GCTJ* 4, nos. 2–3 (1932): 99–102, 181–87; and *GCTJ* 5, no. 1 (1933): 39–44; also cf. A.E.A. Asiamah, *The Mass Factor in Rural Politics: The Case of the Asafo Revolution in Kwahu Political History* (Accra: Ghana Universities Press, 2000).

63. Richard Jeffries, *Class, Power and Ideology in Ghana: The Railwaymen of Sekondi* (Cambridge: Cambridge University Press, 1978), 33, 36.

64. Jeff Crisp, *The Story of an African Working Class: Ghanaian Miners' Struggle, 1870–1980* (London: Zed, 1984), 77. Cf. Frederick Cooper, *Decolonization and African Society: The Labor Question in French and British Africa* (Cambridge: Cambridge University Press, 1996), 248–60.

65. Jeffries, *Class, Power and Ideology,* 36.

66. In the High Court a "judgement was delivered in favor of Kwasi Nyarko, Nifahene of Kwawu." The following month Addo went again to Accra because of this case (Addo-Diaries, February 15, 1933, and March 22, 1933). Addo recalled witnessing this case (November 24, 1994).

67. Addo Diaries, March 26, 1934. The controversy rested on the powers granted to the governor not only to prevent the import of "seditious literature" like the Communist journal *Negro Worker* from North America but also "to make the possession of a [seditious] book, newspaper, or document a crime"; the latter seemed "really apprehensive" to Dr. Nanka-Bruce, Legislative Council member of Cape Coast; see Legislative Council debate of March 14, 1934, in extracts published in *Gold Coast Times,* November 17,

1934; and "Governor's Extraordinary Minute," *Gold Coast Times*, March 3–10, 1934. Cf. Newell, *Literary Culture in Colonial Ghana*, 93–94.

68. Addo-Diaries, September 30, 1934; and Addo, November 24, 1994. See Newell, *Literary Culture in Colonial Ghana*, 46–49; and Busia, *Position of the Chief*, 132–33.

69. Great Britain, Colonial Office, *Report of the [Nowell] Commission on the Marketing of West African Cocoa* (London: His Majesty's Stationery Office, 1938). Cf. Roger Southall, "Polarisation and Dependence in the Gold Coast Cocoa Trade, 1890–1938," *Transactions of the Historical Society of Ghana* 14, no. 1 (1975): 93–113; Gareth Austin, "Capitalist and Chiefs in the Cocoa Hold-ups in South Asante, 1927–1938," *IJAHS* 21, no. 1 (1988): 63–95; and Rod Alence, "The 1937–1938 Gold Coast Cocoa Crisis," *African Economic History* 19 (1991): 77–104. The hold-up had severe consequences for the Gold Coast government, since the colony received 100 percent of its revenue through indirect taxes, most of which came from custom duties; cocoa was the single most important export crop.

70. A. K. Boakye Yiadom, Abetifi, November 15, 1994.

71. Boakye Yiadom, "MOL," 1:11.

72. Boakye Yiadom, November 15, 1994. When explaining the expression "*ɔbarima pa*—a valiant man," he noted: "Sometimes, something has happened in this town that a *brave* man should go forward with a gun, or to do something, then we say *ɔyɛ ɔbarima pa*." For an exploration of silences in the "production of history," see David William Cohen, *The Combing of History* (Chicago: University of Chicago Press, 1994), 17, passim.

73. For a passionate argument about the relevance of subjectivity and subjective reality for the social historian, see Luisa Passerini, "Work Ideology and Consensus under Italian Fascism," *History Workshop* 8 (1979): 85–86.

74. For the aftermath of the riots in Kwawu, especially the looting of European firms in Nkawkaw, and various rumors about the looting of Kwawu stores in Koforidua, Nsawam, and Accra, see intelligence reports in NAG-K, ADM/KD 29/6/433, "Incidents in Kwahu, March 3–October 29, 1948"; and ADM/KD 29/6/432, "Civil Disturbances 1948 (Confidential)."

75. Watson Commission, 30–49, appendix 15, contains the Ex-Servicemen's Union petition. The arrested "big six" were J. B. Danquah, Kwame Nkrumah, E. Akuffo Addo, W. E. Ofori Atta, E. Ako Adjei, and Obetsebi Lamptey. Cf. Austin, *Politics in Ghana*, 73–92; and Emmanuel Akyeampong, *Drink, Power, and Cultural Change: A Social History of Alcohol in Ghana, c. 1800 to Recent Times* (Portsmouth, N.H.: Heinemann, 1996), 120–24. For press reporting, see the *Ashanti Pioneer*.

76. Watson Commission, 7–8.

77. Ankoma, April 29, 1993. One demonstrator shouted, "this is the last European Governor who will occupy the Castle," in hindsight a prophetic statement since Governor Creasy had only one successor before Ghana became a republic in 1960 (Watson Commission, 12). See Nkrumah's brief telegram to the secretary of state of the colonies with copies to the U.N. secretary general, the *New African*, the *New York Times*, and other newspapers, and Danquah's lengthy note to the secretary of state (Watson Commission, appendices 13, 14). Cf. Austin, *Politics in Ghana*, 75.

78. Boakye Yiadom, November 15, 1994; in the 1950s he was an active party worker, well documented in BYP. Staying with Ankoma in April 1993, we both read and discussed Nkrumah's autobiography.

79. Austin, *Politics in Ghana*, 70, 55.

80. Akyeampong, *Drink, Power, and Cultural Change*, 117, 123.

81. Hunt, *Colonial Lexicon*. Jeffries argued that clerical railway workers were "highly conscious of their superior status to the artisans, and therefore inclined to regard the 'rowdy', militant style of unionism of the latter as very much beneath them" (*Class, Power and Ideology*, 36).

82. Tribunal registrars, crucial brokers in the system of indirect rule, caused much concern among colonial officials who considered them "inefficient" and troublemakers; cf. SNA W.J.A. Jones, *Confidential: History of Legislation in Connection with Native Jurisdiction in the Gold Coast and Suggested Amendments to the Native Administration Ordinance, 1927* (Accra: Government Printer, 1931), 13, NAG-K, ADM/KD 29/6/11. Little work has been done on the tribunal registrar, but see Stephan Miescher, "Of Documents and Litigants: Disputes on Inheritance in Abetifi—a Town of Colonial Ghana," *Journal of Legal Pluralism and Unofficial Law* 39 (1997): 81–118.

83. Kimble, *Political History*, 119; and H.O.A. McWilliam and M. A. Kwamena-Poh, *The Development of Education in Ghana* (London: Longman, 1975), 59; cf. Wilhelm Stamm, Akropong, July 1929, BMA, D-4-3, 1. In 1930 there were 1,184 trained teachers, 1,162 men and 22 women; by 1940 these numbers had increased to 2,189 trained teachers, 1,911 men and 278 women. In comparison, there were 591 primary schools in 1930, 28 government schools, 312 assisted mission schools, and 251 (estimated) unassisted mission schools; in 1940 there were 931 primary schools, 23 government schools, 11 native authority schools, 433 assisted mission schools, and 464 nonassisted mission schools (Gold Coast, *Report of the Education Committee, 1937–1941* [Accra: Government Printer, 1942], 29, 31). Teachers in middle schools, secondary schools, and training colleges—all segregated by sex—were certified. Salaries of graduates from the Presbyterian Training College started at about six pounds per month (Stamm, "Finanzielle Grundlage der Kirche," Akropong, February 3, 1938, BMA D-11, 8).

84. Agyemang, *Century with Boys*, 69; Boakye Yiadom, "Autobiography," 4–5. Cf. the account by S. O. Boateng who taught for one year after receiving his Standard VII certificate, before looking for clerical employment (Abene, July 6, 1993, and July 20, 1993).

85. Sara Berry, *Fathers Work for Their Sons: Accumulation, Mobility and Class Formation in an Extended Yoruba Community* (Berkeley: University of California Press, 1985), 112. For village teachers as "strangers," their presence evoking "rivalry and strife," see Hunt, *Colonial Lexicon*, 101–104.

86. Great Britain, *Memorandum on the Education of African Communities* (London: His Majesty's Stationery Office, 1935), 2.

87. For articles on sanitation and hygiene, see W. M. Howells, "A Pit Latrine for Rural Schools," *GCTJ* 4, no. 3 (1932): 188–98; and "School Water Supplies and the Purification of Drinking Water," *GCTJ* 5, no. 2 (1933): 135–42; D.G.R. Herbert (Achimota College), "Hygiene: A Life to Be Lived," *GCTJ* 5, no. 3 (1933): 175–78; and the Deputy Director of Health Service, H. O'Hara May, "Cleanliness and the Prevention of Disease," *GCTJ* 5, no. 3 (1933): 202–206. For sports and village mobilization, see C. V. Moult, "Football," *GCTJ* 5, nos. 1, 3 (1933): 28–31, 171–74; and Department of Agriculture, "The Co-operative Societies Movement and the Problems of the Gold Coast Cacao Industry," *GCTJ* 5, no. 3 (1933): 158–64. Cf. David Patterson, *Health in Colonial Ghana: Disease, Medicine, and Socio-Economic Change, 1900–1955* (Waltham, Mass.: Crossroads, 1981).

88. F. A. Austin, "The Village School Teacher," *GCTJ* 28, no. 1 (1956): 19–20. Cf. Penelope Roberts, "The Village Schoolteacher in Ghana," in *Changing Social Structure in Ghana*, ed. J. Goody (London: International African Institute, 1975), 245–60.

89. Opusuo, Pepease, December 21, 1992. For school inspectors, see Agyemang, *Century with Boys*, 77.

90. Kwame Gyekye, *An Essay on African Philosophical Thought: The Akan Conceptual Scheme* (Cambridge: Cambridge University Press, 1987), 148–50.

91. Boakye Yiadom, "Autobiography," 5; and November 15, 1994. Teachers formed a close network of colleagues and friends; Boakye Yiadom kept a record of the career paths of his former teachers.

92. Gold Coast, *Education Committee*, 5–6. Cf. McWilliam and Kwamena-Poh, *Development of Education in Ghana*, 71, 83. St. Andrews was first located at Akropong and was then moved to Mampong, Asante, in 1951.

93. Note from St. Andrews' College, December 5, 1949, and report card, both in BYP; and an account of fund-raising in "MOL," 1:64–65, September 14 to November 2, 1950. While at St. Andrews, Boakye Yiadom and other scouts met Lady Baden-Powell in Accra; see "MOL," 1:62, April 21, 1950.

94. Oskar Tschudin, annual report 1954, BMA, D.11, 12. Cf. Tschudin, "Das Katechisten- und Evangelisten Seminar Abetifi," July 1952, BMA, D.11, 12; A. K. Boakye Yiadom, Abetifi, June 27, 1993; and "MOL," 1:79. The blazer is still in Boakye Yiadom's possession. Tschudin's wife described their work as missionaries at the Abetifi seminary during the 1950s (Rosmarie Tschudin-Gehr, Gelterkinden, September 17, 2001).

95. Rev. E.K.O. Asante, Abetifi, May 18, 1993.

96. E. F. Opusuo, Pepease, December 19, 1992, and April 2, 1993.

97. Great Britain, *Memorandum on the Education of African Communities*, 12.

98. E. F. Opusuo, Pepease, August 27, 1994. Cf. the accounts of other Akropong-trained teachers about difficulties with school inspectors: L. M. Date-Ba, Mamfe, January 20, 1993; and G. O. Reynolds, Mamfe, January 6, 1993.

99. Minutes by director of education to acting CS, October 10, 1934, NAG, CSO 18/3/13. First called Accra Assisted Schools Teachers' Union, in 1933, after expansion into the Colony and Ashanti, it was renamed simply Assisted Schools Teachers Union. Government-assisted schoolteachers often earned less than those in government schools and often had no pension; the press supported demands for the same treatment of mission and government teachers; see editorial in the *TWA*, October 10, 1932. Cf. McWilliam and Kwamena-Poh, *Development of Education in Ghana*, 59, 68.

100. Kofi Awoonor's, *This Earth, My Brother: An Allegorical Tale of Africa*. (Garden City, N.Y.: Doubleday, 1971), 48. The Gold Coast Teachers' Union was federated to the National Union of Teachers of England ("Confidential Minutes of the Central Advisory Committee on Education, Second Session 1950," para. 111, NAG-K, ADM/KD 29/6/564). Cf. resolutions of the 14th and 16th annual national conferences, Gold Coast Teachers Union, October 8–10, 1947; January 4–7, 1949, NAG-K, ADM/KD 29/6/224; and file "The Accra Youth Club," NAG, RG/3/1/281.

101. *Gold Coast Independent*, January 12, 1935; for a report on the first conference, see *Gold Coast Spectator*, September 8, 1934. Following Italy's invasion of Ethiopia, Basel Mission school inspector Eugen Haegele commented on an increasing "suspicion" toward Europeans among "educated Africans," particularly teachers, raising questions about unequal pay and the Sedition Bill (Abetifi, September 17, 1936, BMA, D-4-3, 3a).

102. Central Advisory Committee on Education, "Discussion of Manners and Discipline in Schools" (strictly confidential), June 1–2, 1949, NAG-K, ADM/KD 29/6/564. Cf. letters and newspaper clippings in "Anonymous Attacks on the Education Department," NAG, RG, 3/1/682, documenting an anticolonial sentiment, for example, "The Comedy of Colonial Education," *Gold Coast Evening News,* December 22, 1948.

103. Director of education to education officers (strictly confidential), May 9, 1949, NAG-K, ADM/KD 29/6/565.

104. Director of education, strictly confidential, August 15, 1949, NAG-K, ADM/KD 29/6/565.

105. Education Department, "Disciplines and Party Politics in Schools and the Position of Non-Government Teachers in Relation to Politics," October 10, 1949, NAG-K, ADM/KD 29/6/564.

106. Strictly confidential report sheet by education officer, Mpraeso district, submitted to senior DC Birim, Kibi, March 10, 1950, NAG-K, ADM/KD 29/6/564.

107. E. F. Opusuo, Pepease, April 2, 1993. Reverend Asante, Abetifi, May 18, 1993, recalled how he was reprimanded for not complying with the dress code by wearing long trousers instead of the compulsory shorts on a cold day in the mountainous Amanokurom, Akuapem, in 1935.

108. Cited after Fred Agyemang, *Amu—The African: A Study in Vision and Courage* (Accra: Asempa, 1988), 75. David Ghartey-Tagoe, former director of the Ghana Broadcasting System, mentioned the Amu case in a lecture at the University of Michigan, and further elaborated in a conversation on March 23, 1995; cf. Reverend Asante, May 18, 1993. For debates about clothing elsewhere, see Martin, "Contesting Clothes"; John Comaroff and Jean Comaroff, *Of Revelation and Revolution: The Dialectics of Modernity on a South African Frontier,* vol. 2 (Chicago: University of Chicago Press, 1997), 242–44; Hunt, *Colonial Lexicon,* 77–78; and *Clothing and Difference: Embodied Identities in Colonial and Post-Colonial Africa,* ed. Hilde Hendrickson (Durham, N.C.: Duke University Press, 1996).

109. Agyemang, *Amu,* 75.

110. Addo-Diaries, December 18, 1932.

111. Ibid., February, 18, 1933.

112. Kwame Kyeretwic (pseud. J. B. Danquah), "Vignettes of Coming Africans: 1. Mr. E. Amu of Peki," *TWA,* March 21, 1933. See *Gold Coast Independent,* March 18, 1933; *Gold Coast Spectator,* March 18, 1933; and *TWA,* March 14 and 21, 1933. The Palladium performance was on April 29, 1933; cf. Agyemang, *Amu,* 82–87.

113. Editorial, *TWA,* June 26, 1933.

114. Young Presbyterian, *TWA,* July 8, 1933.

115. Kwaku Okae, *TWA,* July 15, 1933.

116. J. Kwesi Ansah, *TWA,* July 14, 1933. Ansah's letter was also published by the *Gold Coast Independent* and triggered more debate (July 15 and 29, 1933). See concerns about the commitment of the Presbyterian Church to nationhood, editorialized by the *TWA,* July 7, 1933.

117. Letter to Synod Committee, July 18, 1933; cited in Agyemang, *Amu,* 88–90.

118. Hendrickson, *Clothing and Difference,* 8. For Epharim Amu's early publications, see his "How to Study African Rhythm," *GCTJ* 5, no. 3 (1933): 154–56; and *GCTJ* 6, no. 2 (1934): 121–25.

119. Rev. E.K.O. Asante, Abetifi, August 16, 1993.

120. Opusuo, Pepease, August 22, 1993; he repeated this story on December 21, 1992, and on April 2, 1993. Cf. Comaroff and Comaroff, *Of Revelation and Revolution,* 2:303–304.

121. Reverend Asante's collection of books is remarkable, ranging from the 1928 *Gold Coast Handbook;* J. B. Danquah, *Gold Coast: Akan Laws and Custom and the Akim Abuakwa Constitution* (London: Routledge, 1928); idem, *Cases in Akan Law* (London: Routledge, 1928); M. J. Field, *Search for Security: An Ethno-Psychiatric Study of Rural Ghana* (London: Faber and Faber, 1960); to Noel Smith, *The Presbyterian Church of Ghana, 1835–1960* (Accra: Ghana Universities Press, 1960), as well as books on theology and human sexuality (Reverend Asante, Abetifi, January 26, 1993, and May 18, 1993). For a history of reading in colonial Ghana, see Newell, *Literary Culture in Colonial Ghana.*

122. Boakye Yiadom, November 15, 1994; E. K. Nyame and Kwesi Pepera are Kwawu musicians in his collection of twenty-two records. For his reading habits, see Miescher, " 'My Own Life.' "

123. See Gold Coast, *Education Rules, 1933* (Accra: Government Printing Office, 1933).

124. Opusuo, March 24, 1993. Cf. Reverend Asante, February 2, 1993; May 18, 1993; and August 17, 1993.

125. Strictly confidential memorandum, "Bribery, Extortion and Misappropriation of Funds in Primary Schools," Education Department, January 15, 1951, NAG-K, ADM/KD 29/6/564. For earlier allegations of extortions by teachers, see confidential letter from Director of Education to provincial education officers and heads of (mission) educational units, March 14, 1946, NAG-K, ADM/KD 29/6/11.

126. Newell, *Literary Culture in Colonial Ghana,* 27–49; cf. Deborah Kallmann, "Projected Moralities, Engaged Anxieties: Northern Rhodesia's Reading Publics, 1953–1964," *IJAHS* 32, no. 1 (1999): 71–117.

5. THE MARRIAGES OF MEN

1. J. G. Christaller, *A Dictionary of the Asante and Fante Language, Called Tschi (Twi),* 2nd ed., rev. and enl. (Basel: Basel Evangelical Missionary Society, 1933), 558.

2. R. S. Rattray, *Religion and Art in Ashanti* (Oxford: Clarendon, 1927), 78. Cf. Edmond Perregaux, "Chez les Achanti," *Bulletin de la Société neuchâteloise de Géographie* 17 (1906): 116–25.

3. R. S. Rattray, *Ashanti Law and Constitution* (Oxford: Clarendon, 1929), 23–31. These included *adehye awadie* (marriage between a free man and a free woman), *afona awadie* (marriage between a free man and a female slave), *awowa awadie* (marriage between a free man and a female pawn), *ayete* (sororate; usually stool wives of a chief), *kuna awadie* (levirate), and *mpena awadie* (open concubinage).

4. Meyer Fortes, "Kinship and Marriage among the Ashanti," in *African Systems of Kinship and Marriage,* ed. A. Radcliffe-Brown and D. Forde (London: Oxford University Press, 1950), 278, 282; cf. idem, "Time and Social Structure: An Ashanti Case Study," in *Social Structure,* ed. M. Fortes (Oxford: Clarendon, 1949), 54–84.

5. T. E. Kyei, *Marriage and Divorce among the Asante: A Study Undertaken in the Course of the Ashanti Social Survey (1945),* Cambridge African Monograph 14 (Cambridge: African Studies Centre, 1992), 14–17, 26. The fate of Kyei's original manuscript, "Some Notes on Marriage and Divorce among the Ashantis," completed in the 1940s, sheds light on the relationship between a colonial anthropologist and his African research

assistant. Fortes considered Kyei's manuscript in a letter to T. E. Barton, director of education, "not suitable to publication by itself," since it needed "considerable additions and elaboration." Fortes added, "It will have to be published within the framework of the publications I am planning for setting out the results of the survey" (June 7, 1946). This correspondence and a copy of Kyei's manuscript are in NAG, RG, 3/1/304.

6. Jean Allman and Victoria Tashjian, "*I Will Not Eat Stone*": *A Women's History of Colonial Asante* (Portsmouth, N.H.: Heinemann, 2000), 53. Cf. Takyiwaa Manuh, "Changes in Marriage and Funeral Exchanges among the Asante: A Case Study from Kona, Afigya-Kwabre," in *Money Matters*, ed. J. Guyer (Portsmouth, N.H.: Heinemann, 1995), 190–92.

7. Eugene Addow, "Notes on Kwahu" (ca. 1927): 12–13, in R. S. Rattray Papers, ms. 102, Royal Anthropological Institute, London. Addow from Kubase, Abetifi, was a tribunal registrar, later an Asafo leader, known as Kwame Mossi (Rev. E.K.O. Asante, Abetifi, September 28 and 30, 1994). Cf. R. S. Rattray's brief publication on Kwawu, "The Mausoleum of 'Ampon Agyei," *Blackwood's Magazine* 223 (1928): 842–53.

8. Rattray, *Religion and Art*, 102; idem, *Ashanti Law*, 26; and idem, *Ashanti* (Oxford: Clarendon, 1923), 41–42. Cf. Kyei, *Marriage and Divorce*, 31. In a marital dispute the husband was forced to cover his senior wife's debt that occurred by her swearing an oath against him in a case of jealousy between the two wives; an expert had to testify about the "Kwabena Atia marriage laws." See *Afua Kisiwaah* v. *Kwasi Manuh*, Native Tribunal of Adɔntenhene, Abetifi, June 21–24, 1937, KTC, 2:280, 296–308. Cf. A. K. Boakye Yiadom, Abetifi, November 10, 1994.

9. Addow, "Notes," 13–15. An elderly informant of Kyei also suggested that the knocking fee was of Fante origin, introduced to Asante around 1900 (*Marriage and Divorce*, 27).

10. Addow, "Notes," 14–15. This festive meal is referred to by Kyei as *aduan-kesec*; God's sheep was presented to the father for "his souls and gods" who had guarded his daughter from childhood to maturity. Now, as a wife, she was under the spiritual protection of her husband, an aspect not mentioned by Addow. See Kyei, *Marriage and Divorce*, 31–32.

11. Addow, "Notes," 16. For an early report of *tiri sika*, see Perregaux, "Chez les Achanti," 116.

12. This is different from Kyei who notes that the return of *tiri nsa* marked the dissolution of the marriage (*Marriage and Divorce*, 30).

13. "New Asafo Laws" of 1917, Appendix D of "Inquiry into Kwawu Native Affairs, 1931–32," NAG, CSO, 21/22/11.

14. Sophy Osafo, "How Children Are Brought Up in Kwahu" (Thesis, Institute of Education, University College, Achimota, 1950–51), 47. Osafo uses the term "*aseda-sika*" (thanking money) (49). For *mpena-twee*, see Kyei, *Marriage and Divorce*, 14; for increase of Asante marriage payments because of higher cocoa prices after 1950, see Manuh, "Changes in Marriage," 193–94.

15. Wolf Bleek, *Marriage, Inheritance and Witchcraft: A Case Study of a Rural Ghanaian Family* (Leiden: Afrika Studiecentrum, 1975), 139, 152, first presented as a master's thesis, University of Ghana, 1972; cf. idem, "Marriage in Kwahu, Ghana," in *Law and Family in Africa*, ed. S. A. Roberts (The Hague: Mouton, 1977), 183–204.

16. Addow, "Notes," 17–18.

17. See K. O. Adinkrah, "Ghana's Marriage Ordinance: An Inquiry into a Legal Transplant for Social Change," *African Law Studies* 18 (1980): 1–42. According to the

Register General, in 1935 there were 399 Ordinance marriages out of a population of ca. 3.1 million; in 1967 there were 494 Ordinance marriages out of a population of ca. 6.7 million (cited after Dorothy Vellenga, "Who Is a Wife? Legal Expression of Heterosexual Conflicts in Ghana," in *Female and Male in West Africa*, ed. C. Oppong (London: Allen and Unwin, 1983), 153 n.

18. Cf. Stephan Miescher, "Of Documents and Litigants: Disputes on Inheritance in Abetifi—a Town of Colonial Ghana," *Journal of Legal Pluralism and Unofficial Law* 39 (1997): 81–119; and Roger Gocking, "Competing Systems of Inheritance before the British Courts of the Gold Coast Colony," *IJAHS* 23, no. 4 (1990): 601–18.

19. Allman and Tashjian, *"I Will Not Eat Stone,"* 54.

20. Ibid., 54, 46. Cf. Penelope Roberts, "The State and the Regulation of Marriage in Sefwi Wiaso (Ghana), 1900–1940," in *Women, State and Ideology*, ed. H. Afshar (London: Macmillan, 1987), 48–69.

21. Vellenga, "Who Is a Wife?" 145. For a fascinating discussion of these contested marriage ideologies in fiction writing, see Stephanie Newell, *Ghanaian Popular Fiction: "Thrilling Discoveries in Conjugal Life" and Other Tales* (Oxford: James Currey, 2000), 59–69.

22. The "overwhelming majority" of women studied by Allman and Tashjian "married outside the church"; most were not associated with a church prior to World War II. Allman and Tashjian did not explore governing bodies of churches that sought to redefine marriage; see *"I Will Not Eat Stone,"* xxxi.

23. Exceptions are Kenda Mutongi, " 'Dear Dolly's' Advice: Representations of Youth, Courtship, and Sexualities in Africa, 1960–1980," *IJAHS* 33, no. 1 (2000): 1–23; Lynn Thomas, *Politics of the Womb: Women, Reproduction, and the State in Twentieth-Century Kenya* (Berkeley: University of California Press, 2003); and, especially, Kyei, *Marriage and Divorce*, 19–25. Concerning the vast scholarship on African marriage, for Ghana see Kyei, *Marriage and Divorce*; Allman and Tashjian, *"I Will Not Eat Stone"*; and Christine Oppong, *Middle Class African Marriage: A Family Study of Ghanaian Senior Civil Servants* (London: Allen and Unwin, 1981). For elsewhere, cf. Barbara Cooper, *Marriage in Maradi: Gender and Culture in a Hausa Society in Niger, 1900–1989* (Portsmouth, N.H.: Heinemann, 1997); Diana Jeater, *Marriage, Perversion, and Power: The Construction of Moral Discourse in Southern Rhodesia, 1894–1930* (Oxford: Clarendon, 1993); Kristin Mann, *Marrying Well: Marriage, Status, and Social Change among the Educated Elite in Colonial Lagos* (Cambridge: Cambridge University Press, 1985); and *Transformations of African Marriage*, ed. David Parkin and David Nyamwaya (Manchester: Manchester University Press, 1987).

24. Okyeame Kwabena Asante, Pepease, August, 27,1993, with the assistance of Joseph Kwakye.

25. Kwaku Marfo, Pepease, September 8, 1993, with the assistance of Douglas Asomani.

26. Okyeame Asante, August 27, 1993. Cf. Kofi Ankoma, Obo, April 29, 1993.

27. Barrington Kaye, *Bringing Up Children in Ghana: An Impressionistic Survey* (London: Allen and Unwin, 1962), 125; cf. Kyei, *Marriage and Divorce*, 14.

28. J. A. Wahyee, Kwadwo Donkor, and E. V. Osei Addo, Abetifi, October 31, 1994, with the assistance of Joseph Kwakye. Kaye noted that mock marriages were "sometimes said to lead to sexual experimentation, or to actual intercourse." Those caught by parents were "severely punished, by being beaten, or by having red pepper rubbed on their genitals, or by both" (*Bringing Up Children in Ghana*, 125).

29. Wahyee, Donkor, and Osei Addo, October 31, 1994. Cf. spinning bees in German peasant villages where unmarried youth met for work, pleasures, and courtship; see Hans Medick, "Village Spinning Bees: Sexual Culture and Free Time among Rural Youth in Early Modern Germany," in *Interest and Emotion,* ed. H. Medick and D. W. Sabean (Cambridge: Cambridge University Press, 1984), 317–39.

30. Addow listed seventeen popular dances, among them *bontuku* ("Notes," 60–61).

31. J. A. Wahyee, Kwadwo Donkor, and E. V. Osei Addo, Abetifi, November 28, 1994, with the assistance of Joseph Kwakye, October 31, 1994.

32. Wahyee, Donkor, and Osei Addo, October 31, 1994. Akua Nimako, Abetifi, July 14, 1993, with the assistance of Joseph Kwakye, recalled her participation in a *bontuku* performance.

33. R. M. Boonzajer Flaes and Fred Gales, "Brass Bands in Ghana," typescript, University of Amsterdam, n.d., 23–24; thanks to Paul Jenkins for this citation. Boonzajer Flaes and Gales added, "Although no recordings were made of this music, the descriptions suggest a strong similarity with the earlier East African *Beni* and South African *Amalaita* forms of street music. *Konkomba* was short lived however, invented by a generation coming of age on the eve of the Second World War, and conveniently used by the British in Ghana to recruit soldiers." Cf. Terence Ranger, *Dance and Society in Eastern Africa, 1890–1970: The Beni Ngoma* (London: Heinemann, 1975).

34. Ɔkyeame Kwabena Asante, Pepease, October 29, 1994, and November 27, 1994, with the assistance of Kwame Fosu.

35. A. K. Boakye Yiadom, Abetifi, November 15, 1994; cf. Kwaku Marfo, Pepease, September 19, 1994, with the assistance of Douglas Asomani.

36. E. F. Opusuo, Pepease, August 27, 1994.

37. J. A. Wahyee, Abetifi, September 18, 1994, with the assistance of Joseph Kwakye. Kyei noted a "typical" courtship story by the drummer Kwaku M., who met his future wife at a "dancing place." Young, unmarried women arrived in groups of friends; Kwaku admired Afua "dancing gracefully in a ring among dancers." Late in the night, he "escorted her to the entrance of her house." Kwaku commented, "But we had to part. . . . There never was a longer night. I lay awake, haunted by the imagined presence of the nymph" (*Marriage and Divorce,* 19).

38. Wahyee, Donkor, Osei Addo, October 31, 1994. Cf. Karl Hartenstein, *Anibue: Die "Neue Zeit" auf der Goldküste und unsere Missionsaufgabe* (Stuttgart: Evangelischer Missionsverlag, 1932), 37.

39. Perregaux, "Chez les Achanti," 181–82. This stereotype of African male sexuality is widespread in colonial discourse, critiqued by Frantz Fanon, "For the majority of the white men the Negro represents the sexual instinct (in its raw state)" (*Black Skin, White Masks,* trans. C. L. Markmann [New York: Grove, 1967 (1952)], 177). For European hysteria of "black peril," see Elizabeth Schmidt, *Peasants, Traders, and Wives: Shona Women in the History of Zimbabwe, 1870–1939* (Portsmouth, N.H.: Heinemann, 1991), 169–73. African female sexuality became a "subject of distinct interest when it could no longer be contained by African men" (Megan Vaughan, *Curing Their Ills: Colonial Power and African Illness* [Stanford, Calif.: Stanford University Press, 1991], 21–22; and Schmidt, *Peasants, Traders, and Wives,* 100–101).

40. *JB* 93 (1908): 47. The Twi word *dɛ* (sweet) was often misunderstood in missionary writing, emphasizing solely its sensual connotations yet neglecting the notion of being pleasant, well-suited. A sweet tongue connotes eloquence; see Kwesi Yankah,

"Proverbs: The Aesthetics of Traditional Communication," *Research in African Literatures* 20, no. 3 (1989): 328.

41. CEP C. N. Curling to SNA, November 12, 1908, NAG, ADM 11/1/1445.

42. Curling, November 12, 1908, was concerned about Asafo companies challenging chiefs and the *Aberewa* cult; cf. Jarle Simensen, "The Asafo Movement of Kwahu, Ghana: A Mass Movement for Local Reform," *IJAHS* 8, no. 3 (1975): 383–406. Boonzajer Flaes and Gales mentioned the *osibi saba* dance ("Brass Band," 14). Allman and Tashjian have argued that adultery in Asante "was always about power and subordination: chiefs over commoners, Kumase over Asante's periphery, and husbands over wives" (*"I Will Not Eat Stone,"* 182). Yet while these conflicts consumed Asante from the 1920s on, in Kwawu they dominated tensions between commoners and chiefs over the first three decades of the twentieth century.

43. Wahyee, Donkor, and Osei Addo, November 28, 1994.

44. Emmanuel Akyeampong, *Drink, Power, and Cultural Change: A Social History of Alcohol in Ghana, c. 1800 to Recent Times* (Portsmouth, N.H.: Heinemann, 1996), 153.

45. Addow, "Notes," 16–17, 19.

46. Fortes, "Kinship and Marriage," 269; and Addow, "Notes," 13–14.

47. Phil Bartle, "Urban Migration and Rural Identity: An Ethnography of an Akan Community, Obo, Ghana" (Ph.D. dissertation, University of Ghana, 1978), 383–84. For female initiation, see Peter Sarpong, *Girls' Nubility Rites in Ashanti* (Accra: Ghana Publishing, 1977); Rattray, *Religion and Art*, 69–75; and Osafo, "How Children Are Brought Up in Kwahu," 40–43.

48. Bartle, "Urban Migration," 383–84. Cf. Bleek, *Marriage, Inheritance, and Witchcraft*, 168–72. In the absence of male initiation in precolonial Asante, Sarpong noted the custom marking adulthood, "which consisted in the presentation by the father of a cutlass, a gun, a tool, or an instrument of trade to a son who was mature enough to be able to marry." The father might also "inform the boy, that he had 'married for him,'" that is, had "a girl in mind for his son to marry, and the boy in turn usually complied with the father's wishes" (*Girls' Nubility*, 11). Cf. Kyei, *Marriage and Divorce*, 11.

49. Kofi Ankoma, Obo, April 29, 1993.

50. Okyeame Kwabena Asante, October 29, 1994.

51. Yaw Mensa (b. 1918), Nkwantanan, July 27, 1993, with the assistance of Abena Pearl Ofosu.

52. Marfo, September 8, 1993.

53. Okyeame Asante, November 27, 1994, October 19, 1994, and August 27, 1993. Wolf Bleek noted that the "rule" of a woman being married in Kwawu before first becoming pregnant is more often broken than observed; see his "Sexual Relationships and Birthcontrol in Ghana: A Case Study of a Rural Town" (Ph.D. dissertation, University of Amsterdam, 1976), 73.

54. See *Alfred Mensa v. Francis Cofie*, November 30, 1930, KTC, 1:192–208. Discussing this case, Rev. E.K.O. Asante confirmed the validity of this practice (Abetifi, May 18, 1993).

55. Okyeame Kwabena Asante, November 27, 1994. Most migrant cocoa farmers around Coaltar came from Akuapem; cf. Polly Hill, *The Migrant Cocoa-Farmers of Southern Ghana: A Study in Rural Capitalism* (Cambridge: Cambridge University Press, 1963), 199, 230.

56. Allman and Tashjian, *"I Will Not Eat Stone,"* 148–50.

57. "District Record Book, Mpraeso," 1:38, March 31, 1943, and June 30, 1943,

NAG, ADM 34/5/3; and the correspondence in "Kwawu State Unmarried Women Movement Control By-Laws," which includes a detailed letter by Akuamoa VI, Ɔman-hene of Kwawu, August 25, 1930, describing the practice of rounding up unmarried women and forcing them into marriage (NAG, CSO 21/22/229). In Agogo unmarried women were forced into marriage by the chief, as Gertrud Goetz reported (Semi-annual report of 1935, BMA, D-11, 3). Allman and Tashjian discuss a similar measure in Asante towns and villages, particularly Effiduasi, between 1929 and 1933 (*"I Will Not Eat Stone,"* 151–58); cf. Jean M. Allman, "Rounding Up Spinsters: Gender Chaos and Unmarried Women in Colonial Asante," *JAH* 37, no. 2 (1996): 195–214; and Roberts, "State and Regulation of Marriage," 61. African elders' concern about prostitution was not unique to Ghana; see Schmidt, *Peasants, Traders, and Wives,* 117.

58. Ɔkyeame Asante, November 27, 1994. For fathers and school fees, cf. Fortes, "Kinship and Marriage," 268.

59. Kofi Ankoma, Obo, April 28 and 29, 1993.

60. Kofi Ankoma, Obo, March 28, 1993. This eroticized life on the road is well expressed in Cameron Duodu's novel *The Gab Boys* (London: Deutsch, 1967), 102. The narrator mentioned not only the practice of buying bread for "girls" but elaborated on the effects of cigarettes: "Smoking does make you look like a man and the girls like somebody who acts like a man."

61. These proverbs are listed by J. G. Christaller, *Twi Mmebusɛm: Mpensa-Ahansia Mmoaano—A Collection of Three Thousand and Six Hundred Tshi Proverbs* (Basel: Basel Evangelical Missionary Society, 1879), as Nos. 294 and 167. For a slightly different translation, see Kofi Lange, *Three Thousand Six Hundred Ghanaian Proverbs (From the Asante and Fante Language)* (Lewiston, N.Y.: Edwin Mellen, 1990). Akan proverbs derive their meanings only through specific contexts; see Kwesi Yankah, *The Proverb in the Context of Akan Rhetoric: A Theory of Proverb Praxis* (Bern: Peter Lang, 1989).

62. According to Christaller's Christian ideology, *osigyafo* has a negative connotation; "an unmarried person . . . who is not in the state of regular marriage. As such a state with the natives is hardly ever one of abstinence, the word rather includes than excludes *irregular intercourse with the other sex*" (Christaller, *Dictionary,* 456; my emphasis).

63. Ɔkyeame Asante, October 29, 1994.

64. Ibid. In Twi divorce, *aware gyae,* is literally translated as "stop marrying" and can refer to the end of any sexual relationship.

65. Akua Nimako, Abetifi, April 8, 1993, with the assistance of Joseph Kwakye.

66. For the "sexual connotation of cooking" in Asante, see Gracia Clark, *Onions Are My Husband: Survival and Accumulation by West African Market Women* (Chicago: University of Chicago Press, 1994), 344–48; and Allman and Tashjian, *"I Will Not Eat Stone,"* 65–66. In Twi the same verb, *di,* is used for eating and having sex. The wife's preparation of her husband's food is a central obligation in marriage in many African societies; see Claire Robertson, *Sharing the Same Bowl: A Socioeconomic History of Women and Class in Accra, Ghana* (Bloomington: Indiana University Press, 1984), 184; and Karen Tranberg Hansen, "Cookstoves and Charcoal Braziers: Culinary Practice, Gender and Class in Zambia," in *African Encounters with Domesticity,* ed. K. T. Hansen (New Brunswick, N.J.: Rutgers University Press, 1992), 281.

67. Nimako, April 8, 1993. In Akan marriages it was rather unusual for co-wives to share one household; see Katharine Abu, "The Separateness of Spouses: Conjugal Resources in an Ashanti Town," in *Female and Male in West Africa,* ed. C. Oppong (London: Allen and Unwin, 1983), 160.

68. J.W.A. Amoo, "The Effect of Western Influence on Akan Marriage," *Africa* 16, no. 2 (1946): 229. Amoo's observation of the senior wife accompanying the new co-wife to the market "advising her what to buy and how much to spend" seems, at least in Nimako's account, too benign (231). Fortes was more aware of the "great jealousy" among co-wives ("Kinship and Marriage," 281); cf. Kyei, *Marriage and Divorce,* 62.

69. Nimako, April 8, 1993. See Bartle, "Urban Migration"; and Victoria Tashjian, "'It's Mine' and 'It's Ours' Are Not the Same Thing: A History of Marriage in Rural Asante, 1900–1957" (Ph.D. dissertation, Northwestern University, 1995), 120–25.

70. Nimako, April 8, 1993. Probably she referred to the attempted cocoa hold-up of 1934, which "was badly organized and never became fully effective"; low prices for cocoa continued through the mid-1930s, and producers suffered (Roger Southall, "Polarisation and Dependence in the Gold Coast Cocoa Trade, 1890–1938," *Transactions of the Historical Society of Ghana* 14 [1975]: 109).

71. See Allman and Tashjian, *"I Will Not Eat Stone,"* 61–65; and Dorothy Vellenga, "Matrilinity, Patrilinity and Class Formation among Women Cocoa Farmers in Two Rural Areas of Ghana," in *Women and Class in Africa,* ed. C. Robertson and I. Berger (New York: Holms and Meier, 1986), 62–77.

72. Nimako, April 8, 1993.

73. "District Record Book," 151–54, September 30, 1938, and September 30 and December 31, 1940, NAG, ADM 34/5/3. For Opoku Yao's work as tribunal registrar in Abetifi, cf. the above-mentioned case, *Afua Kisiwaah* v. *Kwasi Manuh.*

74. Nimako, April 8, 1993. For a description of the divorce procedure, see Addow, "Notes," 17; and Kyei, *Marriage and Divorce,* 64–69. Nimako did not mention whether she had to return all the *awaredeɛ* (gifts, cloths, etc., given by the husband) and the brideprice, *tiri sika.*

75. Nimako, July 14, 1993. His son Yao Annor (now Nana Annor Boama II, Aduanahene of Abetifi) recalled Opoku Yao's aspirations (Abetifi, January 1, April 3, and November 16, 1993). Opoku Yao's involvement with his own lineage is well documented in a case he brought to the DC, claiming £64, 21 from lineage members for medical and funeral expenses for the late Kwasi Asante, former *Kurontihene* of Aduamoa; Magistrate Court, Mpraeso, *M. J. Opoku Yao and Kwasi Addo* v. *Ɔkɔmfo Kwasi Anim et al.,* April 10, 1940, NAG, ADM 34/4/5.

76. Nimako, July 14, 1993, and April 8, 1993. Her expectations correspond to Addow's listing of a husband's obligations ("Notes," 16–17, 19). Cf. Kyei, *Marriage and Divorce,* 41; and Robertson, *Sharing the Same Bowl,* 182.

77. Nimako, April 8, 1993. For the "feminization of the marketplace," see Clark, *Onions Are My Husband,* 318, who noted for Asante that, "during the 1920s and 1930s, both fish and game sales gradually became female-identified." Men preferred cocoa farming which offered a higher income.

78. Tegare shrines were popular in Kwawu during the late 1940s and early 1950s. See confidential police reports of June 11 and December 15, 1944, about Nkwantanan and Abetifi, NAG-K, ADM/K 29/6/69; and J. A. Cowley, "The Tegare Fetish" (1949), RH, MSS. Afr. s. 1051.

79. Nimako, April 8, 1993; for the "multiform" of divorce in Kwawu, see Bleek, *Marriage, Inheritance, and Witchcraft,* 188; for the deteriorating conditions of cocoa, cf. Gwendolyn Mikell, *Cocoa and Chaos in Ghana* (New York: Paragon, 1989), 145.

80. Nimako, April 8, 1993. Upon Mensa's death, his brother and successor de-

manded the remaining money; less than a week later the brother was also dead, discouraging further claims.

81. Mikell, *Cocoa and Chaos*, 120.

82. Allman and Tashjian, *"I Will Not Eat Stone,"* 139.

83. Presbyterian Church of the Gold Coast, *Regulations Practice and Procedure*, revised 1929, 19, BMA, D-9.1c, 13d (hereafter, *Regulations*).

84. Cf. the exclusion for one year of Pastor Akoto's daughter, Rebecca, after she had given birth to a child out of wedlock. Since the child's father—E. V. Mamphey, a pastor's son—refused to marry her, he had to pay six pounds for maintenance and sixteen pounds in compensation ("Nkawkaw Chronicle," January 9, 1942, PCA 6/9). Another case of exclusion involved Charles Adame, for marrying a second wife; three years after divorcing the second wife, the session of Abetifi was not willing to reaccept him and decided to reconsider the case in one year ("Session Minute Book," Abetifi Presbyterian Church, November 4, 1963, APC).

85. Cases from the Abetifi Native Tribunal document this practice; see *Alfred Mensa* vs. *Francis Kofi*, November 18, 1930, KTC, 1:192–208. Cf. Rev. E.K.O. Asante, Abetifi, March 30, 1993; and Boakye Yiadom, November 15, 1994.

86. Amoo, "Akan Marriage," 228, reported that a man who "possesses" wives and children "in considerable numbers is acknowledged as rich and deserving respect." For conjugal expectations within marriage, see Rattray, *Religion and Art*, 76–87; Fortes, "Kinship and Marriage"; Tashjian, " 'It's Mine'," 194–230; and Allman and Tashjian, *"I Will Not Eat Stone,"* chaps. 2, 3.

87. *Salome Owusua* v. *Charles Gyeni*, Native Tribunal of the Adɔntenhene, Abetifi, August 26, 1936, KTC, 2:87–88, 95–125. Accusations of prostitution were frequent in the interwar period, an expression of a "gender chaos" (Allman and Tashjian, *"I Will Not Eat Stone,"* 150–61.

88. Wahyee, September 18, 1994; and Wahyee, Donkor, and Addo, October 31, 1994. Cf. Addow, "Notes," 13–16.

89. *Regulations*, 17.

90. The Marriage Ordinance No. 14, 1884, excluded the "customary family" from inheritance, causing much criticism by Gold Coast lawyers as undermining local "family" obligations (NAG 4/1/7). Because of this opposition, the Marriage Ordinance was amended, granting two-thirds of a deceased's estate, according to English law, to a man's wife and children, and one-third "in accordance with the provisions of the native customary law" (Marriage [Amendment] Ordinance, No. 2, 1909, sect. 15 NAG, 4/1/38). See Roger Gocking, *Facing Two Ways: Ghana Coastal Communities under Colonial Rule* (Lanham, Md.: University Press of America, 1999), 88–105; and "Systems of Inheritance," cf. Adinkrah, "Marriage Ordinance." For a fictional representation about the controversy among the coastal elite, serialized in 1880s newspapers, see Stephanie Newell, *Marita: or the Folly of Love. A Novel by A. Native* (Leiden: Brill, 2002).

91. See Rev. George R. Akwa, Asamankese, October 1917, reporting that "marriage under the Marriage Ordinance . . . is quite distasteful to many young men" (BMA D-3.8). Inspector Oettli noted the unpopularity of Ordinance marriage because of the restrictions placed on divorce (*JB* 103 [1918]: 34).

92. E. K. Addo, Abetifi, September 28, 1994, with the assistance of Kwame Fosu. In the early 1930s £70 was a huge sum of money; Boakye Yiadom, as an assistant weighing clerk, earned £18 per annum in 1938; salaries of teachers with four years of training started at £71 in government-assisted schools and at £48 in government schools;

cf. Gold Coast, *Report on the Education Committee, 1937–1941* (Accra: Government Printer, 1942), 16–17.

93. E. K. Addo, Abetifi, November 24, 1994. The marriage certificate is dated July 18, 1931 (AP). Cf. Tashjian's account of a customary marriage performed in "grand style," an indication of having achieved the "status of '*barima pa*', that is, a financially successful 'big man' " (" 'It's Mine'," 101).

94. *Regulations*, 18.

95. For the *ɔbirɛmpɔn* title in precolonial Asante, and the meaning of wealth, see T. C. McCaskie, *State and Society in Pre-Colonial Asante* (Cambridge: Cambridge University Press, 1995), 42–49, 275; and Ivor Wilks, *Forest of Gold: Essays on the Akan and the Kingdom of Asante* (Athens: Ohio University Press, 1993), 136–44.

96. Kristin Mann, "The Danger of Dependence: Christian Marriage among Elite Women in Lagos Colony, 1880–1915," *JAH* 24, no. 1 (1983): 46; and idem, *Marrying Well*. For postcolonial Ghana, cf. Oppong, *Middle Class African Marriage*, 65–72.

97. Wahyee, September 18, 1994; and Wahyee, Donkor, and Addo, November 28, 1994. For a similar pattern of decreasing dependence on lineage labor and children, replaced by northern wage laborers, in the Sunyani district, see Mikell, *Cocoa and Chaos*, 127, 129–30. For labor migration's impact in colonial Burkina Faso, cf. Elliot Skinner, "Labour Migration and Its Relation to Socio-cultural Change in Mossi Society," *Africa* 30, no. 4 (1960): 275–301; for swollen shoot disease, cf. Hill, *Migrant Cocoa Farmers*, 23–25.

98. E. K. Addo's Diaries, July 11, 1932, and December 23, 1934, AP.

99. Kwabena Ofori Atta Addo, Abetifi, August 20, 2000, and September 1, 2001.

100. Addo, September 28, 1994. Edna completed the Presbyterian senior primary school of Nsawam in 1947, Andrews the Abetifi boys' boarding school in September 1955 (AP).

101. Wahyee, September 18, 1994; his daughter, for example, was sponsored by her employer, a bank, to work and study abroad; one of his sons became a lawyer. For Kwawu migrations, see Stephan Miescher and Leslie Ashbaugh, "Been-to Visions: Transnational Linkages among a Ghanaian Dispersed Community in the Twentieth Century," *Ghana Studies* 2 (1999): 57–76.

102. E. K. Addo, Abetifi, July 21, and Accra, July 28, 1997; Edna Sampong, Seattle, January 11, 1998. For a discussion of Edna's migration, see Miescher and Ashbaugh, "Been-to Visions."

103. Letters to Addo by John E. Kwakye, London, August 20, 1961; and by Yaw Nathan Sampong, August 26, 1961, AP (Addo, November 24, 1994).

104. Andrews to Addo, London, September 17, 1962; cf. Andrews to Addo, London, March 5 and 31, 1962, and March 3, 1963, AP.

105. Kwame Fosu, Abetifi, September 28, 1994. For Ghanaians' international migrations, see Emmanuel Akyeampong, "Africans in the Diaspora: The Diaspora and Africa," *African Affairs* 99, no. 395 (2000): 204–13; Takyiwaa Manuh, " 'This Place Is Not Ghana': Gender and Rights Discourse among Ghanaian Men and Women in Toronto," *Ghana Studies* 2 (1999): 77–95; Gerrie ter Haar, *Halfway to Paradise: African Christians in Europe* (Cardiff: Cardiff Academic Press, 1998); and Margaret Peil, "Ghanaians Abroad," *African Affairs* 94, no. 376 (1995): 345–67.

106. Addo-Diaries, December 16, 1933. Two days later he left together with Asante, providing him with lorry fare to Nsawam. Cf. Rev. E.K.O. Asante, Abetifi, November 24, 1994.

107. Salome Kwakye to Addo, Keta, April 19, 1949, AP.

108. Addo, September 28, 1994, and November 24, 1994. Among I. O. Sampong's children, Paulina Sampong wrote about her school experiences at the Presbyterian Women's Training College, Agogo, asking for clothes, November 11, 1950; Hilda Sampong acknowledged a gift, April 19, 1951, as did the aforementioned Yaw Nathan Sampong, London, August 26, 1961, AP. I. O. Sampong, once a prominent teacher, is still widely remembered in Abetifi.

109. Addo, November 24, 1994. GNT stores replaced retail outlets of European companies under Nkrumah's nationalization policies; see Ofori Atta Addo, August 23, 2000.

110. Paulina Ago Acheampong, November 21, 1994; and Addo, November 24, 1994.

111. Paulina Ago Acheampong, Abetifi, September 1, 2001, with the assistance of Abena Pearl Ofosu. See also Ofori Atta Addo, August 20, 2000. Cf. Wambui Wa Karanja, " 'Outside Wives' and 'Inside Wives' in Nigeria: A Study of Changing Perceptions in Marriage," in *Transformations of African Marriage*, ed. D. Parkin and D. Nyamwaya (Manchester: Manchester University Press, 1987), 247–61.

112. *Regulations*, 19, 22.

113. Ibid., 18.

114. *Gold Coast Leader*, May 29, 1926. In nineteenth-century Europe, terms like "comradery," "comrade love," and "comradeship" were used as code words of sexual relations among men; "comrade" to name an intimate male friend. For the U.S. context, see Jonathan Katz, *Love Stories: Sex between Men before Homosexuality* (Chicago: University of Chicago Press, 2001), 152, 273.

115. E. F. Opusuo, Pepease, December 21, 1992, and August 22, 1993. Cf. Ankoma, April 29, 1993. See Bleek, "Sexual Relationships," 50, who did not find any evidence for sexual relations among men.

116. Great Britain, *Memorandum on the Education of African Communities* (London: HMSO, 1935), 12.

117. Hartenstein, *Anibue*, 107.

118. Rev. E.K.O. Asante, Abetifi, August 17, 1993.

119. Elizabeth Ntim, Abetifi, August 26, 1993, with the assistance of Abena Pearl Ofosu.

120. Adelaide Opong, Abetifi, April 14, 1993, with the assistance of Joseph Kwakye.

121. Felicia Asante, Abetifi, August 22, 2000, with the assistance of Abena Pearl Ofosu.

122. Reverend Asante, November 24, 1994. For the color symbolism in Kwawu, see Phil Bartle, "The Universe Has Three Souls: A Few Notes on Learning Akan Culture" (Leiden: Afrika Studiecentrum, 1980), 11, 30–31.

123. Carol Summers, *Colonial Lessons: Africans' Education in Southern Rhodesia, 1918–1940* (Portsmouth, N.H.: Heinemann, 2002), 181.

124. Opong, April 14, 1993.

125. Reverend Asante, Abetifi, September 7, 1994, and December 3, 1994.

126. Felicia Asante, August 22, 2000.

127. Ibid. Cf. Abu, "Separateness of Spouses," 166.

128. Helen Haegele-Schlatter (missionary wife of the resident school inspector) to Basel, Abetifi, March–April 1939; Haegele-Schlatter noted that Felicia Asante practiced

the "old custom" of seclusion for several weeks after giving birth (BMA, D-11, 10). See Felicia Asante, August 22, 2000, and Opong, April 14, 1993.

129. "Prospectus Presbyterian Girls Middle School Agogo," dated July 11, 1953, ASP.

130. Opong, April 14, 1993.

131. Oppong, *Middle Class African Marriage*, 90–93.

132. For example, *J. D. Ofori* vs. *S. W. Antwi*, October 1932, KTC, 1:329, 343–59. Hartenstein noted congregation members' strong sexual drives, "the sin of Africa" (*Anibue*, 66). Fighting unwanted "carnal desires" and practices of polygynous marriages was at the center of the missionary project, and complaints about "fallen scholars" and "immoral behavior" are persistent themes in their writing; see Inspector Oehler, *JB* 103 (1918): 34–35, or Rev. D. E. Akwa's reports about exclusions as a result of "adultery" and "fornication between a teacher and a school girl," Abetifi, February 15, 1916, and February 22, 1917, BMA, D-3, 6, 7.

133. E. F. Opusuo, Pepease, April 2, 1993, and August 27, 1994.

134. Amoo, "Akan Marriage," 228. Contraceptives began to arrive in Africa along with concerns about population increase and family planning in the postwar period. See Thomas, *Politics of the Womb*, 110–11; and Amy Kaler, *Running after Pills: Politics, Gender, and Contraception in Colonial Zimbabwe* (Portsmouth, N.H.: Heinemann, 2003). For Kwawu in the 1970s, see Bleek, "Sexual Relationships," 241, who argued that "birthcontrol is predominantly practised outside marriage, between lovers and partners in secret liaisons. It does not belong to the world of public morality and lawfulness."

135. Opusuo, August 27, 1994.

136. This is based on a perusal of advice columns in the *Daily Graphic and Sunday Mirror*, the *Evening News*, the *African Morning Post*, and the *Ashanti Pioneer*. Thanks to Colin Nickerson for help in this research. Cf. Gustav Jahoda, "Love, Marriage, and Social Change: Letters to the Advice Columns of a West African Newspaper," *Africa* 29, no. 2 (1959): 177–90; for more explicit sexual advice in the 1960s and 1970s in *Drum*, see Mutongi, " 'Dear Dolly's' Advice."

137. Hillary Hill, Family Planning Association, to J. Rettie, Regional Secretary, International Planned Parenthood Federation, Europe and Near East Region, January 30, 1966, Wellcome Institute for the History of Medicine, London, FPA/A10/8/Box 305. I am grateful to Lynn Thomas for this reference.

138. Opusuo, Pepease, April 2, 1993, and August 22, 1993.

139. Opusuo, August 22, 1993.

140. Opusuo, April 2, 1993. For Kwawu divorce practices, see Addow, "Notes," 17; cf. Kyei, *Marriage and Divorce*, 64–75.

141. See Karanja, "Outside Wives."

142. A. K. Boakye Yiadom, "My Life History: The Autobiography of Akasease Kofi Boakye Yiadom," n.d. (hereafter, "Autobiography"), 5, 7, BYP.

143. A. K. Boakye Yiadom, "Autobiography: My Own Life" (hereafter, "MOL"), BYP; and Boakye Yiadom, Abetifi, August 28, 1994, and November 15, 1994. Cf. Stephan Miescher, " 'My Own Life': A. K. Boakye Yiadom's Autobiography—Writing and Subjectivity of a Ghanaian Teacher-Catechist," in *Africa's Hidden Histories: Person, Text, and the Colonial State*, ed. K. Barber (Bloomington: Indiana University Press, 2006).

144. Boakye Yiadom, November 15, 1994.

145. A. K. Boakye Yiadom, Abetifi, June 27, 1993.

146. In April 1957 the oldest son, Yaw Obeng, challenged Boakye Yiadom's authority over a conflict with his younger sister. Boakye Yiadom "handed Obeng over to his relatives" and stopped paying school fees; a few days later the case was "amicably settled" by local elders and a teacher. In March 1963 Boakye Yiadom helped Obeng during a visit with ten pounds to purchase a " 'foot machine' for his tailoring work" as an apprentice at Nkawkaw and paid two pounds, ten shillings, for transport ("MOL," 1: 90–91, 118).

147. Boakye Yiadom, November 15, 1994. Cf. "MOL," 1:110.

148. Jean Allman, "Fathering, Mothering and Making Sense of *Ntamoba:* Reflections on the Economy of Child-Rearing in Colonial Asante," *Africa* 67, no. 2 (1997): 308.

149. Boakye Yiadom, June 27, 1993, and November 15, 1994.

150. Boakye Yiadom, June 27, 1993. Cf. "MOL," 1:14–15.

151. Boakye Yiadom, "MOL," 1:19. The birth took place "by the help of Mrs. D. Riggs, a famous well known Government Certificated Midwife" who charged twenty-three shillings for her services.

152. Boakye Yiadom, June 27, 1993; cf. *Regulations,* 19–20.

153. Boakye Yiadom, April 27, 1993.

154. Arthur Jehle's letters from Abetifi to his parents and to Basel Mission Inspector Oehler, written in 1906 and 1907, which documents his search for a suitable wife. Thanks to Manfred Jehle for giving me access to transcripts of his grandfather's correspondence. For a historical account of the *Missionsfrau,* see the biographical portrait of Rosina Widmann (1826–1909), in Waltraud Haas, *Erlitten und erstritten: Der Befreiungsweg von Frauen in der Basler Mission, 1816–1966* (Basel: Basileia Verlag, 1994), 82–93.

155. Boakye Yiadom, April 27, 1993.

156. Boakye Yiadom, "MOL," 1:112–13, and 2:10.

157. "MOL," 2:23, 56, 82–88, 108–109, 116, 119–22, 126–27, 142.

158. Boakye Yiadom, August 25, 2001.

159. Noel Smith, *The Presbyterian Church of Ghana, 1835–1960* (Accra: Ghana Universities Press, 1966), 173; and Gold Coast, *Accelerated Development Plan for Education, 1951* (Accra: Government Printer, 1951). Cf. Philip Foster, *Education and Social Change in Ghana* (Chicago: University of Chicago Press, 1965), 182–90.

160. Boakye Yiadom, November 15, 1994; and Opusuo, April 2, 1993, and August 22, 1993.

161. Letters by the solicitor of the Synod Clerk, Presbyterian Church, to Boakye Yiadom, June 15, 1971, "to quit the Mission House" at Amuana-Praso; and Boakye Yiadom's forceful reply, June 28, 1971, as well as other correspondence, BYP.

162. Allman and Tashjian, *"I Will Not Eat Stone,"* 70–78; cf. Manuh, "Changes in Marriage," 196; and Roberts, "State and Regulation of Marriage."

163. Abu, "Separateness of Spouses," 158.

164. Allman and Tashjian, *"I Will Not Eat Stone,"* 122–25.

165. Karanja, "Outside Wives."

166. See Alessandro Portelli, *The Death of Luigi Trastulli and Other Stories: Form and Meaning in Oral History* (Albany: State University of New York Press, 1991), 50. For an interpretation of Boakye Yiadom's oral and written recollections as different "narrative genres," see Stephan Miescher, "The Life Histories of Boakye Yiadom (Akasease Kofi of Abetifi, Kwawu): Exploring the Subjectivity and 'Voices' of a Teacher-Catechist

in Colonial Ghana," in *African Words, African Voices*, ed. L. White, S. F. Miescher, and D. W. Cohen (Bloomington: Indiana University Press, 2001), 165–66.

6. Speaking Sensibly

1. J. G. Christaller, *A Dictionary of the Asante and Fante Language, Called Tschi (Twi)*, 2nd ed., rev. and enl. (Basel: Basel Evangelical Missionary Society, 1933), 375.

2. Ɔkyeame Kwabena Asante, Pepease, October 29, 1994, with the assistance of Kwame Fosu.

3. Rev. E.K.O. Asante, Abetifi, May 18, 1993. Literally *animonyam* refers to the "splendour of the face," translated as "glory, spendour, brilliancy, excellency, celebrity, honour, dignity" (Christaller, *Dictionary*, 354).

4. J. B. Danquah, *The Akan Doctrine of God: A Fragment of Gold Coast Ethics and Religion* (London: Lutterworth, 1944), 121–22.

5. A. K. Boakye Yiadom, Abetifi, June 27, 1993.

6. E. F. Opusuo, Pepease, August 27, 1994, and August 21, 1993. Cf. T. E. Kyei, *Marriage and Divorce among the Asante: A Study Undertaken in the Course of the Ashanti Social Survey (1945)*, Cambridge African Monograph 14 (Cambridge: African Studies Centre, 1992), 141–43.

7. Phil Bartle, "Urban Migration and Rural Identity: An Ethnography of a Kwawu Community, Obo, Ghana" (Ph.D. dissertation, University of Ghana, 1978), 375–76.

8. Sjaak van der Geest, "Ɔpanyin: The Ideal of Elder in the Akan Culture of Ghana," *CJAS* 32, no. 3 (1998): 454–56.

9. Ibid., 490 n. See also Sjaak van der Geest, "The Elder and His Elbow: Twelve Interpretations of an Akan Proverb," *Research in African Literatures* 27, no. 3 (1996): 110–18; and "Money and Respect: The Changing Value of Old Age in Rural Ghana,"*Africa* 67, no. 4 (1997): 534–59.

10. Ɔkyeame Asante, October 29, 1994.

11. Arhin Brempong (Kwame Arhin) refers to the same notion of "going to consult *aberewa*" in his discussion of the *ɔhemaa* (queenmother), considered "wisdom personified." He notes that, as the *aberewa* of the town, "the *ɔhemaa* was the moral guardian of the females of the political community and a kind of moral censor: she examined adolescent girls before the main puberty rites which ushered them into adulthood and licensed their marriage" ("The Role of Nana Yaa Asantewaa in the 1900 Asante War of Resistance," *Ghana Studies* 3 [2000]: 106).

12. D. E. Akwa, Abetifi, August 12, 1916, BMA, D-3.7 (hereafter, Rev. Akwa Report). At the end Arthur Jehle, the senior missionary, commented, "interesting enough to be sent home to be used in publications." For the pattern of conversion stories, see Marcia Wright, *Strategies of Slaves and Women: Life Histories from East/Central Africa* (New York: Lynne Barber, 1993); and Edward Alpers, "The Story of Swema: Female Vulnerability in Nineteenth-Century East Africa," in *Women and Slavery in Africa*, ed. C. C. Robertson and M. A. Klein (Madison: University of Wisconsin Press, 1983), 185–219.

13. Rev. Akwa Report, 2, 5–6. For Atta's baptism, see Mrs. R. Werner-Niehans, Abetifi, June 16, 1878, BMA, D-1.30, 254, published in *HB* 51, no. 10 (1878): 75–76. Male congregation members, at least twenty years old, elected presbyters; see *Ordnung*

für die Evangelischen Gemeinden der Basler Mission auf der Goldküste, revidiert 1902, 11–14, BMA, D-9.1c, 13b (hereafter, *Gemeindeordnung*). Across colonial Africa, many converts had initially lived as domestic servants with missionaries; see Nancy Hunt, *A Colonial Lexicon of Birth Ritual, Medicalization, and Mobility in the Congo* (Durham, N.C.: Duke University Press, 1999); John Comaroff and Jean Comaroff, *Of Revelation and Revolution: The Dialectics of Modernity on a South African Frontier,* vol. 2 (Chicago: University of Chicago Press, 1997); and Elizabeth Schmidt, *Peasants, Traders and Wives: Shona Women in the History of Zimbabwe, 1870–1939* (Portsmouth, N.H.: Heinemann, 1992).

14. Rev. Akwa Report, 10–12, 18; DC H. J. Hobbs to CEP, October 10, 1911, about building a road between New Mankrong and Kwawu Tafo; Hobbs noted "merchants trading on Volta," like Mr. Phillips of Millers Ltd. who claimed that Kwawu people "would transport any tools for this road work from Akuse to Mankrong free of charge." On July 14, 1913, Hobbs added that "natives have promised if the aid suggested is granted they will give free labor towards the works" (NAG, ADM 1/11/298). J. Y. Atta is identified as the founder of Mankrong in J. R. Wallis, "The Kwahus: Their Connection with the Afram Plain," *Transactions of the Gold Coast and Togoland Historical Society* 1, no. 3 (1953): 23; and Peter Garlick, "The Development of Kwahu Business Enterprise in Ghana since 1874: An Essay in Recent Oral Tradition," *JAH* 8, no. 3 (1967): 469. According to Rev. E.K.O. Asante, Abetifi, August 17, 1993, only descendants of Abetifi Christians could farm in Amamma, the village founded by Atta.

15. Reverend Akwa commented, "His advices, and decisions are like prophecy; whatever he utters, it comes to pass" (Rev. Akwa Report, 12–13). His importance in politics is well documented: former Ɔmanhene Kwasi Diawuo reported that his uncle, J. Y. Atta, had helped negotiate his destoolment (Kwasi Diawuo to governor, Mangoase, March 21, 1916, NAG, ADM 11/1/1445). For middlers, see Hunt, *Colonial Lexicon;* and J.D.Y. Peel, *Religious Encounter and the Making of the Yoruba* (Bloomington: Indiana University Press, 2000).

16. Rev. Akwa Report, 14, 19–20. Expenses were amassed owing to the Kwawu-Kumawu (Agogo) land dispute and Kwasi Diawuo's installation as ɔmanhene. For Diawuo's enstoolment in 1909 and destoolment in 1915, see NAG, ADM 11/1/1445. For the Kwawu-Kumawu land dispute, see NAG, ADM 11/1/242; and Sara Berry, *Chiefs Know Their Boundaries: Essays on Property, Power, and the Past in Asante, 1896–1996* (Portsmouth, N.H.: Heinemann, 2001), 12, 173. For the 1905/06 Asafo crisis, see A.E.A. Asiamah, *The Mass Factor in Rural Politics: The Case of the Asafo Revolution in Kwahu Political History* (Accra: Ghana Universities Press, 2000), 115–28; cf. Jarle Simensen, "The Asafo Movement of Kwahu, Ghana: A Mass Movement for Local Reform under Colonial Rule," *IJAHS* 8, no. 3 (1975): 393–94.

17. Rev. Akwa Report, 14–15. For Basel Mission marriage rules, see *Gemeindeordnung,* 26–36.

18. Rev. Akwa Report, 15–16. Traveling Commissioner H. M. Hull to CS, August 22, 1898, reported from Kwawu, "Ata was *the* man whom all of Kwahu would have preferred. He is the senior presbyter at the Mission station, one of the best natives I have, & in every way well suited to be King. But he would not consent" (NAG, ADM, 11/1/1445).

19. Rev. Akwa Report, 16–18, 24. For Atta's nominations as ɔmanhene, see Edmond Perregaux, annual report, Abetifi, February 11, 1899, BMA D-1.69, 133; and

Otto Schimming, annual report, Abetifi, February 1906, BMA, D-1.84b. Cf. DC Francis Crowther to SNA, Abetifi, April 12, 1905, NAG, ADM, 11/1/1445.

20. J. A. Wahyee, Abetifi, August 25, 1993, with the assistance of Joseph Kwakye.

21. For example, by Reverend Asante, August 17, 1993. The Basel Mission's official history contains an account of J. Y. Atta rejecting the stool in 1898 and in 1905, Wilhelm Schlatter, *Geschichte der Basler Mission* (Basel: Missionsbuchhandlung, 1916), 3: 118, 120. Cf. Kofi Nkansa-Kyeremateng, *One Hundred Years of the Presbyterian Church in Kwahu* (Accra: Presbyterian Press, 1976), 12.

22. Wahyee, August 25, 1993.

23. See Christaller, *Dictionary*, 30; and Kwame Gyekye, *An Essay on African Philosophical Thought: The Akan Conceptual Scheme* (Cambridge: Cambridge University Press), 90.

24. In 1933 a member of the Presbyterian Church was enstooled as Omanhene Akuamoa Akyeampong; see CEP to SNA, March 3, 1933, NAG, CS0, 21/22/11. His Christian faith caused problems; see Government Agent (GA) Mpraeso's confidential report to GA Birim, April 2, 1953, NAG-K, ADM/KD 29/6/1053. Abetifi's first literate chief, educated at Presbyterian schools, was enstooled as Ohemen Amanfo II, *Adontenhene* of Kwawu, in 1957. Prior to his enstoolment he was a stool revenue collector; see Kwabena Ameyaw-Gyamfi, "The History of Abetifi," unpublished manuscript (n.d.), 42.

25. Luise White commented on the analytical possibilities of gossip, "A self is revealed in talking about others at least as much as it is revealed in introspection" (*Speaking with Vampires: Rumor and History in Colonial Africa* [Berkeley: University of California Press, 2000], 69).

26. Emmanuel Akyeampong, *Drink, Power, and Cultural Change: A Social History of Alcohol in Ghana, c. 1800 to Recent Times* (Portsmouth, N.H.: Heinemann, 1996), 157.

27. Bartle, "Urban Migration," 408.

28. For the investment patterns of Kwawu traders, see Garlick, "Development of Kwahu Business Enterprise," 479. Cf. the discussion on "sojourning" by Victoria Tashjian, " 'It's Mine' and 'It's Ours' Are Not the Same Thing: A History of Marriage in Rural Asante, 1900–1957" (Ph.D. thesis, Northwestern University, 1995), 104–28.

29. J. A. Wahyee, Abetifi, September 18, 1994, with the assistance of Joseph Kwakye.

30. The Presbyterian Church of the Gold Coast, *Regulations, Practice and Procedure*, rev. 1929, 3, BMA, D-9.1c, 13c (hereafter, *Regulations*). Cf. Wahyee, August 25, 1993.

31. J. A. Wahyee and Kwadwo Donkor, Abetifi, November 28, 1994, with the assistance of Joseph Kwakye. On behalf of Wahyee, an Abetifi headmaster wrote to E. K. Addo, "to do the best you can to arrange and bring by this week any number of iron sheets. . . . Half will go to the Senior Boys' and the other half to the Senior Girls!" (Abetifi, July 17, 1940, AP).

32. Rosmarie Tschudin-Gehr who worked with her husband at the Abetifi seminary in the 1950s, Sissach, September 17, 2001, and Paul Rutishauser, a "fraternal worker," during the 1960s, Kreuzlingen, August 2, 2001.

33. Session Minute Book, November 4, 1963, 12, APC (hereafter, Minute Book).

34. Ibid., December 28, 1964, 38.

35. Ibid., June 13, 1966, 68–69.

36. Beatrice Sabea asked for "reacceptance" after she ended her marriage with a married man. Following questions about her marital life, "J. A. Wahyee suggested that the session should not dive too much into her domestic affairs and to accept her. She was accepted with prayer and benediction by the Local Pastor" (Minute Book, November 21, 1966, 73–74).

37. Ibid., February 27, 1967, 81. On a different occasion, Wahyee "advised that the behaviour of the new Christians needs checking during announcement periods on Sunday. He alleged that they still rub shoulders with their heathen friends in manner things" (ibid., February 26, 1968, 100).

38. Ibid., December 26, 1967, 93.

39. Wahyee had cocoa farms first in Nkwantanan, then in Dwerebease (Abene), and finally close to Kwawu-Tafo; after losing the ones in Tafo, he became "discouraged" (J. A. Wahyee, Kwadwo Donkor, and E. V. Osei Addo, Abetifi, October 31, 1994, with the assistance of Joseph Kwakye). There were complaints about Wahyee's farming on church land: the session informed Paulina Anɔbea that "mission land" had been officially allotted to "Op. Wahyee & Sackey" who had paid a certain amount (Minute Book, May 28, 1968, 105–106). For the ups and downs of cocoa farming, see Seth La Anyane, *Ghana Agriculture: Its Economic Development from Early Times to the Middle of the Twentieth Century* (Oxford: Oxford University Press, 1963), 97–111, 172–75. Van der Geest learned from an informant that an ɔpanyin should no longer travel for business and stay elsewhere ("Ɔpanyin," 462).

40. Kofi Ankoma, Obo, April 27, 29, and 30, 1993. John Aglionby, bishop of Accra, provided assistance to acquire the necessary permit from the government to purchase a van.

41. Ankoma, April 27 and 29, 1993. Since the 1930s Swiss entrepreneurs established companies in Ghana: Accra Brewery in 1931; the construction company A. Lang, Ltd., in 1945; in addition to the older UTC (Union Trading Company, former Missions-Handlungs-Gesellschaft, then Basler Handels-Gesellschaft). By 1960 Swiss expatriates were Ghana's second-largest European community after the British; see René Lenzin, *"Afrika macht oder bricht einen Mann": Soziales Verhalten und politische Einschätzung einer Kolonialgesellschaft am Beispiel der Schweizer in Ghana (1945–1966)* (Basel: Basler Afrika Bibliographien, 1999), 115–49.

42. Kofi Ankoma, Obo, March 25, 1993, and June 1, 1993, and Kwame Asiamah's funeral program, Kofi Ankoma's papers. Cf. Philip Bartle, "Forty Days: The Akan Calendar," *Africa* 48, no. 1 (1978): 80–84.

43. Eugen Haegele, trained as a teacher and employed by the Basel Mission, was posted to Abetifi in 1934 to supervise Presbyterian schools in Kwawu and Asante. For Haegele and the expulsion of the Basel missionaries at the onset of World War II, see Hermann Witschi, *Geschichte der Basler Mission, 1920–40*, vol. 5 (Basel: Basileia Verlag, 1970), 334, 349–50. For Haegele's work see his report, Abetifi, September 17, 1936, BMA, D-4-3, 3a (and D-11, 4).

44. Rev. E.K.O. Asante, Abetifi, May 18, 1993; he narrated the same episode in another conversation, February 4, 1993.

45. Presbyterian rules encouraged married couples to have shared meals: "It would greatly help the growth of a full Christian family life if husbands and wives united in common family meals, although this has not been the custom of the country" (*Regulations*, 19). For other accounts of the Haegeles' deportation, see Alice Ofosuhemaa, Abe-

tifi, August 22, 2000; and Paulina Ago Acheampong, September 1, 2001, with the assistance of Pearl Ofosu.

46. Reverend Asante, May 18, 1993. Opanyin Okra became senior presbyter in 1916; for his influence, see Stephan Miescher, "Of Documents and Litigants: Disputes on Inheritance in Abetifi—a Town of Colonial Ghana," *Journal of Legal Pluralism and Unofficial Law*, 39 (1997): 102–108. Trinity College at Kumase, a joint project of the Presbyterian and Methodist churches, opened in 1943; cf. Noel Smith, *The Presbyterian Church of Ghana, 1835–1960* (Accra: Ghana Universities Press, 1966), 184; and F. L. Bartels, *The Roots of Ghana Methodism* (London: Cambridge University Press, 1965), 224–25.

47. E.K.O. Asante, "The Missionary Work of the Presbyterian Church in Northern Ghana," in *History of the Presbyterian Church in Northern Ghana*, ed. A. A. Berinyuu (Accra: Asempa, 1997), 40–41; cf. the chapter by Fritz Raaflaub, "Mission in Northern Ghana: A Basel Mission Perspective of How It All Began," 11–22. Thanks to Richard Haller for drawing my attention to this book.

48. Annegret Guggenbühl, "Einiges aus dem Durcheinander der Akropong Synode," April 17–24, 1948; and Richard Haller, October 1948, BMA, D-11, 10. The majority of delegates criticized the executive synod committee's acceptance of government plans to build the Presbyterian secondary school near Krobo-Odumase and not in politically tense Accra; young teachers also "rebelled" against the Presbyterian pension fund. Since teachers had become eligible for a state pension in 1946, they demanded return of their capital, now earmarked to cover retired pastors. The discussions were heated and tumultuous, during which two European missionaries resigned from the pension fund committee. For the crisis of 1948, cf. Dennis Austin, *Politics in Ghana, 1946–1960* (London: Oxford University Press, 1964), 70–85. After a visit to Europe, Josef Eichholzer (Basel Mission) wrote to Asante, "Your name is known all over Switzerland and southern Germany in our congregations" (letter of May 26, 1953, ASP). Cf. Smith, *Presbyterian Church*, 203.

49. Asante, "Missionary Work," 43. Rev. Wilhelm Stamm recognized that sending Reverend Rytz to Salaga prior to the arrival of an African missionary created some "anxiety" among "native co-workers," leading to the impression of securing Basel Mission control over this new mission field (confidential annual report, Abetifi, April 15, 1950, BMA D-11, 12).

50. Rev. E.K.O. Asante, Abetifi, September 5, 1994. He completed a three-month first-aid course at the Basel Mission hospital in Agogo as preparation; cf. "Instructions" from Synod Clerk Obeng to Reverend Asante for his work in Salaga, February 2, 1949; for the bicycle, see Otto Rytz to Reverend Asante, March 3, 1949, both in ASP. Also see "A Brief Report on the Mission of the Presbyterian Church in the Northern Territories. An Address by Rev. E.K.O. Asante to the Asante Presbytery at Nkwanta, 23rd August, 1949." A. K. Boakye Yiadom saved a copy of this address (BYP).

51. Cf. Hermann Witschi, "Bericht über den Aufenthalt auf der Goldküste und über die besonderen Fragen betr. Salaga und Dr. Neumann," Agogo, January 17, 1950, BMA, D-4-7, 5; Reverend Asante's note, October 1949, and program of formal opening of mission house in Salaga, December 11, 1950, ASP.

52. Reverend Asante to E. K. Addo, Salaga, March 3 and 23, 1949, AP; and his letter acknowledging receipt of 150 pounds (Reverend Asante to A. K. Addo, Salaga, April 25, 1949, AP). Reverend Asante's former teacher at the Abetifi Boarding School,

A. G. Sakyiama Amoako and wife, by now headmaster of Akropong School for the Blind, donated "five guineas" for buying "Bricks" (May 27, 1950, ASP).

53. "Tribute to the Late Rev. E.K.O. Asante by Mr. E. K. Addo (Sober House, Abetifi), Family Member," memorial brochure, June 1997, AP.

54. See the synod clerk's instructions to Reverend Asante about his appointment to Tamale, December 6, 1950, ASP. The annual licensing fee of the Tamale Urban Council for his bicycle was five shillings, receipt October 23, 1952, ASP.

55. Felicia Asante, Abetifi, August 22, 2000. Some congregation members disapproved of trading, particularly if it involved the pastor. Reverend Asante was asked to explain a slanderous accusation by an anonymous "Christian" that he was "most disinterested in Church Affairs," his "sole object" instead being "trading" (Synod clerk to Reverend Asante, May 19, 1952, ASP). See also Rev. E.K.O. Asante, "Tamale District II: The United Church-Tamale," in *History of the Presbyterian Church in Northern Ghana,* ed. A. A. Berinyuu (Accra: Asempa, 1997), 71–72.

56. Reverend Asante, "Rev. E.K.O. Asante—A Profile" (written after 1981; rev. 1994); letters from Presbyterian Moderator Reverend Asihene approving construction, June 5, 1953, and from Basel Mission secretary, Richard Haller, Kumase, July 29, 1953; all in ASP.

57. Rosmarie Tschudin-Gehr, September 17, 2001, was deeply impressed by the Asante home; vividly she recalled the meals and the clean kitchen of Felicia Asante, who also talked about the "many foreign visitors," August 22, 2000. Decades later the two women met again.

58. See Fritz Raaflaub, "Vierter Goldküstenbericht," Tamale, February 22, 1954, BMA, D-4-7, 5. In an interview Richard Haller, Basel Mission secretary in Kumase during the 1950s, addressed the political tensions about the northern expansion of the Presbyterian Church (Merlingen, September 14, 2001).

59. Fritz Raaflaub, "Fünfter Goldküstenbericht," Tamale, March 3, 1954, BMA, D-4-7, 5.

60. Fritz Raaflaub, "Neunter Goldküstenbericht," Accra, April 8, 1954, BMA, D-4-7, 5. See Lenzin's discussion in *"Afrika macht, oder bricht einen Mann,"* 92–113, about the changing direction of the Basel Mission work in postwar Ghana; many missionaries objected to the integration into the Presbyterian Church and experienced personal frustration at not being able to follow their evangelical calling. Some, for example, Rosmarie Tschudin-Gehr and her husband, were more willing to make this step (September 17, 2001).

61. Raaflaub, "Fünfter Goldküstenbericht"; and George Anafi to Reverend Asante, April 30, 1953, ASP. See also Asante's speech, "Brief Report," in which he sought to overcome negative stereotypes about the north, common among southerners.

62. Asante, "Tamale District," 74. Raaflaub noted that the Presbyterian Church made three appeals "undergirded by some special benefits" to find a candidate to the new pioneer station in Bolgatanga. In 1955, after the only volunteer had resigned before moving north, the synod committee appointed an expatriate missionary, Josef Eichholzer, who stayed on at his post for ten years. That same year the Presbyterian Church received new leadership, more willing to work with the Basel Mission. Prominent for the northern expansion among the new Presbyterian leaders was Synod Clerk Rev. A. L. Kwansa, whom Reverend Asante had replaced in Bekwai (both were classmates at Akropong). See Raaflaub, "Mission in Northern Ghana," 19; and Haller, September 14, 2001.

63. Asante, "A Profile"; and Nkansa-Kyeremateng, *One Hundred Years,* 22.

64. Garlick, "Development of Kwahu Business Enterprise"; and *African Traders and Economic Development in Ghana* (Oxford: Clarendon, 1971). For the impact of wealthy traders on Obo, see Bartle, "Urban Migration."

65. Kofi Nkansa-Kyeremateng, *The Story of Kwawu* (Accra: Presbyterian Press, 1990), 86.

66. Wahyee, September 18, 1994.

67. See the glossy funeral brochure, "In Honour of the Late Ebenezer Agyako Saka, 12th March 1912 to 20th August 2002." I am grateful to Georgina Saka-Siriboe for sending me a copy.

68. T. C. McCaskie, *State and Society in Pre-colonial Asante* (Cambridge: Cambridge University Press, 1995), 37–38. Cf. Ivor Wilks, *Forests of Gold: Essays on the Akan and the Kingdom of the Asante* (Athens: Ohio University Press, 1993), chap. 4; and Kwame Arhin, "Rank and Class among the Asante and Fante in the Nineteenth Century," *Africa* 53, no. 1 (1983): 2–22. For a fascinating account of the history of Yoruba big men, their position depending on reputation, see Karin Barber, *I Could Speak until Tomorrow: Oriki, Women and the Past in a Yoruba Town* (Washington, D.C.: Smithsonian Institution Press, 1991), 183–247.

69. Arhin, "Rank and Class," 4–5. For honoring *askiafoɔ* with the *ɔbirɛmpɔn* title, see McCaskie, *State and Society,* 42–47.

70. McCaskie, *State and Society,* 49.

71. Kwame Arhin defined *akonkofoɔ* as "an intermediary group between office holders and non-holders of office," and as "the earliest bearers of British culture as interpreted in the coastal towns." Following the British conquest of Kumase in 1900, *akonkofoɔ* distinguished themselves "by a distinctive manner of living, by a definite view of colonial rule as vector of 'progress,' and by a certain positive attitude towards Western-style education for their dependents." See Arhin, "A Note on the Asante Akonkofo: A Non-Literate Sub-Elite, 1900–1930," *Africa* 56, no. 1 (1986): 25, 28–29.

72. McCaskie, *State and Society,* 71–72; Kwame Arhin, "Some Asante Views of Colonial Rule: As Seen in the Controversy Relating to Death Duties," *Transactions of the Historical Society of Ghana* 15, no. 1 (1975): 63–84; and Ivor Wilks, *Asante in the Nineteenth Century: The Structure and Evolution of a Political Order* (Cambridge: Cambridge University Press, 1975), 697–717. For Kwawu, see Thomas Lewin, *Asante before the British: The Prepean Years, 1875–1900* (Lawrence: Regents Press of Kansas, 1978), 103–104.

73. Arhin, "Rank and Class," 13. The emerging class of Kwawu traders echoed social stratification along the coast with a delay of fifty years; see Garlick, "Development of Kwahu Business Enterprise," for interviews of some of these traders. Rev. E.K.O. Asante, Abetifi, November 24, 1994, identified J. E. Sampong's prominence among traders who established themselves on the coast, Sampong allegedly being the first to own a car.

74. E. K. Addo's diaries provide evidence of his dedication in attending funerals; see his visit to Abetifi for his aunt's funeral as reported in his diary, August 29–31, 1932, AP.

75. For example, female carriers received two shillings for each heap of sand, sawyers 150 pounds for two hundred Odum (a fine hardwood) scantlings; and two hundred drums of cement cost 275 pounds, transported by a lorry for fifty pounds (expense list for the twenty-six-month period, "Sober House No. 2, Built—1948," AP).

76. E. K. Addo, Abetifi, September 28, 1994, with the assistance of Kwame Fosu, and November 24, 1994. The arrangement of patrilineal inheritance was confirmed in a conversation with his son, Kwabena Ofori Atta Addo, Abetifi, August 20, 2000. An inheritance dispute about a house had recently occurred; see Native Tribunal of the *Adɔntenhene*, Abetifi, *Ɔkyeame Kwame Asong* v. *Kwaku Asong*, June 14, 1943, KTC, 4: 190–210. Cf. Miescher, "Of Documents and Litigants."

77. Nana Kwasi Mireku II, Obomeng, to E. K. Addo, August 10, 1949, AP. According to Addo's son, Mireku became very prosperous (Kwabena Ofori Atta Addo, Accra, August 23, 2000).

78. Headmaster, Aburi, Presbyterian infant junior school, to E. K. Addo, June 30, 1950, AP.

79. E. Boansi, Abetifi secondary school, to E. K. Addo, March 10, 1960, AP.

80. Kofi Nkansa-Kyeremateng (the historian) to E. K. Addo, Abetifi, December 27, 1983, AP.

81. E. K. Addo, Abetifi, November 24, 1994.

82. Richard Rathbone, "Businessman in Politics: Party Struggle in Ghana, 1949–1957," *Journal of Development Studies* 9, no. 3 (1973): 395.

83. K. A. Gbedemah, who once ran a timber and transport business, served in CPP cabinets as minister of health and labor, and then of finance. In 1961, asked by Nkrumah to resign, Gbedemah insisted on his innocence in parliament, criticized the increasingly repressive regime, and fled the country. See Austin, *Politics*, 155 n., 196 n., 251 n., 405–407. Gbedemah's own timber truck was not suitable to carry Nkrumah (Ofori Atta Addo, August 20, 2000).

84. Addo, November 24, 1994.

85. Kwame Nkrumah, *Ghana: The Autobiography of Kwame Nkrumah* (Edinburgh: Nelson, 1957), 135, and plate no. 14, the quote is the original caption; the same photograph hangs in the museum behind Nkrumah's mausoleum in Accra. E. K. Addo repeated the account, Accra, July 1997.

86. Ofori Atta Addo, August 20, 2000.

87. Ibid. Addo provided funds to keep the college in Abetifi, November 22 and 24, 1994.

88. Richard Rathbone, *Nkrumah and the Chiefs: The Politics of Chieftaincy in Ghana, 1951–1960* (Oxford: James Currey, 2000), 30.

89. See extract of an address delivered to the Joint Provincial Council at Dodowa by the acting chief regional officer, Colony, September 16, 1952, NAG-K, ERG 1/13/84. For the Kwawu North Local Council, see NAG-K, ERG 1/13/176; and for the Kwawu South Local Council, see NAG-K, ERG 1/13/83. Cf. Local Government (Gold Coast) Ordinance 29 of 1951.

90. See "Councillors of the Kwahu District Council" (ca. 1953), NAG-K, ERG 1/13/84.

91. GA to chief regional officer, September 17, 1952; and "Address on the Occasion of the Opening of the Kwahu District Council," September 26, 1952, NAG-K, ERG 1/13/84. See Oskar and Rosmarie Tschudin-Gehr, Abetifi, February 9, 1954, "5. Rundbrief," BMA, D-11, 12.

92. GA Mpraeso to GA Kibi, January 1, 1953. Addo signed a memorandum in support of E. I. Preko's appointment, March 30, 1953, NAG-K, ERG 1/13/84. Rosmarie Tschudin Gehr, September 17, 2001, recalled the heated political discussions at the Abe-

tifi seminary and a reluctance among local leaders of the Presbyterian Church to support the CPP.

93. The paramount stool dispute, too complex to fully present here, featured a pretender, supported by a coalition of Kwawu Youth Association, CPP, Abene elders, and three wing chiefs (*Benkum, Nifa,* and *Kyidom*), against Ɔmanhene Akuamoa Akyeampong who had backing of Abetifi, the Presbyterian Church, and businessman P. K. Anim Addo, his "chief supporter," who preferred "the Omanhene to reside in Abetifi rather than Abene." This question of residence was "a real bone of contention." See confidential reports, "Commission of Enquiry into Kwahu Paramountcy," GA Birim to Chief Regional Officer, March 30, 1953; and GA Mpraeso to GA Birim, April 2, 1953, in NAG-K, ADM/KD 29/6/1053. Nkrumah's representative, R. A. Ampadu, was sent to Kwawu to install the new ɔmanhene; see confidential police reports, W. A. Gbolonyo, Mpraeso, June 3 and 6, 1952, NAG-K, ADM/KD 29/6/941. Cf. files in "Kwahu Local Constitutional Affairs—General, 1952–1954," NAG-K, ERG 1/13/98. S. O. Boateng, Abene, October 11, 1994, narrated the Abene version of the conflict. For CPP strategies in chieftaincy disputes, see Rathbone, *Nkrumah and the Chiefs.*

94. Acting Regional Officer, Koforidua, John Duncan to Ministry of Local Government, November 13, 1953, and the latter's response, December 4, 1953, NAG-K, ERG 1/13/84.

95. GA I. E. Cochran to Regional Officer, April 20, 1955, NAG-K, ERG 1/13/127. The Kwawu North Local Council came close to gathering the estimated revenue of seven thousand pounds. After a commission of enquiry declared that Ɔmanhene Akuamoa Akyeampong was "in occupation of the Paramount Stool contrary to native law and custom" (*Gold Coast Gazette,* no. 1449, June 19, 1954), Akyeampong appealed to the Queen, with no success; see confidential report, Regional Officer to GA Mpraeso, October 6, 1955, NAG-K, ADM/KD 29/6/1053. Thus Boateng Akuamoa, enstooled de facto since 1952, was confirmed.

96. GA Mpraeso to Regional Officer, November 29, 1955, and March 3, 1956, NAG-K, ERG 1/13/127. The district council office now houses the Kwawu Traditional Council.

97. E. K. Addo, Abetifi, November 24 and 26, 1994. He saved receipts documenting the work on a public latrine (£4.10) in February 1955 and the post office, "£2191.9.8 plus communal labor," September 1958. Only a few records about the Kwawu North Local Council could be located; see GA quarterly report, December 31, 1955, detailing expenses on market sheds in Hwehwee and Abetifi (government loan of £1,200 and council funds of £100), NAG-K, ERG 1/13/135.

98. Addo, September 28, November 22 and 24, 1994.

99. E. K. Addo to M. D. P&T Corporation, April 6, 1994, AP.

100. Addo, November 26, 1994. Cf. Rev. E.K.O. Asante, Abetifi, December 1, 1994.

101. Koranteng Agyeman Fie to Ɔpanyin Kwame (Anane) Addo (= E. K. Addo), Abetifi, April 12, 1995, AP.

102. Addo, September 28, 1994.

103. E. K. Addo to author, Abetifi, September 9, 1995 (my emphasis).

104. Kwawu Traditional Council to E. K. Addo, February 17, 1998; and Felix Maafo to E. K. Addo, April 27, 1998, AP.

105. Addo, September 28, 1994. See Kwame Arhin, "Monetization and the Asante

State," in *Money Matters*, ed. J. Guyer (Portsmouth, N.H.: Heinemann, 1995), 97–110; and T. C. McCaskie, "Accumulation, Wealth and Belief in Asante History: II. The Twentieth Century," *Africa*, 56, no. 1 (1986): 3–23.

106. See J. A. Cowley, "The Tegare Fetish" (1949), RH, MSS. Afr. s. 1051; James Christensen, "The Tigari Cult of West Africa," *Papers of the Michigan Academy of Science, Arts and Letters* 39 (1954): 389–98; and Hans Debrunner, *Witchcraft in Ghana: A Study on the Belief in Destructive Witches and Its Effects on the Akan Tribes* (Accra: Presbyterian Book Depot, 1959), 106–108. Cf. T. C. McCaskie, "Anti-Witchcraft Cults in Asante: An Essay in the Social History of an African People," *HA* 8 (1981): 125–54; and M. J. Field, *Akim-Kotoku: An Oman of the Gold Coast* (London: Crown Agents, 1948), 171–97.

107. According to Cowley, Tegare was brought to Nkwantanan from Ypala, Ghana's Upper West Region, in 1938 ("Tegare," 2). During the 1940s the Nkwantanan shrine was popular, attracting large crowds every six weeks for Anwona. See Kwaku Marfo, Pepease, September 19, 1993, with the assistance of Douglas Asomani; and Ankoma, June 1, 1993. Cf. the confidential police report, "Tigare alias Gare Fetish," Nkawkaw, June 11, 1944, NAG-K, ADM/KD 29/6/69; Otto Rytz, "Halbjahresbericht," Kumase, August 6, 1943, BMA, D-4-3, 4; and Richard Haller, "Rundbrief," Abetifi, September 29, 1948, BMA, D-4-3, 5.

108. Nana Okyerɛ Ampadu II, *Kyidomhene* of Kwawu, and E. F. Opusuo, Pepease, August 29, 2000, with the assistance of Joseph Kwakye.

109. Kofi Ankoma explained that Gare was "very powerful" and only men were strong enough to hold it (June 1, 1993). Cf. Christensen, "Tigari Cult," 394. A rare example of a female Gare ɔbosomfo is Awo Yaa (Nana Afua Nsiah), whose shrine in Nsiakrom outside Konongo was popular in the late 1970s; see Kofi Appiah-Kubi, *Man Cures, God Heals: Religion and Medical Practice among the Akans of Ghana* (Totowa, N.J.: Allanheld, Osmun, 1981), 41–58.

110. See Ankoma, March 25, 1993; and Nana Okyerɛ Ampadu, August 29, 2000. Many Kwawu traders relied on Tegare when seeking commercial success; see Garlick, *African Traders*, 107–108.

111. Ɔkɔmfo Amma Yeboaa, Ɔkɔmfo Yaa Animwaa, and G. G. Y. Dovi, Pepease, August 10, 2000, with the assistance of Kwame Fosu.

112. E. F. Opusuo, Pepease, August 11, 2000, and the recollection of Yaw Dorsah (b. 1907) who emphasized the dangers of Tegare, Abetifi, August 25, 2000.

113. Otto Rytz, "Jahresbericht," Kumase, March 31, 1944, BMA, D-11, 11. Cf. the pamphlet published by the Christian Council of the Gold Coast, "Tigare or Christ" (Accra: Achimota College Press, 1947), BMA D-4-3, 5. Abetifi session records document the continued importance of Tegare; see cases November 20, 1967, 90, and December 26, 1968, 121, APC.

114. Ɔkyeame Asante, Pepease, August 27, 1993, with the assistance of Joseph Kwakye.

115. Ɔkyeame Asante, Pepease, November 27, 1994, with the assistance of Kwame Fosu, and August, 27, 1993. Rules of Tegare are included in Cowley, "Tegare," 17–20, and Christian Council, "Tigare: A Report Issued by the Christian Council of the Gold Coast" (1947), 2–3, BMA: Sch. 6562, 45.

116. Ɔkyeame Asante, October 29, 1994. For a description of *agorɔ*, see Cowley, "Tegare," 9.

117. According to the ɔmanhene, Kwasi Fofie attracted "upwards of 2000 people"

visiting the Anwona festival every six weeks (Quarterly Report, DC Mpraeso, September 30, 1946, NAG, ADM 32/1/135).

118. Nana Okyere Ampadu, August 29, 2000.

119. Ɔkɔmfo Amma Yeboaa et al., August 10, 2000. Haller, "Rundbrief," noted that Kwasi Fofie had "raised young priests" and sold them for "dear money," spreading the medicine across southern Ghana. The Christian Council, "Tigare," 4, mentioned prices of 300 to 600 pounds in order to acquire Gare. Cf. Cowley, "Tegare," 10.

120. E. F. Opusuo, Pepease, August 29, 2000.

121. Ɔkɔmfo Amma Yeboaa et al., August 10, 2000; Kwasi Agyei, Agya Kwadwo Amoa, Kwasi Dankyi, Kwasi Addae, and Ɔkyeame Kwabena Asante, Pepease, September 22, 1994, with the assistance of Kwame Fosu. Cf. Afua Afriyie and Kwaku Berko, Pepease, September 29, 1994, with the assistance of Kwame Fosu; and James Kwaku Aboagye, Tease, October 13, 1993, with the assistance of Kwame Fosu.

122. Kwasi Addae and G. G. Y. Dovi, Abetifi, August 11, 2000, with the assistance of Kwame Fosu.

123. James Kwaku Aboagye, October 13, 1993.

124. Ɔkɔmfo Amma Yeboaa et al., August 10, 2000. Cf. Debrunner, *Witchcraft in Ghana*, 130–31.

125. William Ofori Atta, "Must We Tolerate the Tigare Cult?" *Ashanti Pioneer*, June 13, 1947.

126. Otmar Auinger, SVD, Tease, October 12, 1993.

127. McCaskie, "Anti-Witchcraft Cults," 138. See the striking similarity between Kwasi Mawu and Awo Yaa, both Gare *abosomfoɔ* and cocoa farmers who provided Western education, electricity, and other modern amenities; see Appiah-Kubi, *Man Cures*, 42–44.

128. Afua Afriyie and Kwaku Berko, September 29, 2000.

129. Marfo, September 19, 1994. He also commented on *"Din pa yɛ sɛn ahonya"* (A good name is better than riches).

130. See Sjaak van der Geest, *"Yebisa Wo Fie:* Growing Old and Building a House in the Akan Culture of Ghana," *Journal of Cross-Cultural Gerontology* 13, no. 4 (1998): 333–59.

131. Rev. E.K.O. Asante, August 16, 1993.

132. E. F. Opusuo, Pepease, December 21, 1992.

133. Cf. the accounts about building houses by other Akropong-trained teachers, L. M. Date-Ba, Mamfe, January 23, 1993; and B. E. Ofori, Akropong, January 5, 1993.

134. The Department of Social Welfare and Housing, established in 1946, provided "social housing" in urban areas of colonial Ghana. See G. A. Atkins, "African Housing," *African Affairs* 49, no. 196 (1950): 230, 235.

135. For the absence of flowers in African cultures, see Jack Goody, *The Culture of Flowers* (Cambridge: Cambridge University Press, 1993), 11. This is only a brief discussion of architecture and the creation of homes by *akrakyefoɔ*, but see the "dialectics of domesticity," in Comaroff and Comaroff, *Of Revelation and Revolution*, 2:274–322; cf. Hunt, *Colonial Lexicon*, 117–58.

136. Ofori Anyinam, Pepease, May 2, 1993.

137. Boakye Yiadom recorded funeral expenses and other responsibilities toward his *abusua;* cf. Stephan Miescher, " 'My Own Life': A. K. Boakye Yiadom's Autobiography—Writing and Subjectivity of a Ghanaian Teacher-Catechist," in *Africa's Hidden Histories: Person, Text, and the Colonial State*, ed. K. Barber (Bloomington: Indiana University Press, 2006).

138. Boakye Yiadom, June 27, 1993.

139. We visited the site the day after his ninetieth birthday party, August 28, 2000.

140. Kofi Ankoma, Obo, June 1, 1993, considered it a good omen for the house project that both of us had the same names. His "Christian" name, only used at school, was Stephen; I was also born on a Friday, called Kofi in Kwawu.

141. Throughout Abetifi and other Kwawu towns, older buildings are associated with men and women who have passed away. Prominently in Abetifi's Christian Quarters are the Kru Memorial Villa, named after Elizabeth Kru, who died in 1925 and left behind funds to erect a building for her *abusua* on her behalf; the large building of the former *Ɔmanhene* Akyeampong, who died in 1971; and the house of trader Yaw Boateng, who passed away around 1990. Cf. van der Geest, *"Yebisa Wo Fie."*

142. On November 23, 1994, Reverend Asante and I visited his *abusua* home built by *wɔfa* Kwabena Adofo in Abetifi's old section. With pride, he showed improvements like additional rooms.

143. Interview with Reverend Asante, Abetifi, March 23, 1993. During a visit of a German-Ghanaian evaluation team, board chairman Reverend Asante and center manager Hubert Weinberg invited board member E. K. Addo as "Nkoanim Fekuo Representative" (business community) to attend the reception in honor of the guests, March 30, 1984, AP.

144. Reverend Asante, Abetifi, January 26, March 30, and May 18, 1993. As a boy he served his *wɔfa*, the Akwamuhene of Kwawu. His interest in Akan customs led him to purchase books by J. B. Danquah, M. J. Field, and others. In the 1990s elders at the Abetifi *ahenfie* directed foreign researchers, including myself, to Reverend Asante's house.

145. *Afahye*, when Kwawu subchiefs pay respect to the *ɔmanhene* in Abene, is the Kwawu version of the Akan *odwira* festival. Cf. Michelle Gilbert, "Aesthetic Strategies: Politics of Royal Ritual," *Africa* 64, no. 1 (1994): 99–125, who explored the relation between *odwira* and political conflicts in contemporary Akuapem; for *odwira* in precolonial Asante, see McCaskie, *State and Society*, 144–242.

146. Reverend Asante, September 27, 1994, provided a woolen blanket from Mali, bought in Tamale in the 1950s, to wrap the *Akwamuhene's* palanquin. Cf. *The Invention of Tradition*, ed. Eric Hobsbawm and Terence Ranger (Cambridge: Cambridge University Press, 1983).

147. Local Government Law (PNDC Law 207) of 1988. See Paul Nugent, *Big Men, Small Boys and Politics in Ghana: Power, Ideology and the Burden of History, 1982–1994* (London: Pinter, 1995), 177.

148. Richard Crook, "Four Years of the Ghana District Assemblies in Operation: Decentralization, Democratization, and Administrative Performance," *Public Administration and Development* 14 (1994): 358.

149. Maxwell Owusu, "Democracy and Africa: A View from the Village," *Journal of Modern African Studies* 30, no. 3 (1992): 391.

150. *Ghanaian Times*, July 11, 1992, cited after Owusu, "Democracy and Africa," 392.

151. E. F. Opusuo, Pepease, September 28, 1993. Opusuo's assessment is closer to Paul Nugent's who noted the PNDC government's attempts to decentralize *and* broaden its support by reaching to "the most influential power brokers at the community level" (*Big Men*, 205).

152. A district assembly candidate "shall present himself to the electorate as an individual, and shall not use any symbol associated with any political party." Political

parties "shall not endorse, sponsor, offer a platform to or in anyway campaign for or against a candidate seeking election to a District Assembly." See *Constitution of the Republic of Ghana, 1992* (Accra: Ghana Publishing, 1992), 153, chap. 20, para. 247–48.

153. E. F. Opusuo, Pepease, August 22, 1993.

154. E. F. Opusuo's letter to author, Pepease, March 20, 1996.

155. There is a great gender inbalance in these institutions: during the 1990s, in Ghana's Fourth Republic, only 8 percent of parliamentarians and less than 8 percent of district assembly members were women; see Mansah Prah, "Gender Issues in Ghanaian Tertiary Institutions: Women Academics and Administrators at Cape Coast University," *Ghana Studies* 5 (2002): 85.

156. See Bartle, "Urban Migration," 391–400. A family might decide to wear white in order to celebrate a long and successful life.

157. Arhin "Rank and Class," 9; cf. McCaskie, *State and Society,* 79.

158. T. E. Kyei, "Some Notes on Marriage and Divorce among Ashantis," n.d. (ca. 1945), 27, NAG, RG 3/1/304; this sentence is missing in the published version; cf. R. S. Rattray, *Religion and Art in Ashanti* (Oxford: Clarendon, 1927), chap. 14; and Meyer Fortes, "Kinship and Marriage among the Ashanti," in *African Systems of Kinship and Marriage,* ed. A. Radcliffe-Brown and D. Forde (London: Oxford University Press, 1950), 256; for other Akan societies, see J. B. Danquah, *Gold Coast: Akan Laws and Customs, and the Akim Abuakwa Constitution* (London: Routledge, 1928), 230–38; Field, *Akim-Kotoku,* 138–50; and Michelle Gilbert, "The Sudden Death of a Millionaire: Conversion and Consensus in a Ghanaian Kingdom," *Africa* 58, no. 3 (1988): 281–305. See also Kwame Appiah, *In My Father's House: Africa in the Philosophy of Culture* (New York: Oxford University Press, 1992), 181–92.

159. J. H. Nketia, *Funeral Dirges of the Akan People* (Accra: Achimota, 1955), 5.

160. Bartle, "Urban Migration," 392; and R. S. Rattray, *Ashanti Proverbs* (Oxford: Clarendon, 1916), 51.

161. Sjaak van der Geest, "Funerals for the Living: Conversations with Elderly People in Kwahu, Ghana," *ASR* 43, no. 3 (2000): 113.

162. I attended both, one in Pepease, August 6–9, 1993, and one in Tease, October 11–13, 1993. For classification of funerals, see Bartle, "Urban Migration," 393; and Field, *Akim-Kotoku,* 147–48. For the relation between honor and war in precolonial Asante, see Arhin, "Rank and Class," 13.

163. Listed in the printed program, "Order of Service for the Burial, Memorial & Thanksgiving Service for the Late Chief Kwadwo Donkor at the Abetifi Presbyterian Church," October 2, 1993 (hereafter, "Burial Service").

164. "Burial Service"; for the practice of elaborate appellations at Akan funerals, see Nketia, *Funeral Dirges,* 187, 30–38. For praise poetry of "big men," interpreted as a source of history, see Barber, *I Could Speak,* 183–247.

165. "Burial Service."

166. During the 1950s Ɔmanhene Akuamoa Akyeampong's Presbyterian faith, as well as his refusal to live in Abene and perform stool rites, were partially responsible for a constitutional crisis; see files in NAG-K, ADM/KD 29/6/941 and 1031, and ERG 1/13/98.

167. Additional funeral rites were performed forty days, eighty days, and one year after Donkor's death.

168. Wahyee, September 18, 1994.

169. E. K. Addo, Abetifi, November 22, 1994.

170. Kwame Arhin, "The Economic Implications of Transformations in Akan Funerals," *Africa* 64, no. 3 (1994): 308, 318.

171. Members of Christian churches usually select the white lace, whereas chiefs and those participating in local religious practices opt for Kente. In Kwawu towns, bars do most of their business during funeral weekends. See Arhin's account and his detailed list of expenses incurred during the funerals of his late mother and father in, respectively, 1989 and 1991, "Economic Implications," 314–16. Cf. Takyiwaa Manuh, "Changes in Marriage and Funeral Exchanges among the Asante: A Case Study from Kona, Afigya-Kwabre," in *Money Matters*, ed. J. Guyer (Portsmouth, N.H.: Heinemann, 1995), 188–201.

172. Rev. Akwa Report, 24–25.

173. E. K. Addo, November 22, 1994, and Kofi Boakye Yiadom, Abetifi, November 15, 1994.

174. Reverend Asante, January 26, 1993.

175. Akua Nimako commented on the near-nudity of these female dancers, while reminiscing about herself wearing only waist beads with a loin cloth as a young girl in the 1910s (Nimako Abetifi, July 14, 1993, with the assistance of Joseph Kwakye, who considered these dancers' outfits "quite daring").

176. Reverend Asante, January 26, 1993. Bartle noted that "occasionally" there might be a profit after a funeral: "Then it is expected that it would be kept for serving refreshments to latecomers and for the subsequent memorial services" ("Urban Migration," 398).

177. Arhin, "Economic Implications," 317.

178. Ɔpanyin Yaw Opoku Annor (Nana Annor Boama III), Abetifi, July 21, 1997. Arhin expressed skepticism about funeral deficits: "many people make a profit but officially announce debt because it is said to be customary to incur a debt to be paid by members of the lineage" ("Economic Implications," 320 n.).

179. E. K. Addo, November 22, 1994; cf. Boakye Yiadom, November 15, 1994, and E. F. Opusuo, Pepease, April 2, 1993. In the nineteenth century coffins for common people "were fashioned out of the great flat buttress roots of the silk cotton tree, *onyina*, freely obtained and purchased"; when a coffin was not used, the body was wrapped in mats (see Arhin, "Economic Implications," 312; and Rattray, *Religion and Art*, 159).

180. "Funeral Instructions of Me, Mr. Emmanuel Kwame Addo to the Elders and Head of My Family," November 7, 1996, AP.

181. Addo informed his renters, should they find him dead, to place his body on the bed, close the door, and call the pastor for some final prayer over his corpse. The next day he should be buried. Pearl Ofosu, July 22, 1997.

182. E. K. Addo, Abetifi, July 21, 1997.

183. E. K. Addo, Accra, July 28, 1997.

184. Ofori Atta Addo, August 20, 2000. The composer Ephraim Amu also requested that his relatives should not "hire an expensive bed; nor waste a fortune on his funeral." Yet, despite his wishes, he was granted a state funeral with special performances in Ghana's national theater. See Fred Agyemang, *Amu—the African: A Study in Vision and Courage* (Accra: Asempa, 1988), 186; and David Ghartey-Tagoe's report about Amu's funeral, Ann Arbor, March 23, 1995.

185. Kwame Gyekye, *Tradition and Modernity: Philosophical Reflections on the African*

Experience (New York: Oxford University Press, 1997), 51–52. Meyer Fortes noted, "Understandably, it is in funeral rites that the intersection of individual, self and personhood is most dramatically represented"; see Fortes, "The Concept of the Person among the Tallensi," in *La notion de personne in Afrique noire*, ed. G. Dieterlen (Paris: Éditions du Centre Nationale de la Recherche Scientifique, 1973), 303.

186. Addo had asked a carpenter to take his measurements and make a coffin out of *wawa* wood (the cheapest) to his size so there would be no extra space "to stuff it with expensive cloth," Ofori Atta Addo, August 20, 2000.

187. See "In Evergreen Memory of the Late Emmanuel Kwame Addo, 1904–1998" (AP); my emphasis.

188. For similar accounts of Addo's funeral, which cost twelve million cedis, see Ofori Atta Addo, August 20, 2000, and Abetifi, September 1, 2001, as well Abena Pearl Ofosu and Yaw Douglas Asomani, Abetifi, August 10, 2000. Cf. Addo's brother, Yaw Dorsah, September 2, 2000.

189. Reverend Asante, "A Profile."

190. Andreas Riis, founder of the first Basel Mission congregation on the Gold Coast in 1843, is remembered as *ɔsii adan* (he built houses); see C. C. Reindorf, *History of the Gold Coast and Asante* (Basel: Missionsbuchhandlung, 1895), 225. The topos of presenting service for the Presbyterian Church as a series of successfully completed building projects also appears in A. K. Boakye Yiadom, "My Life History: The Autobiography of Akasease Kofi Boakye Yiadom," BYP.

191. The *nsumankwaahene* is responsible for the royal *asuman* (charms, amulets, and talismans); Ɔpanyin Kwaku Marfo, Pepease, December 2, 1994.

192. Ɔkyeame Asante, November 27 and October 29, 1994.

193. Boakye Yiadom, "My Life History."

194. A. K. Boakye Yiadom, "Autobiography: My Own Life," 1:10–11, BYP.

195. Boakye Yiadom, June 27, 1993. For attempts to enter Trinity College, see letters September 13, 1963, and June 23, 1967; for petitioning field ordination, see letter to District Pastor, Japekrom, October 7, 1963, BYP. Additional petitions followed in the 1970s.

196. Boakye Yiadom's appeal was reported in *The Presbyterian* 1, no. 1 (1985): 1.

197. Boakye Yiadom to Synod Committee, May 2, 1994, BYP.

198. Presbyterian Church Konongo (asked by the synod clerk to decide the matter) to Boakye Yiadom, March 28, 1995, BYP. Boakye Yiadom appealed immediately on April 27, 1995, and then again petitioned the Synod Committee, December 28, 1995, July 29, 1996, and August 26, 2000, BYP.

199. BYP and A. K. Boakye Yiadom, Abetifi, July 23, 1997.

200. A. K. Boakye Yiadom, Abetifi, August 12, 2000.

201. Ofori Atta Addo, August 20, 2000, and September 1, 2001.

202. The Pepease *Akɔmfoɔhene* has been a woman for years: Ɔkɔmfo Yaa Animwaa, Pepease, June 4, 1993, with the assistance of Joe Acquah, and Ɔkɔmfo Yaa Animwaa and Ɔkɔmfo Amma Yeboaa, Pepease, November 3, 1994, with the assistance of Kwame Fosu. For big women, see Emmanuel Akyeampong, " 'Wo pe tam won pe ba' ('You like cloth but you don't want children'): Urbanization, Individualism and Gender Relations in Colonial Ghana, c. 1900–39," in *Africa's Urban Past*, ed. D. M. Anderson and R. Rathbone (Oxford: James Currey, 2000), 230; and Asante commodity queenmothers (commodity group leaders, like the yam queenmother as the leader of all yam sellers)

studied by Gracia Clark, *Onions Are My Husband: Survival and Accumulation by West African Market Women* (Chicago: University of Chicago Press, 1994), 248–82.

203. Jean Allman and Victoria Tashjian, *"I Will Not Eat Stone": A Women's History of Colonial Asante* (Portsmouth, N.H.: Heinemann, 2000), 20, 24; also see Takyiwaa Manuh, "The Asantehemaa's Court and Its Jurisdiction over Women," *Research Review* (New Series) 4, no. 2 (1988): 50–66.

204. Adelaide Opong, Abetifi, April 14, 1993, with the assistance of Joseph Kwakye, who served as presbyter in Abetifi.

205. See T. C. McCaskie, *Asante Identities: History and Modernity in an African Village, 1850–1950* (Edinburgh: Edinburgh University Press, 2000), 109.

206. GA Mpraeso to GA Birim in a confidential report, April 2, 1953, in NAG-K, ADM/KD 29/6/1053.

207. There is a larger story that I cannot explore here; in addition to archival material cited above, see the file documenting Akuamoa Akyeampong's second reign until 1967, NAG-K, ERG 1/13/139.

208. Barber, *I Could Speak,* 243.

209. McCaskie, "Accumulation, Wealth and Belief in Asante History II," 12.

210. Sjaak van der Geest, "Money and Respect," 355.

211. Gyekye, *Tradition and Modernity,* 59.

212. Van der Geest, "Funerals for the Living," 112. Cf. the conflict about the right to bury a Kenyan big man between his Luo patrilineage and his wife and children, in David William Cohen and E. S. Atieno Odhiambo, *Burying SM: The Politics of Knowledge and the Sociology of Power in Africa* (Portsmouth, N.H.: Heinemann, 1992).

EPILOGUE

1. R. W. Connell, *Masculinities* (Berkeley: University of California Press, 1995), 199–200; for a shift from the local to the global, see his "Masculinities and Globalisation," in *The Life of Brian: Masculinities, Sexualities, and Health in New Zealand,* ed. H. W. Worth, A. Paris, and L. Allen (Dunedin, New Zealand: University of Otago Press, 2002), 27–42.

2. Elisabeth Debrunner, who taught in Ghana from 1948 to 1972, commented in her annual report on the loss of respect for teachers, Agogo, January 16, 1972, BMA D-11, 15.

3. David Brokensha, *Social Change at Larteh, Ghana* (Oxford: Clarendon, 1966), 261.

4. T. C. McCaskie, *Asante Identities: History and Modernity in an African Village, 1850–1950* (Edinburgh: Edinburgh University Press, 2000), draws on unpublished material produced by Meyer Fortes's research assistants.

5. See the *AHR* forum, especially the contributions by Frederick Cooper, "Conflict and Connection: Rethinking Colonial African History," *AHR* 95, no. 5 (1994): 1516–45; and Gyan Prakash, "Subaltern Studies as Postcolonial Criticism," 1475–90; cf. Dipesh Chakrabarty, "Postcoloniality and the Artifice of History: Who Speaks for the 'Indian' Past?" *Representations* 37 (1992): 1–26.

6. But see Lisa Lindsay, *Working with Gender: Wage Labor and Social Change in Southwestern Nigeria* (Portsmouth, N.H.: Heinemann, 2003); and Nancy Hunt, *A Co-*

lonial Lexicon of Birth Ritual, Medicalization, and Mobility in the Congo (Durham, N.C.: Duke University Press, 1999).

POSTSCRIPT

1. Ɔpanyin J. A. Wahyee and Kwadwo Donkor, Abetifi, November 28, 1994, with the assistance of Joseph Kwakye.

2. Appellation of Ɔnyame, the supreme god.

3. Appellation of Tegare.

4. Ɔkyeame Kwabena Asante, Pepease, November 27, 1994, with the assistance of Kwame Fosu.

Bibliography

Interviews

All interviews were taped, except those that are marked with an asterisk, and were conducted either in English, Twi, or Swiss German. During most interviews in Twi, I was supported by a research assistant who helped in transcribing and translating the texts of the interviews.

Ghana

Abbas, Muhammed. Abetifi, April 10, 1993.*
Aboakye, James. Tease, October 10, 1993. With the assistance of Kwame Fosu.
Acheampong, Paulina Ago. Abetifi, November 21, 1994.*
————. Abetifi, September 1, 2001. With the assistance of Pearl A. Ofosu.
Adamu Nyanko, Nana. Bepong, June 27, 1993.
Addae, Kwasi, and G.G.Y. Dovi. Abetifi, August 11, 2000. With the assistance of Kwame Fosu.
Addo, E. K. Abetifi, September 28, 1994. With the assistance of Kwame Fosu.
————. Abetifi, November 22, 1994.*
————. Abetifi, November 24, 1994.
————. Abetifi, July 21, 1997.*
————. Accra, July 28, 1997.*
Addo, Kwabena Ofori Atta. Abetifi, August 20, 2000.*
————. Accra, August 23, 2000.*
————. Abetifi, September 1, 2001.
Addo, Kwadwo. Abetifi, July 3, 1993. With the assistance of Douglas Asomani.
Addo, Paulina. Abetifi, April 18, 1993. With the assistance of Douglas Asomani.
Afriyie, Afua, and Kwaku Berko. Pepease, September 29, 1994. With the assistance of Kwame Fosu.
Agyei, Kwasi, Agya Kwadwo Amoa, Kwasi Dankyi, Kwasi Addae, and Ɔkyeame Kwabena Asante. Pepease, September 22, 1994. With the assistance of Kwame Fosu.
Ako-Addo, Rev. Akropong, January 21, 1993.
Anim, Yaw Emmanuel. Abetifi, June 29, 1993. With the assistance of Douglas Asomani.
Animwaa, Ɔkɔmfo Yaa. Pepease, June 4, 1993. With the assistance of Joe Acquah.
Animwaa, Ɔkɔmfo Yaa, and Ɔkɔmfo Amma Yeboaa. Pepease, November 3, 1994. With the assistance of Kwame Fosu.
Ankoma, Kofi. Obo, March 4, 1993.
————. Obo, March 25, 1993.

Bibliography

———. Obo, March 28, 1993.*
———. Obo, April 27–28, 1993.
———. Obo, April 29, 1993.
———. Obo, April 30, 1993.*
———. Obo, May 25, 1993.
———. Obo, June 1, 1993.
———. Obo, November 24, 1993.
———. Obo, August 23, 1994.
———. Obo, September 30, 1994.
Annoa, Yaa. Abetifi, April 17, 1993. With the assistance of Douglas Asomani.
Annor, Yao Edward Opoku. Abetifi, January 1, 1993.
———. Abetifi, April 3, 1993.
———. Abetifi, November 16, 1993.
———. Abetifi, July 21, 1997.*
Annor, Yao Edward Opoku (Nana Annor Boamah III). Abetifi, September 2, 2001.
Anɔbea, Ɔkɔmfo Adwoa. Abetifi, April 24, 1993. With the assistance of Joseph
      Kwakye.
———. Abetifi, July 5, 1993. With the assistance of Joseph Kwakye.
Asante, Rev. E.K.O. Abetifi, January 19, 1993.*
———. Abetifi, January 26, 1993.
———. Abetifi, February 2, 1993.
———. Abetifi, March 30, 1993.
———. Abetifi, May 18, 1993.
———. Abetifi, June 7, 1993.
———. Abetifi, August 16, 1993.
———. Abetifi, September 27, 1994.
———. Abetifi, September 28, 1994.*
———. Abetifi, September 30, 1994.
———. Abetifi, October 18, 1994.*
———. Abetifi, October 21, 1994.*
———. Abetifi, November 23, 1994.*
———. Abetifi, November 24, 1994.*
———. Abetifi, December 3, 1994.*
Asante, Felicia. Abetifi, August 22, 2000. With the assistance of Pearl A. Ofosu.
Asante, Ɔkyeame Kwabena. Pepease, August 27, 1993. With the assistance of Joseph
      Kwakye.
———. Pepease, October 29, 1994. With the assistance of Kwame Fosu.
———. Pepease, November 27, 1994. With the assistance of Kwame Fosu.
Auinger, Otmar, SVD. Tease, October 12, 1993.
Boateng, S. O. Abene, July 6, 1993.
———. Abene, July 20, 1993.
———. Abene, October 11, 1994.*
Daaku, Nana Atta. Abetifi, December 30, 1992.
———. Abetifi, August 10, 1993.*
———. Abetifi, August 12, 1993.
Date-Ba, L. M. Mamfe, January 20, 1993.
———. Mamfe, January 21, 1993.
———. Mamfe, September 19, 1993.
Debra, Gilbert F. Abetifi, April 13, 1993.

Dorsah, Yaw. Abetifi, August 25, 2000. With the assistance of Joseph Kwakye.
———. Abetifi, September 2, 2000. With the assistance of Joseph Kwakye.
Marfo, Opanyin Kwaku. Pepease, August 5, 1993. With the assistance of Douglas Asomani.
———. Pepease, September 15, 1993. With the assistance of Douglas Asomani.
———. Pepease, September 19, 1994. With the assistance of Douglas Asomani.
———. Pepease, December 2, 1994.*
Mensa, Yaw. Nkwantanan, July 27, 1993. With the assistance of Pearl A. Ofosu.
Nimako, Akua. Abetifi, April 8, 1993. With the assistance of Joseph Kwakye.
———. Abetifi, July 14, 1993. With the assistance of Joseph Kwakye.
Ntim, Elizabeth. Abetifi, August 26, 1993. With the assistance of Pearl A. Ofosu.
Ofori Anyinam. Pepease, May 5, 1993.
Ofori, Benjamin E. Akropong, January 5, 1993.
———. Akropong, October 31, 1993.
Ofosu, A. K., *Adehyeehene* of Abene, and *mpanyinfoo* (elders). Abene, June 15, 1993.
    With the assistance of Yaw Tweneboa.
Ofosu, Pearl A. Abetifi, July 22, 1997.*
Ofosu, Pearl A., and Douglas Asomani. Abetifi, August 10, 2000.*
Ofosuhemaa, Alice. Abetifi, August 22, 2000. With the assistance of Pearl A. Ofosu.
Okyere Ampadu II, *Kyidomhene* of Kwawu, and E. F. Opusuo. Pepease, September 12,
    1994. With the assistance of Kwame Fosu.
———. Pepease, August 29, 2000. With the assistance of Joseph Kwakye.
Opong, Adelaide Saka. Abetifi, April 14, 1993. With the assistance of Joseph Kwakye.
Opusuo, Emmanuel Frempong. Pepease, December 19, 1992.*
———. Pepease, December 21, 1992.
———. Pepease, March 24, 1993.
———. Pepease, April 2, 1993.
———. Pepease, August 22, 1993.
———. Pepease, September 28, 1993.*
———. Pepease, August 27, 1994.
———. Pepease, August 11, 2000.*
———. Pepease, August 29, 2000.
Osei, Rev. T. A. Akropong, January 5, 1993.
Reynolds, G. O. Mamfe, January 6, 1993.
Sampong, Agnes. Abetifi, August 22, 2000. With the assistance of Pearl A. Ofosu.
Wahyee, J. A. Abetifi, September 18, 1994. With the assistance of Joseph Kwakye.
Wahyee, J. A., and Kwadwo Donkor. Abetifi, August 25, 1993. With the assistance of
    Joseph Kwakye.
———. Abetifi, November 11, 1994. With the assistance of Joseph Kwakye.
Wahyee, J. A., Kwadwo Donkor, and E. V. Osei Addo. Abetifi, October 31, 1994. With
    the assistance of Joseph Kwakye.
Yeboaa, Okomfo Amma. Nkwantanan, September 20, 1993.*
———. Pepease, July 19, 1993. With the assistance of Joe Acquah.
Yeboaa, Okomfo Amma, Okomfo Yaa Animwaa, and G.G.Y. Dovi. Pepease, August 10,
    2000. With the assistance of Kwame Fosu.
Yiadom, Akasease Kofi Boakye. Abetifi, June 27, 1993.
———. Abetifi, August 28, 1994.
———. Abetifi, November 8, 1994.*
———. Abetifi, November 15, 1994.
———. Abetifi, December 5, 1994.*

Bibliography

————. Abetifi, July 23, 1997.
————. Abetifi, August 12, 2000.
————. Abetifi, August 25, 2001.*

Switzerland

Bassi, Rev. Bruno. Meggen, October 13, 1992.*
Haller, Rev. Richard. Merlingen, September 14, 2001.
Rutishauser, Rev. Paul. Kreuzlingen, August 2, 2001.
Tschudin-Gehr, Rosmarie. Sissach, September 17, 2001.

United States

Adamson, William. Newark, Delaware, December 26, 1995.*
Ghartey-Tagoe, David. Ann Arbor, Michigan, March 23, 1995.
Sampong, Edna. Seattle, Washington, January 11, 1998.*

ARCHIVAL SOURCES

Basel Mission Archive, Basel/Switzerland (BMA)

Note: All translations from German and French are mine.
D-1: Incoming correspondence from the Gold Coast, 1875–1914.
D-3: Records of the Gold Coast Mission, 1915–1918.
D-4-3: Gold Coast reports from the first three quarters of each year, 1926–1950.
D-4-4: Correspondence with missionaries.
D-4-7, 4: Inspektionsreise Hartenstein, 1931.
D-4-7, 5: Inspektionsreise Kellerhals (1933–1934), Witschi (1948–1949, 1950), Raaflaub (1954).
D-9.1c, 11a: *Ordnung für die evangelischen Gemeinden in Ostindien und Westafrika,* 1865.
D-9.1c, 13b: *Ordnung für die Evangelischen Gemeinden der Basler Mission auf der Goldküste,* revidiert 1902.
D-9.1c, 13d: *The Presbyterian Church of the Gold Coast: Regulations, Practice and Procedure,* revised 1929.
D-11: Letters from the Gold Coast/Ghana, 1931–1983.
Sch. 6473, 21: *Worship in School* (Accra: Scottish Mission Book Depot, 1933).
Sch. 6562, 45: Tigare: A Report Issued by The Christian Council of the Gold Coast (1947).
Q-9.22: *Verordnung für die Basler Missionsstationen: VI. Schulordnung,* 1869.
No call number: Tertialberichte, 1955–1967.

Kwawu Traditional Council, Mpraeso/Ghana (KTC)

An inventory of forty-four volumes is in Stephan Miescher, "Becoming a Man in Kwawu: Gender, Law, Personhood, and the Construction of Masculinities in Colonial Ghana, 1875–1957" (Ph.D. dissertation, Northwestern University, 1997), 620–24.
Vol. 1, "Native Tribunal of Adontenhene of Kwahu, Abetifi." Civil cases, April 16, 1928–December 1932, pp. 2–500.
Vol. 2, "Native Tribunal of Adontenhene of Kwahu, Abetifi." Civil cases, March 21, 1936–January 5, 1939, pp. 1–493.

Vol. 4, I. "Native Tribunal of Adontenhene of Kwahu, Abetifi." Civil cases, August 1, 1941–March 28, 1945, pp. 1–377.
Vol. 7, "Native Tribunal of Adontenhene of Kwahu, Abetifi." Criminal cases, November 14, 1930–December 12, 1934, pp. 1–730.
Vol. 43, I. "Judicial Proceedings of Kwahu State Council, held at Abetifi, Mpraeso, Nkwatia," January 12, 1939–November 31, 1944, 1–162.

National Archives of Ghana, Accra (NAG) (now called Public Records and Archives Administration Department [PRAAD])

ADM 4/1/ . . . Ordinances, Acts.
ADM 11/1/ . . . Files of the Secretary of Native Affairs:
  ADM 11/1/206, "Pepease (Kwahu) Native Affairs, 1910–1945."
  ADM 11/1/242, "Kwahu-Kumawu Land Dispute, 1908–1920."
  ADM 11/1/298, "Road Kwahu-Tafo to New Mankrong, 1911–1913."
  ADM 11/1/598, "Kwahu (Abene) Native Affairs, 1888–1929."
  ADM 11/1/738, "Kwahu, Asafo, Origins of the Powers of, 1907–1928."
  ADM 11/1/1445, "Kwahu District, Native Affairs, 1880–1923."
  ADM 11/1/1639, "Kwahu Traders, Restrictions placed on, 1923–1931."
ADM 32/1/ . . . District Records, Kibi:
  ADM 32/1/127, "Kwahu Native Affairs, 1940–1946."
  ADM 32/1/135, "Quarterly Reports Kwahu District, 1931–1946."
ADM 34/ . . . District Records Mpraeso:
  ADM 34/4/5, "Civil Record Book, March 22, 1939–May 26, 1941."
  ADM 34/5/2, "District Record Book, 1923–1928."
  ADM 34/5/3, "District Record Book, 1937–1940."
CSO . . . Colonial Secretary Office:
  CSO 18/3/13, "Assisted School Teachers Union, 1934."
  CSO 18/5/17, "Strikes in Schools, 1941."
  CSO 21/22/11, "Kwahu Native Affairs, 1931–1932."
  CSO 21/22/229, "Kwahu State Unmarried Women Movement Control By-Laws, 1930–1943."
  CSO 25/1/84, "Boy Scouts, 1933–1934."
RG 3/1/ . . . Ghana (Gold Coast) Education Service:
  RG 3/1/144, "Handbook for Ghana Teachers, 1931."
  RG 3/1/249, "Survey of Facilities for Education in the Kwahu District, 1944."
  RG 3/1/281, "The Accra Youth Club, 1944–1945."
  RG 3/1/304, Thomas E. Kyei, "Some Notes on Marriage and Divorce among the Ashantis," n.d. (ca. 1945).
  RG 3/1/333, "Agreements between Native Authorities and Youth for Free Education, 1945–1953."
  RG 3/1/682, "Anonymous Attacks on the Education Department, 1948."

National Archives of Ghana, Koforidua (NAG-K)

ADM KD 29/6/ . . . Regional Administrative Office, Koforidua:
  ADM/KD 29/6/11, "Confidential Papers, Civil Disturbances."
  ADM/KD 29/6/69, "Fetishes and Charms, 1930–1952."
  ADM/KD 29/6/224, "Gold Coast Teachers Union, 1947–1949."
  ADM/KD 29/6/432, "Civil Disturbances 1948 (Confidential)."

Bibliography

ADM/KD 29/6/433, "Incidents in Kwahu, March 3–October 29, 1948."
ADM/KD 29/6/564, "Education and Schools General—Confidential, 1948–1953."
ADM/KD 29/6/565, "Education Confidential, 1949–1959."
ADM/KD 29/6/941, "Native Affairs Kwahu, Confidential, 1952."
AMD/KD 29/6/1053, "Kwahu State Affairs, Strictly Confidential, 1953–55."
ERG 1/ . . . Regional Administration:
ERG 1/13/83, "South Kwahu Local Council, 1952–1960."
ERG 1/13/84, "Kwahu District Council, 1952–1960."
ERG 1/13/98, "Kwahu Local Constitutional Affairs—General, 1952–1954."
ERG 1/13/127, "Kwahu District Council, 1954–1959."
ERG 1/13/135, "Quarterly Reports, Kwahu District, 1955–1956."
ERG 1/13/139, "Kwahu Local Constitutional Affairs, General, 1955–1967."
ERG 1/13/176, "Kwahu Local Council, 1960–1962."

Presbyterian Church Archive, Accra/Ghana (PCA)

3/ . . . Publications.
6/ . . . Chronicles.
7/ . . . Diaries.
8/ . . . Minutes.
9/ . . . Announcement Books.
10/ . . . Diaries.

Abetifi Presbyterian Church, Abetifi/Ghana (APC)

Property Records ("Landkäufe, 1876–1898").
"Session Minute Book, 1963–1970."

Rhodes House, Oxford University/United Kingdom (RH)

Henry Venom Cusack papers, MSS Afr. s. 318.
J. A. Cowley papers, MSS Afr. s. 1051.

Personal Papers

Germany

Rev. Manfred Jehle:
Letters of Rev. Dr. Arthur Jehle.

Ghana

E. K. Addo (AP):
Diaries (1932–1934).
Letters, receipts, photos.
Rev. E.K.O. Asante (ASP):
"Rev. E.K.O. Asante: A Profile" (ca. 1980, rev. 1994).
Letters, photos.
E. F. Opusuo (OP):
Photos.
A. K. Boakye Yiadom (BYP):
"Autobiography: My Own Life." 2 vols. (1946–1981).

"My Life History: The Autobiography of Akasease Kofi Boakye Yiadom" (n.d., after 1978).
Letters, receipts, notebooks, photos.

Royal Anthropological Institute, Museum of Mankind, London
R. S. Rattray Papers:
Eugene Addow. n.d. "Notes on Kwahu." Ms. 102: 1 (ca. 1927).

PUBLISHED GOVERNMENT SOURCES

Cardinall, A. W. *The Gold Coast, 1931: A Review of Conditions in the Gold Coast in 1931 as Compared with Those of 1921, Based on Figures and Facts Collected.* Accra: Government Printer, 1932.
Ghana, Republic of. *Constitution of the Republic of Ghana, 1992.* Accra: Ghana Publishing, 1992.
Gillespie, W. H. *A History of the Gold Coast Police, 1844–1955.* Accra: Government Printing Office, 1955.
Gold Coast. *Accelerated Development Plan for Education, 1951.* Accra: Government Printer, 1951.
———. *Achimota College: Report of the Committee Appointed in 1932 by the Governor of the Gold Coast to Inspect the Prince of Wales' College and Schools, Achimota.* London: Crown Agents for the Colonies, 1932.
———. *Census of the Population, 1911.* Accra: Government Press, n.d.
———. *Census of the Population, 1948.* London: Crown Agents, 1950.
———. *Census Report 1921 for the Gold Coast Colony, Ashanti and Northern Territories and the Mandated Area of Togoland.* Accra: Government Press, 1923.
———. *Education Rules, 1933.* Accra: Government Printing Office, 1933.
———. *The Gold Coast Census, 1931, Appendices, Containing Comparative Returns and General Statistics of the 1931 Census.* Accra: Government Printer, 1932.
———. *Report on the Census of the Gold Coast Colony for the Year 1891.* London: Waterlow, 1891.
———. *Report on the Census for the Year 1901.* London: Waterlow, 1902.
———. *Report of the Education Committee, 1937–1941.* Accra: Government Printer, 1942.
———. *Scheme for the Employment of Two Hundred Selected Ex-Servicemen as Teachers and for Their Subsequent Training in Teacher-Training Colleges* (Colony and Ashanti). Accra: Government Printing Department, 1945.
Great Britain. Colonial Office; Advisory Committee on Education in the Colonies. *Memorandum on Education Policy in British Tropical Africa.* London: His Majesty's Stationery Office, 1925.
———. *Memorandum on the Education of African Communities.* London: His Majesty's Stationery Office, 1935.
———. *Report of the [Nowell] Commission on the Marketing of West African Cocoa.* London: His Majesty's Stationery Office, 1938.
———. *Report of the [Watson] Commission of Enquiry into the Disturbances in the Gold Coast, 1948.* London: His Majesty's Stationery Office, 1948.
Guggisberg, Sir Frederick Gordon. *The Gold Coast: A Review of the Events of 1920–1926 and the Prospects of 1927–1928.* Accra: Government Printing Works, 1927.

Bibliography

Maxwell, John, ed. *The Gold Coast Handbook, 1928.* 3rd ed. London: Crown Agents of the Colonies, 1928.

NEWSPAPERS AND OTHER SERIALS

African Morning Post, 1939, 1950
Ashanti Pioneer, 1946–1960
Daily Graphic and Sunday Mirror, 1953–1955, 1964
Gold Coast Independent, 1918–1940
Gold Coast Leader, 1926
Gold Coast Spectator, 1932–1934
Gold Coast Times, 1934–1935
Gold Coast Teachers' Journal, 1932–34, 1956
Evangelischer Heidenbote, 1850–1914
Evening News, 1960–1964
Jahresbericht der Evangelischen Missions-Gesellschaft zu Basel, 1850–1960
Times of West Africa, 1932–1935

PUBLISHED WORKS

Abu, Katherine. "The Separateness of Spouses: Conjugal Relationships in an Ashanti Town." In *Female and Male in West Africa,* ed. C. Oppong, 156–68. London: Allen and Unwin, 1983.

Abun-Nasr, Sonia. *Afrikaner und Missionar: Die Lebensgeschichte von David Asante.* Basel: P. Schlettwein, 2003.

Achebe, Nwando. " 'And She Became a Man': King Ahebi Ugbabe in the History of Enugu-Ezike, Northern Igboland, 1880–1948." In *Men and Masculinities in Modern Africa,* ed. L. A. Lindsey and S. F. Miescher, 52–68. Portsmouth, N.H.: Heinemann, 2003.

Acquah, Ioné. *Accra Survey.* London: University of London Press, 1958.

Adams, Rachel, and David Savran, eds. *The Masculinity Studies Reader.* Malden, Mass.: Blackwell, 2002.

Adinkrah, Kofi Oti. "Ghana's Marriage Ordinance: An Inquiry into a Legal Transplant for Social Change." *African Law Studies* 18 (1980): 1–42.

Agyemang, Fred M. *Amu—The African: A Study in Vision and Courage.* Accra: Asempa, 1988.

———. *A Century with Boys: The Story of the Middle Boarding School in Ghana, 1867–1967.* Accra: Waterville, 1967.

Aidoo, Agnes Akosua. "Asante Queen Mothers in Government and Politics in the Nineteenth Century." In *Black Women Cross-Culturally,* ed. F. C. Steady, 65–77. Cambridge, Mass.: Schenkman, 1988.

Akyeampong, Emmanuel Kwaku. "Africans in the Diaspora: The Diaspora and Africa." *African Affairs* 99, no. 395 (2000): 183–215.

———. *Between the Sea and the Lagoon: An Eco-social History of the Anlo of Southeastern Ghana, c. 1850 to Recent Times.* Athens: Ohio University Press, 2001.

———. "Bukom and the Social History of Boxing in Accra: Warfare and Citizenship in Precolonial Ga Society." *International Journal of African Historical Studies* 35, no. 1 (2002): 39–60.

——. *Drink, Power, and Cultural Change: A Social History of Alcohol in Ghana, c. 1800 to Recent Times*. Portsmouth, N.H.: Heinemann, 1996.

——. "Sexuality and Prostitution among the Akan of the Gold Coast, c. 1650–1950." *Past and Present* 156 (1997): 144–73.

——. "What's in a Drink? Class Struggle, Popular Culture and the Politics of *Akpeteshie* (Local Gin) in Ghana, 1930–67." *Journal of African History* 37, no. 2 (1996): 215–36.

——. "*'Wo pe tam won pe ba'* ('You like cloth but you don't want children'): Urbanization, Individualism and Gender Relations in Colonial Ghana, c. 1900–39." In *Africa's Urban Past*, ed. D. M. Anderson and R. Rathbone, 222–34. Oxford: James Currey, 2000.

Akyeampong, Emmanuel, and Pashington Obeng. "Spirituality, Gender, and Power in Asante History." *International Journal of African Historical Studies* 28, no. 3 (1995): 481–508.

Akyeampong, Emmanuel, and Charles Ambler. "Leisure in African History: An Introduction." *International Journal of African Historical Studies* 35, no. 1 (2002): 1–16.

Alaimo, Kathleen. "Childhood and Adolescence in Modern European History." *Journal of Social History* 24, no. 3 (1991): 591–602.

Alegi, Peter C. "Playing to the Gallery? Sport, Cultural Performance, and Social Identity in South Africa, 1920s–1945." *International Journal of African Historical Studies* 35, no. 1 (2002): 17–38.

Alence, Rod. "The 1937–1938 Gold Coast Cocoa Crisis." *African Economic History* 19 (1991): 77–104.

Allen, Judith A. "Men Interminably in Crisis? Historians on Masculinity, Sexual Boundaries, and Manhood." *Radical History Review* 82 (2002): 191–207.

Allman, Jean Marie. "Fathering, Mothering and Making Sense of *Ntamoba:* Reflections on the Economy of Child-Rearing in Colonial Asante." *Africa* 67, no. 2 (1997): 296–321.

——. "Making Mothers: Missionaries, Medical Officers and Women's Work in Colonial Asante, 1924–1945." *History Workshop Journal* 38 (1994): 23–47.

——. "Rounding up Spinsters: Gender Chaos and Unmarried Women in Colonial Asante." *Journal of African History* 37, no. 2 (1996): 195–214.

——. *The Quills of the Porcupine: Asante Nationalism in an Emergent Ghana*. Madison: University of Wisconsin Press, 1993.

Allman, Jean, and Victoria Tashjian. *"I Will Not Eat Stone": A Women's History of Colonial Asante*. Portsmouth, N.H.: Heinemann, 2000.

Allman, Jean, Susan Geiger, and Nakanyike Musisi, eds. *Women in African Colonial Histories*. Bloomington: Indiana University Press, 2002.

Alpers, Edward A. "The Story of Swema: Female Vulnerability in Nineteenth-Century East Africa." In *Women and Slavery in Africa*, ed. C. C. Robertson and M. A. Klein, 185–219. Madison: University of Wisconsin Press, 1983.

Amadiume, Ifi. *Male Daughters, Female Husbands: Gender and Sex in an African Society*. London: Zed, 1987.

Ameyaw-Gyamfi, Kwabena. "Kwahu: An Early Forest State." *Ghana Notes and Queries* 9 (1966): 39–45.

Amoo, J.W.A. "The Effect of Western Influence on Akan Marriage." *Africa* 16, no. 2 (1946): 228–37.

Bibliography

Anyane, Seth La. *Ghana Agriculture: Its Economic Development from Early Times to the Middle of the Twentieth Century.* Oxford: Oxford University Press, 1963.

Appiah, Kwame Anthony. *In My Father's House: Africa in the Philosophy of Culture.* New York: Oxford University Press, 1992.

Appiah-Kubi, Kofi. *Man Cures, God Heals: Religion and Medical Practice among the Akans of Ghana.* Totowa, N.J.: Allanheld, Osmun, 1981.

Arhin, Kwame. "Asante Military Institutions." *Journal of African Studies* 7, no. 1 (1980): 22–30.

———. "The Asante Praise Poems: The Ideology of Patrimonialism." *Paideuma* 32 (1986): 163–97.

———. "The Economic Implications of Transformations in Akan Funerals." *Africa* 64, no. 3 (1994): 307–21.

———. "The Missionary Role on the Gold Coast and in Ashanti: Reverend F. A. Ramseyer and the British Take-Over of Ashanti, 1869–1894." *Research Review* 4, no. 2 (1968): 1–15.

———. "Monetization and the Asante State." In *Money Matters: Instability, Values and Social Payments in the Modern History of West African Communities,* ed. J. Guyer, 97–110. Portsmouth, N.H.: Heinemann, 1995.

———. "A Note on the Asante Akonkofo: A Non-Literate Sub-Elite, 1900–1930." *Africa* 56, no. 1 (1986): 25–31.

———. "The Political and Military Roles of Akan Women." In *Female and Male in West Africa,* ed. C. Oppong, 91–98. London: Allen and Unwin, 1983.

———. "Rank and Class among the Asante and Fante in the Nineteenth Century." *Africa* 53, no. 1 (1983): 2–22.

———. "The Role of the Presbyterian Church in the Economic Development of Ghana." *Research Review* (New Series) 1, no. 2 (1985): 152–65.

———. "Some Asante Views of Colonial Rule: As Seen in the Controversy Relating to Death Duties." *Transactions of the Historical Society of Ghana* 15, no. 1 (1975): 63–84.

———. "The Structure of Greater Ashanti (1700–1824)." *Journal of African History* 8, no. 1 (1967): 65–84.

———. *West African Traders in Ghana in the Nineteenth and Twentieth Centuries.* London: Longman, 1979.

Arhin Brempong (Kwame Arhin). "The Role of Nana Yaa Asantewaa in the 1900 Asante War of Resistance." *Ghana Studies* 3 (2000): 97–110.

Asante, E.K.O. "The Missionary Work of the Presbyterian Church in Northern Ghana." In *History of the Presbyterian Church in Northern Ghana,* ed. A. A. Berinyuu, 40–46. Accra: Asempa, 1997.

———. "Tamale District II: The United Church-Tamale." In *History of the Presbyterian Church in Northern Ghana,* ed. A. A. Berinyuu, 71–74. Accra: Asempa, 1997.

Asiama, A.E.A. *The Mass Factor in Rural Politics: The Case of the Asafo Revolution in Kwahu Political History.* Accra: Ghana Universities Press, 2000.

Atieno-Odhiambo, E. S. "Luo Perspectives on Knowledge and Development: Samuel G. Ayany and Paul Mbuya." In *African Philosophy as Cultural Inquiry,* ed. I. Karp and D. A. Masolo, 244–57. Bloomington: Indiana University Press, 2000.

Atkins, G. Anthony. "African Housing." *African Affairs* 49, no. 196 (1950): 228–37.

Atkins, Kaletso E. *The Moon Is Dead! Give Us Our Money! The Cultural Origins of an African Work Ethic, Natal, South Africa, 1843–1900.* Portsmouth, N.H.: Heinemann, 1993.

Austin, Dennis. *Politics in Ghana, 1946–1960.* London: Oxford University Press, 1964.

Austin, Gareth. "Capitalists, Chiefs in the Cocoa Hold-ups in South Asante, 1927–1938." *International Journal of African Historical Studies* 21, no. 1 (1988): 63–95.

———. "Human Pawning in Asante, 1800–1950: Markets, Coercion, Gender and Cocoa." In *Pawnship in Africa: Debt Bondage in Historical Perspective,* ed. T. Falola and P. E. Lovejoy, 119–59. Boulder: Westview, 1994.

———. " 'No Elders Were Present': Commoners and Private Ownership in Asante, 1807–96." *Journal of African History* 37, no. 1 (1996): 1–30.

Awoonor, Kofi. *This Earth, My Brother: An Allegorical Tale of Africa.* Garden City, N.Y.: Doubleday, 1971.

Barber, Karin. *The Generation of Plays: Yoruba Popular Life in Theater.* Bloomington: Indiana University Press, 2000.

———. *I Could Speak until Tomorrow: Oriki, Women and the Past in a Yoruba Town.* Washington, D.C.: Smithsonian Institution Press, 1991.

———. "Literacy, Improvisation, and the Public in Yoruba Popular Theatre." In *The Pressures of the Text: Orality, Texts, and the Telling of Tales,* ed. S. Brown, 6–27. Birmingham: Centre of West African Studies, University of Birmingham, 1995.

Barber, Karin, ed. *Africa's Hidden Histories: Person, Text, and the Colonial State.* Bloomington: Indiana University Press, 2006.

Bartels, F. L. *Roots of Ghana Methodism.* London: Cambridge University Press, 1965.

Bartle, Philip F. W. *Cyclical Migration and the Extended Community: A West African Example.* Leiden: Afrika Studiecentrum, 1980.

———. "Forty Days: The Akan Calendar." *Africa* 48, no. 1 (1978): 80–84.

Bederman, Gail. *Manliness and Civilization: A Cultural History of Gender and Race in the United States, 1880–1917.* Chicago: University of Chicago Press, 1995.

Behar, Ruth. *Translated Woman: Crossing the Border with Esperanza's Story.* Boston: Beacon, 1993.

Beidelman, T. O. *Colonial Evangelism: A Socio-historical Study of an East African Mission at the Grassroots.* Bloomington: Indiana University Press, 1982.

———. *The Cool Knife: Imagery of Gender, Sexuality, and Moral Education in Kaguru Initiation Ritual.* Washington, D.C.: Smithsonian Institution Press, 1997.

Berry, Sara. *Chiefs Know Their Boundaries: Essays on Property, Power, and the Past in Asante, 1896–1996.* Portsmouth, N.H.: Heinemann, 2001.

———. *Fathers Work for Their Sons: Accumulation, Mobility and Class Formation in an Extended Yoruba Community.* Berkeley: University of California Press, 1985.

———. *No Condition Is Permanent: The Social Dynamics of Agrarian Change in Sub-Saharan Africa.* Madison: University of Wisconsin Press, 1993.

Bleek, Wolf. *Marriage, Inheritance and Witchcraft: A Case Study of a Rural Ghanaian Family.* Leiden: Afrika-Studiecentrum, 1975.

———. "Marriage in Kwahu, Ghana." In *Law and Family in Africa,* ed. S. A. Roberts, 183–204. The Hague: Mouton, 1977.

Boahen, A. Adu. *Yaa Asantewaa and the Asante-British War of 1900–1.* Accra: Sub-Saharan Publishers, 2003.

Boateng, F. Yao. "The Catechism and the Rod: Presbyterian Education in Ghana." In *African Reactions to Missionary Education,* ed. E. H. Berman, 75–91. New York: Teachers' College Press, Columbia University, 1975.

Bonnell, Victoria E., and Lynn Hunt, eds. *Beyond the Cultural Turn: New Directions in the Study of Society and Culture.* Berkeley: University of California Press, 1999.

Bourdieu, Pierre. *Outline of a Theory of Practice.* Translated by R. Price. Cambridge: Cambridge University Press, 1977 [1972].

Bourret, F. M. *The Gold Coast: A Survey of the Gold Coast and British Togoland, 1919–1945.* Stanford, Calif.: Stanford University Press, 1949.

Bozzoli, Belinda, with Mmantho Nkotsoe. *Women of Phokeng: Consciousness, Life Strategy, and Migrancy in South Africa, 1900–1983.* Portsmouth, N.H.: Heinemann, 1991.

Brokensha, David W. *Social Change at Larteh, Ghana.* Oxford: Clarendon, 1966.

Brown, Carolyn. "A 'Man' in the Village Is a 'Boy' in the Workplace: Colonial Racism, Worker Militance, and Igbo Notions of Masculinity in the Nigerian Coal Industry." In *Men and Masculinities in Modern Africa,* ed. L. A. Lindsay and S. F. Miescher, 156–74. Portsmouth, N.H.: Heinemann, 2003.

Burke, Timothy. *Lifebuoy Men, Lux Women: Commodification, Consumption and Cleanliness in Modern Zimbabwe.* Durham, N.C.: Duke University Press, 1996.

Burman, Sandra, and Pamela Reynolds, eds. *Growing Up in a Divided Society: The Contexts of Childhood in South Africa.* Johannesburg: Ravan, 1986.

Burton, Andrew. "Urchins, Loafers and the Cult of the Cowboy: Urbanization and Delinquency in Dar es Salaam, 1919–61." *Journal of African History* 42, no. 2 (2001): 199–216.

Busia, Kofi A. *The Position of the Chief in the Modern Political System of Ashanti: A Study of the Influence of Contemporary Social Changes on Ashanti Political Institutions.* London: Oxford University Press for the International African Institute, 1951.

Butler, Judith. *Gender Trouble: Feminism and the Subversion of Identity.* New York: Routledge, 1990.

Caplan, Pat. *African Voices, African Lives: Personal Narratives from a Swahili Village.* London: Routledge, 1997.

Carrithers, Michael, Steven Collins, and Steven Lukes, eds. *The Category of the Person: Anthropology, Philosophy, History.* Cambridge: Cambridge University Press, 1985.

Cartry, Christiane. "Jeux d'enfants Gourmantché." In *Systèmes de signes. Textes réunis en hommage à Germaine Dieterlen,* 73–78. Paris: Hermann, 1978.

Chakrabarty, Dipesh. "Postcoloniality and the Artifice of History: Who Speaks for the 'Indian' Past?" *Representations* 37 (1992): 1–26.

Christaller, Johann Gottlieb. *A Dictionary of the Asante and Fante Language, Called Tschi (Twi).* 2nd ed. Revised and enlarged. Basel: Basel Evangelical Missionary Society, 1933.

———. *Twi Mmebusɛm: Mpensa-Ahansia Mmoaano—A Collection of Three Thousand and Six Hundred Tshi Proverbs.* Basel: Basel Evangelical Missionary Society, 1879.

Christensen, James B. "The Tigari Cult of West Africa." *Papers of the Michigan Academy of Science, Arts and Letters* 39 (1954): 389–98.

Clark, Gracia. *Onions Are My Husband: Survival and Accumulation by West African Market Women.* Chicago: University of Chicago Press, 1994.

Clayton, Anthony, and David Killingray. *Khaki and Blue: Military and Police in British Colonial Africa.* Athens: Ohio University Center for International Studies, 1989.

Cohen, David William. *The Combing of History.* Chicago: University of Chicago Press, 1994.

Cohen, David William, and E. S. Atieno Odhiambo. *Burying SM: The Politics of Knowledge and the Sociology of Power in Africa.* Portsmouth, N.H.: Heinemann, 1992.

Cohen, David William, Stephan Miescher, and Luise White. "Introduction: Voices, Words, and African History." In *African Words, African Voices: Critical Practices in*

Oral History, ed. L. White, S. F. Miescher, and D. W. Cohen, 1–27. Bloomington: Indiana University Press, 2001.

Cole, Catherine M. *Ghana's Concert Party Theatre.* Bloomington: Indiana University Press, 2001.

Collins, John. *West African Pop Roots.* Philadelphia: Temple University Press, 1992.

Comaroff, Jean, and John Comaroff. *Of Revelation and Revolution: Christianity, Colonialism, and Consciousness in South Africa.* Vol. 1. Chicago: University of Chicago Press, 1991.

Comaroff, John L., and Jean Comaroff. *Of Revelation and Revolution: The Dialectics of Modernity on a South African Frontier.* Vol. 2. Chicago: University of Chicago Press, 1997.

Connell, R. W. *Masculinities.* Berkeley: University of California Press, 1995.

———. "Masculinities and Globalisation." In *The Life of Brian: Masculinities, Sexualities, and Health in New Zealand,* ed. H. W. Worth, A. Paris, and L. Allen, 27–42. Dunedin, New Zealand: University of Otago Press, 2002.

Cooper, Barbara. *Marriage in Maradi: Gender and Culture in a Hausa Society in Niger, 1900–1989.* Portsmouth, N.H.: Heinemann, 1997.

Cooper, Frederick. "Colonizing Time: Work Rhythms and Labor Conflicts in Colonial Mombasa." In *Colonialism and Culture,* ed. N. Dirks, 209–45. Ann Arbor: University of Michigan Press, 1992.

———. "Conflict and Connection: Rethinking Colonial African History." *American Historical Review* 95, no. 4 (1994): 1516–45.

———. *Decolonization and African Society: The Labor Question in French and British Africa.* Cambridge: Cambridge University Press, 1996.

———. "Industrial Man Goes to Africa." In *Men and Masculinities in Modern Africa,* ed. L. A. Lindsay and S. F. Miescher, 128–37. Portsmouth, N.H.: Heinemann, 2003.

———. "Urban Space, Industrial Time, and Wage Labor in Africa." In *Struggle for the City: Migrant Labor, Capital, and the State in Urban Africa,* ed. F. Cooper, 7–50. Beverly Hills: Sage, 1983.

Coplan, David. "Go to My Town, Cape Coast! The Social History of Ghanaian Highlife." In *Eight Urban Musical Cultures: Tradition and Change,* ed. B. Nettl, 96–114. Urbana: University of Illinois Press, 1978.

Cornwall, Andrea, and Nancy Lindisfarne. "Dislocating Masculinity: Gender, Power and Anthropology." In *Dislocating Masculinity: Comparative Ethnographies,* ed. A. Cornwall and N. Lindisfarne, 11–47. London: Routledge, 1994.

Crisp, Jeff. *The Story of an African Working Class: Ghanaian Miners' Struggles, 1870–1980.* London: Zed, 1984.

Crook, Richard C. "Four Years of the Ghana District Assemblies in Operation: Decentralization, Democratization, and Administrative Performance." *Public Administration and Development* 14 (1994): 339–64.

Crowther, Francis. "Notes on a District of the Gold Coast." *Quarterly Journal of the Institute of Commercial Research in the Tropics* (Liverpool University) 3 (1906): 167–82.

Danquah, J. B. *The Akan Doctrine of God: A Fragment of Gold Coast Ethics and Religion.* London: Lutterworth, 1944.

———. *Cases in Akan Law.* London: Routledge, 1928.

———. *Gold Coast: Akan Laws and Customs and the Akim Abuakwa Constitution.* London: Routledge, 1928.

Bibliography

Davison, Jean, and the Women of Mutira. *Voices from Mutira: Changes in the Lives of Rural Gikuyu Women, 1910–1995*. Boulder: Lynne Rienner, 1996.

Debrunner, Hans. *Witchcraft in Ghana: A Study on the Belief in Destructive Witches and Its Effects on the Akan Tribes*. Accra: Presbyterian Book Depot, 1959.

Denzer, La Ray. "Gender and Decolonization: A Study of Three Women in West African Public Life." In *People and Empires in African History*, ed. J. F. Ade Ajayi and J.D.Y. Peel, 217–36. London: Longman, 1992.

Dickson, Kwamina B. *A Historical Geography of Ghana*. Cambridge: Cambridge University Press, 1969.

di Leonardo, Micaela. "The Female World of Cards and Holidays: Women, Families, and the Work of Kinship." *Signs* 12, no. 3 (1984): 440–53.

Du Bois, W.E.B. "Education in Africa: A Review of the Recommendations of the African Educational Committee." *The Crisis* 30 (June 1926): 86–89.

———. *The Souls of Black Folk*. Chicago: McClurg, 1903.

Dumett, Raymond E. *El Dorado in West Africa: The Gold Mining Frontier, African Labor, and Colonial Capitalism in the Gold Coast, 1875–1900*. Athens: Ohio University Press, 1998.

Dumett, Raymond, and Marion Johnson. "Britain and the Suppression of Slavery in the Gold Coast Colony." In *The End of Slavery in Africa*, ed. S. Miers and R. Roberts, 71–116. Madison: University of Wisconsin Press, 1988.

Duodu, Cameron. *The Gab Boys*. London: Deutsch, 1967.

Elbourne, Elizabeth. "Word Made Flesh: Christianity, Modernity, and Cultural Colonialism in the Work of Jean and John Comaroff." *American Historical Review* 108, no. 2 (2003): 435–59.

Evans-Pritchard, E. E. "Nuer Time Reckoning." *Africa* 12, no. 2 (1939): 189–216.

Fair, Laura. "Kickin' It: Leisure, Politics and Football in Colonial Zanzibar, 1900s–1950s." *Africa* 67, no. 2 (1997): 224–251.

———. *Pastimes and Politics: Culture, Community, and Identity in Post-Abolition Urban Zanzibar, 1890–1945*. Athens: Ohio University Press, 2001.

Fanon, Frantz. *Black Skin, White Masks*. Translated by Charles Lam Markmann. New York: Grove, 1967 [1952].

Field, M. J. *Akim-Kotoku: An Oman of the Gold Coast*. London: Crown Agents, 1948.

———. *Search for Security: An Ethno-Psychiatric Study of Rural Ghana*. London: Faber and Faber, 1960.

Fieldhouse, David K. *Merchant Capital and Economic Decolonization: The United Africa Company, 1929–1987*. Oxford: Clarendon, 1994.

Fortes, Meyer. "The Ashanti Social Survey: A Preliminary Report." *The Rhodes-Livingstone Journal* 6 (1948): 1–37.

———. "The Concept of the Person among the Tallensi." In *La notion de personne in Afrique noire*, ed. G. Dieterlen, 283–319. Paris: Éditions du Centre Nationale de la Recherche Scientifique, 1973.

———. "Kinship and Marriage among the Ashanti." In *African Systems of Kinship and Marriage*, ed. A. Radcliffe-Brown and D. Forde, 252–84. London: Oxford University Press, 1950.

———. "Time and Social Structure: An Ashanti Case Study." In *Social Structure: Studies Presented to A. R. Radcliffe-Brown*, ed. M. Fortes, 1–32. Oxford: Clarendon, 1949.

Foster, Philip J. *Education and Social Change in Ghana*. Chicago: University of Chicago Press, 1965.

Foucault, Michel. *Discipline and Punish: The Birth of the Prison.* Translated by A. Sheridan. New York: Vintage, 1977 [1975].

Fraser, A. G. "The Cult of the Kwahu Hunter on the Question of the Sasa Animals, Especially the Elephant." *The Gold Coast Review* 4, no. 2 (1928): 155–71.

Gaitskell, Deborah. "Devout Domesticity? A Century of African Women's Christianity in South Africa." In *Women and Gender in Southern Africa to 1945,* ed. C. Walker, 251–72. Cape Town: David Philip, 1990.

Garlick, Peter. *African Traders and Economic Development in Ghana.* Oxford: Clarendon, 1971.

———. "The Development of Kwahu Business Enterprise in Ghana since 1874: An Essay in Recent Oral Tradition." *Journal of African History* 8, no. 3 (1967): 463–80.

Gaudio, Rudi. "Male Lesbians and Other Queer Notions in Hausa." In *Boy-Wives and Female Husbands,* ed. S. O. Murray and W. Roscoe, 115–28. New York: St. Martin's, 1998.

Geertz, Clifford. "Deep Play: Notes on a Balinese Cockfight." *Daedalus* 101 (1972): 1–37.

Geiger, Susan. *TANU Women: Gender and Culture in the Making of Tanganyikan Nationalism, 1955–1965.* Portsmouth, N.H.: Heinemann, 1997.

———. "Women's Life Histories: Method and Content." *Signs* 11, no. 2 (1986): 234–51.

Gengenbach, Heidi. "Truth-Telling and the Politics of Women's Life History Research in Africa: A Reply to Kirk Hoppe." *International Journal of African Historical Studies* 27, no. 3 (1994): 619–27.

Giddens, Anthony. "Notes on the Concepts of Play and Leisure." *Sociological Review* 12, no. 1 (1964): 73–89.

Gilbert, Michelle. "Aesthetic Strategies: The Politics of a Royal Ritual." *Africa* 64, no. 1 (1994): 99–125.

———. "The Sudden Death of a Millionaire: Conversion and Consensus in a Ghanaian Kingdom." *Africa* 58, no. 3 (1988): 281–305.

Ginzburg, Carlo. "Mikro-Historie: Zwei oder drei Dinge, die ich von ihr weiss." *Historische Anthropologie* 1, no. 2 (1993): 169–92.

Glaser, Clive. *Bo-Tsotsi: The Youth Gangs of Soweto.* Portsmouth, N.H.: Heinemann, 2000.

Gluck, Sherna Berger, and Daphne Patai, eds. *Women's Words: The Feminist Practice of Oral History.* New York: Routledge, 1992.

Gluckman, Max. "Analysis of a Social Situation in Modern Zululand." *Bantu Studies* 14 (1940): 1–30, 147–74.

Gluckman, Max, J. C. Mitchell, and J. A. Barnes. "The Village Headman in British Central Africa." *Africa* 19, no. 2 (1949): 89–101.

Gocking, Roger. "Competing Systems of Inheritance before the British Courts of the Gold Coast Colony." *International Journal of African Historical Studies* 23, no. 4 (1990): 601–18.

———. *Facing Two Ways: Ghana Coastal Communities under Colonial Rule.* Lanham, Md.: University Press of America, 1999.

Goody, Esther. *Parenthood and Social Reproduction: Fostering and Occupational Roles in West Africa.* Cambridge: Cambridge University Press, 1982.

Goody, Jack. "Anomie in Ashanti?" *Africa* 27, no. 4 (1957): 356–63.

———. *The Culture of Flowers*. Cambridge: Cambridge University Press, 1993.

Gould, Peter R. *The Development of the Transportation Pattern in Ghana*. Evanston, Ill.: Department of Geography, Northwestern University, 1960.

Grant, Faye Woodward. *The Nutrition and Health of Children in the Gold Coast*. Chicago: University of Chicago Press, 1955.

Gray, Natasha. "Witches, Oracles, and Colonial Law: Evolving Anti-Witchcraft Practices in Ghana, 1927–1932." *International Journal of African Historical Studies* 34, no. 2 (2001): 339–63.

Grier, Beverly. "Pawns, Porters, and Petty Traders: Women in the Transition to Cash Crop Agriculture in Colonial Ghana." *Signs* 17, no. 2 (1992): 304–28.

Gyekye, Kwame. *An Essay on African Philosophical Thought: The Akan Conceptual Scheme*. Cambridge: Cambridge University Press, 1987.

———. *Tradition and Modernity: Philosophical Reflections on the African Experience*. New York: Oxford University Press, 1997.

Haas, Waltraud Ch. *Erlitten und erstritten: Der Befreiungsweg von Frauen in der Basler Mission, 1816–1966*. Basel: Basileia Verlag, 1994.

Haenger, Peter. *Slaves and Slave Holders on the Gold Coast: Towards an Understanding of Social Bondage in West Africa*. Translated by C. Handford. Basel: P. Schlettwein, 2000 [1997].

Haizel, E. A. "Education in Ghana, 1951–1966." In *The Life and Work of Kwame Nkrumah*, ed. K. Arhin, 53–81. Trenton, N.J.: Africa World Press, 1993.

Handler, Richard. "An Interview with Clifford Geertz." *Current Anthropology* 32, no. 5 (1991): 601–13.

Hansen, Karen Tranberg. "Cookstoves and Charcoal Braziers: Culinary Practice, Gender and Class in Zambia." In *African Encounters with Domesticity*, ed. K. T. Hansen, 266–89. New Brunswick, N.J.: Rutgers University Press, 1992.

Hantover, Jeffrey. "The Boy Scouts and the Validation of Masculinity." *Journal of Social Issues* 34, no. 1 (1978): 184–95.

Harries, Patrick. *Work, Culture, and Identity: Migrant Laborers in Mozambique and South Africa, c. 1860–1910*. Portsmouth, N.H.: Heinemann, 1994.

Harris, Grace Gredys. "Concepts of Individual, Self, and Person in Description and Analysis." *American Anthropologist* 91 (1989): 599–612.

Hartenstein, Karl. *Anibue: Die "Neue Zeit" auf der Goldküste und unsere Missionsaufgabe*. Stuttgart: Evangelischer Missionsverlag, 1932.

Hendrickson, Hilde, ed. *Clothing and Difference: Embodied Identities in Colonial and Post-Colonial Africa*. Durham, N.C.: Duke University Press, 1996.

Herbert, Eugenia W. *Iron, Gender, and Power: Rituals of Transformation in African Societies*. Bloomington: Indiana University Press, 1993.

Heywood, Colin. *Childhood in Nineteenth-Century France: Work, Health, and Education among the "Classes Populaires."* Cambridge: Cambridge University Press, 1988.

Hill, Polly. *The Migrant Cocoa-Farmers of Southern Ghana: A Study in Rural Capitalism*. Cambridge: Cambridge University Press, 1963.

Hobsbawm, Eric, and Terence Ranger, eds. *The Invention of Tradition*. Cambridge: Cambridge University Press, 1983.

Hodgson, Dorothy, and Sheryl McCurdy, eds. *"Wicked" Women and the Reconfiguration of Gender in Africa*. Portsmouth, N.H.: Heinemann, 2001.

Hofmeyr, Isabel. "John Bunyan, His Chair, and a Few Other Relics: Orality, Literacy, and the Limits of Area Studies." In *African Words, African Voices: Critical Practices in Oral History,* ed. L. White, S. F. Miescher, and D. W. Cohen, 78–90. Bloomington: Indiana University Press, 2001.

———. *"We Spend Our Years as a Tale That Is Told": Oral Historical Narrative in a South African Chiefdom.* Portsmouth, N.H.: Heinemann, 1994.

Hollbrook, Wendell P. "Oral History and the Nascent Historiography for West Africa and World War II: A Focus on Ghana." *International Journal of Oral History* 3 (1982): 148–166.

Honey, John Raymond de Simons. *Tom Brown's Universe: The Development of the Victorian Public School.* London: Millington, 1977.

Hoppe, Kirk. "Whose Life Is It, Anyway? Issues of Representation in Life Narrative Texts of African Women." *International Journal of African Historical Studies* 26, no. 3 (1993): 623–36.

Howard, Thomas C. "West Africa and the American South: Notes on James E. K. Aggrey and the Idea of a University for West Africa." *Journal of African Studies* 2, no. 4 (1975): 445–65.

Hughes, Heather. " 'A lighthouse of African womanhood': Inanda Seminary, 1869–1945." In *Women and Gender in Southern Africa to 1945,* ed. C. Walker, 197–220. Cape Town: David Philip, 1990.

Huizinga, Johan. *Homo Ludens: A Study of the Play Element in Culture.* New York: Harper and Row, 1970.

Hunt, Nancy Rose. "Colonial Fairy Tales and the Knife and Fork Doctrine in the Heart of Africa." In *African Encounters with Domesticity,* ed. K. T. Hansen, 143–71. New Brunswick, N.J.: Rutgers University Press, 1992.

———. *A Colonial Lexicon of Birth Ritual, Medicalization, and Mobility in the Congo.* Durham, N.C.: Duke University Press, 1999.

———. Introduction to "Gendered Colonialism in African History." *Gender and History* (special issue) 8, no. 3 (1996): 323–37.

———. "Letter-Writing, Nursing Men and Bicycles in the Belgian Congo: Notes toward the Social Identity of a Colonial Category." In *The Paths towards the Past: Essays in Honor of Jan Vansina,* ed. R. W. Harms et al., 187–210. Atlanta: African Studies Press, 1994.

———. "Placing African Women's History and Locating Gender." *Social History* 14, no. 3 (1989): 359–379.

Imam, Ayesha, Amina Mama, and Fatou Sow, eds. *Engendering African Social Sciences.* Dakar: CODESRIA, 1997.

Jackson, Michael. *Minima Ethnographica: Intersubjectivity and the Anthropological Project.* Chicago: University of Chicago Press, 1998.

Jackson, Michael, and Ivan Karp, eds. *Personhood and Agency: The Experience of Self and Other in African Cultures.* Washington, D.C.: Smithsonian Institution Press, 1990.

Jahoda, Gustav. "Love, Marriage, and Social Change: Letters to the Advice Columns of a West African Newspaper." *Africa* 29, no. 2 (1959): 177–90.

Jeater, Diana. *Marriage, Perversion, and Power: The Construction of Moral Discourse in Southern Rhodesia, 1894–1930.* Oxford: Clarendon, 1993.

Jeffries, Richard. *Class, Power and Ideology in Ghana: The Railwaymen of Sekondi.* Cambridge: Cambridge University Press, 1978.

Jenkins, Paul. "The Basel Mission in West Africa and the Idea of the Christian Village Community." In *Wholeness in Christ: The Legacy of the Basel Mission in India,* ed. G. Shir, 13–25. Balmatta, Mangalore: Karnataka Theological Research Institute, 1985.

Jenkins, Paul, ed. *The Recovery of the West African Past: African Pastors and African History in the Nineteenth Century, C.C. Reindorf and Samuel Johnson*. Basel: Basler Afrika Bibliographien, 1998.

Johnson, Marion. "The Slaves of Salaga." *Journal of African History* 27, no. 3 (1986): 341–62.

Jones, Adam. " 'My Arse for Akou': A Wartime Ritual of Women on the Nineteenth-Century Gold Coast." *Cahiers d'Études africaines* 132, nos. 33–34 (1993): 545–66.

Jones, T. Jesse. *Education in Africa: A Study of West, South and Equatorial Africa by the African Education Commission*. New York: Phelps-Stokes Fund, 1922.

Kaler, Amy. *Running after Pills: Politics, Gender, and Contraception in Colonial Zimbabwe*. Portsmouth, N.H.: Heinemann, 2003.

Kallmann, Deborah. "Projected Moralities, Engaged Anxieties: Northern Rhodesia's Reading Publics, 1953–1964." *International Journal of African Historical Studies* 32, no. 1 (1999): 71–117.

Kaphagawani, Didier. "Some African Conceptions of the Person." In *African Philosophy as Cultural Inquiry*, ed. I. Karp and D. A. Masolo, 66–79. Bloomington: Indiana University Press, 2000.

Karanja, Wambui Wa. " 'Outside Wives' and 'Inside Wives' in Nigeria: A Study of Changing Perceptions in Marriage." In *Transformations of African Marriage*, ed. D. Parkin and D. Nyamwaya, 247–61. Manchester: Manchester University Press, 1987.

Karlinger, Felix. *Grundzüge einer Geschichte des Märchens im deutschen Sprachraum*. Darmstadt: Wissenschaftliche Buchgesellschaft, 1983.

Karp, Ivan, and D. A. Masolo, eds. *African Philosophy as Cultural Inquiry*. Bloomington: Indiana University Press, 2000.

Katz, Jonathan Ned. *Love Stories: Sex between Men before Homosexuality*. Chicago: University of Chicago Press, 2001.

Kay, G. B. *The Political Economy of Colonialism in Ghana: A Collection of Documents and Statistics, 1900–1960*. Cambridge: Cambridge University Press, 1972.

Kaye, Barrington. *Bringing Up Children in Ghana: An Impressionistic Survey*. London: Allen and Unwin, 1962.

Kea, Ray. *Settlements, Trade, and Politics in the Seventeenth-Century Gold Coast*. Baltimore, Md.: Johns Hopkins University Press, 1982.

Keegan, Tim. *Facing the Storm: Portraits of Black Lives in Rural South Africa*. London: Zed, 1988.

Killingray, David. "Guarding the Extending Frontier: Policing the Gold Coast, 1865–1913." In *Policing the Empire*, ed. D. M. Anderson and D. Killingray, 106–25. Manchester: Manchester University Press, 1991.

———. "Imagined Martial Communities: Recruiting for the Military and Police in Colonial Ghana, 1860–1960." In *Ethnicity in Ghana: The Limits of Invention*, ed. C. Lentz and P. Nugent, 119–36. London: Macmillan, 2000.

———. "Military and Labour Recruitment in the Gold Coast during the Second World War." *Journal of African History* 23, no. 1 (1982): 83–95.

Kimble, David. *A Political History of Ghana: The Rise of Gold Coast Nationalism, 1850–1928*. Oxford: Clarendon, 1963.

Kratz, Corinne A. "Conversations and Lives." In *African Words, African Voices: Critical Practices in Oral History*, ed. L. White, D. W. Cohen, and S. F. Miescher, 127–61. Bloomington: Indiana University Press, 2001.

Kyei, Thomas E. *Marriage and Divorce among the Asante: A Study Undertaken in the*

Course of the Ashanti Social Survey (1945). Cambridge African Monographs 14. Cambridge: Cambridge African Studies Centre, 1992.

———. *Our Days Dwindle: Memories of My Childhood Days in Asante*. Portsmouth, N.H.: Heinemann, 2001.

Landau, Paul Stuart. *The Realm of the Word: Language, Gender, and Christianity in a Southern African Kingdom*. Portsmouth, N.H.: Heinemann, 1995.

Lange, Kofi Ron, ed. *Three Thousand Six Hundred Ghanaian Proverbs (From the Asante and Fante Language)*. Compiled by J. G. Christaller. Translated by K. R. Lange. Lewiston, N.Y.: Edwin Mellen, 1990.

Lawler, Nancy. *Soldiers, Airmen, Spies and Whisperers: The Gold Coast in World War II*. Athens: Ohio University Press, 2002.

Lenz, Carola, and Veit Erlmann. "A Working Class in Formation? Economic Crisis and Strategies of Survival among Dagara Mine Workers in Ghana." *Cahiers d'Études africaines* 113, nos. 29–30 (1989): 69–111.

Lenzin, René. *"Afrika macht oder bricht einen Mann": Soziales Verhalten und politische Einschätzung einer Kolonialgesellschaft am Beispiel der Schweizer in Ghana (1945–1966)*. Basel: Basler Afrika Bibliographien, 1999.

Lewin, Thomas J. *Asante before the British: The Prepean Years, 1875–1900*. Lawrence: Regents Press of Kansas, 1978.

Lindsay, Lisa A. "Money, Marriage, and Masculinity on the Colonial Railway." In *Men and Masculinities in Modern Africa*, ed. L. A. Lindsay and S. F. Miescher, 138–55. Portsmouth, N.H.: Heinemann, 2003.

———. *Working with Gender: Wage Labor and Social Change in Southwestern Nigeria*. Portsmouth, N.H.: Heinemann, 2003.

Lindsay, Lisa A., and Stephan F. Miescher, eds. *Men and Masculinities in Modern Africa*. Portsmouth, N.H.: Heinemann, 2003.

Long, Norman. *Social Change and the Individual: A Study of the Social and Religious Responses to Innovation in a Zambian Rural Community*. Manchester: Manchester University Press, 1968.

MacDonald, Robert H. *Sons of the Empire: The Frontier and the Boy Scout Movement, 1890–1918*. Toronto: University of Toronto Press, 1993.

McCaskie, Thomas C. "Accumulation, Wealth and Belief in Asante History: II. The Twentieth Century." *Africa* 56, no. 1 (1986): 3–23.

———. "Anti-Witchcraft Cults in Asante: An Essay in the Social History of an African People." *History in Africa* 8 (1981): 125–54.

———. *Asante Identities: History and Modernity in an African Village, 1850–1950*. Edinburgh: Edinburgh University Press, 2000.

———. "People and Animals: Constru(ct)ing the Asante Experience." *Africa* 62, no. 2 (1992): 221–47.

———. "R. S. Rattray and the Construction of Asante History: An Appraisal." *History in Africa* 10 (1983): 187–206.

———. "State and Society, Marriage and Adultery: Some Considerations towards a Social History of Precolonial Asante." *Journal of African History* 22, no. 4 (1981): 477–94.

———. *State and Society in Pre-Colonial Asante*. Cambridge: Cambridge University Press, 1995.

McKittrick, Meredith. *To Dwell Secure: Generation, Christianity, Colonialism in Ovamboland*. Portsmouth, N.H.: Heinemann, 2002.

McWilliam, H.O.A., and M. A. Kwamena-Poh. *The Development of Education in Ghana.* London: Longman, 1975.

Mager, Anne Kelk. *Gender and the Making of a South African Bantustan: A Social History of the Ciskei, 1945–1959.* Portsmouth, N.H.: Heinemann, 1999.

Mama, Amina. *Beyond the Masks: Race, Gender, and Subjectivity.* London: Routledge, 1995.

Mandala, Elias. *Work and Control in a Peasant Economy: A History of the Lower Tchiri Valley in Malawi, 1859–1960.* Madison: University of Wisconsin Press, 1990.

Mandela, Nelson. *Long Walk to Freedom: The Autobiography of Nelson Mandela.* Boston: Little, Brown, 1994.

Mangan, James A. "Ethics and Ethnocentricity: Imperial Education in British Tropical Africa." In *Sport in Africa: Essays in Social History,* ed. W. J. Baker and J. A. Mangan, 138–71. New York: Africana, 1987.

———. *The Games Ethic and Imperialism: Aspects of the Diffusion of an Ideal.* New York: Viking, 1986.

Mann, Gregory. "Old Soldiers, Young Men: Masculinity, Islam, and Military Veterans in Late 1950s Soudan Français (Mali)." In *Men and Masculinities in Modern Africa,* ed. L. A. Lindsay and S. F. Miescher, 69–85. Portsmouth, N.H.: Heinemann, 2003.

Mann, Kristin. "The Danger of Dependence: Christian Marriage among Elite Women in Lagos Colony, 1880–1915." *Journal of African History* 24, no. 1 (1983): 37–56.

———. *Marrying Well: Marriage, Status, and Social Change among the Educated Elite in Colonial Lagos.* Cambridge: Cambridge University Press, 1985.

Manuh, Takyiwaa. "The Asantehemaa's Court and Its Jurisdiction over Women." *Research Review* (New Series) 4, no. 2 (1988): 50–66.

———. "Changes in Marriage and Funeral Exchanges among the Asante: A Case Study from Kona, Afigya-Kwabre." In *Money Matters: Instability, Values and Social Payments in the Modern History of West African Communities,* ed. J. Guyer, 188–201. Portsmouth, N.H.: Heinemann, 1995.

———. "Women and Their Organizations during the Convention People's Party Period." In *The Life and Work of Kwame Nkrumah,* ed. K. Arhin, 101–27. Trenton, N.J.: Africa World Press, 1993.

———. " 'This Place Is Not Ghana': Gender and Rights Discourse among Ghanaian Men and Women in Toronto." *Ghana Studies* 2 (1999): 77–95.

Marks, Shula, ed. *Not Either an Experimental Doll: The Separate Worlds of Three South African Women.* Bloomington: Indiana University Press, 1987.

Martin, Phyllis M. "Contesting Clothes in Colonial Brazzaville." *Journal of African History* 35, no. 3 (1994): 401–26.

———. *Leisure and Society in Colonial Brazzaville.* Cambridge: Cambridge University Press, 1995.

Mbiti, John S. *African Religions and Philosophy.* 2nd ed. Portsmouth, N.H.: Heinemann, 1990.

Medick, Hans. "Village Spinning Bees: Sexual Culture and Free Time among Rural Youth in Early Modern Germany." In *Interest and Emotion: Essays on the Study of Family and Kinship,* ed. H. Medick and D. W. Sabean, 317–39. Cambridge: Cambridge University Press, 1984.

Menkiti, Ifeanyi. "Person and Community in African Traditional Thought." In *African Philosophy: An Introduction,* ed. R. A. Wright, 157–68. 2nd ed. Washington, D.C.: University Press of America, 1979.

Middleton, John. "One Hundred and Fifty Years of Christianity in a Ghanaian Town." *Africa* 53, no. 3 (1983): 2–19.

Miescher, Stephan F. " 'Called to Work for the Kingdom of God': The Challenges of Presbyterian Masculinity in Colonial Ghana." In *Readings in Gender in Africa*, ed. A. Cornwall, 187–95. Bloomington: Indiana University Press, 2005.

———. "Of Documents and Litigants: Disputes on Inheritance in Abetifi—a Town of Colonial Ghana." *Journal of Legal Pluralism and Unofficial Law* 39 (1997): 81–119.

———. "The Life Histories of Boakye Yiadom (Akasease Kofi of Abetifi, Kwawu): Exploring the Subjectivity and 'Voices' of a Teacher-Catechist in Colonial Ghana." In *African Words, African Voices: Critical Practices in Oral History*, ed. L. White, S. F. Miescher, and D. W. Cohen, 162–93. Bloomington: Indiana University Press, 2001.

———. "The Making of Presbyterian Teachers: Masculinities and Programs of Education in Colonial Ghana." In *Men and Masculinities in Modern Africa*, ed. L. A. Lindsay and S. F. Miescher, 89–108. Portsmouth, N.H.: Heinemann, 2003.

———. " 'My Own Life': A. K. Boakye Yiadom's Autobiography—Writing and Subjectivity of a Ghanaian Teacher-Catechist." In *Africa's Hidden Histories: Person, Text, and the Colonial State*, ed. K. Barber. Bloomington: Indiana University Press, 2006.

Miescher, Stephan F., and Leslie Ashbaugh. "Been-to Visions: Transnational Linkages among a Ghanaian Dispersed Community in the Twentieth Century." *Ghana Studies* 2 (1999): 57–76.

Miescher, Stephan F., and Lisa A. Lindsay. "Introduction: Men and Masculinities in Modern African History." In *Men and Masculinities in Modern Africa*, ed. L. A. Lindsay and S. F. Miescher, 1–29. Portsmouth, N.H.: Heinemann, 2003.

Mikell, Gwendolyn. *Cocoa and Chaos in Ghana*. New York: Paragon, 1989.

Miller, Jon. *The Social Control of Religious Zeal*. New Brunswick, N.J.: Rutgers University Press, 1994.

Mirza, Sarah, and Margaret Strobel, eds. *Three Swahili Women: Life Histories from Mombasa, Kenya*. Bloomington: Indiana University Press, 1989.

Moore, Decima, and Major F. G. Guggisberg. *We Two in West Africa*. London: Heinemann, 1909.

Moore, Sally Falk. *Anthropology and Africa: Changing Perspectives on a Changing Scene*. Charlottesville: University Press of Virginia, 1994.

Morrell, Robert. "Boys, Gangs, and the Making of Masculinity in the White Secondary Schools of Natal, 1880–1930." *Masculinities* 2, no. 2 (1994): 56–82.

———. "Of Boys and Men: Masculinity and Gender in Southern African Studies." *Journal of Southern African Studies* 24, no. 4 (1998): 605–30.

Morrell, Robert, ed. "Masculinities in Southern Africa." *Journal of Southern African Studies* (special issue) 24, no. 4 (1998).

———, ed. *Changing Men in Southern Africa*. London: Zed, 2001.

Mutongi, Kenda. " 'Dear Dolly's' Advice: Representations of Youth, Courtship, and Sexualities in Africa, 1960–1980." *International Journal of African Historical Studies* 33, no. 1 (2000): 1–23.

Ndambuki, Berida, and Claire C. Robertson. *"We Only Come Here to Struggle": Stories from Berida's Life*. Bloomington: Indiana University Press, 2000.

Newell, Stephanie. *Ghanaian Popular Fiction: "Thrilling Discoveries in Conjugal Life" and Other Tales*. Oxford: James Currey, 2000.

———. *Literary Culture in Colonial Ghana: "How to play the game of life."* Bloomington: Indiana University Press, 2002.

———. *Marita: or the Folly of Love. A Novel by A. Native.* Leiden: Brill, 2002.

Nkansa-Kyeremateng, Kofi. *One Hundred Years of the Presbyterian Church in Kwahu.* Accra: Presbyterian Press, 1976.

———. *The Story of Kwawu.* Accra: Presbyterian Press, 1990.

Nketia, J. H. *Drumming in Akan Communities of Ghana.* London: Thomas Nelson, 1963.

———. *Funeral Dirges of the Akan People.* Accra: Achimota, 1955.

Nkrumah, Kwame. *Ghana: The Autobiography of Kwame Nkrumah.* Edinburgh: Nelson, 1957.

Nthunya, Mpho 'M'atsepo Nthunya. *Singing Away the Hunger: Stories of Life in Lesotho.* Pietermaritzburg: University of Natal Press, 1996.

Nugent, Paul. *Big Men, Small Boys and Politics in Ghana: Power, Ideology and the Burden of History, 1982–1994.* London: Pinter, 1995.

Obeng, Pashington. "Gendered Nationalism: Forms of Masculinity in Modern Asante of Ghana." In *Men and Masculinities in Modern Africa,* ed. L. A. Linsday and S. F. Miescher, 192–208. Portsmouth, N.H.: Heinemann, 2003.

Oduyoye, Mercy Amba. *Daughters of Anowa: African Women and Patriarchy.* Maryknoll, N.Y.: Orbis, 1995.

Oldham, J. H. "Christian Education in Africa." *Church Missionary Review* 75 (June 1925): 305–14.

Oppong, Christine. *Middle Class African Marriage: A Family Study of Ghanaian Senior Civil Servants.* London: Allen and Unwin, 1981.

Ottenberg, Simon. "Boys' Secret Societies at Afikpo." In *African Religious Groups and Beliefs,* ed. S. Ottenberg, 170–84. Cupertino, Calif.: Folklore Institute, 1982.

Ouzgane, Lahoucine, ed. "African Masculinities." *Journal for Men's Studies* (special issue) 10, no. 3 (2002).

Owusu, Maxwell. "Democracy and Africa: A View from the Village." *Journal of Modern African Studies* 30, no. 3 (1992): 369–96.

Owusu-Ansah, David. "History of Islamic Education in Ghana: An Overview." *Ghana Studies* 5 (2002): 61–81.

Packard, Randall. "The 'Healthy Reserve' and the 'Dressed Native': Discourses on Black Health and the Language of Legitimation in South Africa." *American Ethnologist* 16, no. 4 (1989): 686–703.

Parker, John. *Making the Town: Ga State and Society in Early Colonial Accra.* Portsmouth, N.H.: Heinemann, 2000.

Parkin, David, and David Nyamwaya, eds. *Transformations of African Marriage.* Manchester: Manchester University Press, 1987.

Parsons, Timothy H. *Race, Resistance, and the Boy Scout Movement in British Colonial Africa.* Athens: Ohio University Press, 2004.

Passerini, Luisa. "Work Ideology and Consensus under Italian Fascism." *History Workshop* 8 (1979): 82–108.

Patterson, David K. *Health in Colonial Ghana: Disease, Medicine, and Socio-Economic Change, 1900–1955.* Waltham, Mass.: Crossroads, 1981.

———. "The Influenza Epidemic of 1918–19 in the Gold Coast." *Journal of African History* 24, no. 3 (1983): 485–502.

Paul, Sigrid. "The Wrestling Tradition and Its Social Functions." In *Sport in Africa: Essays in Social History,* ed. J. Baker and J. A. Mangan, 23–46. New York: Africana, 1987.

Peil, Margaret. "The Apprenticeship System in Accra." *Africa* 60, no. 2 (1970): 137–50.

————. *The Ghanaian Factory Worker: Industrial Man in Africa.* Cambridge: Cambridge University Press, 1972.

————. "Ghanaians Abroad." *African Affairs* 94, no. 376 (1995): 345–67.

Peacock, James L., and Dorothy C. Holland. "The Narrated Self: Life Stories in Process." *Ethos* 21, no. 4 (1993): 367–83.

Peel, J.D.Y. *Religious Encounter and the Making of the Yoruba.* Bloomington: Indiana University Press, 2000.

Personal Narratives Group, ed. *Interpreting Women's Lives: Feminist Theory and Personal Narratives.* Bloomington: Indiana University Press, 1989.

Perregaux, Edmond. "Chez les Achanti." *Bulletin de la Société neuchâteloise de Géographie* 17 (1906): 7–312.

————. "A Few Notes on Kwahu." *Journal of the African Society* 2, no. 8 (1903): 444–50.

Portelli, Alessandro. *The Death of Luigi and Other Stories: Form and Meaning in Oral History.* Albany: State University of New York Press, 1991.

Prah, Mansah. "Gender Issues in Ghanaian Tertiary Institutions: Women Academics and Administrators at Cape Coast University." *Ghana Studies* 5 (2002): 83–122.

Prakash, Gyan. "Subaltern Studies as Postcolonial Criticism." *American Historical Review* 95, no. 5 (1994): 1475–90.

Prodolliet, Simone. *Wider die Schamlosigkeit und das Elend der heidnischen Weiber. Der Export des europäischen Frauenideals in die Kolonien durch die Basler Frauenmission.* Zurich: Limmat Verlag, 1987.

Raaflaub, Fritz. "Mission in Northern Ghana: A Basel Mission Perspective of How It All Began." In *History of the Presbyterian Church in Northern Ghana,* ed. A. A. Berinyuu, 11–22. Accra: Asempa, 1997.

Ranger, Terence O. *Are We Not Also Men? The Samkange Family and African Politics in Zimbabwe 1920–64.* Portsmouth, N.H.: Heinemann, 1995.

————. *Dance and Society in Eastern Africa, 1890–1970: The Beni Ngoma.* London: Heinemann, 1975.

Rathbone, Richard. "Businessman in Politics: Party Struggle in Ghana, 1949–1957." *Journal of Development Studies* 9, no. 3 (1973): 391–401.

————. *Murder and Politics in Colonial Ghana.* New Haven, Conn.: Yale University Press, 1993.

————. *Nkrumah and the Chiefs: The Politics of Chieftaincy in Ghana, 1951–1960.* Oxford: James Currey, 2000.

Rattray, R. S. *Akan-Ashanti Folk-Tales.* Oxford: Clarendon, 1930.

————. *Ashanti.* Oxford: Clarendon, 1923.

————. *Ashanti Law and Constitution.* Oxford: Clarendon, 1929.

————. *Ashanti Proverbs.* Oxford: Clarendon, 1916.

————. "The Mausoleum of 'Ampon Agyei." *Blackwood's Magazine* 223 (1928): 842–53.

————. *Religion and Art in Ashanti.* Oxford: Clarendon, 1927.

Reefe, Thomas Q. "The Biggest Game of All: Gambling in Traditional Africa." In *Sport in Africa: Essays in Social History,* ed. W. J. Baker and J. Mangan, 47–78. New York: Africana, 1987.

Reindorf, Carl Christian. *History of the Gold Coast and Asante: Based on Traditions and Historical Facts, Comprising a Period of More Than Three Centuries from about 1500 to 1860.* Basel: Missionsbuchhandlung, 1895.

Rennstich, Karl. *Handwerks-Theologen und Industrie Brüder als Botschafter des Friedens:*

Entwicklungshilfe der Basler Mission im 19. Jahrhundert. Stuttgart: Missionsverlag, 1985.

Reynolds, Pamela. *Dance Civet Cat: Child Labor in the Zambezi Valley.* Athens: Ohio University Press, 1991.

Riesman, Paul. "The Person and the Life Cycle in African Social Life and Thought." *African Studies Review* 29, no. 2 (1986): 71–138.

Roberts, Penelope. "The State and the Regulation of Marriage in Sefwi Wiaso (Ghana), 1900–1940." In *Women, State and Ideology: Studies from Africa and Asia,* ed. H. Afshar, 48–69. London: Macmillan, 1987.

———. "The Village Schoolteacher in Ghana." In *Changing Social Structure in Ghana,* ed. J. Goody, 245–60. London: International African Institute, 1975.

Robertson, Claire. "Post-Proclamation Slavery in Accra: A Female Affair." In *Women and Slavery in Africa,* ed. C. Robertson and M. Klein, 220–45. Madison: University of Wisconsin Press, 1983.

———. *Sharing the Same Bowl: A Socioeconomic History of Women and Class in Accra, Ghana.* Bloomington: Indiana University Press, 1984.

Rosenbaum, Heidi. *Formen der Familie: Untersuchungen zum Zusammenhang von Familienverhältnissen, Sozialstruktur und sozialem Wandel in der deutschen Gesellschaft des 19. Jahrhunderts.* Frankfurt am Main: Suhrkamp, 1982.

Rosenthal, Michael. *The Character Factory: Baden-Powell and the Origins of the Boy Scout Movement.* New York: Pantheon, 1986.

Sarpong, Peter K. *Ghana in Retrospect: Some Aspects of Ghanaian Culture.* Accra: Ghana Publishing, 1974.

———. *Girls' Nubility Rites in Ashanti.* Accra: Ghana Publishing, 1977.

Schlatter, Wilhelm. *Geschichte der Basel Mission, 1815–1915.* 3 vols. Basel: Missionsbuchhandlung, 1916.

Schlumbohm, Jürgen, ed. *Kinderstuben: Wie Kinder zu Bauern, Bürgern, Aristokraten wurden, 1700–1850.* München: Deutscher Taschenbuch Verlag, 1983.

Schmidt, Elizabeth. *Peasants, Traders, and Wives: Shona Women in the History of Zimbabwe, 1870–1939.* Portsmouth, N.H.: Heinemann, 1992.

Seigel, Jerrold. "Problematizing the Self." In *Beyond the Cultural Turn: New Directions in the Study of Society and Culture,* ed. V. E. Bonnell and L. Hunt, 281–314. Berkeley: University of California Press, 1999.

Shaw, Rosalind. " 'Tok A, Lef Af': A Political Economy of Temne Techniques of Secrecy and Self." In *African Philosophy as Cultural Inquiry,* ed. I. Karp and D. A. Masolo, 25–49. Bloomington: Indiana University Press, 2000.

Shear, Keith. " 'Not Welfare or Uplift Work': White Women, Masculinity and Policing in South Africa." *Gender and History* 8, no. 3 (1996): 393–415.

Shire, Chenjerai. "Men Don't Go to the Moon: Language, Space and Masculinities in Zimbabwe." In *Dislocating Masculinity: Comparative Ethnographies,* ed. A. Cornall and N. Lindisfarne, 147–58. London: Routledge, 1994.

Shostak, Marjorie. *Nisa: The Life and Words of a !Kung Woman.* Cambridge, Mass.: Harvard University Press, 1981.

Skinner, Elliot. "Labour Migration and Its Relation to Socio-cultural Change in Mossi Society." *Africa* 30, no. 4 (1960): 375–401.

Simensen, Jarle. "The Asafo Movement of Kwahu, Ghana: A Mass Movement for Local Reform under Colonial Rule." *International Journal of African Historical Studies* 8, no. 3 (1975): 383–406.

———. "Rural Mass Action in the Context of Anti-Colonial Protest: The Asafo Movement of Akim Abuakwa, Ghana." *Canadian Journal of African Studies* 8, no. 1 (1974): 25–41.

Sinha, Mrinalini. *Colonial Masculinity: The "Manly Englishman" and the "Effeminate Bengali" in the Late Nineteenth Century.* Manchester: Manchester University Press, 1995.

Smith, Edwin W. *Aggrey of Africa: A Study in Black and White.* London: Student Christian Movement, 1929.

Smith, M. F. *Baba of Karo: A Woman of the Muslim Hausa.* London: Faber and Faber, 1954.

Smith, Noel. *The Presbyterian Church of Ghana, 1835–1960.* Accra: Ghana Universities Press, 1966.

Southall, Roger J. "Polarisation and Dependence in the Gold Goast Cocoa Trade, 1890–1938." *Transactions of the Historical Society of Ghana* 14, no. 1 (1975): 93–113.

Spitzer, Leo. *The Creoles of Sierra Leone: Responses to Colonialism, 1870–1945.* Madison: University of Wisconsin Press, 1974.

———. *Lives in Between: Assimilation and Marginality in Austria, Brazil, West Africa, 1780–1945.* Cambridge: Cambridge University Press, 1989.

Springhall, John O. *Youth, Empire and Society: British Youth Movements, 1883–1942.* London: Croom Helm, 1977.

Summers, Carol. *Colonial Lessons: Africans' Education in Southern Rhodesia, 1918–1940.* Portsmouth, N.H.: Heinemann, 2002.

Tashjian, Victoria B. " 'It's mine' and 'It's ours' Are Not the Same Thing: Changing Economic Relations between Spouses in Asante." In *The Cloth of Many Colored Silks: Papers on History and Society, Ghanaian and Islamic, in Honor of Ivor Wilks,* ed. J. Hunwick and N. Lawler, 205–22. Evanston, Ill.: Northwestern University Press, 1996.

ter Haar, Gerrie. *Halfway to Paradise: African Christians in Europe.* Cardiff: Cardiff Academic Press, 1998.

Thomas, Lynn. *Politics of the Womb: Women, Reproduction, and the State in Twentieth-Century Kenya.* Berkeley: University of California Press, 2003.

Thompson, E. P. "Time, Work-discipline and Industrial Capitalism." *Past and Present* 38 (1967): 56–97.

Thompson, Paul. *The Voice of the Past: Oral History.* 3rd ed. Oxford: Oxford University Press, 2000.

Tonkin, Elizabeth. *Narrating Our Pasts: The Social Construction of Oral History.* Cambridge: Cambridge University Press, 1992.

van der Geest, Sjaak. "The Elder and His Elbow: Twelve Interpretations of an Akan Proverb." *Research in African Literatures* 27, no. 3 (1996): 110–18.

———. "Funerals for the Living: Conversations with Elderly People in Kwahu, Ghana." *African Studies Review* 43, no. 3 (2000): 103–29.

———. "Money and Respect: The Changing Value of Old Age in Rural Ghana." *Africa* 67, no. 4 (1997): 534–59.

———. "Ɔpanyin: The Ideal of Elder in the Akan Culture of Ghana." *Canadian Journal of African Studies* 32, no. 3 (1998): 449–93.

———. "*Yebisa Wo Fie:* Growing Old and Building a House in the Akan Culture of Ghana." *Journal of Cross-Cultural Gerontology* 13, no. 4 (1998): 333–59.

van Onselen, Charles. "The Reconstruction of a Rural Life from Oral Testimony: Critical

Bibliography

Notes on the Methodology Employed in the Study of a Black South African Share-cropper." *Journal of Peasant Studies* 20, no. 3 (1993): 494–514.

———. *The Seed Is Mine: The Life of Kas Maine, a South African Sharecropper, 1894–1985.* New York: Hill and Wang, 1996.

Vansina, Jan. *The Tio Kingdom of the Middle Congo, 1880–1892.* London: Oxford University Press, 1973.

Vaughan, Megan. *Curing Their Ills: Colonial Power and African Illness.* Stanford, Calif.: Stanford University Press, 1991.

Vellenga, Dorothy Dee. "Matrilinity, Patrilinity and Class Formation among Women Cocoa Farmers in Two Rural Areas of Ghana." In *Women and Class in Africa,* ed. C. Robertson and I. Berger, 62–77. New York: Holms and Meier, 1986.

———. "Who Is a Wife? Legal Expressions of Heterosexual Conflicts in Ghana." In *Female and Male in West Africa,* ed. C. Oppong, 144–55. London: Allen and Unwin, 1983.

von Gnielinski, Stefan. *Ghana: Tropisches Entwicklungsland an der Oberguineaküste.* Darmstadt: Wissenschaftliche Buchgesellschaft, 1986.

von Laue, Theodore H. "Anthropology and Power: R. S. Rattray among the Ashanti." *African Affairs* 75, no. 298 (1976): 33–54.

Walker, A. J. "The Kwahus." *Gold Coast Review* 1, no. 1 (1925): 15–28.

Wallis, J. R. "The Kwahus: Their Connection with the Afram Plain." *Transactions of the Gold Coast and Togoland Historical Society* 1, no. 3 (1953): 10–26.

Ward, Barbara E. "Some Observations on Religious Cults in Ashanti." *Africa* 26, no. 1 (1956): 47–61.

Warren, Allen. "Popular Manliness: Baden Powell, Scouting and the Development of Manly Character." In *Manliness and Morality: Middle-Class Masculinity in Britain and America, 1800–1940,* ed. J. A. Mangan and J. Walvin, 199–219. Manchester: Manchester University Press, 1987.

Werbner, Richard. *Tears of the Dead: The Social Biography of an African Family.* Washington, D.C.: Smithsonian Institution Press, 1992.

Werbner, Richard, ed. *Postcolonial Subjectivities in Africa.* London: Zed, 2002.

White, Landeg. *Magomero: Portrait of an African Village.* Cambridge: Cambridge University Press, 1987.

White, Luise. *The Comforts of Home: Prostitution in Colonial Nairobi.* Chicago: University of Chicago Press, 1990.

———. "Separating the Men from the Boys: Constructions of Gender, Sexuality, and Terrorism in Central Kenya, 1939–1959." *International Journal of African Historical Studies* 23, no. 1 (1990): 1–25.

———. *Speaking with Vampires: Rumor and History in Colonial Africa.* Berkeley: University of California Press, 2000.

White, Luise, Stephan F. Miescher, and David William Cohen, eds. *African Words, African Voices: Critical Practices in Oral History.* Bloomington: Indiana University Press, 2001.

Wilkie, Arthur W. "An Attempt to Conserve the Work of the Basel Mission to the Gold Coast." *International Review of Missions* 9 (1920): 86–94.

Wilks, Ivor. *Asante in the Nineteenth Century: The Structure and Evolution of a Political Order.* London: Cambridge University Press, 1975.

———. *Forests of Gold: Essays on the Akan and the Kingdom of Asante.* Athens: Ohio University Press, 1993.

Williamson, Sidney George. *Akan Religion and Christian Faith*. Accra: Ghana Universities Press, 1965.

Witschi, Hermann. *Geschichte der Basler Mission, 1914–1919*. Vol. 4 (after a manuscript by W. Schlatter). Basel: Basileia Verlag, 1965.

———. *Geschichte der Basler Mission, 1920–1940*. Vol. 5. Basel: Basileia Verlag, 1970.

Wright, Marcia. *Strategies of Slaves and Women: Life Histories from East/Central Africa*. New York: Lynne Barber, 1993.

Wood, John C. *When Men Are Women: Manhood among Gabra Nomads in East Africa*. Madison: University of Wisconsin Press, 1999.

Yankah, Kwesi. *The Akan Trickster Cycle: Myth or Folklore?* Bloomington: Indiana University African Studies Program, 1983.

———. "To Praise or Not to Praise the King: The Akan *Apaeε* in the Context of Referential Poetry." *Research in African Literatures* 14, no. 3 (1983): 381–400.

———. *The Proverb in the Context of Akan Rhetoric: A Theory of Proverb Praxis*. Bern: Peter Lang, 1989.

———. "Proverbs: The Aesthetics of Traditional Communication." *Research in African Literatures* 20, no. 3 (1989): 325–46.

———. *Speaking for the Chief: Ɔkyeame and the Politics of Akan Royal Oratory*. Bloomington: Indiana University Press, 1995.

Yarak, Larry. *Asante and the Dutch, 1794–1873*. Oxford: Clarendon, 1990.

Yeboa-Dankwa, J. *Presbyterian Training College, Akropong-Akwapim (Founded 1948): 125th Anniversary Celebrations*. Accra: Waterville, 1973.

Dissertations, Theses, Seminar Papers, and Unpublished Manuscripts

Ameyaw-Gyamfi, Kwabena. "History of Abetifi." Unpublished manuscript, n.d.

Bartle, Philip F. W. "The Universe Has Three Souls: A Few Notes on Learning Akan Culture." Afrika Studiecentrum, Leiden, 1980.

———. "Urban Migration and Rural Identity: An Ethnography of a Kwawu Community, Obo, Ghana." Ph.D. dissertation, University of Ghana, 1978.

Bleek, Wolf. "Sexual Relationships and Birthcontrol in Ghana: A Case Study of a Rural Town." Ph.D. dissertation, University of Amsterdam, Netherlands, 1976.

Boonzajer Flaes, Robert M., and Fred Gales. "Brass Bands in Ghana." University of Amsterdam, Netherlands, n.d.

Haenger, Peter. "Die Basler Mission im Spannungsbereich afrikanischer Integrationsversuche und europäischer Kolonialpolitik. Vorbereitung und Anfangszeit der 'Asante Mission' in Abetifi, Kwawu." Master's thesis, University of Basel, Switzerland, 1989.

Hollbrook, Wendell P. "The Impact of the Second World War on the Gold Coast, 1939–1945." Ph.D. dissertation, Princeton University, 1978.

Laumann, Dennis H. "Remembering and Forgetting the German Occupation of the Central Volta Region of Ghana." Ph.D. dissertation, University of California, Los Angeles, 1999.

Lindsay, Lisa A. "Putting the Family on Track: Gender and Domestic Life on the Colonial Nigerian Railway." Ph.D. dissertation, University of Michigan, 1996.

Miescher, Stephan F. "Becoming a Man in Kwawu: Gender, Law, Personhood, and the Construction of Masculinities in Colonial Ghana, 1875–1957." Ph.D. dissertation, Northwestern University, 1997.

Bibliography

Osafo, Sophy L. A. "How Children Are Brought Up in Kwahu." Thesis, Institute for Education, University College, Achimota, Ghana, 1950–51.

Simensen, Jarle. "Commoners, Chiefs and Colonial Government." Ph.D. dissertation, University of Trondheim, 1975.

Tashjian, Victoria B. " 'It's Mine' and 'It's Ours' Are Not the Same Thing: A History of Marriage in Rural Asante, 1900–1957." Ph.D. dissertation, Northwestern University, 1995.

Index

Index

adehyeɛ (royals of stool/office), 8, 228n79
Adofo, Kwabena (uncle of Rev. Asante), 29,
    30–31, 60, 141
Adofo, Kwadwo (uncle of Kofi Ankoma), 32,
    95, 97, 162
adolescence, 155
Adoma, Florence, 161
Adonso village, 27
Adu, Rev. C. M., 60, 68
Adu, E. S., 81
Adu, Kwaku (father of E. F. Opusuo), 27, 61,
    69
Aduamoa, town of, 8, 58, 132
aduanan (forty-day cycle), 33
adult masculinity, 11, 12, 15, 45, 126, 140; fa-
    therhood and, 146, 151, 155; marriage
    and, 152, 257n48; resilience of Akan
    culture and, 199. See also masculinity;
    senior masculinity
adultery, 12, 18, 214n19; dances and, 123; fees
    paid for, 115, 145; native tribunal and,
    134; power and, 257n42
aduro owura (medicine person), 51
aduru (medicine), 7, 174, 176
adwuma (work), 20, 32, 65, 221n13; herbal
    knowledge, 24; hunting profession, 21.
    See also work
afahye festival, 31, 172, 180, 183, 225n44
afoofi (leisure), 34, 37, 41, 45, 47; boarding
    schools and, 65; time and, 33
Afram Plains, xvii, 5, 20, 21, 52; cocoa planta-
    tions in, 176–77, 197; Kwawu Water
    Project and, 167–68
Afram River, 19
Africa, colonial, 2, 47, 48, 68, 72, 202; histori-
    ography of, 201; marriage in, 141;
    "middle figures" in, 84–85; scouting in,
    75–76
Africa, postcolonial, 2, 202
Africa, precolonial, 14, 19, 220n4
African Americans, 72, 238n92
African Universal Church, 105
Africanists, 13
Africanization, 86, 103, 109–11, 166
Aggrey, J.E.K., 88, 242n131, 245n25
Agogo, town of, 23, 70, 71, 91, 140
agorɔ (games, play, dancing, singing, ritual per-
    formance), xxvi, xxix, 43; children's
    games, 34; Tegare cult and, xvii, 162–
    63, 176, 177
agriculture, 3, 30; as academic subject, 107;
    cash crops, 50, 58, 66, 153, 177; chil-
    dren's work obligations and, 20; cocoa,
    3, 7, 11; shift to artisanship, 50; taught
    in boarding schools, 67
aguma (wrestling), 34
agya (father), 17
Agyei, Ampon, 8, 31, 225n45

Agyeiwa, Adwoa (mother of E. K. Addo), 25
Agyeman, Nana Asiedu, III, 172
ahemaa. See ɔhemaa (queenmother)
ahenfie (chief's palace), xvii, 5, 9, 28, 30, 153,
    178; Christian Quarters and, 157, 160;
    elderhood and, 195, 197; funerals and,
    186, 191; patrilineage and, 49; postco-
    lonial institutions and, 184
ahenkwaa (palace attendant), 197
ahyiko dance, 43–45, 46, 123, 229n91
Akan societies, xix, xxii, 3–13, 62, 169; calen-
    dar, xxix, 33, 225n47; cosmology, 8;
    dancing, 123; elderhood in, 153; eth-
    nography of Asante, 17; funerals, 184–
    91; gendered occupations, 49; impo-
    tence in, 155; initiation rites in, 125;
    left hand, significance of, 25, 223n27;
    male "traditional" dress, 77, 109–10;
    marriage forms in, 115, 133–34, 150–
    51; masculinity in, 2; paternal obliga-
    tions in, 69; personhood in, 15, 41;
    proverbs, xv, xvii, 223n27; public ora-
    tion as performance in, 203. See also
    Twi language
akɔbo ɔpon (knocking fee), 117
akɔmfoɔ (diviners), 8, 23, 24, 123. See also ɔk-
    ɔmfo (diviner)
Akɔmfoɔhene (chief diviner), xxvi, 279n202
akonkofoɔ (traders), 168, 271n71
Akoto, John, 144
akpeteshie (local gin), xxxii
akrakyefoɔ (clerks, scholars, school graduates),
    11–12, 54, 71, 75, 84–86, 112–14;
    competing masculine identities and, 199–
    200; elderhood and, 163; houses of,
    178–79; marriage and, 116, 130, 151;
    military service in World War II, 91–
    95, 96, 97–99; nationalism and, 110;
    politics and, 99–105; Presbyterian mas-
    culinity and, 83; social position of, 111–
    12; as teachers, 105; women, 90; writ-
    ing and, 87–91. See also middle figures
Akropong, town of, 65, 77, 79, 80, 235n50
Akropong Boarding School, 85
Akuapem state, xvi, 7, 28, 54, 79; cocoa culti-
    vation in, 59; Presbyterian churches of,
    110
Akwa, Rev. D. E., 156–58, 160, 195
akwakora (old man), 155, 162
Akwamuhene, 31, 180
akwantufoɔ (travelers), 44, 45
Akwasidae Sunday, xxix, 162
Akwasihu, town of, 28, 29, 61
Akyeampong, Emmanuel, 19, 160
Akyeampong, Ɔmanhene Akuamoa, 195–96
Akyem Abuakwa, state of, 28, 59, 99
Akyem state, 7
Akyemang, S. L., 81

312

Index

Index

Kwakye, J. K. (brother of E. K. Addo), 88, 90, 91, 135, 194; Addo as apprentice of, 54–55; as itinerant trader, 26; residence of, 169

Kwakye, Joseph, xv, 124, 131, 203

Kwawu District Assembly, xxvi, 181

Kwawu state, xvi, 1, 8, 30; Akan societies in, 3–13; apprenticeships in, 50; Asafo Laws, 12; childhood in, 17; Christian Quarters, xviii, 62; "Christian state" in, 196; cocoa cultivation in, 59; courtship rites in, 119–24; customary marriage in, 124–33; integrated into Gold Coast, 19; Kwawu ridge, 3, 3; leisure activities in, 41–45; map of, 161; marriage practices in, 115, 116–20; paramount chief of, xvii; political organization of, 170–72; population dispersal from, 137; protectorate treaty with Britain, 5, 57; roads in, 188, 235n50; schools in, 56–60; sports (football) in, 73; Unmarried Women Movement Control By-Laws, 127

Kwawu-Tafo, town of, 28, 53, 162, 210n8

Kwawu Traditional Council, xxxii

Kwawu Water Project, 168, 172

Kwawu Youth Association, 196

Kyebi, town of, 99

Kyei, T. E., 23, 35, 116, 184, 222n19

Kyidomhene, xxvi

labor, conjugal, 38

labor, wage, 5, 12, 45, 86

Labor Railway Union, 100

Lang, A., 161, 268n41

lawyer-mercant class, 84–85

legacy, 160, 191–94

libations, xix, 9, 159, 203, 204–205, 221n11. *See also* alcohol

Liberia, 43, 44, 79, 80

life cycle, 13, 200

life histories, xvii–xix, 13–16, 200–201

Lindsay, Lisa, 211n6

literacy, 23, 58, 59, 67, 83; *akrakyefoɔ* and, 88, 93–94; authority and, 113; greeting card exchange and, 87–88, 89; middle figures and, 86; police force and, 97; prestige attached to, 84; skilled technical work and, 100; status and, 105; teaching of, 15

Local Government Ordinance (1951), 170

London Family Planning Association, 144

Maafo, Rev. Felix, 173

Mager, Ann, 36

Makrong, town of, 19

Mali, 94

Mampong, Kwasi, 122

Mangan, James, 73

Mankesim-Dominase, towns of, 23

manliness, 72–76, 139

Mann, Gregory, 94

Mann, Kristin, 136

Marfo, Ɔpanyin Kwaku, 5, 42, 126, 151–52, 192; apprenticeship of, 50, 51–52, 55, 82; childhood memories, 23–25; on courtship practices, 120; introduction to, xxvi, *xxviii*, xxix; marriages of, 125; as *odunsini* (herbalist), 198; positions held by, 197–98; Tegare shrines and, xvi, 174, 176

marriage, xvi, 8, 11, 71; Christian marriage, 133–39, 268n45; cross-cousin, 116; customary, 115, 124–33; female perspective on, 130; mock marriage game, 37, 67, 120–21, 255n28; monogamous, 70; multiple forms of, 115–19, 253n3; Ordinance marriage, 119, 133, 135, 136, 144; of Presbyterian teachers, 139–41, *142,* 143–50, *149;* unmarried status, xviii, 127, 129, 140, 258n62. *See also* polygyny

masculinity, xviii, 82, 202; *akrakyefoɔ* and, 84, 85, 114; in Ananse stories, 38, 41; Basel Mission and, 5; big-man status, 7; colonialism and, 1; female, 19, 32; funerals and, 185; gambling and, 42–43; gender studies and, 1–2; government schools and, 64; hegemonic, 2, 12; life histories and, 13–16; marriage and, 119, 124–33; military service and, 93, 94–95; mission schools and, 57, 58; sports and, 72–75; uniforms and, 13; warrior ideal, 8–9, *10. See also* adult masculinity; Presbyterian masculinity; senior masculinity

masturbation taboo, 18

matriclans (*mmusua kɛseɛ*), 8

matrilineage. *See abusua* (matrilineage)

Mau Mau fighters, 1

Mawu, Ɔbosomfo Kwasi, 7, 174, *175,* 176–77, 197, 213n13; economic success of, 198; funeral of, 185

medicine, 26, 51

men: Akan dress style, 77; dress and clothing styles, 109–11; gender studies and, 1–2; greeting card exchange among, 88; male wage labor, 12; self-presentation of, xvi, 2, 12, 14; subjectivity, 2, 13–16. *See also* manliness; masculinity

Men and Masculinities in Modern Africa, 2

Mensa, Nana Owusu, 61, 174

Mensa, Yaw, 132–33

Mensa, Yaw (of Nkwantanan), 125–26

Mensah, E., *81*

Mensah, Marjorie, 86

Index

ɔdame (draught game), 41, 42
ɔdekuro (headman), 57, 87
Odiawuo, Nana, 8
Odonkor, Rev. S. S., 164
odunsini (herbalist), xxix, 52, 53, 192, 198
odwira festival, 31
Ofin-Pra basin, 8
ɔhemaa (queenmother), 9, 194, 228n79, 265n11, 279n202
ɔhene (chief), 20
Ohenewaa (mother of Rev. Asante), 29, 141
Okae, Kwaku, 110
ɔkatakyie (hero), 9, 185
ɔkɔmfo (diviner), 32, 33, 42, 51, 133, 174; children of, 44, 63; possessed by lesser gods, 222n23. See also akɔmfoɔ (diviners)
Okra, Joseph, 164
ɔkrawa (barren man), 155
ɔkyeame (spokesperson), xxix, 53, 159, 174, 176, 186, 204
oman (Akan state), 8, 9
ɔmanhene (paramount chief), xvii, xxvi, 31, 69; adultery cases and, 123; community service and, 184; dispute resolution and, 157; enstoolment of, 158, 159, 195, 267n24; funerals and, 190, 198; native tribunals and, 100
ɔmanheneba (child of paramount chief), 27
ɔnimdefo (man of special knowledge), 54
Ɔnyame dua (god's tree, place for libations), 9
Ɔnyame (supreme god), 8
ɔpanyin (elder), xvii, xx, 51, 154–56, 194–98; as adviser to young men, 17; apprenticeship and, 54; child rearing and, 30; community service and, 180, 181–84; death of, 187, 198; life and death of, 156–60; process of becoming, 153, 160–67; respect for, 25; storytelling and, 228n79; Tegare shrines and, 174. See also elders
Opoku, E. K., xxvi
Opoku, Yaw, 161–62
Opong, Adelaide, 62, 70–71, 140, 143, 151
Opong, Kwabena Mensa (uncle of Boakye Yiadom), 61, 87
Opong, Kwadwo (uncle of Boakye Yiadom), 29, 60–61, 87
Oppong, Christine, 143–44
Opusuo, E. F., xvi, 5, 65; on Ananse stories, 39–40; childhood memories, 26–28; on children's games, 36–37; community service and, 181, 183, 183; conversion to Christianity, 67–68; on dances, 121; education of, 59, 61–62, 70, 82; elderhood and, 163, 183, 196; house of, 178–79; introduction to, xxvi, xxvii; mar-

riages, 144–46, 151; at Presbyterian Training College, 77–78, 81–82; on scouting, 76; on sports at school, 73–74; as teacher, 105, 107, 109, 111, 112
oral genres, xvi, 209n2
oral history, xvi–xix, 8, 14, 152, 201
Ordinance marriage, 119, 133, 135, 136; civil servants and, 144; Presbyterian teachers and, 139; prevalence of, 255n17
Ormsby-Gore, W.G.A., 101
Osafo, Kwadwo (father of Rev. Asante), 29, 141
Osafo, Sophy, 19–20, 50, 70, 118
osafo. See pastors
Osu (part of Accra), 65
ɔtɔfo wu (accidental/unexpected death), 184–85
ɔware (board game), xxxii, 41, 43, 46
Owusu, Maxwell, 181
Owusua, Salome, 134

palm-wine guitar music, 44
pastors, xx, 55, 60, 61, 88, 107
patriarchy, 2, 8, 194
patrilineage, 13, 20, 49, 127, 150, 155
pawning, 12, 42, 56–57, 233n29
peasants, 103
Pentecostal Church, 133
Pepease, town of, 8, 18, 53; chiefs in, xvii; Christian Quarters, xvi, xix, 62, 178; dancing in, 122; elders in, xxvi, xxvii–xxviii, xxix, xxx, 5, 26, 78; Tegare shrine, 154
performance, xvi. See also agorɔ
Perregaux, Edmond, 34, 43, 69, 123
personhood, 5, 13, 15, 154, 190–91, 200
Phelps-Stokes Commission, 72, 73
Pietism, xviii, 88, 245n26
Pilgrim's Progress, The (Bunyan), 62, 236n54
play, 33, 46
police, 13, 26, 84, 86, 162, 247n53; Disturbances of 1948 and, 99, 102–103; marriage rules and, 115; surveyor police, 53; training of, 95; uniforms, 97–98; women in, 98–99
politics, 181, 183, 276–77n152; akrakyefoɔ and, 84, 99–105; collision of Western and local systems, 13; independence struggle, 170–72, 171; masculinization of, 194; women and, 194–95, 277n155
polygyny, 29, 115, 129, 150; missionaries' opposition to, 157, 263n132; as ruling form of marriage, 119. See also concubinage
postcolonial institutions, 184
praise poetry and songs, 9, 22–23, 28
Preko, Beatrice Ohenewa (wife of E. K. Addo), 135

STEPHAN F. MIESCHER

is Associate Professor of History at the University of California, Santa Barbara. He is co-editor of *African Words, African Voices: Critical Practices in Oral History* with Luise White and David William Cohn and of *Men and Masculinities in Modern Africa* with Lisa A. Lindsay.